Reading:
Foundations and
Instructional Strategies

Contributors

Richard Arnold, Purdue University

Carolyn Burke, Indiana University

Emerald Dechant, Fort Hays State College

William Eller, State University of New York at Buffalo

Anna Rose Geary, Rockingham County Public Schools

Yetta Goodman, University of Arizona

Frank J. Guszak, University of Texas

Roselmina Indrisano, Boston University

Dale Johnson, University of Wisconsin

Bjorn Karlsen, California State College, Sonoma

James Laffey, Madison College

Pose Lamb, Purdue University

John Miller, Wichita State University

Alden J. Moe, Purdue University

Lloyd Ollila, University of Victoria

Peggy Ransom, Ball State University

Darryl Strickler, Indiana University

Reading:
Foundations and
Instructional Strategies

Edited by

Pose Lamb and Richard Arnold
Purdue University

Wadsworth Publishing Company, Inc.
Belmont, California

Designer: Nancy Benedict

Education Editor: Roger Peterson

Production Editor: Larry Olsen

Copy Editor: Jeanne DuPrau

ISBN 0–534–00423–7

L. C. Cat. Card No. 75–23505

Printed in the United States of America

2 3 4 5 6 7 8 9 10—80 79 78 77 76

Preface

Scholars agree that progress in understanding and teaching reading will only occur when knowledge from many disciplines is gathered and synthesized. The knowledge explosion of recent years is forcing interdisciplinary dependence. It is no longer possible for one person to be expert in all of the disciplines related to reading. Experts in such disciplines as cognitive psychology, linguistics, sociology, and psychometrics are bringing new perspectives to an understanding of the reading process, and teachers of reading are adapting these insights in developing new methods and materials for instruction.

Recognizing the limitations of a text written by one person, the editors have asked several authors with demonstrated competencies in specific disciplines related to reading to contribute chapters to a new text on reading methods. The result is *Reading: Foundations and Instructional Strategies*, a basic reading methods text which combines extensive syntheses of reading theory with discussions of the latest methods of reading instruction. *Reading* is intended to serve as a basic aid for all who are interested in methods of teaching reading—prospective teachers as well as in-service teachers.

In a book of this type the reader can expect to find differences in approach and emphasis among the various contributors. The editors consider this to be a strong point rather than a weakness, as the reader will be challenged to compare, contrast, and synthesize the various approaches. The editors believe that every teacher of reading must develop a theoretical understanding of the reading process and the basic principles of reading instruction. At the same time, teachers must remain flexible with regard to the needs and capacities of individual pupils. The variety of approaches presented here will allow teachers to formulate their own theory of reading and help them to select appropriate methods and materials for a variety of classroom situations.

The text has been organized to help the reader attain this goal. Part One: Foundations is devoted to a discussion of theoretical foundations, including the physical, psychological, sociocultural, and psycholinguistic bases of reading. Included in this part are discussions of:

1. The basic elements of the reading process.
2. The linguistic problems of blacks, chicanos, American Indians, Puerto Ricans, Appalachians, Cubans, and other minorities, and reading programs designed especially for these groups.
3. The organization of a reading curriculum, including both long and short-term learning objectives, within the context of the total school program.
4. Self-actualization and the problems of teacher expectations.
5. The use of teaching assistants and other aides in the classroom.
6. The use of diagnostic tools in reading assessment.

The authors of these chapters present the rationale, the "why," which determines what the teacher does with the pupil. Contrary to some currently popular beliefs, the editors are convinced that this fundamental knowledge is equally as important as knowledge of techniques, materials, and direct experience with children.

Part Two: Instructional Strategies is devoted to discussions of reading instruction, including:

1. Various approaches to teaching reading, including basal reader approaches, the language-experience approach, individualized instruction, linguistic approaches, programmed materials, computer-assisted instruction, and others.
2. An analysis of the reasons why readers prefer certain materials, and suggestions for stimulating interest in reading.
3. A discussion of the various skills required for successful reading of "content area" materials.

Part Two provides the extensive exposure to methods and materials that teachers must have to develop a sound, flexible reading curriculum. Thus, the organization of this book reflects the two parallel dimensions, the "why" and the "how" of reading.

The editors have provided extensive prefaces in the Preview sections at the beginning of each chapter. Each Preview is followed by an Objectives section, which the reader may use as a self-check to be sure the main points of the chapter have been mastered. The References sections at the end of each chapter provide documentation for references in the text, as well as serving as a guide for further reading. The reader will find the Index at the back of the book particularly useful in comparing the treatment of key concepts by different authors.

The editors would like to thank all who have contributed to this volume, including Diane Monson, University of Washington; S. Jay Samuels, University of Minnesota; and Sam Sebesta, University of Washington, for their helpful comments and suggestions in preparing the text.

Pose Lamb and Richard Arnold

Contents

Chapter Six
Reading: Assessment and Diagnosis of Abilities   *146*

Bjorn Karlsen, California State College, Sonoma

Part Two: Instructional Strategies

Chapter Seven
Reading: Current Approaches, Part One   *194*

Dale Johnson, University of Wisconsin

Chapter Eleven
Reading: Comprehension Skills   *362*

Frank J. Guszak, University of Texas

Chapter Twelve
Reading: Specialized Skills   *400*

Roselmina Indrisano, Boston University

Chapter Thirteen
Reading: Attitudes and Interests   *448*

Darryl Strickler, Indiana University
William Eller, State University of New York at Buffalo

Index   **491**

Part One:
Foundations

Chapter
One

Preview

Many educators feel that a discussion of reading at the theoretical level is unnecessary, and in the past, many texts on reading instruction omitted such discussions. The author feels, however, that without a theoretical orientation and a philosophical foundation, a teacher will be directionless and confused in applying principles of reading instruction.

In this era of accountability, teachers are increasingly responsible for justifying instructional practices. It is indeed unfortunate if teachers do not know why they selected the methods and materials they are using. Those concerned with the educational process have come to expect more than this from professional educators.

In this chapter Lamb presents several different theoretical points of view and their methodological implications for teaching reading. While she emphasizes that each position can be justified, she does *not* suggest that an effective reading program will operate from diverse and sometimes discordant theoretical bases. The best reading program is one on which teachers work together.

This chapter is designed to provide a framework within which rational decision making in reading programs can occur. The author shows that the teacher's definition of reading will have a significant impact on teaching strategies.

Reading: Definitions, Models, and Beliefs

Pose Lamb, Purdue University

Objectives

After you have read this chapter, you should be able to:

1. State two major implications which result from one's definition of reading.
2. Select two sets of reading materials, designed to be used at beginning levels, which reflect contrasting definitions of reading; state the definitions upon which the materials are based.
3. Identify two specific teaching techniques which are characteristic of each contrasting definition. Use suggestions from the teacher's guides that accompany the materials chosen for Objective 2.
4. Identify and list at least three general characteristics of a comprehensive model of the reading process.
5. Write your own definition of the reading process, and list specific components in your definition which are similar to components of the definitions discussed in the chapter.

The term *reading* can be defined in many ways. One *reads* the expression on another's face. The weather, changes in foliage, and the behavior of birds and squirrels are *read* for signs of seasonal change. A mother very quickly learns to *read* her infant's cries, to distinguish a cry of pain from a cry of hunger. So, too, does an infant learn to *read* his mother's behavior for signals indicating satisfaction, displeasure, or affection. Clocks, calendars, road maps, and wordless picture books are *read*. In its broadest sense, then, reading can be viewed as a process of discrimination and interpretation, whether or not printed or even oral codes are involved.

While the classroom teacher is aware of these facets of the reading process, his central concern is with the printed page, and his goal is helping the learner deal with print with increasing effectiveness, efficiency, and pleasure.

Reading the expression on a person's face and reading a paragraph from a book are processes which have certain common elements. Both involve perception, memory, cognition, and comprehension. The observer must find relationships between the immediate sensory input and previous experience. These relationships, which will be based at least in part on attitude or affect, are ordered, rearranged, and expanded, and some preconceptions may be discarded.

A major difference between reading the expression on a face and reading print is that in the case of print, the code to be cracked is linguistic: words are involved. Printed words are arranged according to certain conventions. In American English, one reads from *left* to *right,* from the *top* of the page to the *bottom,* and from the *front* of a book to the *back.* Furthermore, these words represent, to some degree, the sounds of our language.

A definition of reading that focuses on language—specifically written language—as the medium of communication is a narrower definition of the term; but it is still by no means specific enough for the classroom teacher, or anyone else seriously concerned about the reading process. Even within this narrower, linguistically oriented context, there is controversy concerning the nature of this process. Although the task is difficult and complex, no teacher should avoid the responsibility of searching for a reasonably satisfactory and practical, although tentative, definition of reading. A definition of reading will give focus and structure to the teaching-learning process.

Two terms frequently used for purposes of contrast in describing the basic components of the reading process are *decoding* and *meaning.* The term *decoding* usually refers to the techniques that a reader uses to relate the printed words on a page to the language sounds these represent. A clear grasp of the relationships between sounds and symbols, operating at an efficient, even automatic level, is obviously essential to the reading process. Decoding skills are not sufficient in themselves, however. Understanding meaning—the concepts the words represent—is also necessary. Meaning can be viewed as operating on several levels, from literal comprehension to interpreting, reacting to, and evaluating what has been decoded.

The relationship between these two major components of the reading process has definite instructional implications. If reading is viewed primarily as a decoding process, the reading lesson will be far different from one in which the emphasis is on meaning and comprehension. Different materials will be used, and the questions asked and the tasks required of pupils will also be different. The materials used by a teacher who emphasizes decoding will be prepared and selected with primary concern for the basic word analysis skills pupils should develop as they are taught to read. Such skills will be presented in a carefully arranged sequence which the teacher is directed to follow, varying only the rate of presentation, and skipping little for fear of leaving gaps in the child's array of reading competencies. In contrast, when meaning and comprehension strategies receive more emphasis, work on decoding skills is supplemented or even replaced by materials designed to cause children to think about what they have read. In classrooms where meaning and comprehension are emphasized, experience charts, trade books, newspapers, and appropriate periodicals become basic teaching tools and learning resources.

Most of the questions asked of pupils in the "decoding emphasis" class have answers which are clearly correct or incorrect: the word is *pit,* or *pet,* or *pot.* In the classroom where understanding, interpreting, and evaluating receive a great deal of emphasis, the questions asked may not have right or wrong answers. After reading Ezra Jack Keats's *The Snowy Day,* a child might be asked to respond to the following: "*Why* did Peter put the snowball in his pocket? Do you think he ever knew what happened to it? Do you think he is likely to do something like that again?" In other words, questions are designed to stimulate children's thinking.

It is obviously a gross oversimplification to cite only two extreme views of the nature of reading and to note the results of operating at one of these two extremes. Ruddell (1974) [1] writes:

> During the last decade a wide variety of reading-language programs has been developed, and teachers have used these programs in organizational plans ranging from totally individualized efforts to instruction of large numbers of youngsters. These programs can be roughly characterized . . . in the following ways:
>
> 1. Programs emphasizing control of grapheme-phoneme correspondence and letter-sound patterns for decoding and encoding.
> 2. Programs emphasizing language structure (relational meaning) designed to enhance reading-listening comprehension and oral and written expression.
> 3. Programs emphasizing conceptual (lexical meaning), interpretative (semantic interpretation), and problem-solving abilities (cognitive strategies basic to reading-listening comprehension and oral and written expression).
> 4. Programs emphasizing reading-language interests and attitudes (affective mobilizers).
> 5. Programs attempting to integrate the previous components in a systematic manner.

[1] From Robert B. Ruddell, *Reading–Language Instruction: Innovative Practices,* © 1974, pp. 116–117. By permission of Prentice-Hall, Inc., Englewood Cliffs, New Jersey.

Clearly, few reading programs are limited strictly to either decoding or comprehension skills. Most programs consist of strategies designed to develop both kinds of skills, as well as encourage positive attitudes toward reading. Nevertheless, by observing the materials and methods most frequently and consistently used by a reading teacher, we can gather significant evidence regarding the teacher's operational (if not theoretical) definition of reading.

Maturation and the Reading Process: Changing Emphases

The teacher concerned with beginning reading instruction will almost certainly place more emphasis upon decoding or relating speech to print than will the teacher of older children. It seems logical to assume that most nine- to twelve-year-old children have broken the code. They have some concept of letter-sound relationships. The teachers of children in upper elementary and junior high school can and should place more emphasis on interpreting, reacting to, and determining author purpose in what is read. However, the teacher of older children must not ignore those who still need help in basic word analysis skills, just as teachers of young children must not force their pupils to remain at the decoding stage any longer than is necessary.

While the emphasis a teacher places on the various facets of the reading process will vary with the maturity of the student, neither decoding nor comprehension should be emphasized to the exclusion of the other. Both decoding and comprehension are of concern to teachers at all levels, although the emphasis will change as the reader matures. However, the fact that a teacher's understanding of the reading process changes with reference to the maturity of the pupils he is teaching should not be an excuse for devoting less attention to the teaching of reading with older children. Very few adults have reached full maturity in the reading process; most could profit by further developing flexibility in rate, selective retention of major points, and those skills loosely categorized as critical reading skills.

Briefly then, the writer believes that each teacher *must* work toward a definition of reading that is consistent with his beliefs about children and youth, is consonant with his understanding of how children acquire language, and comprehends the intimate relationship between thought, language, and that use of language we call reading.

Working toward a practical, rational definition of reading is important because a teacher's concept of reading influences the materials he will select and the manner in which he will use them.

Various Ways of Viewing the Reading Process

One's definition of reading should not remain static. An effective teacher is constantly growing, stretching, and learning in this area as in other areas. Furthermore, an alert teacher will quickly discover that authors who write for textbooks on reading or who write articles for journals do *not* agree on what reading is, or what facets of the reading process should be emphasized at various levels of a child's development. Edmund B. Huey wrote in 1908 that

> . . . to completely analyze what we do when we read would indeed be the acme of a psychologist's achievements, for it would describe very many of the most intricate workings of the human mind as well as unravel the tangled story of the most remarkable specific performance that civilization has learned in all its history (p. 6).

Nevertheless, the search for a definition of the reading process is important. It results in growth on the part of the teacher and a more effective program for children.

George and Evelyn Spache (1973) have written an excellent book, *Reading in the Elementary School.* Rather than defining reading, they list the "components" of reading. After writing that "reading is obviously a multifaceted process, a process that, like a chameleon, changes its nature from one developmental stage to the next" (p. 3), the authors list the following as descriptive of reading or points of view toward reading:

1. Reading is skill development, beginning with word recognition and proceeding to critical or evaluative reading.
2. Reading is a visual act, a successive series of eye movements, fixations, and regressions (hopefully, not too many of the latter).
3. Reading is a perceptual act, the recognition of a word and assigning to it a meaning, based upon past experience.
4. Reading is a reflection of cultural background. (This hardly needs to be noted, in these times.) "Elevator" means one thing to a rural child, another to a child who lives in the city. The preadolescent who follows the crops reads and reacts to *The Loner* from one point of view, the well cared-for suburban child from another.
5. Reading is a thinking process. The questions teachers ask and the questions good readers ask themselves, before, during, and after reading, reflect previous thinking and stimulate mental growth. Reading as a cognitive ("thinking") process is receiving a great deal of attention from

reading researchers and theorists. In discussing the models presented in
The Literature of Research in Reading with Emphasis on Models (Davis,
1971) Williams writes:

The most promising type of model seems to be one with a cognitive
framework; most recent models are of this nature. I am including in this
group the information processing models discussed by Hansen. Moreover,
two more traditional approaches, operant learning and associative learning, are currently undergoing modification in directions that are definitely
in line with the cognitive approach. The notion of reading as a complex
skill or set of skills often goes hand in hand with a cognitive point of view
(p. 44).

6. Reading is information processing. Reading is conceived of as a visual
   scanning directed by the child's general information store (or long-term
   memory, as it is called) and the information derived from the material
   being read (which is temporarily stored in short-term memory). According to this concept of reading, new material is assimilated into past
   experiences of related nature . . . (Spache and Spache, 1973, p. 35).
7. Reading is associational learning. Those who hold this view of the
   reading process emphasize directing the child's attention to distinctive
   features of letters and words. Samuels (1972) writes that:

When the beginning reader uses strategies such as recognizing words as
sight words, using unusual characteristics of words and word shape as
cues, he is learning strategies which not only are not useful for transfer
but will have to be abandoned if he is to progress to the point where he
can decode words on his own.

He adds:

If there is anything which discrimination studies indicate, it is that
children select the easiest cue for recognition and the easiest cue is
frequently just a single letter of a word or some incidental detail. Children
do not ordinarily attend to a total pattern nor to all the letters in a word. It
is only when single letter cues fail to distinguish one word from another
that children attend to all the letters (p. 27).

Many consider reading as associational learning to be a limited view
most pertinent to beginning word perception.

It is interesting to note how little emphasis was given to language in
general and to speech, especially phonology, in the list of components just
summarized. If vision deserves special mention, and it does, shouldn't
auditory discrimination and perception be stressed, too?

Theodore Clymer (1967), the senior author of a major publisher's basal reading series, approaches a definition of reading by citing four major "aspects" of the reading process. The reader's first task, he says, is that of *decoding* the author's message. The reader's next task is *understanding* the author's message. Unless the reader has been involved in both the decoding and understanding processes, reading has not occurred.

The third aspect of reading, according to Clymer, is interpretation and *critical evaluation* of the author's message. Finally, reading involves *incorporating the author's message* into one's own behavior. One might question whether the evaluative and incorporative stages are always present. Does one invariably evaluate the accuracy of the printed directions on a dress pattern, a recipe, or an interstate highway sign? It is probably true that some visually-processed information is accepted rather uncritically. One might also question the extent to which a reader's behavior changes as a result of evaluating the material he has read. Try to recall the last book you read which profoundly, or even minimally, changed your beliefs or overt behavior. If such change occurs, it is probably both gradual and cumulative. Few readers incorporate even an author's direct messages into their behavior. It seems a bit naïve to assume that voters' decisions are greatly influenced by newspaper editorials, or that everyone who reads the Surgeon General's warning on a pack of cigarettes stops smoking.

Thus, while decoding and understanding appear to be fundamental to the reading process, evaluation and incorporation may occur less commonly. The fact that readers too seldom evaluate or incorporate material which has been read may well represent a serious indictment of reading instruction designed for older children and adolescents. As has been noted before, reading instruction should not be concluded when pupils have acquired basic word analysis and comprehension skills. In a more recent publication (1968) Clymer writes:

> Most educators with special interest in reading assign relatively broad goals or outcomes to reading instruction. The implied principle seems to be that, if reading instruction can make an important contribution to an outcome, even if it is not necessarily a unique contribution, the outcome is a legitimate objective of the reading program. This view places a broad range of outcomes within the province of the reading program.
>
> What are the outcomes or goals which are customarily assigned to reading and how much agreement on these goals does the literature reveal? The answer to this question is not easily obtained. While the following statements may be oversimplified, it seems that four relatively separate but major outcomes of the reading program can be listed. . . . The four outcomes might be listed as: (a) decoding, which corresponds to . . . "word perception"; (b) grasping the author's meaning . . . "literal interpretation"; (c) testing and recombining the author's message with the understanding and background of the reader; (d) application of ideas and values to decisions and actions and extension of author's ideas to new settings.

These outcomes differ greatly in their complexity, with decoding the least complex application and extension the most complex. The characteristic of complexity seems to bear a direct relationship to the agreement in the literature that the outcome is a legitimate concern of the reading program. The less complex the outcome, the more general is the agreement in the literature on its inclusion as an objective for reading. The broad goals are often excluded from the reading program by some specialists such as linguists, psychologists, and others.

The lack of definite information on all factors should not obscure one fact of enormous importance to teachers and educators: Our definition of reading and the outcomes we hold for the reading program have immediate and important implications for how we teach reading and what we teach in it. There is no question more important to ask than: "What is reading?" (pp. 27–29).

For purposes of sharp contrast, the definitions of reading provided by Russell Stauffer (1969) and Leonard Bloomfield (1961) might be examined. According to Clarence Barnhart, Bloomfield believed that "Reading involves nothing more than the correlation of a sound image with its corresponding visual image, that is, the spelling" (Bloomfield and Barnhart, *Let's Read*, jacket cover).

Russell Stauffer is in almost complete disagreement with Bloomfield. He writes in *Directing Reading, Maturity as a Cognitive Process*:

. . . reading is a mental process requiring accurate word recognition, ability to call to mind particular meanings, and ability to shift or reassociate meanings—until the constructs or concepts presented are clearly grasped, critically evaluated, accepted and applied, or rejected. This means that knowledge gained through reading can increase understanding and, in turn, influence social and personal adjustment, enrich experience, and stimulate thinking (p. 16).

Stauffer includes the *uses* of reading in his definition; Bloomfield does not.

Arthur Heilman (1972) notes that reading is a complex process and is difficult to define. However he says most experts agree that ". . . reading is a language function that involves more than the mechanical process of correctly pronouncing words—it involves the recognition of meaning" (p. 5). Such a definition is general enough to offend no one. However, it does not provide very effective guidelines for teachers searching for appropriate methods and criteria for the selection of materials.

Arthur Heilman is not the only one who relates the reading process to its linguistic origins. In *Reading: A Psycholinguistic Guessing Game*, Kenneth Goodman (1970) writes:

. . . reading is a selective process. It involves partial use of available minimal language cues selected from perceptual input on the basis of the reader's expectation. As this partial information is processed, tentative decisions are made to be confirmed, rejected, or refined as reading progresses. More simply stated, reading is a psycholinguistic guessing game. It involves an interaction between thought and language. Efficient reading does not result from precise perception and identification of all elements, but from skill in selecting the fewest, most productive cues necessary to produce guesses which are right the first time. The ability to anticipate[2] that which has not been seen, of course, is vital in reading, just as the ability to anticipate what has not yet been heard is vital in listening (p. 260).

Implications for the Teacher

What difference does all of this make? Should the teacher be advised just to *teach*, without a clear-cut definition of reading, but following certain commonly accepted principles and practices, such as individualized instruction, a flexible program, and continuous diagnosis? This is, of course, much easier than struggling to develop a rational, theoretically sound, yet practical definition. But can the issue be avoided so easily? One's beliefs *do* make a difference. If a teacher operates primarily from a decoding framework, then learning is viewed in narrow terms. Specific facets of cognitive development may be neglected while others are stressed, and the affective domain may be de-emphasized or even ignored.

If, on the other hand, the teacher operates basically from a "meaning" framework, the child may never develop the fundamental word analysis skills he needs for independence in reading. Maturity in reading clearly involves the ability to relate printed words to speech and to the concepts represented by speech.

The Author's Viewpoint

The reading process begins with the child's acquisition of language and with the experiences this language symbolizes. It involves the ability to associate specific sound elements with appropriate graphic symbols. The effective reader demonstrates his understanding of the complexity of language by making necessary adjustments when sounds or words occur in unfamiliar settings.

---

[2] Accordingly, *home* would probably be a higher level (and less serious) miscue for the printed word *house* than would *horse* because it would indicate more accurate anticipation and a more sophisticated application of context clues.

Obviously the competent reader will apply his understanding of both the general and the specific meanings of the words he reads. As he defines the terms he reads, he will rely upon his previous experiences with the concepts these terms symbolize. As he reacts to what he has read, the effective reader will apply the appropriate interpretive and evaluative criteria. He will *think* about what is being read.

Without question, reading involves decoding, or if one prefer's Goodman's term, recoding. This process includes both auditory and visual perception and discrimination at very high levels. Even the broadest definition of reading as a basis for instruction will take into account the significance of this vital phase of the reading act.

Reading is also, without question, understanding or comprehending the material read. The major purpose of decoding is to facilitate comprehension. Decoding does not exist as an end in itself. A case can be made for placing interpretation and reaction to what is read on the periphery of the reading process. However, the reading act cannot be said to be complete if the reader is consistently unselective, uncritical, apathetic, or antagonistic in his responses to what is read.

It seems clear that a teacher has a professional obligation to know *why* he's teaching as he is. Without developing a definition of reading it is difficult to formulate a useful set of objectives or to arrange these objectives in order of importance. Without such objectives, evaluation becomes a rather pointless, expensive exercise. One cannot diagnose until one has determined what areas of strength and weakness are of greatest concern. Is Johnny, who cannot determine the main idea of a paragraph, in more or less serious trouble than Bill, who confuses *-ed* and *-ing* endings? One's definition of reading should help to answer this question.

Models of the Reading Process

As noted before, it is misleading to characterize reading as *either* decoding *or* searching for meaning. Unfortunately, some reading experts have categorized methods and materials used at the beginning levels of instructions as representative of either a coding emphasis or a meaning emphasis (Chall, 1967). Such views are not very useful to a teacher concerned with instructional methods and materials.

A simple representation of the reading process might well be a continuum with decoding skills at one extreme and meaning or comprehension at the other. Such a representation is called a model.

Gephart (1970) defines a model as follows: "A model is a representation of a phenomenon which displays the identifiable structural elements of that phenomenon, the relationships among these elements, and the processes involved in the natural phenomenon" (p. 38). The models presented here were selected because they appear to meet most or all of the criteria specified by Athey (1971, p. 6–3): parsimony, coherence, correspondence with reality, and heuristic value. The *Theoretical Models* reference and the Davis reference are particularly valuable and are suggested for those with strong interests in this area.

Several models of the reading process will be presented. The models to be discussed are complex and present a fairly representative view of what occurs in the reading act. They are somewhat controversial, but should provide the pre-professional and professional with additional insights into the reading process.

Goodman's Model

Kenneth Goodman (1968) has devised a series of diagrams representing his model of what occurs in reading at three levels of proficiency.

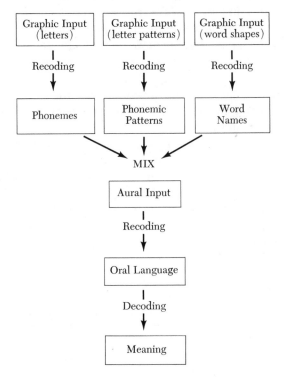

Figure 1.1   Proficiency Level 1.

Source: Kenneth S. Goodman, *The Psycholinguistic Nature of the Reading Process*, p. 17. Copyright © 1968 by Wayne State University Press. Reprinted by permission of the publisher and the author.

Graphic input refers to the print selected by the author. As noted, such print can be interpreted at three levels, *letters, letter patterns,* and *word shapes.* A teacher's instructional strategies influenced by the definition upon which he operates, will determine which of these three types of graphic clues a child will use most frequently. An efficient, well-instructed reader will learn to use several kinds of graphic clues and not rely exclusively upon one.

Before children learn to read, they have learned to listen and to speak. They have acquired some understanding of the phonological, morphological, syntactic, and semantic features of their language. All of this is implied in Goodman's use of the term *aural input.* Goodman notes that there may be a difference between what is spoken and what is heard. What the speaker utters may or may not closely resemble what the listener hears.

The term *phoneme* refers to the thirty-eight to forty-eight significant, distinctive, and contrastive sound units of our language. There are separate phonemic representations for the initial sounds in *sip* and *zip,* in *bit* and *pit,* to indicate the meaning differences represented. The initial, medial, and final sounds represented by the letter *p* in *pie, pepper,* and *lip* differ slightly in most dialects. Because meaning would *not* be affected if the sounds were identical, these differences are not typically represented by different phonemic symbols.

By *word names* Goodman apparently means the assignment of a name to a word pre-existing in the child's speaking vocabulary without analysis of the phonemes involved.

In explaining the *interrelationships* of the parts of the model, Goodman writes (1968), "In the early stages of reading the process may involve a stretching out so that graphic input is *re*-coded (not decoded) into aural input which is eventually decoded for meaning" (p. 16). Goodman and others contend that the task of learning to read will be more easily accomplished if the language the child reads closely resembles the language he hears and speaks.

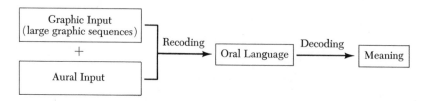

Figure 1.2   Proficiency Level 2.

Source: Kenneth S. Goodman, *The Psycholinguistic Nature of the Reading Process,* p. 18. Copyright © 1968 by Wayne State University Press. Reprinted by permission of the publisher and the author.

Goodman suggests that the process is considerably faster at Proficiency Level 2. Larger units are processed almost simultaneously in terms of graphic and aural input. The reader at this level no longer concentrates upon isolated sounds, letters, and words, although when he is faced with an unfamiliar word, he may return to a more fundamental level and work with word parts (sounds and letters).

This view of reading in larger meaningful units is not held by those who cite evidence from studies of visual perception. Some of those concerned primarily with reading as a visual process would seriously question the ability of a child to grasp large units of print even when segmented into meaningful parts. Eye camera evidence is cited by Dechant (1970, p. 22) to support the claim that the beginning reader makes two fixations or stops per word. How then can one claim that reading occurs in large units—clauses, phrases, or sentences?

It is appropriate to discuss at this point Goodman's use of the term *meaning*. Meaning serves as the focal point of the models representing all three proficiency levels. Goodman feels that isolated phonemes and graphic symbols have no independent meaning, but acquire meaning with reference to the child's language development and background of experiences.

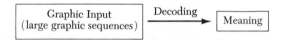

Figure 1.3   Proficiency Level 3.

Source: Kenneth S. Goodman, *The Psycholinguistic Nature of the Reading Process*, p. 19. Copyright © 1968 by Wayne State University Press. Reprinted by permission of the publisher and the author.

At Proficiency Level 3, according to Goodman (1968),

. . . recoding and decoding become simultaneous so that, except in passages where the phrasing is complex or ambiguous, the reader is virtually decoding meaning directly from graphic input (p. 18).

Silent reading assumes greater significance at Proficiency Level 3. The child is no longer limited to the rate at which he can speak. The mature reader makes use of minimal cues and learns to utilize only those which are most essential.

Perhaps the most significant features of Goodman's view of the reading process are the following:

1. The focus is always upon meaning. The acquisition of a large number of generalizations regarding grapheme-phoneme correspondence serves

only one purpose: that is, enabling the reader to accurately interpret the author's message.

2. The mature reader streamlines the reading process. The recoding and decoding processes are quite automatic, and graphic input is rarely returned to speech.
3. The child's response to print is strongly influenced by his oral language. When there is great divergence between the language a child speaks and hears and that which he reads, reading will be less effective and efficient.

Kenneth Goodman's model is an interesting and provocative way of representing the reading process. It is unlikely that a teacher who accepts his model and operates on the basis of it will concentrate on isolated letter-sound drills or will devote much effort to teaching linguistic patterns, particularly if these patterns are meaningless (i.e., *sic, pic, dic* as examples of a consonant-vowel-consonant pattern).

Ruddell's Model

Robert Ruddell's communication model (Ruddell and Bacon, 1972) concentrates on *decoding* strategies, *meaning* strategies, and *interpretation* abilities (see Figure 1.4). This communication model may be analyzed in terms of five basic components.

Category I: Oral and Written Language Forms This category refers to letters, letter patterns, and the relationship of these to sounds and sound patterns. It also includes work typically classified as the development of sight vocabulary and that ordinarily considered structural analysis as well. Ruddell makes it clear that work with sounds, letters, and patterns of each is done within the context of the word. It should be noted that the feature of Goodman's model called *aural re-coding*, relating print to speech, is not emphasized in this model.

Category II: Aspects of Meaning In this category several aspects of the meaning process are identified. First the child relates the syntax he encounters in print to the syntactical structures in his own oral language. Then he may select an appropriate meaning of the term he has encountered from all the meanings with which he is familiar. The child's handling of form and structure words (*of, the, for*) affects the process of getting meaning, as does the interaction of nonlinguistic information, such as illustrations with print.

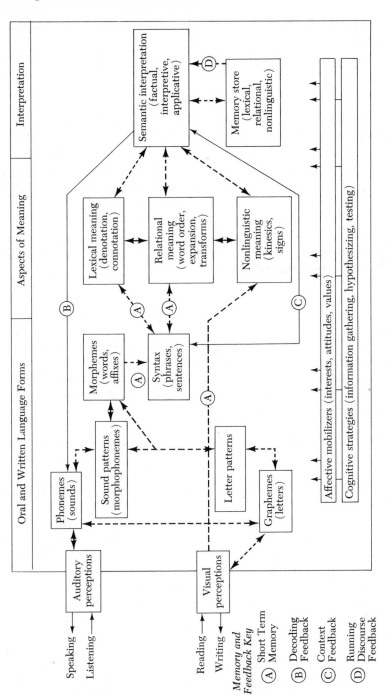

Figure 1.4   The Communication Framework.

Source: Robert Ruddell. *Reading–Language Instruction: Innovative Practices*, © 1974, p. 41. By permission of Prentice-Hall, Inc., Englewood Cliffs, New Jersey.

It is interesting to note that Ruddell and Bacon consider the interpretation of illustrations to be a very significant context clue.[3] This is in contrast with the position taken by some linguists (Fries, 1962) that the reading process is inhibited when children rely on illustrations rather than print for meaning.

Category III: Interpretation Interpretation is seen as an integrative process. In this process, the linguistic and thinking skills of the child are integrated. This integration produces what are commonly termed more sophisticated responses to print, or critical reading skills. Questioning the author's purpose, evaluating the logic of the arguments the author presents, comparing one author's ideas with another's, and recognizing propaganda techniques would be among the results of this process of integration.

It has been noted before (see Clymer's discussion of evaluating the author's message, pp. 9–10) that readers do not invariably react critically to what has been read, nor is such reaction always expected.

Category IV: Memory and Feedback In evaluating or analyzing what has been read, the reader relies upon what is termed the *memory store,* his previous experiences with the concepts, objects, or events described in print. The memory store is enriched and grows larger as a result of new cognitive and linguistic input. This facet of the reading process is very similar to and perhaps could be considered a logical extension of the interpretation process.

Category V: Affective Mobilizers and Cognitive Strategies Ruddell (1972, pp. 176–177) states that "throughout the various stages of the communication process, the reader's participation is directed by his interests, attitudes, and values. . . ." The term *affective mobilizers* is used to describe these influences.

The questions a reader asks prior to reading, whether these are set forth by the reader himself, the writer of the material he is reading, or the teacher, will help to determine his reaction to this material. Such questions can be asked at several levels, and Ruddell and Bacon have devised a taxonomy of comprehension skills, as has Barrett.[4]

A person's attitudes, interests, and values influence the way he thinks about what he reads, and the thinking strategies he employs will have an effect upon his attitudes toward the material. It is appropriate that these two be discussed together.

[3] See Arnold and Miller's discussion of picture clues in Chapter Ten.
[4] See Guszak's discussion of Barrett's taxonomy in Chapter Eleven.

Ruddell's model appears to be comprehensive enough to include most if not all the cognitive and linguistic activity which comprises the reading process. It is indeed complex, and although it may be modified in light of future research findings, it is difficult to see what aspects of the reading act are not accounted for.

He writes the following summary description of his communication model:

> The communication model may be arranged into five basic categories. The first, Oral and Written Language Forms, includes the phonological, graphological, morphological, and syntactic components. The second category, Aspects of Meaning, includes the meaning components—lexical, relational, and nonlinguistic. The third category, Interpretation, integrates the various meaning forms through factual, interpretive, and applicative processes. The fourth category, Memory and Feedback, provides for storing and transferring information from one part of the model to another to formulate and evaluate interpretations. The fifth category is Affective Mobilizers and Cognitive Strategies. These dual components interact with and serve to direct all dimensions of communication as the individual identifies specific goals and objectives and directs his thinking processes to achieve the established goals and objectives so as to culminate in the third category, Interpretation (p. 90).

The Ruddell and Goodman Models Compared

Teachers operating on the basis of Ruddell's model will be particularly aware of the cognitive skills they are developing. It may well be that Ruddell gives more attention to the child's thinking skills, to reading as a cognitive act, than Goodman does. It may also be true that Goodman pays somewhat more attention to the child's linguistic background as this influences and is influenced by his reading. Goodman accounts for increasing sophistication through the use of his three Proficiency Levels. He also appears to be very much aware of the merging of certain components of the reading process as the reader matures. Ruddell's model does not account for the stage of oral recoding as Goodman's does.

The differences between the models, however, are of much less significance to the classroom teacher than the areas of agreement. Both models conceptualize reading as both a linguistic and a cognitive process. Both models take a similar approach to the acquisition and development of word analysis skills. Neither Goodman nor Ruddell would support drill on isolated letter-sound relationships.

Goodman emphasizes the value of promoting a close relationship between the language a child speaks and hears and the language he reads to the point where one might automatically associate Goodman's name with the "language experience" approach (see Chapter Six). It may be more accurate to say that Goodman is less concerned with specific methodology than he is with making full use of the child's language in helping the child learn to read.

Summary

The process of answering the question "What is reading?" is more than an intellectual exercise. One's beliefs about reading and the way one conceives of the reading process strongly influence the methods and materials one uses in teaching. It follows that a teacher's definition of reading will influence the types of readers his pupils become. It is not an accident that over-analytic readers—readers who isolate sounds, apply unnatural pitch and stress patterns, and have difficulty blending sounds into something resembling natural speech—consistently come from the same teachers' classrooms. Children have been taught to read this way. Children from other classrooms may consistently demonstrate positive attitudes toward reading but have inadequate decoding or word analysis skills. These conditions are also the result of learning.

As a teacher learns more about the complex process of reading, his definition of reading should change. Such growth will occur as one studies the reading process, as one learns more about language and the development of the cognitive processes, and as one studies and learns more about children.

Goodman's three Proficiency Levels exemplify the fact that reading is not the same at all stages of development. Reading for a six-year-old is not quite the same process as it is for a ten- or a sixteen-year-old. One's definition should probably account for this.

It may appear to the reader that the models presented are unduly complex and difficult to interpret. As a result of reacting to these models, however, one should have a clearer notion of what occurs in the reading act. The models presented are comprehensive and interactive. Both clearly demonstrate that reading is a dynamic process.

References

Bloomfield, L., and Barnhart, C. *Let's Read: A Linguistic Approach.* Detroit: Wayne State University Press, 1961.

Chall, J. *Learning to Read: The Great Debate.* New York: McGraw-Hill, 1967.

Clymer, T. "What Is 'Reading'?" *Elementary School Notes, Language Arts Issue.* Boston: Ginn, 1967.

Clymer, T. "What Is 'Reading'?: Some Current Concepts." In *Innovation and Change in Reading Instruction.* 67th Yearbook of the National Society for the Study of Education, edited by Helen M. Robinson. Chicago: University of Chicago Press, 1968, pp. 7–29.

Davis, F. B., ed. *The Literature of Research in Reading with Emphasis on Models.* New Brunswick, N.J.: Rutgers Graduate School of Education, 1971.

Dechant, E. V. *Improving the Teaching of Reading.* Englewood Cliffs, N.J.: Prentice-Hall, 1970.

Fries, C. C. *Linguistics and Reading.* New York: Holt, Rinehart and Winston, 1962.

Gephart, W. J. *Application of the Convergence Technique to Basic Studies of the Reading Process.* Bloomington, Ind.: Phi Delta Kappa, 1970.

Goodman, K. S. "The Psycholinguistic Nature of the Reading Process." In *The Psycholinguistic Nature of the Reading Process*, edited by K. S. Goodman. Detroit: Wayne State University Press, 1968.

Goodman, K. S. "Reading: A Psycholinguistic Guessing Game." In *Theoretical Models and Processes of Reading*, edited by H. Singer and R. B. Ruddell. Newark, Del.: International Reading Association, 1970.

Heilman, A. W. *Principles and Practices of Teaching Reading.* Columbus, Ohio: Charles E. Merrill, 1972.

Huey, E. B. *The Psychology and Pedagogy of Reading.* New York: Macmillan, 1908.

Keats, E. J. *The Snowy Day.* New York: Viking Press, 1962.

Otto, W.; Chester, R.; McNeil, J.; and Myers, S. *Focused Reading Instruction.* Reading, Mass.: Addison Wesley, 1974.

Robeck, M. C., and Wilson, J. A. R. *Psychology of Reading: Foundations of Instruction.* New York: John Wiley, 1974.

Ruddell, R. *Reading–Language Instruction.* Englewood Cliffs, N.J.: Prentice-Hall, 1974.

Ruddell, R. B., and Bacon, H. G. "The Nature of Reading: Language and Meaning." In *Language and Learning to Read: What Teachers Should*

Know About Language, edited by R. E. Hodges and E. H. Rudorf. Boston: Houghton Mifflin, 1972.

Singer, H., and Ruddell, R., eds. *Theoretical Models and Processes of Reading.* Newark, Del.: International Reading Association, 1971.

Spache, G. D., and Spache, E. *Reading in the Elementary School.* Boston: Allyn and Bacon, 1973.

Stauffer, R. G. *Directing Reading Maturity as a Cognitive Process.* New York: Harper and Row, 1969.

Wier, E. *The Loner.* New York: David McKay, 1963.

Chapter
Two

Preview

In this chapter Emerald Dechant continues the discussion of theories and models of reading initiated in Chapter One. His focus is primarily upon the psychological contributions to a theory of reading, and he discusses several of the most important models. The discussion of models is prefaced by comments on the physiology of reading, the sign system, language structures, and the psychology of cognition. An attempt is made to place theories of reading within a comprehensive theory of child development.

The reader who is unfamiliar with the concepts and vocabulary may have some difficulty with this chapter, but the editors feel that the material is well worth the effort.

Dechant's treatment of the psychological bases of reading represents a new synthesis of some of the recent contributions of cognitive psychology and psycholinguistics. This chapter reflects a good deal of the thinking regarding the interdisciplinary convergence on the reading process occurring today.

Reading:
Psychological Bases

Emerald Dechant, Fort Hays State College

Objectives

After you have read this chapter, you should be able to:

1. Describe the theories of the reading process discussed by the author.
2. Describe the relationship between cognition and perception, as these relate to reading.
3. Compare and contrast the cue systems in reading.
4. Compare and contrast two of the models of the reading process discussed in the chapter.
5. List and discuss the most significant physiological limitations which can (and often do) inhibit success in reading.

Reading is an exceedingly complex process and specialized skill. It is a type of human behavior that should be studied and analyzed by psychologists, but perhaps because it is a form of behavior that is not directly observable, it has not been given the attention by learning theorists that it deserves. For this reason, Kingston (1968) feels that at present a systematic, well-formulated psychology of reading does not exist and that what is available is inadequately structured to be of much value to the classroom teacher.

Psychology has nonetheless had a profound effect on such concepts as readiness, developmental reading, practice, sensation, and evaluation of student progress, and on our understanding of perception, cognition, and learning.

Kingston (1968) keynotes the purpose of this chapter. He notes that a major contribution of psychology to reading is to provide the impetus needed to develop a more adequate theory of reading. We are on the verge of some significant movement in this direction.

The Nature of the Reading Process

Reading is a *language and communication process.* It is the process of putting the reader in contact with the ideas of the writer as expressed through the symbols of written language. The nature of the reading process will become clearer as this chapter develops. Here let us comment briefly upon three aspects: the sign system in reading, the decoding process, and the role that language structures play in decoding. Our reason for doing so is that reading always involves a sign system—the words or symbols on the printed page; it involves decoding—association of meaning with the symbols; and it involves language structures—a syntax that mediates between the surface structure and meaning.

The Sign System

Reading is a sensory process. The reader must learn to identify and learn to respond to graphic symbols. Reading is a *word-identification* process, and one aspect of the beginning reader's problem is to discover the critical differences between letters and words. He needs to learn the distinctive features of written language. These distinctive features—the visual con-figuration of the letters—form the raw material of reading (Smith, 1971, p. 4).

For many years, reading research has focused on the skills required for developing quick recognition responses to our alphabetic writing. Research was designed to develop the child's ability to see the significant contrastive features of the separate letters (Cooper, 1965). Research therefore emphasized feature analysis of the written symbols, or the *surface structure* of the language. The reading teacher spent most of his time and energy teaching children to identify letters and words.

Within the space of this chapter, it is impossible even to sample the thousands of studies on the sensory aspects of reading or the many methods of letter and word identification. We can, however, examine the major findings of this research. Studies indicate that eye-movement patterns reflect the maturity that the reader has attained. The poor reader makes extra fixations and regressions as he reads a line of print. The studies also clearly indicate that successful methods of word identification generally combine the best of both *surface structure* analysis (letter, sound, or syllable identification) and *deep structure* analysis (identification from context). The beginning reader has to rely on feature analysis much more than the fluent reader, because he is unable to make full use of the context information, both syntactic and semantic (Smith, 1971, p. 221). The beginning reader must deduce meaning primarily from surface structure analysis rather than deep structure analysis.

The Importance of Decoding

Theorists and practitioners have been quick to point out that reading is much more than simply recognizing the graphic symbols. It is even more than pronouncing the words on the printed page, or matching the written code with the spoken code. This is *recoding,* but it is not *decoding.* *Decoding* occurs only when the reader *associates meaning* with the written symbol (Goodman, 1971) and *understands the meaning* that the writer intended. A team of experts, under the sponsorship of the United States Office of Education, has therefore tentatively defined reading as "a term used to refer to an interaction by which meaning *encoded* in visual stimuli by an author becomes meaning in the mind of the reader."

Reading of graphic symbols consists of two processes: the visual process involved in bringing the stimuli to the brain and the mental process involved in interpreting the stimuli after they get to the brain. When the light rays from the printed page hit the retinal cells of the eyes, signals are sent along the optic nerve to the visual centers of the brain. Before this can be called reading, however, the reader must bring *meaning* to the graphic symbol. The critical element in reading often is not what is on the page, but rather what the graphic symbols signify to the reader. So reading might be described as the process of giving the significance intended by the writer to the graphic symbols by relating them to one's own fund of experiences (Dechant, 1970, p. 19).

Reading is thus a *perceptual process* as well as a *conceptual process.* The reader interprets what he reads by associating it with his past experience. Reading is a process of forming tentative judgments and interpretations, and verifying, correcting, and confirming guesses.

Reading for comprehension is something more than reading for word identification. Smith (1971, p. 4) suggests that it is possible to read for comprehension without actually identifying individual words. He adds (1971, p. 222) that the decoding that the skilled reader performs is not to transform visual symbols into sound, but to transform the visual representation into meaning.

The Importance of Language Structures

Recently, descriptions of the reading process have broadened to focus on language structures. Birkley (1970), for example, defines reading as "the recognition and perception of language structures as wholes in order to comprehend both the *surface* and *deep meanings* which these structures communicate." This definition will be dealt with in detail later in the chapter; here we will point out only its main emphasis.

The advocates of Birkley's view generally agree on what reading is not. They do not perceive reading as a precise process, consisting of exact, detailed, sequential perception and identification of letters, words, and spelling patterns. They emphasize, rather, the conceptual nature of the reading process—specifically, how meaning is acquired and conveyed through the *deep structures* of language.

Goodman (1967) notes that reading is a selective process, involving partial use of available minimal language clues (graphic, semantic, and syntactic) selected from perceptual input on the basis of the reader's expectation. The reader, as he processes this partial information, confirms, rejects, or refines his tentative decisions as reading progresses. Goodman points out that a common misconception is that graphic input is precisely and sequentially recoded as phonological input and then decoded bit by bit. He notes that readers utilize all three kinds of information—graphic, semantic, and syntactic—simultaneously. *Certainly without the graphic input there would be no reading, but the reader uses syntactic and semantic information as well.*

Smith (1971) points out that a fluent reader depends more on cues contained in context than on feature analysis. He operates at a *deep structure* level and predicts as he reads, sampling the *surface structure* as he tests out his predictions. When his predictions are not confirmed, he returns to feature analysis.

Smith (1971, p. 44) does not see reading as a matter of decoding printed symbols into sounds and then extracting meaning from the sounds. He suggests that the fluent reader generally is unable to do this because fluent reading is accomplished too fast for the translation into sound to occur. The decoding that the reader does transforms the graphic symbols directly into meaning. *Decoding is effected through syntax;* syntax mediates between the visual surface structure and meaning (Smith, 1971, p. 222).

Wardhaugh (1969) suggests that when a person reads he discovers meaning by using the visual clues of spelling, his knowledge of probabilities of letter and word occurrence, his knowledge of context, and his syntactic and semantic competence to give a meaningful interpretation to the text. He notes that the reader does not process visual signals just to convert these signals into some kind of covert speech. This conversion is merely the beginning of the process; semantic and syntactic processing are also necessary. In support of his view he points out that one cannot read a foreign language by simply being able to vocalize the print.

The Psychology of Cognition

Because reading obviously requires the association of *meaning* with graphic input, a psychology of reading concerns itself with the nature of perception, cognition, and thinking. It also concerns itself with the role that language plays in thought. Language is a system of responses by which individuals communicate with each other (inter-individual communication). Language is also a system of responses that facilitates thinking and cognition (intra-individual communication).

The Role of Language in Thinking

The close relationship between language and thought has always been acknowledged. The Greek word *logos,* for example, is the symbol for both reason and speech. Kant wrote: "To think is to speak to oneself." Watson (1920) referred to thought as "subvocal use of language." DeLaguna (1929) notes that "If an animal cannot express its thoughts in language, that is because it has no thoughts to express; for thoughts which are not formulated are something less than thoughts." Langer (1948, p. 103) writes: "In language we have the free, accomplished use of symbolism, the record of articulate conceptual thinking; without language there seems to be nothing like explicit thought whatever." Laurita (1973) notes that speech is not merely a by-product of thinking but is also a means of thought.

Implicit speech seems to accompany thinking as well as much reading. Jacobsen (1932) suggests that when a person is imagining an object, the muscles controlling his eyes contract as though he were actually looking at it. When the person imagines that he is performing a muscular act, a contraction occurs in the muscle fibers that would normally be involved in that act. When the person thinks, the muscles of the tongue or upper lip vibrate as if he were speaking words.

Edfelt (1960), studying the electromyographic records of university students and adults, found that all these people engaged in silent speech while reading. Good readers engaged in less silent speech than poor readers, and the more difficult the material, the more silent speech occurred. This, of course, does not mean that reading without silent speech is impossible. It simply means that in these experiments silent speech was always present. Beginning readers may depend almost totally upon speech; more fluent readers probably depend on it less.

There is little doubt that a certain amount of vocal behavior and lip and tongue movement accompany many thought processes and most reading. Experiments show that students preparing for an examination actually become hoarse after four hours of intensive study. Hebb (1958, pp. 59–60) suggests that some verbal behavior may play a vital role in problem solving. Intensive thought is much more than a simple brain function. He adds (1958, p. 60), however, that sentence construction shows that thought and speech are not entirely the same process. Thought processes run well ahead of our articulations. Van Riper and Butler (1955, p. 100) note that "just as there is an eye-voice span in oral reading, so, too, there is a similar scanning process preceding utterance. Our minds keep looking ahead of our mouths, scanning our memory drums for the words which will be needed." We know that aphasics, although unable to speak, do think and do learn to read. However, it is much more difficult for them to do so.

Even though the evidence shows a close relationship between thought and language and between implicit speech and reading, it is not always necessary to go through the auditory-vocal counterparts of the printed symbol to proceed from graphic symbol to meaning. A beginning reader often uses this technique, although it may be of very little use to him once he becomes a fluent reader.

The Psychology of Cognition

Later in this chapter we shall examine the cognitive model in detail. Here we will comment on only one aspect of it: namely, that *perception and cognition always go beyond the information given.*

Since the words on the printed page cannot provide meaning by themselves, the reader must be perceiving something beyond what he sees. He must be—and is—using information that is not present to the senses. The reader does not see the object, person, or experience of which the author writes. And yet as he reads he attributes meaning to the word. His reaction to the printed word is determined by the experiences that he has had with the objects or events which the symbol represents. This is what is meant by perception (Hebb, 1958). Perception is a consciousness of the experiences evoked by a symbol.

The cognitive theorist emphasizes that both the external stimulus and the central cerebral process (cognition) determine behavior. There simply is not sufficient information in the external stimulus alone to explain the response of the perceiver. The central cerebral processes bring in past learning experiences which are not present in the immediate stimulus at all. The individual perceives his world in terms of "what he is" as much as "what it is." William James (1890, p. 103) pointed out years ago that "Whilst part of what we perceive comes through our senses from the object before us, another part always comes . . . out of our head."

Horn (1937) points out that the writer does not really convey ideas to the reader; he merely stimulates him to construct them out of his own experience. And, the reader who brings the most to the printed page gains the most. Chall (1947) gave an information test on the subject of tuberculosis to about one hundred sixth and eighth graders. She then had them read a selection on tuberculosis and gave them a test on the selection. Those children who already knew the most about tuberculosis also made the best comprehension scores on the reading selection. Chall noted that we read in order to gain experience, and yet it is also true that we get more out of reading if we have more experience.

Emerging from cognitive research is a picture of man as an active and selective information-gatherer who both gains and creates knowledge. His brain is constantly processing information, and incoming information is continually being tested, reformulated, and acted upon in the light of prior experience.

We have further evidence that the learner, the perceiver, or reader interprets incoming data on the basis of rules already stored in the brain (Smith, 1971, p. 81).

Identification and Association

Bruner (1957) notes that readers can recognize words when certain letters are deleted or can recognize missing numbers in a sequence. In the sequence 3, 9, 12, _____, for example, a reader will see that the numbers are multiples of three and realize that the missing number is fifteen. In the sentence, "George _____ was our first president," the word *Washington* is readily filled in.

Similar examples occur in grammar (Osgood, 1957, p. 87). A singular subject calls for a verb ending in *s* (Jack sits); a time element calls for an appropriate tense (*Today, I am* king); a dependent clause calls for an independent clause (If you see him, call me); and the order of words itself is set (The boy sat on the log—the log sat on the boy). Changing the order usually alters the meaning.

Bruner (1957, p. 44) believes that, in situations like the above, the *perceiver learns certain formal schemata that are used to order the probabilistic relationships between the data.* In support of his assumption, Bruner (1957, p. 47) refers to a study by William Hull. Hull found that in learning to spell, the good speller learned a general "coding system" which permitted him to reconstruct the sequence of letters. Similarly, Bruner notes that while the poor speller learned words by rote, the good speller learned a set of rules based on the transitional probabilities that characterize letter sequences in English.

The letters in the language are used in a way that permits us to reconstruct them from what we know about the surrounding letters. The letters follow one another in a predictable order. Some sequences never occur in English; others occur frequently. The letter *q*, for example, is invariably followed by *u*. The chances are rather good that the letter *p* completes the word *com act*—the probability of occurrence of *p* is greater than that of any other letter. Readers often infer missing words or letters from the context.

In the same way, grammatical forms are inferred. The three-year-old is using the context or the transitional probabilities that characterize the English language when he uses regular endings such as *selled, runned,* or *mans* for the irregular *sold, ran,* or *men,* and so does the first grader who reads *come* as /kōm/. Although linguists still have not adequately constructed the rules of grammar, the child of three and a half knows them (Dechant, 1970, p. 147). Children learn language in a rapid, smooth, and predictable sequence (Ervin and Miller, 1963; Kean and Yamamoto, 1965), indicating that they are equipped biologically both *to use* and *to learn* language (Smith, 1971, p. 49).

Language learning appears to be largely instinctive—a part of our biological inheritance. Any child can learn any of the world's languages because he spontaneously emits the sounds of all languages (Emans, 1973). The acquisition strategy is the same for all babies everywhere in the world (Gunderson, 1973). The child is born ready to speak a language—namely, the babytalk of childhood—which he gradually modifies to approximate the language of his parents. He appears to be systematically trying out alternative rules, constantly testing them against his parents' language.

Piaget's work has contributed additional evidence to support the view that basic language skills are innate. He has shown that very little language learning is attributable to imitation. Children's utterances simply do not approximate those of the adults about them. They gradually change their constructions to conform to adult language, but they do this by starting with a language of their own, not by starting from nothing (Smith, 1971, p. 51). Furthermore, the sequence in which they learn language is orderly and systematic and is closely related to physical and motor aspects of development.

The Cue Systems in Reading

It is clear from what we have said so far that many different factors can cue meaning (Smith, Goodman, and Meredith, 1970), factors both outside and inside the reader. Cues inside the reader are basically experience and the innate rules of language; cues outside the reader are cue systems within words, cue systems in the flow of language, and cue systems that are external both to the reader and to the language.

Even though the reader does not necessarily use all the cue systems when he reads, reading instruction must not ignore any of these systems. Reading is message reconstruction, and for the most part comprehension of meaning consists of using all the cues available.

The various cue systems that operate in reading to cue meaning are the following (Smith, Goodman, and Meredith, 1970):

1. Cue systems within words
   a. Letter-sound relationships (grapheme-phoneme correspondences)
   b. Shape (word configuration or physiognomy)
   c. Known little words in new words or comparison of new words to known words
   d. Affixes, prefixes, and suffixes
   e. Recurrent spelling patterns, phonograms
   f. Diacritical marking systems, color coding
   g. Legibility factors
2. Cue systems in the flow of language
   a. Patterns of word order or function order (subject, predicate)
   b. Inflectional endings (*ed, s, es, ing*)
   c. Function words (articles, auxiliary verbs, prepositions, conjunctions)
   d. Intonation patterns (pitch, stress, juncture)
   e. Verbal or grammatical context in which the word or words are placed
   f. Redundancy clues (In the sentence, "The boys eat their lunches," there are at least four cues that the subject is plural.)
   g. Grammatical and syntactical patterns
   h. Punctuation marks
3. Cues external to the reader and to language
   a. Pictures, art activities, dramatization, tracing, etc.
   b. Prompting (telling the child what the word is)
   c. Concrete objects
4. Cues within the reader
   a. Language facility (especially innate rules of language)
   b. Dialect differences (cultural factors)
   c. Physiology (biological-neurological and maturational factors)
   d. Learned responses to graphic cues or the perceptual skill of the learner
   e. Experiential and socioeconomic background of the learner
   f. Intellectual and conceptual development of the learner
   g. Physical, social, and emotional factors

The last category (cues within the reader) leads us to a discussion of the developmental process.

The Developmental Process

A psychology of reading must be concerned with child development. Reading cannot be completely understood until the perceptual, cognitive, and developmental aspects of living and learning in general are understood.

A great deal of research has been done on maturational and environmental learning influences. Psychologists have studied intelligence, physical development, sensory development, auditory and visual discrimination, psychomotor abilities, personality, social-emotional adjustment, socioeconomic status, and neurological functioning. In general, we have found that the human system can be programmed in three ways: structurally (genetically and through hereditary endowment); environmentally (by the environment with which it interacts); and by learning processes (Blake, 1970, p. 94). The basic assumption underlying all this research is that reading is a learned process and that learning to read, like all learning, is interrelated with the learner's total growth and development.

There are both biological and environmental determinants of readiness for and achievement in reading. The student reads with his biology and his geography, with his nature and his nurture. Growth and development are variable and so is achievement in reading. There is for each child a most teachable moment for learning to read and for the learning of every subsequent reading skill. The teachable moment depends on many developmental factors, especially on those identified above.

The obvious inference we can make from the research is that without adequate maturation the child cannot learn to read and that without experiences he has nothing from which to learn. The teacher must not, however, overemphasize either maturation or experience. Placing too much emphasis on maturation may lead to useless postponing of what could be learned; on the other hand, too much emphasis on experience may lead to futile attempts at teaching something for which the child is not ready. How close the pupil comes to attaining his potential, however, depends upon his experiences and the use he makes of them.

Bruner (1962) adds a slightly different dimension when he observes that readiness for learning depends more on our ability to translate ideas into the language and concepts at the age level we are teaching than on maturation.

Piaget and Cognitive Development

To illustrate how developmental factors relate to reading achievement, let us examine one concept, cognitive development, and restrict our discussion to one psychologist, Piaget, who has probably done the most impressive work in the field of cognitive development. Piaget's model is particularly significant because it supports the linguists' scientific approach to an explanation of the reading process.

Piaget's hypothesis (Avdul, 1974; Piaget, 1969, 1961, 1957, 1952; Inhelder, 1963; Inhelder and Piaget, 1958) is that cognitive development, and by extension the concrete operation of cognition including language development, is "an integrated process of successive equilibrations of cognitive structures, each structure . . . deriving logically and inevitably from the preceding one" (Flavell, 1963). Piaget, positing four interrelated stages of cognitive development, perceived the process of development as structured sequentially. Organisms develop and evolve in a patterned fashion. The process of change is neither cyclic nor linear; it is spiral. In a linear order it is possible to jump over one stage and still get to the next one. According to Piaget, each stage integrates the preceding stage and prepares the way for the following one (Jennings, 1967).

Development is therefore a series of different stages of complex behaviors related in a continuous progression (Svoboda, 1973). The stages are *lawful* in that they are invariant in their developmental sequence from sensory-motor to formal operations; and they are *hierarchical* in that each successive stage is dependent upon prior development and integration of each preceding stage (Laurita, 1973).

Piaget focused his research on cognition, that one function which distinguishes behavior as human. Like other developmental functions, cognition was perceived as developing in a logical, dialectically patterned process. Piaget sees the individual as learning about patterns, growing in knowledge, and building in his own mind the structures of thought which the Gestaltists believe are innately acquired (Emans, 1973). He suggests that children at different ages have different ways of thinking about the world. The child is perceived as a constructor who acts on the world, not as passive reactor to the environment (Gardner, 1973).

Piaget suggests that mental acts reflect *structives*, or coherent systems of actions that evolve at certain points in a child's development (Gardner, 1973). His cognitive theory starts from the central postulate that motor action is the source from which mental operations emerge (Tuddenham, 1966). Intelligence is born of action: the organism must act to acquire the knowledge that it needs to function in the world.

A second central postulate, as indicated earlier, is that intellectual operations, which are acquired by interaction between the organism and the environment, are acquired in a lawful sequence. Piaget's intent has been more to elucidate the sequence of stages rather than to establish exact age norms for the stages of development.

Sensory-Motor Period In the first stage, the *Sensory-Motor Period* (from birth to age two), the child adapts to his environment and manifests his intelligence through sensory-motor action rather than through symbolic means. This stage carries the child from inborn reflexes to acquired behavior patterns, from a body-centered or self-centered world to an object-centered one. The child's mental activity during this stage consists of establishing relationships between sensory experiences and action by physically manipulating the world. The child's sensory-motor actions on objects and his interaction with the environment thus result in knowledge of the perceptual invariants of his environment. The objects he perceives tend to stay within him even when not in view. If the appropriate linguistic forms are associated with these perceptual invariants, he begins to use these linguistic forms to identify objects and to represent his actions on them. At about twelve months he can say two words.

Preoperational Period The *Preoperational Period*, from approximately ages two to seven, covers the important period when rapid growth of language occurs. During the *pre-conceptual period* (ages two to four) the child rapidly learns to represent objects and the world by symbolic means such as language and mental images. For example, 50 percent of children age two can identify common objects, such as a cup or the parts of the body of a doll. At this age the child can normally repeat two numbers. However, the child tends to orient his activities on the basis of appearances. He is easily misled by what he sees. To him language is not something apart from objects and experience. The name of the thing inheres in the thing itself. A chair is called a chair; a rocker is something else entirely (Raven and Salzer, 1971). Every event is new. At age four children can repeat a nine- to ten-word sentence and name a variety of objects.

In the latter part of stage two, ages four to seven (the *intuitive period*), the child moves from nearly total dependence on sensation and perception to the initial stages of logical thought. He can now group objects into classes by noting similarities and differences, but he still pays attention to one aspect of an object to the neglect of other aspects. This tendency is termed *centration*. He can form the concept of "fruit," relating "orange" and "apple." He has intuitively learned and uses the grammar of the language spoken in his environment. He uses all the parts of speech and can transform his vocabulary into a variety of utterances. He has a vocabulary of from 2,500 to 7,500 words, has learned the physical relationships of time and space, and has some idea of causality. His causal reasoning, however, is dependent upon his perceptions and therefore is often in error because his attention is centered on irrelevant or insufficient attributes. For example, he concludes that a narrow, tall glass contains more liquid than a wide, short glass, even though he has seen the same amount of liquid poured from one glass into the other.

Piaget feels that a mental age of four is all that is required to manage reading skills (Furth, 1970), and in fact most children begin learning to read during this period. By age seven, the child is capable of producing simple, active, declarative sentences and can apply inflectional rules. However, the child during this period will still experience difficulty (1) with sounds that occur in the middle or final position of a word; (2) with certain consonant sounds; and (3) with such clusters of consonants as *lfth* (twe*lfth*). The child is gradually consolidating language structures and is just beginning to comprehend the passive construction. He seldom uses the passive in his own spontaneous speech (Palermo and Molfese, 1972).

Concrete Operational Period Beginning about age seven, the *Concrete Operational Period*, the child develops the capability of carrying out logical operations. He can classify according to one or more criteria, he can order in a series, and he can number. In fact, because the child has developed the logical structure of groups, he can organize his cognitive activities much better. He develops some concept of linear measure and weights about age nine. He is less dependent upon his own perceptions and motor actions and shows a capacity for reasoning. He can internalize actions that represent physical objects and relationships. For example, the child can use his imagination to mentally reverse actions; he can break a candy bar in half and he can mentally put the parts together. He also can now make transformations. He will notice that, in pouring liquid from a short glass into a tall glass, nothing is added and nothing has been taken away. He can also transform and manipulate sentences. Such operations suggest that in this period thought and language are freed from dependence upon sensation and perception, but the child's mental activity is still tied to concrete or physical situations or experiences.

Formal Operational Period Between about eleven and fifteen, the *Formal Operational Period,* a child attains the fourth and mature stage of mental development. He can imagine possible and potential relationships, can intellectually manipulate the purely hypothetical, and can think in terms of formal propositions. He can deal with abstract relationships instead of just with things. Whereas the concrete operational child reasons only from directly observed data, his older counterpart is freed from dependence on directly experienced events and begins to deal with conditional, suppositional, and hypothetical statements and propositions.

Although the sequence of these stages of cognitive development is the same for everyone, not all children pass through the stages of intellectual growth exactly in the same way or exactly at the same rate. As a child acquires more experience, his concepts broaden, become clearer, and are hierarchically organized. His concepts also are less egocentric, and they take on conventional significance. Each person passes from a sensory-motor stage, to a preoperational stage, to a concrete operational stage, to a formal operational stage in his own way. As the concepts of individuals become consistent with the concepts of their culture, they can and do communicate more effectively and efficiently.

Children whose experience is more limited, who have less verbal interchange with adults, or who are asked to deal with content that is unfamiliar to them are less likely to attain the *information, linguistic forms*, and *syntax* for organizing and communicating new experiences. Their understanding will not go much deeper than the making of a few verbal associations. Because of some gaps in the materials, in their experience, or in their thinking, they often cannot communicate effectively in certain content areas, even though they have the requisite mental capabilities.

Palermo and Molfese (1972) note that the research data in fact indicate a steady development of linguistic ability from age five to adolescence, with the ages of five to eight and ten to thirteen being special transitional points in which significant development occurs. These are precisely the periods in cognitive development that are reported by Piaget to be transition points from preoperational to concrete operational (between five and eight) and from concrete operational to formal operational (between ten and thirteen). It is during these periods that we note large increases in grammatical constructions and high error rates on some constructions.

Because cognition precedes expression in language, and because numerous studies have shown that cognitive development is closely related to reading achievement, it becomes increasingly clear that a theory of language development must be articulated within the larger context of a theory of cognitive development.

The Physiology of Reading

Reading is a physical act, requiring the reader to respond to graphic symbols. Certain physiological factors may prohibit the reader from making the appropriate response:

1. The reader must first *see* and *identify* the words before he can take meaning to them. He may be inhibited from doing this by inadequate vision: lack of single vision or clear vision, lack of visual coordination or muscular imbalance, restrictions of the visual-information processing system, or tunnel vision.

   Tunnel vision occurs because the amount of information that can be picked up in a single glance is limited. There is a limitation on the rate at which information can be processed from a *sensory store* (immediate memory), or from the number of distinctive features required to identify four or five unrelated letters three or four times every second. The *output* from a single fixation may be four or five letters, two unrelated words, or four or five words in a meaningful sequence (Smith, 1971, p. 218).

The simple fact is that the more difficulty a reader experiences with reading, the more he must rely on feature analysis. He is forced to analyze all the constituents of the surface structure to be able to apply his syntactic skills (Smith, 1971, p. 222).

2. The reader must have adequate auditory acuity, auditory discrimination, auditory blending, and auditory comprehension. Inhibitory factors are intensity deafness and tone deafness (as from a conductive hearing loss stemming from a punctured eardrum or a malfunction of the three small bones in the middle ear, or from a nerve loss resulting from an impairment of the auditory nerve). Intensity deafness and tone deafness cause difficulty with sounds represented by *f, v, s, sh, zh, th, t, d, b, p, k,* and *g.* The pupil will have difficulty with phonics and with oral reading.

3. The reader must have adequate neural functioning. Inhibitory factors are brain damage, inadequate development of the brain, lack of (or crossed) cerebral dominance, or lack of neurological organization generally.

Most physiological deficits make it difficult to read fluently and at an appropriate rate. Rate is important apart from its economy because it helps the pupil to comprehend by discovering the syntactic rules.

Theoretical Models of Reading

Following the lead of Williams (1973), we categorize theoretical models of reading instruction as follows:

I. Taxonomic Models
II. Psychometric Models
III. Psychological Models
    A. Behavioral
    B. Cognitive
IV. Information Processing Models
V. Linguistic Models
    A. Early Formulations
    B. Transformational-Generative Grammar

Taxonomic Models

Taxonomic (classification) models identify the basic skills needed for successful reading. Gray (1950, 1960) gives a purely descriptive model. He describes reading as consisting of four skills: word perception, comprehension, reaction, and assimilation.

Psychometric Models

The statistically-determined models of Holmes (1965) and Singer (1969), constructed by the use of substrata analysis, are designed to determine the combination of hierarchically-organized subsystems that form a working system for attaining speed and power of reading. Models have been developed for college, high school, and elementary levels. The four systems, accounting for 89 percent of the variance in power of reading, are word recognition, word meaning, morphemic analysis, and reasoning in context. Three subtests (reasoning in context, auditory vocabulary–word meaning, and phrase perception discrimination) accounted for 77 percent of the variance in speed of reading.

The model suggests that silent reading ability is divisible into two major interrelated components, speed and power of reading. As the reader changes from speed to power of reading, he reorganizes his set of systems (and subsystems) from emphasizing the visuo-motor perceptual system to one stressing morphemic and word recognition systems.

Psychological Models: Behavioral Models

Learning theories are proper content for a psychology of reading because learning to read is representative of learning in general. Learning theorists have sought to discover and specify the experimental variables that control and determine behavioral changes that occur with practice, experience, or perception, and furthermore they have tried to formulate the functional interrelationships or laws that hold between these variables.

All theorists agree that the observable response is a function of the physical and social world and the condition of the organism. Furthermore, as we observe responses, we note changes in response and infer that these are accompanied by certain internal changes. These internal changes or hypothetical learning factors in turn affect present performance. Theorists agree that the character of these internal events is partly determined by the impinging stimulus and partly by various organic states and past experience; they disagree, however, in their conceptions of these hypothetical learning factors.

Learning theories can be divided into Stimulus–Response Theories and Field Theories:

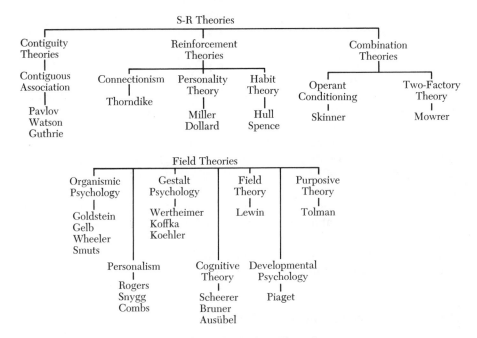

Figure 2.1   Learning Theories.

Smith (1971, p. 71) notes that learning to read cannot be explained if only one of the theories of learning is adopted.

The behavioral model holds that all learning is habit formation, a connection between a stimulus and a response. The connection is referred to as an S–R bond. The S–R theorist focuses on the response or the observable action; the learner learns an action or a response. The S–R theorist asserts his predilection for conditioning, which to him is the clearest and most simple instance of a response to a stimulus. Learning is defined as the acquisition of new behavior patterns or the changing of behavior either by strengthening or weakening of old patterns as a result of practice or training.

The best contemporary exponent of behaviorism is B. F. Skinner. In Skinnerian terminology, all behavior can be understood, predicted, and controlled in terms of *habits* established or shaped by a process of successive approximation by the reinforcement of a response in the presence of a particular stimulus.

Reinforcement determines whether conditioning in fact takes place. A particular S–R bond will be established only if the organism is reinforced in a particular way while responding in the presence of a stimulus.

The type of conditioning in Skinner's experiments is called *operant conditioning* in contrast to *classical conditioning*. In this type of conditioning, the reinforcement occurs after the behavior that is to be conditioned. For Skinner, the behavior had first to be emitted before reinforcement could occur.

The process of setting up the type of behavior that it is desired to reinforce is known as *shaping*. Shaping of behavior does not wait until the learner's response is exactly correct. Operant learning may be quite gradual. At first, it may be necessary to reinforce gross approximations to the final response. Behavior is thus molded into shape by a process of successive approximation. It is through shaping that the very fine discriminations required in reading are produced. Through a process of *chaining*, elaborate sequences of behavior—like those required in reading—are built up.

The behaviorist view explains *why* learning takes place (by reinforcement), and once the habit is established, we find that habits have their own momentum. The very exercise of the habit (reading) reinforces and consolidates the habit. The simple opportunity to engage in the habit is an effective reinforcer (Smith, 1971, pp. 61–66).

Psychological Models: Cognitive Models

Recently, there has been a resurgence of interest in the psychology of cognition, in thinking, and in cognitive styles. Psychologists dealing with this aspect of psychology are grouped into the neobehaviorists (Hebb, Staats), cognitive theorists (Bruner, Ausübel), and the developmentalists (Piaget, Vygotsky).

In *Improving the Teaching of Reading* (Dechant, 1970, pp. 365–374), the author discussed cognitive functioning in detail as the process of moving from percept through perceptual schematism, contextual perception, and perception of differences, to concept and categorization. The course of development of thinking is described as moving from the concrete toward the more decentralized, analytical, and abstract.

The cognitive model, representing as it does the second significant explanation of learning, perceives the learner as a consumer of information (Smith, 1971, pp. 68–79). The cognitive theorist does not believe that language skills can be explained as habits established by the conditioning of S–R bonds. Rather he points out that the reader extracts meaning from what he reads on the basis of the visual information (the surface structure of the language) but also on the basis of all the deep structure of language and the knowledge and experiences contained within his brain (Smith, 1971, p. 69). Language and what is read cannot be comprehended unless the reader (listener) makes this critical, active contribution. Therefore (as we saw earlier), one of the principal tenets of the cognitive theorist is that perception is a constructive process, adding something to the stimulus aspects. Cognition is defined as the integrative activity of the brain, overriding reflex response behavior and freeing behavior from sense dominance (Hebb, 1974). Cognition is the central brain process that determines the reader's particular reaction to graphic symbols.

The cognitive theorist speaks of restructuring perceptions or relationships. The pupil is taught a system of attacking new words, and he uses this system to make an insightful response to a new word. He does not have to be conditioned to come up with the correct response. The reaction to a word (perception of meaning) is an indication that the learner has organized his experiences in a specific way. The response is a sign that perceptual organization or learning has occurred.

The cognitive theorist emphasizes cognitive processes, purposive behavior, and the organizational nature of the learning process. He is interested more in what the child *knows* and *understands* than in what he *does.* He believes strongly that learning is guided by intervening mental processes which are labelled cognition, thought, or perception. Cognition organizes the incoming sensory data into a meaningful pattern. To the cognitive psychologist, what is interesting is the unobservable manner in which information is acquired and organized by the brain (Smith, 1971, p. 60).

Smith (1971, pp. 68–80) rejects the behaviorist view because:

1. There is no simple correspondence between sound (writing) and meaning.
2. Skill in language production and comprehension cannot have developed through the establishment of S–R bonds because practically all the sentences we speak or read are novel ones.
3. Perception is a constructive process, adding something to the stimulus aspects. A reader extracts meaning on the basis of the visual information (the surface structure of the language) and of the deep structure of the language and the knowledge in the brain. The reader makes decisions on the basis of two kinds of evidence: *current* information received from the environment by his receptor systems and the *stored* information that is available in memory. Writing cannot be comprehended unless the reader makes this critical, active contribution. Our fund of knowledge about the world is given a variety of technical names (cognitive schemata, cognitive structures, cognitive maps).
4. Since sentence meaning cannot be determined on a sequential word-by-word basis, information from several printed words has to be held in

short-term memory. The load on short-term memory is reduced by "chunking" information into larger units—by storing words rather than letters, or meanings rather than words (Smith, 1971, pp. 78–79).

The cognitive theorist postulates an internal store of information, and distinguishes three stages of memory function:

1. A *sensory store* (or a *visual image*) or *immediate memory* in which the raw material of perception is briefly stored, perhaps for a quarter of a second or more. Information received decays rapidly as new information is taken in.
2. A *short-term memory* in which the information is held while it is being processed. The information is much less than in the sensory store, perhaps no more than four or five items and generally is retained for only a few seconds. A person wanting to make a telephone call often finds that he looks up the number but in the midst of the dialing, forgets it, and has to look it up again. How much is retained depends on *how* it is formed, either single letters, single words, or a related set of words. The learner can also commit the information to long-term memory by repeating the information to himself.
3. A *long-term memory* in which information may be stored permanently.

That a short-term memory and a long-term memory do in fact exist is shown by neural injury. A neural injury often obliterates long-term memory but leaves intact events learned within a fifteen-minute time span prior to the injury. Conversely, electrical stimulation of a surgically exposed brain while a person is awake can cause the individual to remember experiences long thought forgotten. The same thing can happen during hypnosis.

Yanoff (1972) separates the cognitive process into four major functions:

1. *Input* (sensory-motor)
    a. The stimulation of the sense organs.
    b. Reception and discrimination of the stimulus.
    c. Stimulus-redefinition—the passing of accurate messages to the brain.

    Cognition begins with appropriate perception, and perception begins with a sensory stimulation.

2. *Integration*
    a. Neural excitement—the brain receives electrical impulses, the redefined stimulus, and acts upon it.
    b. Imprinting templates—if the incoming data are congruent with previous experiences, or fit previously formed templates, they are

assimilated. When *new* templates are formed, the process is termed *accommodation*. Accommodation is a restructuring of concepts that enables the person to assimilate formerly discrepant events (Suchman, 1969). The brain is thus perceived as an information-processing system. A template allows one to record an idea or experience. Templates form the structure of the brain. As data bombard the brain, it either *recalls* previously-formed templates, *connects* previously-formed templates, or *develops* new templates. Templates allow the brain to test and evaluate all incoming data. This makes the brain different from the computer, which can only store data. The brain actually decides which sensations the perceiver will attend to. The creative individual is one who takes existing templates and restructures them. Seeing is only input; visualization combines input and integration.

   c. Neural redefinition—the ideas or templates from the brain are redefined as electrical impulses.

3. *Output*

The electrical impulses are carried to the neuro-muscular system where they are redefined and exhibited as:

   a. Communication—any form of language-based interaction.
   b. Product—the construction of an idea.
   c. Performance—an exhibition of an ability such as singing a song or giving a speech.

Output is the only measure that we have of cognition, and unfortunately it can never fully represent what has occurred in the integrative process: concepts are lost because we cannot express them; muscular incoordination can keep us from drawing what we have visualized.

4. *Feedback*

   a. Reward.
   b. Reinforcement.
   c. Self-evaluation of the information.

Feedback is the recycling of a person's thinking. The effect of the output is fed back into the system as input. When a person sings, hearing is his feedback, and he tends to adjust his singing according to what he hears.

Feedback fixes the template. Reward and reinforcement are feedback that strengthen the tendency for a particular response to follow a specific stimulus. The major feedback agent is the person's self-evaluation of the information—it permits him to constantly test information.

Information Processing Models

One of the best descriptions of reading as information processing is offered by Smith (1971, pp. 12–27).

A key principle in the psychology of reading is that reading is a communications process, and the purpose of all communication is the sharing of meanings. Reading takes place only when the reader shares the ideas that the writer intends to convey. Writing has no purpose without a reader. The graphic symbol must carry the burden of meaning between the communicator and the receiver of the communication. For this reason a knowledge of theories of communication and information and signal detection theory are relevant to a study of the psychology of reading. The terminology of communication theory is especially useful in describing a theory of reading. Two points stand out:

1. Reading is an active process—the reader must make an active contribution to the information-seeking process. In fact, the information acquired by a receiver is much more than is actually present in the physical representation of that information in the form of graphic symbols.
2. All information acquisition in reading, from the identification of individual letters or words to the comprehension of a passage, is a reduction of uncertainty.

Terms from communication theory that have special significance in understanding reading are: *communication channel, limited channel capacity, noise, information,* and *redundancy.*

Communication Channel The writer (transmitter) and the reader (receiver) are two ends of a communication channel along which information flows. As a message passes through the communication channel, it takes on a variety of forms. At each part of the communication process, it is possible that the message will be changed in some way.

Limited Channel Capacity Just as in a communication system, there also is a *limited channel capacity* in the communication system of the reader. There is a limit to the speed at which the eye can travel over a passage of text making information-gathering fixations and to the amount of information that can be acquired in a single fixation.

Noise A message or communication may be confused or made less clear by extraneous signals called *noise.* Because all communication channels have limited capacities, noise may overload the system and prevent the transmission of informative signals. In reading, noise may be a type face that is difficult to read, poor illumination, or distraction of the reader's attention. Smith (1971, p. 16) notes that because of noise, reading is intrinsically more difficult for the beginning reader than for the experienced reader. Everything is much "noisier" for the beginner. Anything that one lacks the skill or knowledge to understand automatically becomes noise.

Information *Information* is defined as a reduction of uncertainty. In reading, information exists when the reader can reduce the number of alternative possibilities and can discriminate a given letter from the other twenty-five possibilities. If he can eliminate all alternatives except one, then the amount of information transmitted is equal to the amount of uncertainty that existed.

Redundancy Redundancy exists whenever information is duplicated by more than one source—that is, whenever alternatives can be eliminated in more than one way. Presenting a word both visually and orally is a form of redundancy that helps the learner. In reading, it is immediately apparent that the larger the context, the greater the redundancy. And the more redundancy there is, the less visual information the skilled reader requires (Smith, 1971, p. 23).

The application of redundancy to reading, of course, suggests that the skilled reader does not need a fixed amount of information to identify a word or to ascertain the meaning. The amount of information he will need depends on the difficulty of the passage, the reader's skill, and the reader's decision-making criteria. Does he demand absolute certainty before venturing a guess? Is he willing to take a chance? Setting his criteria too high for word identification may mean that he can't identify a word quickly enough to comprehend it. The beginning reader may not venture a guess for fear of being wrong and so become a very inefficient reader. Generally, readers establish relatively low criteria for words that are common in their experience and require more information if the word is one that appears infrequently (Smith, 1971, p. 26).

Linguistic Models: Early Formations

The early linguistic models were developed by Bloomfield, Fries, and Lefevre. In general, Bloomfield (1942) emphasized that beginning reading should present only regular correspondences between orthography and speech. Fries (1963) stressed letter-sound relationships. Lefevre stressed syntactical cues, both intra-word (such as inflections) and inter-word (such as sentence structure). Lefevre (1964, p. 68) noted that "grasp of meaning is integrally linked to grasp of structure—intonation gives the unifying configuration." Genuine reading proficiency is described as the ability to

read language structure. The best reader is aware of the stresses, elonga-
tions of words, changes of pitch, intonation, and rhythms of the sentences
that he reads. If he reads a sentence the way the writer would like it to have
been said, true communication of meaning may be possible. Fries and
Bloomfield concentrated on letters, sounds, and words as the prime units in
reading; Lefevre makes the sentence the key unit in reading.

Bloomfield and Fries define reading as the act of turning the stimulus
of graphic shape on a surface back into speech (Edwards, 1966). Bloomfield
differentiated between the *act of reading* (recognition of grapheme-
phoneme correspondences) and the *goal of reading* (comprehension).

The central thesis of the Bloomfield-Barnhart (1961) method is that
there is an inseparable relationship between the graphic symbols and the
sounds for which the letters are conventional signs, and that converting
letters to meaning requires from the beginning a concentration upon letter
and sound to bring about an automatic association between them as rapidly
as possible. Bloomfield's system is a linguistic system of teaching reading
which separates the problem of the study of word-form from the study of
word-meaning. He notes that children come to school knowing how to
speak the English language, but they do not know how to read the form of
words.

Lefevre, whose emphasis is different from Bloomfield's, adapted
linguistic ideas to teaching reading. He suggests an analytical method of
teaching reading emphasizing language patterns. He emphasizes that
meaning comes only through grasping the language structure of a sentence.
Meaning therefore depends on the intonation, the word and sentence order,
the grammatical inflections, and certain key function words. Intonation, or
the pauses and stresses in oral language, are represented (1) by capital
letters, periods, semi-colons, and question marks, (2) by the order of the
words, (3) by grammatical inflections signaling tense, number, and posses-
sion, and (4) by such function words as *the, when, nevertheless,* or *because.*
Only by reading structures can the reader attain full meaning. Or, to put it
another way, unless the reader correctly translates the printed text into the
intonation pattern of the writer, he may not be getting the meaning
intended.

Bloomfield felt that initial teaching of reading for meaning is incorrect, and that meaning will come quite naturally as the student learns the
alphabetic code. Lefevre is critical of Bloomfield's approach, criticizing him
for confining himself largely to phonemic analysis and for neglecting
intonation and syntax.

The early linguists focused primarily on the problems of beginning
reading and more specifically on the problems of word recognition (Chall,
1969). Both Bloomfield and Fries subscribed to the primacy of the spoken
word over the written word, with the written form being essentially a
representation of the spoken form. Reading is thus basically described by

Bloomfield and Fries as decoding printed symbols into sound and then extracting meaning from sound. Smith (1971, pp. 44–45) rejects this view because:

1. Fluent reading is accomplished too fast for the translation into sound to occur.
2. It does not follow that reading must go through sound: deaf people do learn to read.
3. Writing is not necessarily speech written down; it might be meaning written down.

Linguistic Models:
Transformational-Generative Grammar

The theorists in this group (Chomsky, 1957, 1968, 1970; Goodman, 1966, 1970) reject the notion that reading is simply sequential word recognition. Reading is perceived as a psycholinguistic process, *only superficially different* from the comprehension of speech. The beginning reader is thought to use abstract rules about language structure to arrive at comprehension. They emphasize the linguistic competence of the reader while the structuralists (Bloomfield and Fries, for example) emphasize *what* the reader must learn (Weber, 1970).

This approach emphasizes that all languages and hence all sentences have a *surface structure* and a *deep structure.* Sounds or written words are the surface representation of a message; meaning, syntactic and semantic interpretation are the deep level. The deep structure gives the meaning of the sentence; the surface structure gives the form (Jacobs and Rosenbaum, 1968).

The first fact that strikes the student of language is that there is no simple correspondence between the surface structure of language (phonology) and meaning (Smith, 1971, p. 29). There are aspects of meaning which are not in the written word.

The transformational-generative grammar model suggests that grammar—the rules of syntax—is a set of rules by which sense is made out of language, or by which words are arranged into sentences. *Grammar is the link between sound and meaning.*

Chomsky hypothesized that human beings have an innate rational ability to generate the underlying rules or syntax of their language after having been sufficiently exposed to it. The rules are identified as deep structures which are transformed to surface structures while being given phonological and semantic flesh (Vogel, 1974). Children, even at an early age, appear to be rule-producing learners. They can construct sentences they have never heard but which are nevertheless well-formed in terms of general rules. They can produce novel sentences.

Language consists of phonemes, words, and utterances. *Phonemes*, of which there are about forty-six in English, are not single sounds; they are rather collections of sounds. They are a class of closely related sounds constituting the smallest unit of speech that will distinguish one utterance from another (Smith, 1971, p. 31). They are perhaps better described as a network of differences between sounds (Hockett, 1958, p. 24). A *grapheme* (the counterpart of the phoneme) is a letter or a group of letters constituting the smallest unit of writing that will distinguish one word from another.

Language thus is a continuum of sound classified into a limited number of permitted single sounds called phonemes that join in a limited number of permitted combinations (Jolly, 1972).

A *morpheme* is the smallest linguistic unit in our language that has meaning. The unit has lexical meaning if it has a meaning of its own (as do, for example, prefixes and suffixes), and it has relational meaning if it has a grammatical meaning. For example, in the sentence, "She insists on it," the *in* in *insists* has lexical meaning. It has meaning wherever it occurs; the *s* at the end of the word has no meaning of itself. It has meaning only to the extent that it makes the verb a third person singular. It is said to have relational meaning. The *s* may also take on a relational meaning when it changes a noun from the singular to the plural or when it denotes the possessive case.

Words are the smallest meaningful linguistic units that can stand alone in a sentence. The study of how words are constructed is called *morphology*. An *utterance* is a series of words spoken at one time. The manner in which words are grouped into utterances is called *syntax*. And syntax and morphology compose the *grammar* of a language. Grammar has only one basic function: to make our utterances clearer. It is an aid to the expression and interpretation of meaning. Figure 2.2 illustrates the relationships existing among the various factors.

Morphology, for example, allows us to introduce minute changes into a word to bring out a special meaning. The various uses of *s* given above are examples of this. Syntax permits us to group words to suggest certain nuances of meaning. For example, the same words might be grouped in two ways to suggest two meanings: "The weak girl is playing a game of tennis," or "The girl is playing a weak game of tennis"; "The boy sat in a chair with a broken arm," or "The boy with a broken arm sat in a chair"; "The lion in the cage roared at the man," or "The lion roared at the man in the cage." The formal distinction between *runs* as a verb and *runs* as a noun ("He *runs* home"; "There were six *runs* on the bank") is syntactic (Ives, 1964). The reader must first recognize the distinction in arrangement before he can perceive the distinction in meaning. An adjective can become a noun by syntax: "The *best* is not good enough for him." To read the word *lead*, the reader must know whether it is a noun or a verb (Reed, 1965).

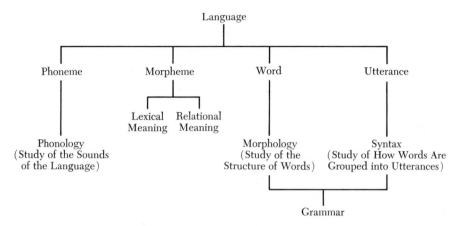

Figure 2.2   Language Structure.

Punctuation in writing and pauses in speech are not so much an aid to writing and speaking as they are to reading and listening. The writer knows what the sentences mean; he does not need punctuation aids to get the meaning.

In addition to phonemes, morphemes, and words, there are certain characteristics about the utterance that add to and develop meaning. The loudness of the voice changes or certain words are stressed more than others. We give a heavy, medium, light, or weak stress. The pitch is either low, normal, high, or extra high. High pitch is often associated with heavier stress. In speaking, utterances are combined by what are termed *plus junctures*; they are ended by *terminal junctures*. The plus junctures separate words; the terminal junctures are usually accompanied by falls or rises in pitch, and differentiate one phrase unit from another or one type of sentence from another. The declarative sentence has a slight drop in pitch at the end. Phrasing depends on the placement of the junctures.

Words do not give meaning to sentences; rather, words receive their meaning from the sentence or the verbal context of which they are a part. The pupil who has become a word reader has fallen into the error of not reading the phrase or sentence unit that gives meaning to the word. The word must be looked upon merely as *one* element in a series of elements that constitute a sentence. The sentence circumscribes the word, giving it the distinct meaning intended by the speaker or writer.

Grammatical transformations are special ways of converting the deep structure of a sentence into a variety of surface representations; transformational rules, conversely, permit the reader to move from the surface structure to the deep structure or meaning. Transformational grammar is nothing more than "a finite set of rules that generates an infinite number of grammatical sentences of a language . . ." (Jacobs and Rosenbaum, 1968). The role of syntax, to mediate between visual surface structure and meaning, is precisely the function that generative-transformational grammarians attribute to it (Smith, 1971, p. 222).

Recent Research

The position of Smith and others of the psycholinguistic school is supported by recent research and by the observations of other reading specialists. Denner (1970) found that problem readers (grades three to four) and children expected to be poor readers (grade one) performed more poorly than normal children on tasks requiring representational and syntactic competence.

MacNamara (1972), producing evidence from syntax, lexicon, and phonology, concluded that infants learn their language by determining the meaning that a speaker intends to convey to them and then working out the relationship between meaning and language. The child uses meaning as a clue to language rather than language as a clue to meaning. He notes that children's thinking is more advanced than their language.

Walcutt, Lamport, and McCracken (1974, pp. 41–42), noting that syntax concerns itself with meaning-bearing patterns, point out that "The word *dogs* can be easily understood on a surface level as two morphemes that express a recognized relationship among certain animals. But consider the differences among 'Dogs make good pets,' 'It's a dog's life,' and 'He's gone to the dogs,' all of which employ the same two morphemes. Meaning comes to us through syntax by intonation, patterns, word form changes, and the use of structure and function words."

Steiner, Wiener, and Cromer (1971) found that poor readers fail to extract contextual clues essential for word identification, and they fail to utilize such cues in identification even when they are presented with them. "They seem to be identifying words as if the words were unrelated items unaffected by syntactical or contextual relationships."

Bever and Bower (1966) report that the best readers among able college students do not read sentences in linear fashion, but in terms of their deep syntactic structure.

Hittelman (1973) suggests that the cloze procedure, which involves the deletion of every *n*th word in a selection and the evaluation of the success a reader has in supplying the deleted word, may measure only an entity within the surface features of the reading. These measurements may be only partly representative of those factors which determine readability.

Weber (1967) found that an analysis of errors on the syntactic and semantic level suggests that even early readers can successfully make use of preceding verbal context. It is apparent that they do not depend solely on graphic representation to make a response.

Burke and Goodman (1970), using Goodman's Taxonomy of Cues and Miscues in Reading, analyzed the reading of a boy named Daniel and concluded that there was little relationship between the miscues and comprehension. Some miscues simply did not result in changed meaning, and they were usually corrected if they did. Miscues tended to be corrected when the resulting syntax was unacceptable.

Vogel (1974) found that dyslexic children with reading comprehension difficulties are deficient in oral syntax.

Summary

We have progressed in our understanding of the reading process and may well be on the threshold of an adequate theory of reading.

The theoretical model that the author began developing in the first edition of *Psychology in Teaching Reading* (and which he leans toward today) is basically a psycholinguistic model, but it is surely eclectic in that it has some elements of the taxonomic model, the psychometric model, the psychological models (both behavioral and cognitive), the information processing model, and the linguistic models (both the early formulations and the transformational-generative grammar models).

There probably is no pure model. Every model seems to have many elements in common with other models. Singer (1969) notes that probably a series of models is necessary to explain and predict reading performance. We agree with the observations of Williams (1973) that there is a growing rapprochement among theorists toward a view of reading as both a complex cognitive skill aimed at obtaining information and a complex language system.

The psycholinguistic approach, especially in the formulation given by Smith (1971), has perhaps the most to offer in reading instruction. It suggests that reading involves a basic knowledge of language as well as the utilization of complex active perceptual and cognitive strategies of information selection and processing. Reading is an active cognitive skill. It is not merely a simple associative learning process; it is not a passive process "with the graphic input cueing directly and automatically the already learned and therefore instantly meaningful speech code."

Reading requires a sign system in which messages are formulated (the graphic system). Reading thus is a sensory process, requiring discriminative visual responses to graphic symbols. It is a process by which a person reconstructs a message encoded graphically by a writer (Goodman, 1970). Encoding is the process of translating thought messages into written symbols. The reader goes from the written language, visually perceived, to a reconstruction of the message encoded in the written language by the writer. Comprehension occurs when the reconstruction agrees with the writer's intended message.

Language has a surface structure (the sounds and written representations of language) and a deep structure (which gives meaning) (Smith and Goodman, 1971). The basic requirement for reading is for the learner to be able to deal efficiently with both the surface and the deep structure.

Reading is both a perceptual process and a conceptual process. Meaning is supplied by the reader as he processes the symbolic system by relating it to experiences and conceptual structures. Reading is not a process of combining individual letters into words and strings of words into sentences from which meanings spring automatically. Rather, the evidence suggests that, for the fluent reader, the deep-level process of identifying meaning either precedes or makes unnecessary the process of identifying individual words (Smith and Goodman, 1971).

The fluent reader can go directly to meaning by using syntactic and semantic redundancy. He uses the words around a given word (the context) to identify the word. The beginning reader must put letters together to form words; the skilled reader only rarely does this. The fluent reader decodes not from visual symbols into sound, but from visual symbols to meaning. He predicts his way through a passage of text.

The two levels of language (surface and deep structure) are related in a complex way through the rules of grammar (Smith and Goodman, 1971). Grammar is the link between sound and meaning. The rules of syntax determine how the particular visual-semantic associations should be interpreted for a cognitive organization (Smith, 1971, p. 216). Children learn these rules rapidly between the ages of eighteen months and four years (Smith, 1971). The pattern of development of these rules is so systematic and invariant that it is believed that children have an innate predisposition for discovering the rules of language (Smith and Goodman, 1971).

Because the acquisition of language and reading skills occurs in predictable stages of development, the reading teacher needs to develop a theory of reading within a theory of the total process of child development.

References

Avdul, Richard. "Piaget Was a Quarterback." *Teacher* 91 (April 1974): 10–12.

Bever, Thomas, and Bower, Thomas. "How to Read Without Listening." Ithaca: Cornell University, 1966.

Birkley, Marilyn. "Effecting Reading Improvement in the Classroom through Teacher Self-Improvement Programs." *Journal of Reading* 14 (November 1970): 94–100.

Blake, James Neal. *Speech Education Activities for Children.* Springfield: Charles C. Thomas, 1970.

Bloomfield, L. "Linguistics and Reading." *Elementary English Review* 19 (1942): 125–130, 183–186.

Bloomfield, L., and Barnhart, Clarence L. *Let's Read: A Linguistic Approach.* Detroit: Wayne State University Press, 1961.

Bruner, Jerome S. "Going Beyond the Information Given." *Contemporary Approaches to Cognition.* Cambridge, Mass.: Harvard University Press, 1957.

Bruner, Jerome S. *On Knowing.* Cambridge, Mass.: Harvard University Press, 1962.

Burke, Carolyn L., and Goodman, Kenneth S. "When a Child Reads: A Psycholinguistic Analysis." *Elementary English* (January 1970).

Carroll, John B. *Language and Thought.* Englewood Cliffs, N.J.: Prentice-Hall, 1964.

Carroll, John B. "The Nature of the Reading Process." In *Theoretical Models and Processes of Reading,* edited by Harry Singer and R. B. Ruddell. Newark, Del. International Reading Association, 1970, pp. 292–303.

Chall, Jeanne S. "The Influence of Previous Knowledge on Reading Ability." Ohio State University, *Educational Research Bulletin* 26 (December 1947): 225–230.

Chall, Jeanne S. "Research in Linguistics and Reading Instruction: For Further Research and Practice." In *Reading and Realism,* edited by J. Allen Figurel. Volume 13, International Reading Association Conference Proceedings, 1969, pp. 560–571.

Chomsky, Noam. *Syntactic Structures.* The Hague: Mouton, 1957.

Chomsky, Noam. *Language and Mind.* New York: Harcourt Brace and World, 1968.

Chomsky, Noam. "Phonology and Reading." In *Basic Studies in Reading,* edited by Harry Levin and Joanna P. Williams. New York: Basic Books, 1970.

Cooper, Bernice. "Contributions of Linguistics in Teaching Reading." *Education* 85 (May 1965): 529–532.

Dechant, Emerald. *Improving the Teaching of Reading.* Englewood Cliffs, N.J.: Prentice-Hall, 1970.

DeLaguna, Grace. "Perception and Language." *Human Biology* 1 (1929): 555–558.

Denner, Bruce. "Representational and Syntactic Competence of Problem Readers." *Child Development* 41 (1970): 881–887.

Edfelt, Ake W. *Silent Speech and Silent Reading.* Stockholm: Almquist and Wiksell, 1959; Chicago: University of Chicago Press, 1960.

Edwards, Thomas J. "Teaching Reading: A Critique." In *The Disabled Reader,* edited by John Money. Baltimore: Johns Hopkins Press, 1966, pp. 349–362.

Emans, Robert. "Oral Language and Learning to Read." *Elementary English* 50 (September 1973): 929–934.

Ervin, Susan M., and Miller, Wick R. "Language Development." *Child Psychology.* Chicago: University of Chicago Press, 1963.

Flavell, J. H. *The Developmental Psychology of Jean Piaget.* Princeton: D. Van Nostrand, 1963.

Fries, C. C. *Linguistics and Reading.* New York: Holt, Rinehart and Winston, 1963.

Furth, Haus G. *Piaget for Teachers.* Englewood Cliffs, N.J.: Prentice-Hall, 1970.

Gardner, Howard. "France and the Modern Mind." *Psychology Today*, June 1973, p. 59.

Goodman, Kenneth S. "Comprehension-Centered Reading." *Claremont Reading Conference Yearbook* 34 (1970): 125–135.

Goodman, Kenneth S. "Decoding—From Code to What?" *Journal of Reading* 14 (April 1971): 455–462, 498.

Goodman, Kenneth S. "A Psycholinguistic View of Reading Comprehension." In *New Frontiers in College-Adult Reading*, edited by George B. Schick and Merrill M. May. Milwaukee: National Reading Conference, 1966, pp. 188–196.

Goodman, Kenneth S. "Reading: A Psycholinguistic Guessing Game." *Journal of the Reading Specialist* 4 (May 1967): 126–135.

Gray, W. S. "Growth in Understanding of Reading and Its Development Among Youth." *Keeping Reading Programs Abreast of the Times*, Supplementary Educational Monographs, No. 72. Chicago: University of Chicago Press, 1950, pp. 8–13.

Gray, W. S. "Reading and Physiology and Psychology of Reading." In *Encyclopedia of Education Research,* edited by C. W. Marris. New York: Macmillan, 1960, pp. 1086–1088.

Gunderson, Doris V. "New Developments in the Teaching of Reading." *Elementary English* 50 (January 1973): 17–21, 148.

Hansen, Halvor P. "Language Acquisition and Development in the Child: A

Teacher-Child Verbal Interaction." *Elementary English* 51 (February 1974): 276–285, 290.

Hebb, D. O. *A Textbook of Psychology.* Philadelphia: W. B. Saunders, 1958.

Hebb, D. O. "What Psychology Is About." *American Psychologist* 29 (February 1974): 71–79.

Herrick, Judson. *The Evolution of Human Nature.* Austin, Tex.: University of Texas Press, 1956.

Hittelman, Daniel R. "Seeking a Psycholinguistic Definition of Readability." *The Reading Teacher* 26 (May 1973): 783–789.

Hockett, Charles F. *A Course in Modern Linguistics.* New York: Macmillan, 1958.

Holmes, Jack A. "Basic Assumptions Underlying the Substrata-Factor Theory." *Reading Research Quarterly* 1 (1965): 5–28.

Horn, Ernest. *Methods of Instruction in the Social Studies.* New York: Charles Scribner's Sons, 1937.

Inhelder, Bärbel. "Criteria of the Stages of Mental Development." In *Psychological Studies of Human Development*, edited by R. Kuhlen and G. J. Thompson. 2nd ed. New York: Appleton-Century-Crofts, 1963, pp. 28–48.

Inhelder, Bärbel, and Piaget, Jean. *The Growth of Logical Thinking from Childhood to Adolescence.* New York: Basic Books, 1958.

Ives, Sumner. "Some Notes on Syntax and Meaning." *The Reading Teacher* 18 (December 1964): 179–183, 222.

Jacobs, Roderick A., and Rosenbaum, Peter S. *English Transformational Grammar.* Waltham, Mass.: Blaisdell Publishing Co., 1968.

Jacobsen, Edmund. "Electrophysiology of Mental Activities." *American Journal of Psychology* 44 (October 1932): 677–694.

James, William. *Principles of Psychology.* New York: Holt, Rinehart and Winston, 1890.

Jennings, F. "Jean Piaget: Notes on Learning." *Saturday Review*, May 20, 1967.

Jolly, Allison. *The Evolution of Primate Behavior.* New York: Macmillan, 1972.

Kean, John M., and Yamamoto, Kaoru. "Grammar Signals and Assignment of Words to Parts of Speech Among Young Children: An Exploration." *Journal of Verbal Learning and Verbal Behavior* 4 (August 1965): 323–326.

Kingston, Albert J. "The Psychology of Reading." *Forging Ahead in Reading.* IRA Conference Proceedings, International Reading Association, 1968, pp. 425–432.

Langer, Susanne K. *Philosophy in a New Key.* New York: Mentor Books, New American Library, 1948. Originally published by the Harvard University Press.

Langman, Muriel Potter. "The Reading Process: A Descriptive, Interdisciplinary Approach." *Genetic Psychology Monographs* 62 (August 1960): 1–40.

Laurita, Raymond E. "Bringing Order to the Teaching of Reading and Writing." *Education* 93 (February/March 1973): 254–261.

Lefevre, C. *Linguistics and the Teaching of Reading.* New York: McGraw-Hill, 1964.

MacNamara, John. "Cognitive Basis of Language Learning in Infants." *Psychological Review* 79 (January 1972): 1–13.

Miller, G. A. "Psycholinguistics." *Encounter* 23 (July 1964): 29–37.

Miller, G. A. "Some Preliminaries to Psycholinguistics." *American Psychologist* 20 (January 1965): 15–20.

Osgood, Charles E. "A Behavioristic Analysis of Perception and Language as Cognitive Phenomena." *Contemporary Approaches to Cognition.* Cambridge, Mass.: Harvard University Press, 1957.

Palermo, David S., and Molfese, Dennis L. "Language Acquisition from Age Five Onward." *Psychological Bulletin* 78 (December 1972): 409–428.

Piaget, Jean. "The Genetic Approach to the Psychology of Thought." *Journal of Educational Psychology* 52 (1961): 271–276.

Piaget, Jean. *Logic and Psychology.* New York: Basic Books, 1957.

Piaget, Jean. *The Mechanisms of Perception.* New York: Basic Books, 1969.

Piaget, Jean. *The Origins of Intelligence in Children.* New York: International Universities Press, 1952.

Raven, Ronald J., and Salzer, Richard T. "Piaget and Reading Instruction." *Reading Teacher* (April 1971).

Reed, David W. "A Theory of Language, Speech and Writing." *Elementary English* 42 (December 1965): 845–851.

Robinson, H. M. "The Major Aspects of Reading." In *Reading: Seventy-Five Years of Progress,* edited by H. S. Robinson. Chicago: University of Chicago Press, 1966, pp. 22–32.

Singer, Harry. "Theoretical Models of Reading." *Journal of Communication* 19 (June 1969): 134–156.

Smith, E. Brooks; Goodman, Kenneth S.; and Meredith, Robert. *Language and Thinking in the Elementary School.* New York: Holt, Rinehart and Winston, 1970.

Smith, Frank. *Understanding Reading: A Psycholinguistic Analysis of Reading and Learning to Read.* New York: Holt, Rinehart and Winston, 1971.

Smith, Frank, and Goodman, Kenneth S. "On the Psycholinguistic Method of Teaching Reading." *Elementary School Journal* 71 (January 1971): 177–181.

Smith, Henry P., and Dechant, Emerald. *Psychology in Teaching Reading.* Englewood Cliffs, N.J.: Prentice-Hall, 1961.

Steiner, Rollin; Wiener, Morton; and Cromer, Ward. "Comprehension

Training and Identification for Poor and Good Readers." *Journal of Educational Psychology* 62 (December 1971): 506–513.

Suchman, J. Richard. "The Child and the Inquiry Process." *Intellectual Development: Another Look.* Washington, D.C.: Association for Supervision and Curriculum Development, 1969.

Svoboda, Cyril P. "Sources and Characteristics of Piaget's Stage Concept of Development: A Historical Perspective." *Journal of Education* (1973): 28–39.

Tuddenham, Read D. "Jean Piaget and the World of the Child." *American Psychologist* 21 (1966): 207–217.

Van Riper, Charles, and Butler, Katharine G. *Speech in the Elementary Classroom.* New York: Harper and Row, 1955.

Vogel, Susan A. "Syntactic Abilities in Normal and Dyslexic Children." *Journal of Learning Disabilities* 7 (February 1974): 103–109.

Walcutt, Charles C.; Lamport, Joan; and McCracken, Glen. *Teaching Reading.* New York: Macmillan, 1974.

Wardhaugh, Ronald. "Reading: A New Perspective." In *Reading: A Linguistic Perspective,* by R. Wardhaugh. New York: Harcourt Brace Jovanovich, 1969.

Watson, J. B. "Is Thinking Merely the Action of Language Mechanism?" *British Journal of Psychology* 11 (October 1920): 87–104.

Chapter
Three

Preview

The authors of this chapter treat a difficult and sensitive topic with a great deal of concern and objectivity. The issues surrounding the education of culturally different pupils have aroused strong emotions; few people, for example, are apathetic about busing as a means of compensating for de-facto segregation. Unfortunately, the attention given to the educational problems of blacks, American Indians, Mexican-Americans, and other minorities has *not,* to date, significantly narrowed the deficits of these pupils.

The reader of this chapter will find helpful information regarding the general characteristics of members of each of the various groups labelled "culturally different." Further, he will find information about the linguistic problems of these pupils, supplementing the data in the chapter by Goodman and Burke.

Of special value are the detailed discussions of the reading programs designed specifically or adapted for blacks, American Indians, Mexican-Americans, Cubans, Puerto Ricans, and Appalachians, to mention some of the more prominent of the groups categorized as "culturally different"—or, in more pejorative terms, "culturally disadvantaged."

After reading this chapter the teacher of culturally different pupils should be more sensitive to their special educational problems and more knowledgeable about alternative, appropriate solutions.

Reading:
Sociocultural Bases

James Laffey, Madison College
Anna Rose Geary, Rockingham County Public Schools

Objectives

After you have read this chapter, you should be able to:

1. State a definition of "culture" which shows your familiarity with several different ways of looking at that concept.
2. Specify the regional, ethnic, and racial groups who comprise the vast majority of the "culturally different" in American society today.
3. List the most significant effects that "cultural differences" have on school achievement in general and specifically on reading achievement.
4. List the *positive* characteristics of most "culturally different" pupils.
5. Discuss, in detail, at least three reading-language programs designed for the "culturally different" pupil and cite the strengths and weaknesses of each.
6. Review and evaluate the authors' list of characteristics of the successful teacher of the "culturally different" pupil.

For the past decade there has been a national educational effort to provide more effective reading-language programs for the "culturally different." Educators, politicians, students, and the reading public in general have come in contact with terms like "culturally different" or "culturally disadvantaged" time and time again and have interpreted them according to various individual conceptions and misconceptions. Most people interpret "culturally disadvantaged" to mean lacking a cultural background. Others broaden the definition by using "educationally deprived," "underprivileged," "lower class," "lower socioeconomic group," and "disadvantaged" as synonyms for "culturally disadvantaged" or "culturally different" (Riessman, 1962, p. 1).

Whatever its definition, "culturally different" is something that middle-class America is definitely glad that it is *not*. The term conjures up thoughts that are incompatible with the America of the affluent society. Social theorist Michael Harrington has described another America which, although containing forty to fifty million citizens, is an invisible land. This America belongs to the poor, to the "unskilled workers, the migrant farm workers . . . the minorities," who "are pessimistic and defeated" because "they are victimized by mental suffering to a degree unknown in Suburbia" (Harrington, 1962, p. 10). Middle-class America, the dominant class in American society, consciously and unconsciously views its own culture and institutions as positive and those of the lower class as negative. Consequently, any culture other than the dominant one is in danger of losing its identity and becoming a non-culture, while its members are viewed as "culturally deprived," here meaning without a culture.

Definitions of Culture

Can a people be "culturally deprived"—that is, without a culture? Most anthropologists say "no," for reasons that lie in their definitions of the word "culture." Bronislaw Malinowski, for example, defines culture as

> . . . the integral whole consisting of implements and consumers' goods, of constitutional charters for the various social groupings, of human ideas and crafts, beliefs and customs (1944, p. 36).

Frank Riessman defines culture as "the traditions, values, and mores of a specific group, many of which have a long history" (1962, p. 6). His definition of culture includes a people's institutions, structures, and methods of organization.

One of the broader definitions of culture is that of Sophie Elam. She views culture as

> . . . primarily a learning which is begun at birth and which provides the base for living. It permeates all behavior, from the simple fundamentals of eating and dressing and talking to the more complex and involved patterns of communication, use of symbols, and the development of a value system. Culture is also considered to be a determinant of the way one perceives oneself and others. It involves the totality of living from the biological to the social and intellectual. And the greatest complexity of the adjustment lies largely in the social sphere (Elam, 1966, pp. 296–297).

According to the above definitions, culture involves certain activities in which human beings consistently engage in order to cope with the world around them. No human being, therefore, no matter how poor or from what background, is deprived of a culture.

Who Are the Disadvantaged?

Who then are the "culturally disadvantaged"? They are those who do not participate in the life of middle-class America—who do not share the benefits of the affluent society—who are among the 31 percent of the nation's population who are ill-clothed, ill-fed, poorly housed, and poorly educated (Riessman, 1962, p. 3). The culturally disadvantaged are those who are caught in a cycle of despair. Their desire to achieve economic success is thwarted because the access to the means of success is less available to them (Hyman, 1953, p. 427). They find themselves in a cycle of low paying jobs, low income housing, and school failure.

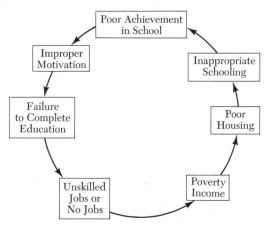

Figure 3.1   Poverty Cycle of Despair.

The culture of the disadvantaged is sometimes equated with their environment. Culture and environment, however, are not the same. Culture is an attempt to cope with one's environment. Often the coping techniques are ineffective because of the various physical, psychological, educational, and economic problems related to poverty. Other times, they are effective. Protest movements are examples of effective coping, as are trade unions, storefront churches, neighborhood clubs, and large extended families (Riessman, 1962, p. 6). It is important that middle America recognize disadvantaged people's struggles and successes in combatting their difficult environment. To see only their ineffectiveness and failures, is to see them one-sidedly.

In the late nineteenth and early twentieth centuries, many of the disadvantaged were found among the ranks of the "hyphenated" Americans, the immigrants who came from Europe and settled primarily in urban areas. These were the city tenement-dwellers who spoke little or no English, who worked at unskilled jobs, who were for the most part uneducated, and who were poor. Gradually, however, these immigrants made their way into the dominant American culture, probably because many of their customs—parental dominance, child obedience, and the passing on of paternal occupations—were similar to American ones (Glazer, 1974, p. 56). Also, the immigrants were of the same race as the dominant group. Their children grew up speaking two languages, and their children's children grew up with the language and cultural patterns of the dominant group. After the third generation, most perceptible evidence of their ethnic origins had disappeared. Along with it went their distinction as a minority group.

Today, the American disadvantaged are primarily the blacks of the urban North and rural South, the Mexican-Americans of Texas and California, the American Indians, the Puerto Ricans of New York City, and the poor white inhabitants of Appalachia. These people are objects of prejudice and discrimination because their race, nationality, customs, religion, or language differ from those of the dominant group, which is white, American, Protestant, English-speaking, and middle class.

If Americans are to realize the dream of a pluralistic society, the disadvantaged must receive schooling which does not perpetuate racial prejudice or undesirable beliefs and attitudes. Teachers—who are, for the most part, members of the middle class—have often dealt with disadvantaged students according to middle-class ideas and consequently have prevented the schools from meeting their needs. It is hoped that the events of the 1960s have effected change in this area. By teaching creativity, decision making, and flexibility, teachers must help the disadvantaged build strong self-concepts and pride in their heritage, and prepare them to act effectively socially, economically, and politically.

The Disadvantaged: Sociocultural Characteristics

Before attempting to structure reading programs for the "culturally disadvantaged," we should take a closer look at the groups which have been lumped together under that banner. For our purposes here we shall consider the sociocultural characteristics of the blacks, Mexican-Americans, Puerto Ricans, American Indians, and poor whites of Appalachia.

Blacks

Between 40 and 50 million Americans live in poverty. We can understand the seriousness of this situation in relation to black Americans only by comparing the number of blacks who live in poverty with the total number of Americans who live in poverty (Johnson, 1970). Of the 22 million blacks in the United States, the number with a yearly income below $4,000 is approximately 13 to 15 million, or 60 to 70 percent of the total black population. Only 26 percent of white families live below this figure (Johnson, 1970, p. 45). It is clear from these statistics that black Americans have largely been excluded from participation in the dominant American culture.

The roots of discrimination against blacks in America go deep—back to their entrance into the colonies as slaves in 1619. It is difficult for a people who for nearly 250 years have been treated as property to suddenly acquire a sense of identity and self-importance. One's self-concept is formed in relation to the rest of society. If the society, as seen on television or in advertisements, is happy, clean, wholesome, well-clothed, and well-fed, as well as white, it becomes obvious to many blacks that they are not able to meet the standards of the society. And so they become submerged more and more in the life of the ghetto or isolated in the rural areas. Many blacks, of course, do participate in the dominant white culture. Yet remnants of discrimination and prejudice persist, and a sense of separation remains. An examination of recent black literature, music, and art shows a preoccupation with themes of alienation, struggle, and the search for an authentic black identity.

The black family finds itself under a great deal of duress when trying to socialize children into the dominant American society. In *Black Families in White America* Andrew Billingsley indicates that the historical development of the black family in the United States, the caste-like qualities of the American stratification system (an informal social system that designates the social pecking order, and which relegates all blacks to inferior status), and economic systems which keep most blacks in the lower economic classes force the black family to teach its children not only how to be human but also how to be black in the white society. This training must also separate blackness and badness, for there is a strong tendency to equate the two (Billingsley, 1968, pp. 28–29). The result is that blacks develop fear and hatred toward the dominant group, and these emotions find their outlets either in explosions such as Watts, Detroit, and Newark or in self-destruction through addiction to drugs and alcohol.

Since the black family has so often been unable to provide for itself because of white discrimination and the unskilled nature of its labor, it has had to turn to government agencies for financial assistance. Unfortunately, assistance has too often depended on the absence of the male head from the family. To some degree, this may account for the fact that 25 percent of black families are headed by women (Johnson, 1970, p. 51). Historically, it has been easier for black women to be employed than black men. The result is that the women tend to be economically independent of the men, and so the family gravitates around the mother.

In 1964, 29 percent of the black male population was unemployed at one time or another (Johnson, p. 53). The income security which the white male takes for granted is denied the black male. Not only is the black father frequently removed from his position as head of the family, as breadwinner, but he also experiences the breakdown of his own self-concept. The breakdown of the family has a tremendous effect upon black children as well. Boys do not have effective male models, and girls learn from their mothers that a black man "ain't no good" (Johnson, 1970, p. 55). Those blacks living in the ghettoes of big cities see not only the breakdown of their families but also the breakdown of the human spirit through disease, hunger, crime, and inadequate housing. The educational implications of this situation, particularly for reading, will be discussed later in this chapter.

Mexican-Americans

Individuals of Spanish origin in the territories encompassing the present states of Arizona, California, Colorado, New Mexico, and Texas were first extended citizenship in 1848 as a result of the Mexican-American War. Ever since, the American people have rather consistently overlooked Mexican-Americans as a group to be assimilated into American society. Only recently, since the decade of the sixties, has the plight of Mexican-Americans been brought to public attention.

Although Mexican-Americans are basically a rural people, a majority of them have migrated to urban areas in order to be present where jobs are available. Research has shown that 80 percent of Mexican-Americans live in urban communities. And of the 80 percent, a large portion (87 percent) live in urban poverty ghettoes in the southwestern United States (Rodriguez, 1969, p. 35).

The *barrios*, Spanish enclaves in the cities, have been pockets of social and residential shelter for Mexican-Americans. There Spanish tradition, with its emphasis on the patriarchal structure of the family, is preserved. The father is the authority figure. He provides a strong male model for the sons to emulate and is expected to represent the family with honor at all times. The mother's role is that of homemaker. She cares for the children, cleans, cooks, and sews. She is expected to show her husband absolute respect. She represents the soul of the family, and for this she is loved and honored. Included within the family structure are relatives such as grandparents, aunts, uncles, cousins, and godparents. These individuals contribute to the close-knit nature of the family by being responsible to and for one another.

The *barrios,* while providing shelter from the outside world, also contain within their walls all the miseries of ghetto life. Children are exposed to poverty, squalor, and disease. They are also witness to the dissolution of the strong family life which is their protection. If the father is unable to find employment, he can no longer provide the image of strength which Spanish tradition insists upon. When the mother seeks employment outside the home in order to provide for the family needs, she steps into a male role. Conflict is likely to ensue as a result of either or both events.

Mexican-Americans have been objects of both economic and educational discrimination in the United States. Economically, they have been exploited in agriculture. American growers have hired smuggled-in Mexican nationals, who will work for very low wages, in preference to Mexican-Americans, thus denying employment opportunities to resident workers.

Educationally, public schools have discriminated arbitrarily against Mexican-Americans. For example, the Spanish language as a medium for teaching was banned by section 288 of the Texas Penal Code (Martinez, 1970, p. 280). Inferior buildings and equipment have been used in schools with high Mexican-American populations. Teachers have not been properly trained to deal with Mexican-American children. As a result, the median level of education among Mexican-Americans is very low—approximately 8.6 years. In Texas, almost 80 percent of students who have Spanish surnames drop out before finishing high school (Rodriguez, 1969, p. 35). In California almost 74 percent of Mexican-American students do not finish high school. Later in this chapter, we will relate these statistics specifically to reading and literature.

Puerto Ricans

Puerto Ricans are another group of Hispanic origin which has sought entrance into life in the United States. They have settled for the most part in New York City. The 1961 census showed that 613,000 Puerto Ricans live in the city. Glazer and Moynihan have described two migratory patterns typical of Puerto Rican families with children. The first is for the father to migrate alone, stay with friends or relatives when he arrives on the mainland, find a job and living quarters for his wife and children, and then bring over his family. The second pattern involves migration of the mother with the children. The father does not accompany them either because he has deserted the mother or because she "has decided to leave home and go to New York, where jobs are plentiful, where the government is reputed to be 'for women and the children' and where relief is plentiful" (Glazer and Moynihan, 1963, pp. 122–123).

Puerto Rican culture is similar to Mexican-American in that boys are raised to exhibit "machismo" or manliness, girls to be mothers, and individuals to be aware of self-pride and dignity. Nevertheless, it is different from Mexican-American culture in two ways:

1. Puerto Rican culture is weak in its ties to Spain, to the folk arts, and to the Catholic Church. The Church, so often the transmitter of culture, was not strong in Puerto Rico because it was viewed as the institution of the rich and because there were too few clergy. Spanish tradition was also weakened by Spain's neglect of Puerto Rico as a colony and by the fact that Puerto Ricans have been citizens of the United States since the turn of the century and have been influenced by American thoughts and ideas.

2. Families of Spanish origin tend to be strong in structure. Not so with the Puerto Rican family. More than a quarter of Puerto Rican marriages are consensual or common-law, with the result that children of these marriages are "illegitimate." Concubinage and male unfaithfulness further weaken the structure. Add to these factors crowded living conditions, unemployment, underemployment, and family members' various stages of entrance into the United States, and we can see how family stability is threatened (Glazer and Moynihan, pp. 88–89).

Acculturation provides educational problems for the Puerto Rican child. Puerto Rican parents would like their children to be well educated, and often hope they will be professionals. School, however, proves to be a frustrating experience to the child, and so educational hopes are often unrealized. Language presents a formidable barrier. In New York City at one time nearly 56,000 children in elementary school could neither speak nor understand English. Most of these children were Spanish-speaking (Glazer and Moynihan, p. 127). Another problem faced by both the Puerto Rican family and school personnel is the difference in opinion concerning the role of the school. Puerto Rican parents fear that the school views itself as a surrogate family, and they frequently consider classroom methods much too informal. These attitudes in combination with the language barrier constitute formidable obstacles which Puerto Rican youngsters and their teachers must overcome if they are to achieve success (Johnson, 1970, pp. 82–83).

American Indians

American Indians are a proud people whose cultural heritage is almost completely different from the dominant white culture. During the colonial period of American history and the period during which Indian tribes were controlled by treaties, the Indian population was decimated and the few people who remained were gradually driven from their land. During the reservation period from 1887 to 1914, the Indian lands were systematically reduced from 138 million acres to 47 million acres. Another phase in the period saw forced assimilation during which, among other things, Indian children were taken from their tribes, placed in boarding schools, and forbidden to use Indian language or practice Indian customs (Marden and Meyer, 1968, p. 363). No attempt was made to adapt the curriculum to the students.

There have been many attempts to deal with the Indian problem since the reservation period. The Indian Reorganization Act in 1934 brought about changes by improving the Indian economic situation, by increasing tribal self-government, and by improving the welfare of the Indians on the whole. The Relocation program of the 1950s was unsuccessful because so many of the Indians who had left the tribal lands to move to industrial centers returned, having found only poor employment and abysmal housing. The Udall Plan of 1966 provided for bringing the Indians into decision-making policies and for upgrading their educational systems (Marden and Meyer, pp. 367–371).

Today, the condition of America's nearly 500,000 Indians is still appalling. The Indians are considered one of the poorest of America's minority groups. Their average income has been estimated at approximately $1,500. Unemployment figures range from 40 to 45 percent, with the Sioux reaching a high of 75 percent. Because of their poverty, Indian children usually come from overcrowded, unattractive homes where privacy, food, and clothing are insufficient (Narang, 1974, pp. 190–191).

The experiences as well as the concepts of the Indian child are limited when measured by the white culture which dominates the schools. The schools have not been successful institutions for the Indians for several reasons: (1) Indian culture does not make room for individualism as it is understood in white society. Since Indians operate in a network of formalized relationships, the individual is important only as a member of the group. (2) Interpersonal relationships stress cooperation rather than competition. (3) Men and women, boys and girls have traditional roles to play; any attempt to violate the arrangement is taboo.

So American culture, with its emphasis on individualism, competition, and, to a certain degree, equality of the sexes, runs completely counter to Indian traditions. If the schools are to be successful, teachers and other school personnel must work with the Indian child in his cultural setting (Kluckhohn, 1962, pp. 339–340). Education must be presented as a means of contributing to Indian society as a whole, not as a means of making money for individuals or of individual assimilation. Only in this manner will the Indians be able to enter American society as a vibrant, viable community.

Appalachians

The term Appalachia often suggests poverty, and rightly so. For many years Appalachia has been an economic problem area. Appalachians, those nearly 10 million people who live in the mountain areas of northern Alabama, Georgia, North and South Carolina, Tennessee, Kentucky, Virginia, West Virginia (and portions of Pennsylvania, western Maryland, and southern New York), have suffered terribly during times of national economic distress and have been unable to benefit from national periods of prosperity. The decline in the area's principal economic activities, especially agriculture and coal mining, is responsible for their almost continuous state of poverty. The employment level in Appalachia's coal mines has declined drastically, according to an analysis of the region done by the Maryland Department of Economic Development. Between 1950 and 1959, 60 percent of the mine workers left their jobs, as did 25 percent of agricultural workers. This decline in employment corresponds to the decline in the region's population. Approximately one and a half million persons, many between eighteen and forty-four, emigrated between 1950 and 1959 (Maryland Department of Economic Development, 1960, p. 5). These emigrants were some of the region's most productive laborers.

Living standards in Appalachia are low in both rural and urban areas. One out of every three families lives on $3,000 or less per year (Crow, 1966, p. 20). At least one worker in six is jobless or is employed only part time. Houses are small and poorly constructed, and in some rural counties only about 2 percent of them have such ordinary conveniences as running water, a bathtub, and a private toilet (Ford, 1962, p. 17). Health standards are low too. Death rates from influenza and pneumonia, tuberculosis, parasitic diseases, and cardiovascular renal diseases are higher in Appalachia than they are in the rest of the nation. The mortality rate from diseases of early childhood also exceeds that of the nation as a whole (Ford, p. 220).

The Appalachian region has been a somewhat mysterious place to the rest of America for a long time. Sometimes it has been depicted as the home of a group of people who speak a language reminiscent of Elizabethan English, sing traditional English ballads, play dulcimers, and spin their own yarn. At other times Appalachia has been pictured as the home of happy hillbillies who take joy in their white lightning and home folks company. And at still other times, the stereotype of the Hatfields and McCoys has dominated the scene.

The people of Appalachia, descendants of peasants and yeomen from England, Ireland, and Scotland, are a proud, hardy, and clannish group. Families are close-knit and strong. The father is head of the family and the main authority figure. The mother, while providing warmth and love for the children, is always mindful of the wishes of her husband. In a description of the Appalachian women a century ago, Harry Caudill embodies the virtues and sufferings which are still so typical of the upcountry womenfolk:

> In their world the man was a tyrant who ruled his house with medieval unconcern for his wife's feelings or opinions. She rarely sat down to eat a meal with him, it being her duty to "wait on" him. When a stranger was present she stayed discreetly out of sight. As a girl she saw her brothers and father "laid away," the victims of feuds, quarrels, logging accidents or disease. Her girlhood was spent in graceless toil and crowned by an early marriage. Wasted by a quarter century of child bearing, she saw a row of graves dug for her children. Often she survived as a widow to fend for the remainder of her brood. She could rarely influence the impetuous decisions of her husband and sons, and, never far from the family graveyard, mourned through long years the results of their efforts (1962, p. 80).

It is from this tradition that the modern Appalachian woman emerges. She is still hardy, still resilient, and, though modern trends and employment in industry have made her less so, still subservient to her husband. Although she may not provide the main income for the family, she is in many ways the motivator of the children, encouraging their education and being held responsible for their failures.

Families are large. Child-rearing practices are on the whole permissive and, although children are responsible for certain chores and duties in the home, they are permitted to roam the hills more or less freely (Giffin, 1972, p. 181). The closeness among kin that results from the extended family system tends to make the mountain people suspicious of outsiders. They often refuse help from organizations or from individuals other than relatives.

How does this isolated background affect the education of Appalachian children? In a survey conducted by Ford to determine the educational aspirations of Appalachians for their children, three out of four said they would like to have a son complete college, and two out of three expressed the same wish for a daughter. Less than 1 percent felt satisfied with merely a high school education for their children. Almost all said they would like to help finance part of their children's college education. This rather surprising revelation indicates that the mountain people realize the importance of formal education in today's industrialized society (Ford, 1962, p. 17).

In contrast to these aspirations are the stark realities of the educational level of the inhabitants of Appalachia. The proportion of adults twenty-five and over whose schooling stopped before the completion of eighth grade is approximately 75 percent in rural areas. In non-rural areas in Appalachia the number reaches approximately two-thirds (Giffin, 1972, p. 182). Related to the dropout problem is retardation—school achievement which is considerably below grade level expectations. In 1930 there were thirteen counties in the Appalachian region in which 55 percent or more of the fourth grade pupils were older than they should have been for their grade (Ford, 1962, p. 189). Today, retardation is not as serious a problem as it was in the past. Nevertheless, better school facilities, staff, and programs are needed to narrow the gap between potential achievement and performance. The Appalachian people tend to be content with school systems as they are. Since school boards in the states concerned have no power to set a tax levy within prescribed legal limits, to support a budget, or to call for a referendum on a slashed budget proposal, the amount of money spent per pupil is lower than in other areas. Indeed, it is approximately 50 percent lower than in the rest of the nation. Federal assistance is vital if the schools are to provide an adequate education.

Education is hampered not only by poverty but by the very attitudes of the children. The strong individualism and freedom of movement which are typical of their background prevent them from easily accepting the authority and confinement of school. Their protests often take the form of sullenness, which makes the teaching of anything, including reading, very difficult.

Common Characteristics of Disadvantaged Groups

The following generalizations can be made about those *not* participating in the dominant American culture:

1. The disadvantaged are isolated by religion, race, ethnic origin, or geography from the American scene. With the exception of the Appalachians, they are not WASPs—White Anglo-Saxon Protestants.
2. The disadvantaged, for the most part, belong to the lowest economic groups because they cannot qualify—or have been prevented from qualifying—for the high-paying jobs.
3. The disadvantaged are prone to sickness and disease because of a lack of nutritious food, well-balanced diets, health care, and adequate housing.
4. The parents of disadvantaged children are frequently bitter and discouraged, more used to defeat than success. They did poorly in school and as a result do not provide an example of success in education for their children.
5. Disadvantaged children often come from crowded, noisy homes where there is a marked lack of privacy. In order to survive in such an environment, they tend to psychologically shut out many stimuli.
6. The language used in the home of the disadvantaged child is generally unlike that which is encountered in the school. It has been estimated that the comprehension vocabulary of the disadvantaged child in the begin-

ning years of school is between one-third and one-half that of the middle-class child.

7. The disadvantaged child often presents a discipline problem to the school because school activities do not sustain his attention, because his parents are unable or unavailable to control him, or because his sense of individualism prevents him from conforming to the middle-class standards of the school.

In spite of these disadvantages, the lifestyle of the culturally different is not totally negative; it also incorporates many strengths. Riessman drew up a balance sheet and listed the following assets (Riessman, 1962, p. 48):

1. Cooperativeness and mutual aid which mark the extended family.
2. Avoidance of strain that accompanies competitiveness and individualism.
3. Equalitarianism, informality, and warm humor.
4. Freedom from self-blame and parental overprotection.
5. Children's enjoyment of each other's company, with a lessened sibling rivalry.
6. Security found in the extended family and in a traditional outlook.

In short, we must realize that those aspects in the lifestyle of the culturally different which appear negative to the dominant American culture are not the result of any genetic inferiority, but simply the result of a life of poverty. And there are few problems which the alleviation of poverty would not cure.

The Language Factor

One of the major problems facing the disadvantaged child as he enters the middle-class environment of the school is that his language does not match that which he encounters in the classroom.[1] He may have come from a home where English is not a native language, as is the case with Mexican-American, Puerto Rican, and American Indian children, or where so-called standard English is not spoken, as in the homes of many blacks and Appalachian white children.

The language of children from such backgrounds often stigmatizes them socially. As indicated by Robert DiPietro, the price for such individu-

[1] Language is discussed in greater detail in Chapter Four, "Reading: Language and Psycholinguistic Bases."

alism in speech has been high in the United States. People who do not speak English or who speak non-standard English have been trapped at the bottom of the economy by being excluded from participation in the full life of the standard English speaking majority. If they are urban, they are ensnared in the ghettoes; if rural, they are caught in a subsistence environment (DiPietro, 1973, p. 37).

People who speak non-standard English or no English must become bidialectal or bilingual in order to communicate with the dominant community. The problem facing them is that their culture and language are of little importance to the majority. As a result, their bilingualism and bidialectalism tend to be transitional steps, taken in order to reduce strife and social tension (DiPietro, p. 38).

The past ten years have seen a change in linguistic attitudes toward non-standard English. As a result of studies by such sociolinguists as Ralph Fasold, William Labov, William Stewart, Roger Shuy, and others, Black English has been identified as a self-contained linguistic system with a set of language norms. Besides indicating that there are "orderly grammatical, phonological, and lexical features which characterize much Black English," these investigators have also illuminated dialectal divergences which exist in so-called standard English (Alatis, 1973, p. 51).

The non-standard language of white Appalachians also reflects an orderly and self-contained set of language norms, different from that of the black dialect speaker. William Stewart (1969, pp. 59, 161) has compared verb forms from these different sets of norms. The present durative form of the verb makes a good example. A speaker of standard English would say the following: "He is working." Mountain children would say: "He's workin'," or "He's a-workin'." Children who speak Black English would say: "He workin'," or "He be workin'." Each of the forms means something different to the speaker. "He's a-workin' " in mountain speech either means the subject has a steady job or that he is away. "He's workin' " means the subject is doing a specific task. In Black dialect, "be" does not necessarily indicate that action is remote in space. "Be" can, however, predicate an adjective (as "He be busy," meaning he is habitually busy) while "a-" cannot be so used in Appalachian speech. The point is that the grammatical rules used by speakers of non-standard English are just as systematized as those of standard English.

Bilingual Education

For years children in American schools who spoke a language other than English were not only forced to communicate in English but were also expected to perform as well as speakers of English. The result was often frustration and failure. The early 1960s saw a new trend in bilingual education. In October 1964, the federal government recognized officially that there were thousands of school children "in the Southwest, on the Atlantic coast and in New England, on American Indian reservations, and in the Trust Territories; in Puerto Rico, Alaska, Texas, Arizona, New Mexico, California, Colorado, Hawaii, New York, New Jersey, Vermont, Maine, Louisiana and Florida—whose mother tongue was other than English and who needed specialized instruction in English if they were fully to understand or participate in the American cultural, social, and economic way of life" (Alatis, 1973, p. 44). Several educational acts—most recently the Bilingual Education Act—have provided instruction for children in American schools who come from homes where English is not the dominant language.

The benefits of bilingual education (meaning the education of students in several subjects in two languages) are many. The school's respect for the individual student's language and culture enhances his self-image and motivates him to learn academic material. When the subject is presented in his mother tongue, the student learns it more easily, and his resistance to learning the second language is not as great. Most students perform better academically in the second language (Modiano, 1969, p. 93).

There are several standard practices for teaching bilingual and bidialectal children. Virginia Allen French has identified them as follows:

1. Contrastive analysis of the target language (or dialect) with the students' home language (or dialect).
2. Acceptance of the target language and students' language as equally valid systems of communication.
3. Emphasis on grammatical structure of the target language, not on vocabulary.
4. Presentation of the linguistic system of the target language in small steps, each issuing from the last.
5. Measurement of success in the target language in terms of oral fluency, not recitation of rules and definitions (Alatis, 1973, pp. 50–51).

As we can see, the emphasis here is upon recognizing that one language is not "better" than another, upon building an understanding of the structure of the target language, and upon the formation of habits in oral fluency.

Teachers working with children who do not speak English often treat these children the same as those who speak a non-standard dialect. James Alatis has indicated, however, that non-standard dialect speakers tend to have motivational, sociological, and psychological problems, while children who speak other languages are more likely to have cultural and linguistic problems (Alatis, p. 51). Techniques used to teach both types of children include mimicry, repetition, and substitution. Problems arise, however, when non-standard dialect speakers are constantly drilled in these areas.

Teachers must remember that it is repetitious and boring to a child who already knows English to repeat constantly such phrases as "This is a red ball" or "This is a book" (Bailey, 1973, p. 107).

What can be done to help teachers deal with the problems of bilingual and bidialectal students? The answer lies in the re-education of teachers and the preparation of new teachers in language arts programs which are geared away from traditional methods and toward the current demand for equal educational opportunities. Drills and exercises should include many opportunities for experimentation with language and for language play. Finally, funds must be provided for school systems to hire the teachers who are creative, imaginative, and professionally equipped to deal with bilingual and bidialectal children, so that these children can succeed in the schools and ultimately in the dominant society (Bailey, pp. 108–114).

Reading Programs for Culturally Different Students

Existing reading programs for culturally different students vary widely in rationale, size, and scope. In fact there are very few common characteristics other than that the majority of such reading programs work toward preventing educational deficits and remediating existing reading problems. These programs are preventive in that they attempt to bridge cultural, language, educational, and reading gaps in the early school period. They are remedial in that there is a sustained effort to hold off the more serious educational and reading deficits that occur at later school periods and to correct problems wherever they occur.

Many of the reading programs designed for culturally different students are based on traditional approaches to teaching reading. We will review some of these traditional approaches here, along with some of the programs which make use of them. This is not an in-depth analysis of all reading approaches and programs available, but only an introduction to some of the materials, approaches, and programs which have been designed for the culturally different. More detailed discussions and analyses are available elsewhere in this text and in some of the references cited in the various bibliographies at the end of each chapter (see, for example, *Approaches to Beginning Reading* by R. C. Aukerman).

Basal Reading Programs

It has been reported that basal reading programs are used in 95 percent of the elementary schools in the United States. There is good reason for this.

Basal programs have many advantages. The following characteristic components of basal reading programs have been listed often in reading textbooks and journal articles. These components also constitute the advantages of such programs from an instructional point of view. The typical basal reading program includes:

1. A systematic and in-depth reading curriculum in word recognition (decoding), vocabulary, comprehension, and study skills. The curriculum is sequential, in that the skills proceed from the easiest skills to the more difficult.
2. A well-rounded selection of high quality literature chosen to meet the varying interests and tastes of children from different cultural and experiential backgrounds.
3. A comprehensive teacher's manual with detailed lesson plans for implementing individual lessons, as well as suggestions for implementing the entire instructional program in reading.
4. Prepared learning activities based upon common childhood experiences and children's interests.
5. Supplementary reading activities and skills workbooks designed to reinforce reading and study skills learned in the basal reading lesson.
6. Supplementary evaluation aids designed to assist the teacher in determining the students' level of mastery in specific reading units. In a number of basal programs, criterion-referenced tests are available to assist the teacher in diagnosing students' specific reading needs.
7. Supplementary audio-visual aids, such as posters, cassette tapes, filmstrips, and bulletin board displays designed to enrich the instructional program. These are provided in only a few basal programs.

While the above list is not comprehensive, it does give the reader a clear idea about the many advantages of the typical basal reading program. One additional advantage is that most basal reading programs integrate reading into a total language curriculum. The prepared lessons demonstrate concretely that reading is only one facet of the language-communication process. But, more important for the culturally different, many reading programs (see the Allyn and Bacon Reading Program, the Ginn 360 Program, the Open Court Reading-Language Program, and the Scott-Foresman Reading System) emphasize not only reading skills but also the language skills which are the foundation stones of any effective instructional program in reading.

In spite of the many advantages of basal reading programs, critics claim that most programs give a distorted view of what American society is all about (Spache, 1973). The critics claim that many basal reading authors fail to recognize the pluralistic, multicultural nature of modern day American society. It is certainly true that a teacher cannot expect to teach all his or her children successfully with a single basal reading program as the only instructional tool. Additional instructional materials and strategies will be needed for students who have different learning styles or serious reading deficiencies. Additional materials will also be needed to enrich the reading curriculum for the very capable students. In other words, in any typical classroom, a teacher should have multiple programs and instructional packets, which should be supplemented with numerous trade books, magazines, reading games, and related language activities.

Linguistic-Phonic Programs

The linguistic-phonic reading programs place a heavy emphasis on decoding skills. Many such programs require students to learn not only the names of the letters of the alphabet, but also the sounds associated with individual letters. Instructional decisions regarding whether students need to learn the letter names as well as the sounds associated with specific letters are often arbitrary, even though there is evidence which suggests that children who have knowledge of letter names are far more successful readers than students who do not have such knowledge (Laffey, 1974).

Lippincott's Reading Series This reading program includes readers for grades one through eight. The first stage of instruction introduces the sounds of the short vowel letters and selected consonants (*m, r,* and *s*). The short vowel sounds and selected consonants are combined in various ways to form words. The words are put into sentences to give the child a successful initial experience with reading words and sentences. As the program progresses, it emphasizes the regular sound symbol patterns (*man, can, tan, fan,* etc.).

The regular linguistic patterns are then supplemented with irregularly patterned sight words. This provides the student with the opportunity to learn words with both linguistically regular and irregular patterns. This approach continues throughout the series. The reading series itself is composed of basic reading books, supplementary workbooks, and a series of supplementary readers for each level.

Structural Reading Program—Random House This program begins instruction with the whole spoken word, since the word has meaning for the child already. The readiness program consists of a series of books in which there are pictures that represent one spoken word. The program continues into a series of graded texts, teaching initial sounds of consonants and vowels first, then later teaching the consonant clusters (*st, sl, sh,* etc.).

After the relationships between sounds and letters have been learned, the student reaches a new level of learning. While the focus remains on the spoken language, the student decodes whole spoken words in the consonant-vowel-consonant (C-V-C) pattern—for example, *can.* Spoken words in this and other patterns are analyzed into their spoken parts—for *can,* /ca/ and /n/, the main part and the ending. The student looking at a picture of a can says *can* and then decodes the word beneath the picture of the can. The student comes to recognize, quite logically, that the structure of the spoken language and the printed word correspond to one another. As a result, he can read a word like *can* because he recognizes its structure. Later, he builds on this knowledge and is able to recognize words like *tan* and *fan* independently.

The central focus of *Structural Reading* is the integration of the skills of reading, listening, writing, and spelling with the spoken language. This is a modified linguistic approach, since it presents linguistically correct rules in sequence. At the same time, it stresses the student's own language-reading discoveries as he is learning to read.

Miami Linguistic Readers This is a language-reading program with a linguistic emphasis. When the program was first prepared, it was intended as a reading program for students from a Spanish-American culture who spoke English as a second language. The original writing efforts were supported by a Ford Foundation grant. The authors' basic purposes here were twofold: (1) to prepare books which were "culture" free and which would have story lines to which children from diverse backgrounds could relate; (2) to write books which would have a high degree of phonemic regularity, since the program was being written primarily for use by children who spoke a language (Cuban-Spanish) which had a high degree of phonemic regularity.

The Miami Linguistic Readers consist of more than twenty small paperback books, as well as a number of workbooks and an accompanying teacher's manual. The specific objectives of the program are:

1. That the content of the materials reflect the true interests of children.
2. That the natural language forms of children's speech be reflected in the books.
3. That the child first have oral-aural control of any materials he is expected to read.
4. That the vocabulary and grammatical structure of the words in the stories be controlled.
5. That the students be required to read by structures.
6. That the central emphasis of the program be directed toward the reading process.
7. That the reading, speaking, and listening experiences be followed by reinforcing writing experiences.
8. That the sound-symbol relationships of the words in the program be related to spelling patterns.

9. That there be an emphasis on learner success throughout the program.
10. That the special nature of the materials determine how much students
    should learn at any given time (Aukerman, 1971).

As the objectives indicate, the Miami Linguistic Readers are more
than a reading program. They comprise a language arts program which
includes some emphasis on the use of regular linguistic patterns. The
program stresses speaking and listening activities in its early stages. This
emphasis reflects the two major goals of the program: to enable students to
acquire some reading competence, and also to enable them to master
English as a second language.

The Distar Reading and Language Program This instructional system is
designed to help students acquire basic concepts and skills in reading and
language. According to the authors of the program, these basic skills will
enable students to succeed in school. The target population of the Distar
Program is the "disadvantaged" (Kim, Berger, and Kratochvil, 1972). While
its authors indicate that the program was designed for the culturally
disadvantaged (that is, culturally different), they fail to indicate which
specific group—the poor black and white of the inner-city ghettoes,
children born to poverty in Appalachia, or American Indians. However, no
single reading and language program could be effective with all the diverse
student populations often incorporated under the descriptive but general
term "culturally different."

The Distar Level I instructional program initiates the student into the
program with a concentrated series of lessons on the language of instruction. Later, students are introduced to the concept that each letter of the
alphabet is associated with a specific sound. An interesting aspect of this
program is that it teaches the student to associate the appropriate sound
with the appropriate letter, but it does not teach letter names. After the
student learns a certain number of sounds, he is taught to blend sounds.
There is a great deal of emphasis placed on successful blending of sounds.
This later enables the student to pronounce whole words.

The teacher's manual for each lesson contains the entire dialogue for
that lesson, along with pictures, questions, and stories. The dialogue is
presented in a step-by-step sequence difficult to deviate from. The guidelines for use of the program suggest that the teacher work with small
groups of children at a time (between five and ten students).

Although this program has many advantages to offer an inexperienced teacher, it also has some disadvantages. To determine both the
strengths and weaknesses of the Distar Program, students in a graduate
seminar at Madison College studied the program intensively during the
summer of 1974. The seminar participants included experienced teachers
who had used the program, reading and language arts supervisors, and a

number of reading specialists. The result of the study was the following list of the *strengths* and *weaknesses* of the Distar Reading and Language Program:

Strengths
1. The program has a positive approach to teaching which includes constant positive reinforcement as part of the program.
2. The nature of the reading and language input in the program is multi-sensory (that is, tactile, auditory, visual).
3. There is an intensive teacher training component.
4. The reading skills are introduced in a sequential order. The teacher uses already learned skills to introduce new skills. (This is not unique to Distar.)
5. The program appears to enhance the student's self-concept and interest students in independent reading. (This is accomplished in most success-ful programs.)
6. The program has built-in curriculum evaluation. The students are evaluated on the basis of the skills taught in the program. (This is also true of many basal programs.)
7. The program was designed for a target population—the disadvantaged.
8. The program uses a directed teaching method which can be highly useful for an inexperienced teacher.

Weaknesses
1. There is some difficulty in maintaining a high level of teacher interest in the program due to the overly prescriptive directions in the teacher's manual. Teacher boredom becomes a factor in successfully implement-ing the program.
2. There is the problem of curriculum consistency in the case where students are transferred to a new school and reading program. This is particularly true of some of the artificial alphabet characters. It is true also in the instances where teaching practices could be dramatically different from the highly teacher-directed learning in the Distar Pro-gram.
3. The highly structured nature of the curriculum does not allow for either student or teacher spontaneity.
4. Even a well-qualified teacher is not encouraged to develop alternative learning activities during the reading-language lessons.
5. The curriculum is not a child-centered curriculum but a teacher-centered curriculum.
6. The heavy emphasis on the decoding skills appears to result in the decoding skills becoming an end in themselves rather than a means to an end—that is, the students seem to decode for the sake of decoding, rather than using decoding as a means to understanding the printed language.

The Distar Reading and Language Instructional System is based on methods developed at the University of Illinois with "culturally disadvantaged" students from large inner-city ghetto environments. Reports of its effectiveness have been made by the publisher of the program (S.R.A., 1971), but further objective evaluations need to be undertaken. An instructional system designed and developed for one culturally different group will not necessarily be effective with other culturally different groups. There are important differences of some educational consequence between cultural groups who are generally referred to as "culturally disadvantaged"; and such differences should certainly be taken into consideration when instructional systems are developed.

Overall, the various phonic-linguistic reading programs now available play a crucial role in instructional programs for the culturally different. They are often highly effective in developing decoding skills among the culturally different groups. The stress on the decoding skills is consistent with the recommendations Jeanne Chall made following her extensive study of instructional methods in reading (Chall, 1967). However, Chall recommends a decoding emphasis only as a beginning reading method—"a method to start the child on" (Chall, p. 307).

Language-Experience Approaches

For years teachers have known that children learn to read quite successfully when their own language is used as a basis for reading instruction. This approach to the teaching of reading views learning to read as a part of language development (Spache, 1973). It stresses the close relationship between listening, speaking, reading, and writing. One scholar (R. Van Allen, 1961) has described the language experience approach from the point of view of the student:

> *What I can think about,*
> *I can talk about.*
> *What I can say, I can write.*
> *What I can write, I can read.*
> *I can read what I write and*
> *what other people can write*
> *for me to read.*

This approach to the teaching of reading brings together all aspects of the communication process into a unified curriculum, using the child's language as the instructional program. This strategy capitalizes on the child's oral language facility, which in turn motivates the child by showing him that what he talks about is important enough to write about, and later on, to read about. When he reads what he has written, the child recognizes that the content of reading is what he thinks about and later expresses.

Usually instruction in the language experience curriculum begins a few days after the students enter school. From the very first day, students are encouraged to express their ideas through such activities as "show and tell." The teacher often records group stories on language experience charts. These stories are then used as instructional reading materials through which the teacher begins teaching words, phrases, selected word perception skills, and some comprehension skills. Later, the teacher puts the children into smaller groups and continues the development of experience stories. At some point, individual children are encouraged to share their ideas so that individual stories can be recorded. These individually recorded experience stories usually motivate students to write their own stories. This natural extension of the language curriculum continues until students are engaged in a wide range of language activities and related art activities.

The language experience approach can be adapted to fit a variety of student needs. Many classroom teachers either use this approach exclusively or integrate it with other teaching approaches. It can be used to provide beginning culturally different readers with materials which match their dialect and/or experiences. These are the steps to follow when using the language experience approach:

1. Have a discussion with a student about an experience he had or one that you shared with him. (You can also use a picture, film, filmstrip, record, tape cassette, or any stimulating object as a basis for a discussion.)
2. Record (in manuscript writing for primary grade students) the story or experience. Let the student see you preparing his/her story.
3. As you write the story do as little editing as possible. If the student speaks in a dialect, record the story in the dialect, using *standard* English spellings, however, since these are what the student will encounter in print.
4. When the story is finished, read it aloud to the student. Then have him read it back to you.
5. At first, keep the stories short—two or three sentences for young students and a paragraph or two for older students.
6. Older students can type their own stories. Allow the students to illustrate any part of their stories. With young children, it is often appropriate to begin with a self-portrait, for example, and record a story about the picture.
7. Ask the student to choose some words he would like to learn.
8. Print the words (and word phrases) on 3″ x 5″ cards to be used for sight word and vocabulary activities.

9. Language experience stories can be used to teach sight words, word analysis skills, readiness skills, and comprehension and vocabulary skills.
10. A skills checklist can be used to identify the skills the student needs, as well as to keep a record of the skills taught.
11. The teacher can have the student color or paint the best illustrations in their stories. Then the stories can be bound or laminated and used as instructional materials for other students.

Most teachers who have used the language experience approach have found it to be an invaluable teaching tool. It is excellent for culturally different students, since it uses oral language for instruction (Hall, 1972). It not only pays attention to the language of the culturally and linguistically different, but it can also extend these students' language and communications skills by correlating writing, reading, and listening activities in a single simplified curriculum.

Individualized Reading Instruction

The individualized approach to reading instruction is received enthusiastically by teachers and pupils alike. The students first seek and select their own reading materials. Second, they decide on both the quantity and quality of materials that they read. This approach to teaching reading places the highest value on individual prerogative and motivation. It emphasizes the development of the individual rather than the significance of the instructional materials (Spache, 1973). The individualized approach to reading recognizes that rates of growth in reading and within specific skills areas in reading are highly variable, and that significant differences not only occur but are inevitable. It is radically different from reading programs in which children are assigned to instructional groups and each group is assigned to a particular text.

Like any other approach, the individualized reading approach requires specific techniques for its successful implementation. We recognize of course, that individualized reading means many things to many people. We recognize also that the procedures we are about to describe are not necessarily recognized and accepted by all teachers who have implemented an individualized reading program. As one authority states, "Individualized reading is not a single method with predetermined steps to be followed" (Jacobs, 1958).

The following are elements of a typical individualized reading program:

1. *Teacher-pupil planning:* Teacher and pupil discuss plans for the reading period, to identify what the student is reading and why.

2. *Reading period:* Individual students select their own materials for reading while other students confer with the teacher.
3. *Teacher's record and history:* Teacher selects an appropriate record keeping format and records pertinent notes on individual students following individual conferences.
4. *Individual pupil conference:* This is the personal conference in which teacher and pupil discuss and review the student's reading activities. It is the period in which there is a close personal interaction between the pupil and teacher. The conference focuses, however, on the student's reading. The student may be asked to read orally. He/she might be requested to review with the teacher some new words or skills.
5. *Student records:* Students write a diary describing their reading activities and identifying their strengths and weaknesses. Typically, teachers as well as pupils maintain records.
6. *Rotating library:* The teacher and students bring to class a large number of books, magazines, and other reading materials. These materials should be rotated monthly.
7. *Group and individual sharing:* There are many opportunities for individual and group sharing. Often the teacher will provide a specific time when books can be shared with the class or with individuals.

While there are common elements to most individualized reading programs, there are no definite procedures for initiating such a program. In fact, we recommend that beginning teachers not attempt to start an individualized reading program. The fact that even experienced teachers initiate such programs only gradually is some indicator of the difficulty of the task.

An exception to the rule is the individualized reading program which has been organized prior to its installation in a school. The Random House High Intensity Learning System is an example of such a program. It not only contains all the elements of an individualized reading program, but it has other elements which add to its strength.

The High Intensity Learning System contains the following:

1. A set of instructional objectives.
2. A catalogue of instructional objectives with accompanying instructional prescriptions.
3. Sets of criterion-referenced tests to go along with the instructional objectives.
4. A library of reading materials from more than forty different publishing firms. Included among the materials are 1,000 trade books, game kits, reading skills kits, workbooks, audio-visual aids, and self-instructional programmed materials.
5. An in-service training program to educate teachers in the use of the program.

6. An update and modification system. A national dissemination network provides input on all effective changes made in the individualized reading system throughout the country.

This reading system is now being used and tested in hundreds of schools throughout the United States. It is too early for us to say that it is an unqualified success, but it does have many of the necessary ingredients of a successful individualized reading program.

Summary of Approaches

We have presented and described a series of different instructional approaches to reading, approaches which can be used successfully with culturally different students. In fact, each of the approaches we have described has been at least *partially* successful with culturally different students (Bond and Dykstra, 1966). No single program, approach, or instructional package, however, has been found to be a panacea for all the instructional problems encountered in schools with a majority of students from culturally different backgrounds.

The Successful Teacher of the Culturally Different

One of the keys to success in reading instruction with culturally different students is the teacher. In fact, the teacher's knowledge and skill are often much more critical than the reading programs being used (Harris, 1967). Some of the teaching qualities which contribute to success are listed below. The successful reading teacher of the culturally different student is:

1. Knowledgeable about the nature of reading and its role in the life of the individual. The teacher's definition of reading will determine how that teacher teaches reading. A teacher with a broad, comprehensive definition will conduct a program in reading that is broad and comprehensive in nature.
2. Either well-informed about the cultural group being taught, or is willing to study the culture and its impact on individuals.
3. Able to identify the different learning styles of individuals within cultural groups.
4. Willing and able to adapt available instructional materials to the

learning styles of different cultural groups. Since it is not possible for textbook publishers to publish textbook materials for all cultural groups and subcultural groups, it is quite essential that the teacher of culturally different groups be capable of using different ways to adapt instructional materials and/or teaching approaches.

5. Aware of the fundamental importance of language facility in learning to read and consequently able to incorporate all aspects of the language-communication process in the instructional program in reading.
6. Aware of teacher beliefs and expectations and their impact on children's learning. It has been found that teachers who believe and expect children in their classrooms to achieve in reading do in fact influence positively their students' achievement in reading (Rosenthal, 1973).
7. Well organized and presents well-organized lessons to the students.
8. A person who sincerely cares about the students he is teaching. This can also be said in an old-fashioned way—the teacher *loves* the children and is a loving person. This quality is all too often ignored in today's teaching world. To begin to consider the importance of loving in teaching, see Jesse Stuart, *To Teach, To Love.*
9. Cognizant of the role of the student's self-concept in learning to read, and as a result enhances the student's self-concept through positive reinforcement on every possible occasion.

The Authors' Viewpoint

We have discussed some aspects of the culture of poverty and have taken a fairly close look at the inhabitants of the ghetto slums, *barrios,* Indian reservations, and hills of Appalachia. We have noted that, as compared with the children of the middle class, children from these backgrounds are at a definite disadvantage in the milieu of the school culture. Because disadvantaged children have not been provided with readiness skills before entering school, they find it difficult to perform the tasks required of them, particularly in the language arts. Many researchers emphasize that the schools must meet the psycho-social and psycho-physical needs of the disadvantaged before they can attempt to teach the children necessary skills. They state that unless feelings of alienation are overcome, unless the psychological strain of broken or overcrowded homes is attended to, and unless a sense of individualism and self-expression is fostered, learning will not take place. While some efforts in these directions are indeed desirable, there are, nevertheless, severe limits to the school's ability to solve economic and cultural problems not of its making. Schools cannot, for example, give work to unemployed fathers, relieve family strains, or cure other ills which impair children's performances. Other social institutions must help here. But schools *should* be able to teach. As S. Alan Cohen in his insightful book *Teach Them All to Read* very strongly asserts, the *raison d'être* of the schools is not to solve the problems of the family, home, and community, but rather to promote literacy (Cohen, 1969, p. 6). Schools cannot and should not be expected to solve the social ills of society; various social institutions are expected to deal with social and moral problems. The *school*'s unique job is to teach the basic skills of reading, writing, and arithmetic. Despite long-winded discussions about why disadvantaged children cannot read, we say with Cohen that in order for breakthroughs to occur in the teaching of reading, teachers must concentrate on methodology. Then and only then will the children of the poor be reading as well as the children of middle America.

Summary

All too often competence in teaching reading to the culturally disadvantaged is equated with different programs and approaches. There are justifiable reasons for this. A number of different approaches which utilize different published reading programs have proven their potential for success with culturally different students. But the success of specific programs depends less on the quality of the instructional programs and the different approaches than it does on the quality and competency of the teacher. The key to high quality reading instruction for culturally different students is the teacher—the teacher who is well-prepared professionally, the teacher who is sensitive, and the teacher who sincerely *cares* for the students he or she teaches.

References

Alatis, James E. "Teaching Standard English as a Second Language or Dialect." In *Teaching English as a Second Language and as a Second Dialect*, edited by Robert P. Fox. Washington, D.C.: National Council of Teachers of English, 1973.

Aukerman, Robert C. *Approaches to Beginning Reading*. New York: John Wiley and Sons, 1971.

Bailey, Beryl L. "Some Principles of Bilingual and Bidialectal Education." In *Teaching English as a Second Language and as a Second Dialect*, edited by Robert P. Fox. Washington, D.C.: National Council of Teachers of English, 1973.

Billingsley, Andrew. *Black Families in White America.* Englewood Cliffs, New Jersey: Prentice-Hall, 1968.

Bond, G. L., and Dykstra, R. "The Cooperative Research Program in First Grade Reading." *Reading Research Quarterly* 2 (1966): 5–138.

Caudill, Harry M. *Night Comes to the Cumberlands.* Boston: Little, Brown, 1962.

Chall, J. *Learning to Read: The Great Debate.* New York: McGraw-Hill, 1967.

Cohen, S. Alan. *Teach Them All to Read.* New York: Random House, 1969.

Crow, Lester D.; Murray, Walter I.; and Smythe, Hugh H. *Educating the Culturally Disadvantaged Child.* New York: David McKay Company, 1966.

DiPietro, Robert J. "Bilingualism and Bidialectalism." In *Teaching English as a Second Language and as a Second Dialect,* edited by Robert P. Fox. Washington, D.C.: National Council of Teachers of English, 1973.

Elam, Sophie L. "Acculturation and Learning Problems of Puerto Rican Children." In *The Disadvantaged Learner,* edited by Staten W. Webster. San Francisco: Chandler Publishing Company, 1966.

Fantini, Mario D., and Weinstein, Gerald. *The Disadvantaged.* New York: Harper and Row, 1968.

Ford, Thomas R. *The Southern Appalachian Region: A Survey.* Lexington, Kentucky: University of Kentucky Press, 1962.

Giffin, Roscoe. "Newcomers from the Southern Mountains." In *Culture and School,* edited by Ronald Shinn. Scranton, Pennsylvania: Intext Educational Publishers, 1972.

Glazer, Nathan. "Ethnicity and the Schools." *Commentary* 58 (1974), pp. 55–59.

Harrington, Michael. *The Other America.* New York: Macmillan, 1962.

Harris, Albert, and Serwer, B. L. "The Craft Project: Instructional Time in Reading Research." *Reading Research Quarterly* 2 (1966): 27–56.

Hyman, Herbert. "The Value Systems of Different Classes: A Social Psychological Contribution to the Analysis of Stratification." In *Class Status and Power,* edited by Reinhard Bendix and Seymour Marinn Lipset. Glencoe, Illinois: The Free Press of Glencoe, 1962.

Jacobs, L. "Individualized Reading Is Not a Thing." In *Individualizing Reading Practices,* edited by Alice Mill. New York: Teachers College Press, Columbia University, 1958.

Johnson, Kenneth R. *Teaching the Culturally Disadvantaged.* Palo Alto, Calif.: Science Research Associates, 1970.

Kim, Y.; Berger, B.; and Kratochvil, D. W. "Product Development Report No. 14—Distar Instructional System." Palo Alto, Calif.: American Institutes for Research, 1972.

Kluckhohn, Clyde. *Culture and Behavior.* New York: The Free Press of Glencoe, 1962.

Laffey, J. L. "An Evaluation Report of a City Reading Program." Mimeographed report, 1974.

Malinowski, Bronislaw. *A Scientific Theory of Culture and Other Essays.* Chapel Hill, North Carolina: The University of North Carolina Press, 1944.

Marden, Charles F., and Meyer, Gladys. *Minorities in American Society.* New York: American Book Company, 1968.

Martinez, Armando. "Literacy Through Democratization of Education." *Harvard Educational Review* 40 (1970): 280–282.

Maryland Department of Economic Development. *The Appalachian Region: A Preliminary Analysis of Economic and Population Trends in an Eleven State Problem Area.* Annapolis, Maryland: Maryland Department of Economic Development, 1960.

Modiano, Nancy. "Where Are the Children?" *Florida F. L. Reporter* 7 (1969): 93.

Narang, H. L. "Improving Reading Ability of Indian Children." *Elementary English* 51 (1974): 190–192.

Riessman, Frank. *The Culturally Deprived Child.* New York: Harper and Row, 1962.

Rodriguez, Armando. "The Mexican-American—Disadvantaged? Ya Basta!" *Florida F. L. Reporter* 7 (1969): 35.

Rosenthal, Robert. "The Pygmalion Effect Lives." *Psychology Today,* September 1973.

Science Research Associates. "Summaries of Case Studies for the Effectiveness of the Distar Instructional System." Palo Alto, Calif.: Science Research Associates, 1971.

Spache, George. *Reading in the Elementary School.* Boston: Allyn and Bacon, 1973.

Stewart, William A. "Urban Negro Speech: Sociolinguistic Factors Affecting English Teaching." *Florida F. L. Reporter* 7 (1969): 58.

Stuart, Jesse. *To Teach, To Love.* New York: World Publishing-Times Mirror, 1970.

Van Allen, R., and Halvorsen, Gladys C. "The Language Experience Approach to Reading Instruction." In *Contributions to Reading.* Lexington, Massachusetts: Ginn and Company, 1961.

Additional References

Baratz, Joan C., and Shuy, Roger W., eds. *Teaching Black Children to Read.* Washington, D.C.: Center for Applied Linguistics, 1969.

Cheyney, Arnold B. *Teaching Culturally Disadvantaged in the Elementary School.* Columbus, Ohio: Charles E. Merrill, 1967.

Cohen, S. Alan, and Cooper, Thelma. "Seven Fallacies: Reading Retardation and the Urban Disadvantaged Beginning Reader." *The Reading Teacher* 26 (1972): 38–45.

Corbin, Richard, and Crosby, Muriel, eds. *Language Programs for the Disadvantaged.* Champaign, Illinois: National Council of Teachers of English, 1965.

Deutsch, Martin. "The Disadvantaged Child and the Learning Process: Some Social Psychological and Developmental Considerations." A paper prepared for Ford Foundation Work Conference on Curriculum and Teaching in Depressed Areas, 10 July 1962, at Columbia University. Mimeographed.

Fasold, Ralph W., and Shuy, Roger W., eds. *Teaching Standard English in the Inner City.* Washington, D.C.: Center for Applied Linguistics, 1970.

Frost, Joe L., and Hawkes, Glenn R., eds. *The Disadvantaged Child.* New York: Houghton Mifflin, 1970.

Hall, Mary Anne. *The Language Experience Approach for the Culturally Disadvantaged.* Newark, Del.: International Reading Association, 1972.

Hawkins, Thomas. *Benjamin: Reading and Beyond.* Columbus, Ohio: Charles E. Merrill, 1972.

Hunt, J. McVicker. *The Challenge of Incompetence and Poverty.* Urbana, Ill.: University of Illinois Press, 1969.

Jensen, Arthur R. "How Much Can We Boost I.Q. and Scholastic Achievement?" *Harvard Educational Review* 39 (1969): 1–123.

Novak, Michael. "Among Middle Class Ethnics—A Great Deal of Bitterness." *U. S. News and World Report,* October 14, 1974, pp. 46–48.

Passow, A. Harry, ed. *Opening Opportunities for Disadvantaged Learners.* New York: Teachers College Press, 1972.

Quick, Donald M. "Toward Positive Self-Concept." *The Reading Teacher* 26 (1971): 468–471.

Rosen, Carl L., and Ortego, Phillip D. "Resources: Teaching Spanish Speaking Children." *The Reading Teacher* 25 (1971): 11–13.

Sepulveda, Betty R. "The Language Barrier and Its Effect on Learning." *Elementary English* 50 (1973): 209–217.

Stensland, Anna Lee. *Literature By and About the American Indian.* Urbana, Ill.: National Council of Teachers of English, 1973.

Williams, Frederick, ed. *Language and Poverty.* Chicago: Markham Publishing Company, 1970.

Chapter
Four

Preview

Professional educators have paid considerable attention to the implications of linguistics for the teaching and learning of reading. Although their points of view differ, very few reading experts deny the importance of the relationship between language development and the reading process. They recognize that the facility with which an individual uses language will have an impact upon his achievement in reading.

The authors of this chapter are experts in the fields of psycholinguistics and sociolinguistics, and they deal here with such topics as language as a symbol system, syntactic system, and semantic system. They state their position on the influence of dialects on reading achievement—currently a matter of considerable professional concern. And, although the chapter is basically theoretical, they also include practical suggestions for the classroom teacher.

Reading:
Language and
Psycholinguistic Bases

Yetta Goodman, University of Arizona
Carolyn Burke, Indiana University

Objectives

After you have read this chapter, you should be able to:

1. Explain the differences between receptive and productive language.
2. State the similarities and differences among listening, speaking, reading, and writing.
3. Provide evidence to show that the purpose of language is communication.
4. Provide evidence to show that reading is an active language process.
5. Explain the essential interrelationships of the semantic, syntactic, and graphophonic systems of American English.
6. Match the concepts and language structures of the child to the concepts and language structures of the child's reading material.

Since the beginning of the twentieth century, psychologists and linguists have studied and analyzed language and how people use it. Psychologists have emphasized the use that people make of language, the ways that language relates to learning and thinking, and how language controls people's behavior. Linguists have analyzed the structural components of language, explored the meanings of words and sentences in different settings, and described how language changes are based on historic, economic, age, geographic, or racial differences.

Around 1960, it became obvious that neither linguistics nor psychology, as separate fields, had an understanding of the scope of the issues and problems involved in how people use language. Linguists began to look to psychology and psychologists began to look to linguistics to learn more about language from each other. The disciplines of communication theory, sociology, and anthropology were also investigated for their contributions to the study of language. As the concepts from all these fields became interrelated, the new field of psycholinguistics emerged.

Much of language difference is related to the social status and role orientation of language users. The study of human reasons for language differences and their functions in society added another field of study known as sociolinguistics. Its development closely parallels that of psycholinguistics, and the fields have many concerns in common.

About 1960, the word *psycholinguistics* began to be used frequently. Now it appears in books and in prominent dictionaries. There are courses at universities in the field of psycholinguistics, and there are professionals who refer to themselves as psycholinguists.

Psycholinguistics is the study of the interrelationship between thought and language processes. It is the study of how people use language, how language affects human behavior, and how language is learned.

Reading is language—and it is the responsibility of those who will teach reading to understand the significance of that statement. Therefore, this chapter will discuss language acquisition and development, the interrelationship among reading, writing, speaking, and listening, and the factors affecting language and cognitive development in the school setting. It will also suggest ways to apply the growing knowledge of psycholinguistics in the classroom.

Language: Systems and Processes

Teachers and students are speaking, listening, writing, and reading continually during the school day. Whenever the term *language* is used in relation to school instruction, all four aspects of language are implied. It is through these four aspects of language that much of human communication takes place. The listener or reader must actively process that which the writer or speaker has actively produced or there will be no communication.

Language Systems

In order to communicate, speakers, listeners, readers, and writers must follow a similar set of rules. These are not rules of which the language user is consciously aware. In fact, in most cases, people cannot state or explain the language rules they use.

For centuries linguists, or more specifically grammarians, have constructed models of these rule systems to show how languages operate. These models are called grammars. All models, including models of language, change as new knowledge is discovered. When, for example, views of the earth became available from space travel, the globe—a scale model of the earth—was changed by geophysicists to accommodate those recent discoveries. Grammatical models, too, have changed over the years as linguists found out more about language. First attempts at explaining the structure of English were made by borrowing archaic Latin grammars (the Romans having already borrowed from earlier Greek grammars). Where differences existed between the two languages, the English was forced into the pre-existing Latin structures (Gleason, 1965, pp. 28–31).

At about this time anthropological linguists began to turn their attention to mapping the structure of a number of languages which did not possess writing systems. This study, focusing its attention upon the unique structural qualities of individual languages, legitimatized describing language as it is spoken in a particular place at a particular time. As a result, the next attempts at explaining English used the techniques of descriptive linguistics (Gleason, 1965, pp. 37–57).

More recently, a new model of grammar is being applied to the study of American English as well as to other languages. Noam Chomsky (1965) has suggested that the study of grammar must be based on the proposition that the language user is a rule learner. The language learner can apply the set of rules to generate statements which he may never have heard uttered before. This set of rules does not simply describe the sounds of the language (the surface structure) but also helps describe how the language user may go from the surface structure to the meaning of the language or to its sense (deep structure). The rules which are employed to go between deep structure and surface structure are called transformations.

The important thing in language learning is not controlling specific sets of sounds or words but controlling a set of rules which can generate any set of sounds or words to express new learnings or new experiences. Hence, this grammar is called a generative-transformational grammar (Wardhaugh, 1972, pp. 98–136; Malmstrom and Weaver, 1973).

Three interrelated language systems are necessary for communication to take place. The word *system* implies that rules are involved.

The Graphophonic System The patterns of sounds and letters which are used to represent language in speaking and writing comprise the graphophonic system. The phonological system consists of the sounds made by speakers. The visual representation of language is called the graphic system. In the English language, the graphic system uses alphabetic symbols to represent significant oral sounds (phonemes or groups of phonemes). Not all written languages use alphabetic graphic systems.

The Semantic System The relationship that words, phrases, clauses, and sentences have to objects and functions as well as to abstract ideas (such as meanings and thoughts) comprises the semantic system of language. This system is the core of the language process. Communication is a language's reason for being. The other two systems of language exist to facilitate this purpose.

The Syntactic System The graphophonic system and the semantic system can be fully related through the order and rules of the syntactic system. The rules which are used to indicate the interrelationship of syntactic structures (words, phrases, clauses, and sentences), the order of these language units, and how these language units are changed to indicate tense, number, and gender are the syntactic, or grammatical, system of language. Meaning (the semantic system) can only be communicated through the graphophonic system by employing the rules of syntax.

These three systems are truly interrelated. For example, the words *boy, runs, mother, to, his,* and *the* can be assigned meaning. But presented as individual words separated by commas, they do not actually communicate what the writer was thinking when they were written. However, when the words are placed in a syntactic pattern ("The boy runs to his mother"), the reader has some understanding of what the writer had in mind. A change in word order or in the inflectional system can convey different meanings. For example: "His mother runs to the boy," or "The boys ran to his mother."

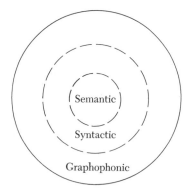

Figure 4.1   The Language Systems.

Language Processes

All aspects of language (reading, writing, speaking, and listening) have the three language systems (graphophonic, syntactic, semantic) in common. When a speaker or a writer is producing language, he is actively doing many things to make sure that his listener or reader will understand what he has produced. For communication to take place, readers and/or listeners must be actively trying to get the message. They use their own language, background, and experience to try to understand the message of the speaker or writer. Language—both oral and written—is an active process.

Oral Language During speaking and listening, it is the phonological system that communicates meaning. Without some kind of mechanical recording device, oral language is fleeting and cannot be recalled exactly as it occurred. Any ideas conveyed through oral language must be recreated if they are to be discussed again later.

Oral language occurs in all human societies. Each language is spoken within a contextual setting common to its speakers, who are together in the same place and know something about the people with whom they are communicating. They share similar experiences; and they can watch each other in order to know whether or not their message is being understood. They use various kinds of body language to enhance their verbal communication. The speaker and listener can interact, ask questions, and explain things to each other when there is a lack of understanding or a breakdown in language communication.

Written Language In writing and reading, the graphic system represents language. Written language is a more permanent system than oral language. It can be perused again and again. An author can continue to rewrite something until it is exactly what he or she would like to express. A reader can reread a passage in order to rethink or redefine it. In written language, the other participant (the reader) is usually not immediately available to the writer. Written language, therefore, must include information regarding people, places, and times, so that whoever comes in contact with the written language will have enough context available to understand the message.

Although reading and writing have the written system in common and listening and speaking have the oral system in common, reading and listening operate in ways that speaking and writing do not.

When people communicate language to others they are producing language. Speaking and writing are the *productive* forms of language. Language producers are concerned with making themselves understood.

Reading and listening are the *receptive* forms of language. When a person is on the receiving end of language, he concentrates not on production but on understanding. He uses strategies to gain the meaning of what the speaker or writer is saying.

By the time a child comes to school, he has spent at least five years of his life using strategies to make himself understood and to understand

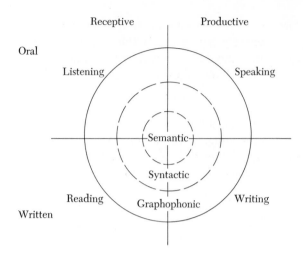

Figure 4.2   The Language Processes.

others. He has usually been successful in communicating with those around him.

Language and Culture

Another aspect of language which teachers of reading must understand clearly is the concept of *dialect.* One way to explain this concept is to draw an analogy. Just as everyone belongs to a particular group of human beings, so everyone speaks a particular dialect of a language. No one is *the* human being or the *normal* human being, with others belonging to a subhuman species. We are simply of various types, which can be classified by differences like sex, race, national origin, or occupation. In the same way, no one speaks *the* language or *a* standard language with all other variations of the language considered substandard or disadvantaged. Each dialect is equally capable of carrying the message of the speaker to others who use the same dialect.

Dialects can be classified by their differences. There are differences between the phonological systems of various dialects, as well as differences between the syntactic and semantic systems. There are different dialects in different geographic regions and for different racial and socioeconomic groups. However, just as there are no clear and distinct lines by which to categorize human groups, there are no clear and distinct lines among dialect groups (Shuy, 1968).

Some dialects are considered to have greater prestige than others and are referred to as standard dialects. Dialects which are not considered prestige dialects are sometimes called non-standard dialects. Socioeconomic criteria—not the "goodness" or "correctness" of the language—usually determine which dialects are prestige or standard. The language of the people who are considered the socioeconomic leaders of a particular community is most often the standard language of that community, even if those people comprise only a small minority. There are probably as many different standard dialects spoken by middle- and upper-class speakers in this country as there are non-standard dialects spoken by poor people.

Speakers of American English dialects can understand each other with a minimum of effort. In general, people can receive a wider range of dialects than they can produce. Speakers of non-standard dialects, particularly in urban areas, usually have broader experiences in receiving standard dialects than speakers of standard dialects have in receiving non-standard dialects. In other words, non-standard speakers probably understand standard speakers better than standard speakers understand non-standard speakers.

The important bond between language and culture is often reflected in the differences between dialects, as well as in the development of thought. Language and thought are shaped by cultural experiences. When cultural groups lack certain experiences, there is no reason for the people to have concepts or language expressions related to those experiences. American middle-class, nuclear families, for example, have little understanding of terms related to extended family relationships—terms like "Big Daddy," "second cousin twice removed," or "kissing cousins."

Experiences stimulate people to think about what is happening to them, and this thinking creates a need for language. At an earlier time in American history, when children were usually looked after within the home, a person needing outside help might have strolled over to a neighbor and said, "Will you sit with my baby while I am gone?" As it became more common for parents to be away from their babies, new language was developed to meet these new experiences, and the term *babysitter* became common: "Will you be my babysitter while I'm gone?" As the concept of babysitting expanded to include various types of roles and duties, it became possible for someone to say: "Will you babysit my dog when I go on my vacation?"

Snow skiing provides another example of the interrelationship of experiences and language. Skiers realize that the way they ski depends on the quality of the snow. When they talk about *corn snow, powder snow,* and *hard packed snow,* they understand—as most non-skiers do not—the significance of such terms.

As children grow up in a particular culture and dialect group, they learn not only to speak the language of that particular group, but also to think and organize their ideas according to the view of the world shared by those with whom they are most intimate (Britton, 1970). *By the time the child enters school he has been communicating successfully in the dialect of his home community for at least three years.* Since language, thought, and cultural view are inextricably intermeshed, attempts to change children's dialect or to reject the way they think about the world will disrupt their learning. The teacher must reach out to understand both the children and the world from which they emerge. This acceptance and respect for what the children are will in turn encourage children to extend their learning and to expand their language (Goodman, 1969).

Learning Language

There is a growing body of research which describes what children do as they learn language. These descriptions are significant for teachers, since they show how the learning of oral language is related to the learning of written language.

Pre-school Years

In early infancy, babies babble in a wide range of sounds, many of which do not appear in their mother tongue (Brown, 1970). Some are sounds that belong to other languages. At about the age of two, children are just starting to speak; but they have been listening for a long time. They have *receptive* control over their language long before they have *productive* control. They have been listening to a multitude of sounds around them. In order to learn to speak, they have distinguished the particular sounds which belong to the language of their own families and have eliminated others from their oral production. They have learned to understand a great deal of what their parents are saying. Even before the age of two, young children will get things that someone asks for, or will point to objects when requested to do so. They indicate specific people when asked to identify "mommy" or "daddy."

As children begin to organize their world, their need for language grows. In turn, their expanded use of language gives them greater opportunities for discussing, interacting, and thinking. And their use of language develops very quickly. They start out with one- or two-word sentences and before they are five are speaking in sentences almost as complex as those spoken by their parents. Though it is very complicated for linguists to describe the syntactic system of any child's or adult's language, it is not difficult for human beings to learn a language during infancy and early childhood. Children's language learning is so precocious that some researchers have been led to hypothesize that language is not learned but is innate (Smith, 1966). It is not necessary to accept the "innate" theory, however, to be impressed with how sophisticated children's language competence becomes.

Children do much more than simply imitate the language they hear. As soon as they begin to produce understandable language, they are generating new language structures which follow systems of rules. When a four-year-old says "He gots my ball," he is showing his control over the rule concerning the *s* endings on verbs following third person singular nouns. But unlike adults' grammar, the child's grammar contains no irregular verb forms. When children produce language which does not conform to adult language, that language often shows that the child is applying a regular rule to an irregular case.

Because children have a social need to communicate and interact, their language moves closer to that of the majority of speakers around them. They accommodate their language to the language of the people with whom they wish to interact. The desire to know about the world around them is another motivation for learning language.

> Necessity is the father of thought. Necessity is the father of speech. But soon speech detaches itself from the motor of need . . . It is not necessity alone that stimulates speech; at an early stage questioning and wonder appear on the scene as well. Next to the cry, "I want to eat," another call is heard, first feebly, then stronger and stronger and more and more frequently: "I want to know" . . . The urge to know is directed towards language; the possession of knowledge requires language; the achievement of knowledge serves as reinforcement in learning language . . . (Hormann, 1971, p. 273).

Five-year-olds will often laugh and think you are telling them a joke if you say that people are animals. They see it as totally incongruous to categorize people within the concept of "animal" that they have developed. Children may call all women "mommy" at two, but within a year they call only their own mother "mommy" or "mom" and begin to put other women in other categories. When they play house, they portray the roles and activities of members of their family, showing that they understand what each one does. They recognize voices and distinguish those they know well from strangers' voices. All these things show that pre-schoolers have already begun to categorize, to differentiate, and to organize their environment (Vygotsky, 1962; Flavell, 1964).

Early School Years

Regardless of community, race, or nationality, all children come to school with language, with a way to think about the world, and with a variety of experiences. Although they acquire some complex aspects of English grammar during the elementary school years, a more significant development is their growing understanding of the relationships among words and what these relationships have to do with their own experience. At age five, children's meanings and concepts do not yet match those of the adult world around them. Any discussion among a group of five-year-olds can reveal the way children view the world.

Mrs. B., a beloved first-grade teacher, started one morning's discussion with "I am a grandmother now." Then she showed the children some pictures of a newborn infant. Pat said, "Now you're old." Barbara said, "Where is your pantsuit and long earrings?" Jimmy, looking unhappy, said, "Now you won't be our teacher any more, and you will have to stay home and babysit the baby."

Each child revealed a different concept of *grandmother,* based on individual experience. Now they began to accommodate into their own thinking the views that the other children and their teacher had about grandmothers. Mrs. B. helped to stimulate this thinking process by asking, "What is a grandmother?" Other children's concepts were added to the discussion. Tom's "grandmother" was an aging widow who lived next door to him and was always giving him fresh baked cookies. But Tom's "grandmother" was not a relative. Jerry's grandmother worked at a factory and was a boss.

The teacher encouraged the children to ask their parents about the term *grandmother,* and they returned the next day with pictures and more ideas. Betty called her mother's grandmother "Grandma" and her own grandmother "Ma." Andy's grandmother didn't like being called "Grandmother" and preferred to be called "Stella." The children talked about all their experiences with grandmothers. No single definition of *grandmother* could fit all they knew, and all they knew did not yet match the concept they would eventually have of grandmothers. But thinking and talking about their experiences expanded their concept of *grandmother,* and the language they used to talk about their new learning was expanded and extended as well.

The greatest aid to children during the elementary school years is a wide range of experiences and a great deal of opportunity to talk about them. By the time children complete the elementary school years, they have developed more differentiated thought categories and an ability to handle more abstract ideas.

Middle School Years

The move into adolescence adds new dimensions to the student's thought and language. Not only do teen-agers want to talk about the things they know, but they begin to examine and evaluate the ideas they have heard around them and the notions about life they have begun to develop. Their thinking becomes more abstract as they examine philosophies of life, religious questions, and political, scientific, and moral issues. This concern about the world and their place in it often brings adolescents into conflict with adults' more stable view of the world. Often adolescents find themselves in conflict with parents and teachers. As teens come together to talk about similar problems and concerns, they often develop unique language that fits some new view of the world which they believe they have discovered. This examination of the world can put the adolescent in the position of a catalyst for cultural change; and this change is often reflected in the dynamic quality of the language of the youth culture. The dialects of the surfer, the motorcycle buff, and the pop music enthusiast exhibit this dynamic quality. The groups farthest removed from the established center of society are less likely to be inhibited in their use of innovative language. It is therefore not surprising that linguistic change seems to be most dynamic among young people.

But adolescents still want and need to communicate with the adult society around them. Although they can use the dynamic language of their peer group, they can also switch easily to the language which is demanded in the classroom or by the adult culture. Teachers who genuinely want to understand and communicate with teen-agers will need to show as much respect for and give as much attention to the youth culture as they do to the various ethnic cultures they find represented in their classroom.

Written Language

Language in its written form plays a central role in technologically advanced cultures. It is chiefly through writing that we communicate with, regulate, and appeal to one another.

Central governments, regulating millions of people over billions of acres of land, are made efficient by rapid communication and rapid transit, but they are made possible by *written* language. The President can appear on television and announce a new tax program. However, because of complexities like long and short form schedules, taxation rates based on varying income, deductions, and capital gains, he can enact the program only through written instructions. In fact, without his own ability to use written language, he could not have "held in mind" the complex relation-ships necessary to have created the program. While the act of taxation is not dependent upon written language, sophistication of taxation is.

We can't take a bus, go shopping, drive, or vote without dealing with written symbols. Often the limits of our ability to participate in the culture are determined by the limits of our ability to deal with written language. Some drivers, for example, seldom or never use the freeways; they are disturbed not only by the speed of traffic, but also by the speed with which they must make decisions to change lanes, exit, or merge, based on some rapidly perceived and minimally cued written information. It can be argued that the most efficient means of discriminating against individuals within our society is to make sure that their facility to receive written language (to read) is not sufficient to meet general public need.

The acquisition of oral language allows people to organize their amorphous perceptions and feelings, to relate their experiences, and to share these experiences with others. The acquisition of written language allows people to reliably expand their relationship to those beyond their physical reach in time and space. Just as a certain complexity of thought is beyond our grasp without the mediating factor of oral language, a level of cultural complexity is dependent upon the use of written language (Winkel-johann, 1973).

It is our culture's ever-increasing dependence on written communica-tion which motivates our concern about the teaching of reading. Recent psycholinguistic research has much to contribute to an examination of written language. We will focus on three of these contributions: the role of perception in reading, a view of initial reading, and the relationship of writing to reading.

Perception and Reading

Because reading involves the processing of visual images (letters, spaces, words, punctuation marks), a reader's visual acuity and visual perception are often diagnosed as factors of reading difficulty.

Visual acuity is simply a measure of how clearly and distinctly visual images are picked up by the optic nerve. Some limitations on visual acuity are corrected by glasses or by surgery. While such common problems as nearsightedness might cause the reader to tire easily, recent studies have indicated that many minor visual acuity problems do not directly affect success in learning to read (Lindsay and Norman, 1972).

Perception is a learned visual task. It involves selective attention to and use of available visual stimuli. We are immersed in a world of color, shape, and texture. If we tried to pay equal attention to all of these stimuli, we would overload the network operating between the eye and the brain.

We would also overreach the brain's capacity to accept, organize, store, and retrieve information. You might say we would "blow a fuse." If we were not selective about the visual stimuli which we take in, we would live in a kaleidoscopic world, with lots of color, texture, and movement but no recognizable or stable relationships (Lindsay and Norman, 1972).

School age children have already developed highly effective visual perception. They have learned to categorize by characteristics instead of paying attention to surface variations. Five-year-olds will recognize as dogs such physically different breeds as chihuahuas, collies, dobermans, and poodles. They will classify a semi, a pick-up, and a van all as examples of truck.

They have intuitively learned to operate by seeking significant characteristics; but if they are to successfully identify the relevant information for any specific category, they must be consciously exposed to the items which are to be classified. A childhood experience of Carolyn Burke's illustrates this point.

> At the age of eight I was a very practiced grocery shopper. It was my job to go to the corner store with a list and pick up all of the miscellaneous items my mother needed between her regular weekly shopping trips. I would always read the list and select the items from the shelves myself. One day I arrived home with the listed items only to have my mother discover that I had bought a cabbage instead of lettuce. I didn't know how to tell the difference between them.
>
> I didn't lack direct contact with these two vegetables. My mother bought one or the other each week and I usually accompanied her to the store. I didn't need perceptual training—I'd been reading since the age of five. I simply had never paid attention to cabbages and lettuces. They had been in my line of vision, but not in my line of perception.

Many adults in our Western culture cannot perceive the differences between makes of cars. They can't tell a Chevrolet from a Ford or a Dodge, much less distinguish between the many different available models. Yet there are ten-year-olds who can use fender shape, grill design, and general lines to make just such distinctions. The adult has simply chosen not to bother learning these distinctions.

Many children coming from social situations labelled "culturally different" or "disadvantaged" do very poorly on perceptual tasks assigned by the school. They seem unable to consistently identify the one duck who is going in the wrong direction out of a line of four ducks,

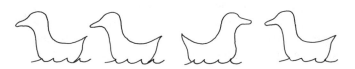

or to note correctly which letter is different:

h   n   h   h

Yet these same children can tell the difference between a bowl full of collard greens and one of turnip greens. They can learn the steps to a new dance by simply watching someone else perform them once or twice. What they lack is not perceptual training but experience in perceiving the specific distinctions which the school intends to use in the teaching of reading. Exposure to these phenomena for a period of time enables them to apply their perceptual strategies to this new experience.

Learning to read need not be dependent, however, upon becoming proficient at these new perceptual tasks. Later in this chapter we will suggest an approach to initial reading in which the perceptual distinctions are developed as an aspect of the reading process.

Visual Images and Meaning One other aspect of perception and its relationship to reading should be considered. Because readers are concerned with the message, they perceive not just the visual images but also meanings.

Paul Kolers, a psychologist (Kolers, in F. Smith, 1972), devised a research study in which he tested this idea. He prepared passages of text which were combinations of English and French writing systems, such as:

Une violente brise was blowing

and asked bilingual readers to read them. He checked their understanding of what they had read against the understanding of people who had read the same text either entirely in French or entirely in English.

He found that the people reading the bilingual text had as comprehensive an understanding of what they had read as did those reading the monolingual texts. He also discovered that the people who had read text containing elements of two languages had no memory of which information had been contained in which language. They had not been perceiving whether the lexical item was French—"brise"—or English—"wind." They had been concerned only with the meaning.

What Paul Kolers discovered when he had people read bilingual text can also be observed in another situation. Sometimes the words that a person reads orally differ from the words in the text. When these unexpected responses are collected from oral reading and examined, they are often found to retain the meaning of the text. The following examples of such reading variations were collected by Kenneth Goodman and his associates as they studied the reading process (Goodman, 1973):

needle[1]
1. He had a hypodermic syringe in one hand.

minute[1]
2. Wait a moment.

engine[1]
3. They put the hoses on the fire truck.

they[2]
4. His class‸was having an outside project.

5. This ⟨is⟩[3] all I'⟨ve⟩[3] got for you tonight.

In each of these cases the reader varied the text without changing the meaning. Like the bilingual readers in Kolers's experiment, these readers have perceived the meaning without concern for its exact surface level representation.

The fourth and fifth examples used above were produced by black dialect speakers. They demonstrate that Kolers's concept of reading meaning and not words works just as well within dialects of a single language as it does between two languages. Recent studies seem to indicate that oral language dialects create no linguistic barriers to reading. *Readers need only be receptive to an author's dialect in order to deal with meaning in print* (Goodman and Buck, 1973; Laffey and Shuy, 1973).

The Reading Miscue Goodman is interested in the unexpected responses produced by readers. He has developed a procedure for studying reading which makes use of two facts:

1. The reader is a language user and must employ the three language systems in order to gain meaning from printed material.
2. All readers create unexpected responses.

He believes that a reader employs the same language cues in producing an unexpected response as he does in producing an expected response. Therefore he calls these unexpected responses *miscues.*

Through miscue analysis Goodman has developed a psycholinguistic view of the reading process (Goodman and Niles, 1970) which suggests that readers predict on the basis of selected cues. (In example 1 listed earlier, the reader predicted *needle* on the basis of the semantic cue *hypodermic.*) If their predictions are confirmed by subsequent cues, they continue reading. However, if those cues indicate that the previous predictions did not produce acceptable language, readers will use various correction strategies. As they predict and confirm, readers simultaneously and continuously integrate the meaning they construct into their own system of knowledge.

[1] Substitution of one word for another
[2] Insertion of a word
[3] Omission of a language unit

Initial Reading

There is one point upon which most people who study reading and reading instruction are agreed—reading is a very complex process. The first section of this chapter pointed out that reading involves using all three of the language systems (phonological, syntactic, and semantic) used in speech, plus learning to relate the set of speech sounds to a set of written letters. Awareness of this complexity has made people very cautious about the initial reading programs which they plan.

A quick look at initial reading programs commonly in use within the schools reveals two major focuses: one on lexical items or words; the other on sound/letter relationships.

Emphasis on Word Attack The first approach directs beginning readers' attention to words. The relationship between oral language units (morphemes) and their written representations (words) becomes the focus for instruction. Readers are encouraged to memorize the written symbols so that they will immediately recall them on sight. The reading text facilitates this recall task by repeated use of selected vocabulary items. Vocabulary is selected on the basis of usage frequency, so that with a small sight vocabulary students are able to read a great deal. They are frequently encouraged to distinguish root words within larger inflected (-ed, -s, -ing), derived (-tion, -ment, -al), and compounded (bird-house, table-cloth, hair-brush) words.

The second approach focuses the students' attention on the relationships between the letters of the alphabet and the sounds of the language. Readers are encouraged to handle or "attack" new words by applying these sound/letter relationships. Individual programs offer varying means for accomplishing this task. Some stress a direct correspondence between individual letters and individual sounds (a one-to-one correspondence); some stress relationships between combinations of letters and possible sequences of sounds (a spelling pattern); some limit themselves to short monosyllabic (one-syllable) words, while others make use of syllable-length units in varying combinations; some use the traditional alphabet, while others introduce an artificial "teaching" alphabet. All of them make exclusive use of the graphophonic system to instruct beginning readers.

These two different approaches to initial reading instruction have the same objective: to enable the student to "read" words. They differ only in their means of accomplishing this goal. Both minimize the reader's use of the syntactic and semantic systems of language. They do this not because they think these systems are unimportant to reading, but because they think that young readers would become confused if they were called upon to pay attention to all three language systems at once. They both conclude that the word is the most simple and direct key to reading—if you can recognize enough words you can string them together like beads and make sentences.

Psycholinguistic Contributions Evidence from psycholinguistic research indicates that these two approaches to initial reading instruction are limited; they fail to take into account information about how people think and about how they learn language.

In planning methods of reading instruction, we need to consider the way that language—listening and speaking—is first learned. The following are key aspects of language development which seem particularly relevant to reading:

1. From birth, infants are surrounded by the ongoing speech of adults.
2. Infants become proficient receivers of oral language long before they effectively produce it.
3. The first speech efforts of toddlers are related to specific ongoing situations which hold great significance for them.
4. Toddlers' first speech reflects their own rule-governed syntactic structures, which they have developed by thoughtfully distilling order from the speech of surrounding adults.

When aspects of oral language development are related to initial reading practices, several ideas emerge.

Pre-school children in our highly literate culture are surrounded by print in many different contexts and are already developing as effective receivers of written language. They have begun to separate alphabetic print from pictures and wordless signs. They have already had experience with print on television commercials and programs. Three-year-olds, accompanying their mother to the store, can pick out their favorite brand of cereal from among all the others by using a combination of picture, color, and word shape clues. Chris, a four-year-old who has been out driving with his father, can tattle to mommy that, "Daddy didn't stop when the sign told him to."

Even the mistakes of pre-schoolers substantiate the fact that they are conscious consumers of print. Another four-year-old boy, having lunch with his family at a quick food restaurant, announced that he wanted to go to the bathroom and that he could use the one right there. He pointed to a door with a small metal signplate. His father informed him that the sign said "private" and not "restroom."

Children thus demonstrate that they react specifically to printed symbols—the cereal name, "STOP," the signplate; that the symbols act as recognized placeholders for meaningful experiences—a food they like, an expected behavior, a need; and that their inexpert use of the symbols is supported by the use of other situational clues—the tiger on the box, the red eight-sided sign at street corners, the door with a signplate in a public building.

The school does not have to initiate reading, but only to support a process which the child has already initiated. The child has used situational context to begin to organize print and to assign meaning to it. He has done this intuitively and naturally as part of a constant effort to understand and participate in the surrounding world.

The language and thought processes which the child is using are abstract and complex. But as a language user he is not called upon to understand them, only to make use of them. This he does in much the same way that people become expert drivers without knowing anything about the operation of the gasoline engine, or create and use electrical power without being able to explain its existence. Models of the language process, theories of propulsion, the relationship of electrons and protons are all very abstract. But cereal names, cars, and lamps are concrete. They are known and understood by the way in which they are used. In the same way, context makes written language concrete and allows the reader to gain reliable meanings for words he does not recognize.

Imagine that you are twelve years old and the teacher has placed the following word on the blackboard and asked you to read it:

krait

You have very few methods available for dealing with this item. You either recognize it or you do not. If you do not recognize it, you cannot even be sure that it is a real word. Because the letters seem to be organized in familiar combinations, you can use the graphophonic system of language. That is, you can try to pronounce the item.

Even your attempts at pronouncing an unknown item will be kept in the context of other items which you already know how to pronounce. So you will try *crate* because you know the word *bait*, or *krite* because of *aisle*, or *kret* because of *said*. But you will not know which one of these pronunciations, if any, is the conventional one, and the pronunciation will not tell you the meaning of the word or its grammatical function. Is it a verb?

I could krait all day if I had to.

Or a noun?

The krait was in my soup.

Or an adjective?

I'll take the krait balloon.

Now imagine that the teacher erases the word from the board, and in its place she writes the following:

> The krait is only about 10 inches long.
> But even though it is small, it is deadly.
> It is a cold-blooded animal and seeks warm
> places to stay. The krait is a relative
> of the cobra.

This does not help you decide which of your attempted pronunciations was correct—only the dictionary or other people's usage can do that—but it does answer more important questions. Krait must be a noun because it is used in slots where nouns are used:

> The krait is . . .
> (car)
> (hose)
> (trunk)

If you know the cobra, you will assume that a krait is a snake. Not knowing the cobra, you can still guess that it is a poisonous reptile (*deadly* and *cold-blooded*).

Now imagine that you are six years old and the teacher places this word on the board:

> dog

You groan to yourself. There's that darn letter again. It looks so much like that other letter, *b*, and you can never remember which sound is associated with which letter. Is the word on the board *bog* or *dog*?

But then the teacher surrounds the item with the following context:

> The dog was Sam's pet.

And now you know. You can read the word and be assured of your choice, without having to be dependent on an isolated component of the process.

In both of these instances the context made all three of the language systems available for the reader's use. Inexpert functioning in one system could be compensated for and supported by cues from the other two systems. The basic criterion for an initial reading program might be stated this way: *Keep written language in context, and keep the structure and meaning predictable.*

Writing in Relationship to Reading

While reading is the receptive expression of written language, writing is its productive expression. A person must, to some limited degree, be a reader in order to write.

Of the four expressions of language, writing is the one least developed when the child enters school. But even here the child has made some initial learning efforts. The child's first conscious efforts at written communication are called scribbling.

A four-year-old will very deliberately sit and fill a page with a series of squiggles, loops, and wavy lines. At times she will choose to do this in place of drawing the houses and trees and people which she has become fairly proficient at representing. Her page filled, she is apt to approach an adult and inform him that she has written a story. Upon request she can then "read" the story she has just written.

This little scribbler has just told us several very important things about her language development.

1. She has grasped the language relationship of reading and writing. She understands that the marks on the page carry meaning. She expects that she could understand these things if they were translated to speech.
2. She is developing a feeling for the purpose of writing. She went to seek a second person because she is aware that she is "acting out" an adult behavior. She also did this because she has some notion that what the author puts down on the page should be accessible and meaningful to some other person who approaches the page as a reader.
3. She is aware of the limitations of her "writing." The person she has sought out is expected to act as a listener/reader. At this point the "author" is the only one who can gain meaning from the page.
4. She has perceived a difference between the written symbols of language and pictures. For this experience she has abandoned her newly developed talents as an artist. She is aware that the symbols of writing do not "picture" the meaning.
5. She has preferred to re-enact a whole message in context rather than to create a piece of "writing" by sitting and meticulously trying to reproduce individual letters from some master copy. She is not interested in the detail.

Informal Learning Experiences By the time children reach school they have already invested five years of intensive study into language learning. As listeners/speakers they are most accomplished. They can listen to and, in varying degrees, understand different dialects, and they can respond to these communication situations effectively with their own dialect. Their oral communication is limited more by lack of experience and conceptual development than by language development.

As readers/writers they already respond to written symbols in context. They expect written symbols to carry meaning and are willing to guess at that meaning on the basis of the life situation in which they find it.

For these five years children have supervised their own learning with only occasional intervention from "outside experts." They were born into a world where everyone was a member of a private club which they could not immediately join. The entrance requirement was language. The club members were receptive to them. They talked, read, and wrote in front of and to the children, but generally left it up to them as to how they could best sort, organize, and develop understanding for the language process.

Children deal with whole messages and always keep them in the context of the situations which generate them. The planned learning experiences of the school will be most supportive to language users if the learning format closely resembles the one the children have already devised and very successfully used in their initial language learning.

The Language Experience Story The language experience story (Lee and Van Allen, 1963; Robinson, 1971; Stauffer, 1970) is one example of a planned situation which makes use of children's favored learning strategies. The characteristics of such a story include the following:

1. The lesson is built directly upon a meaningful experience which the learner has had. This can be done either by encouraging the learner to call to mind something from the past or by planning an activity in which learner and teacher will both participate.
2. The learner is given time to organize and evaluate the experience. Through discussion—thinking out loud—the learner's attitudes can be fully developed and alternate ways of sharing them can be considered.
3. The learner's thought and language are preserved. The teacher writes what the learner wants shared in the learner's preferred language.

The writer and the reader of the first language experience stories are often the same person. The focus is on the interrelationship of the four expressions of language. The learners come to understand how the language expressions support each other and realize that strength in one kind of expression can be used to develop another. At first the teacher offers strong support. She encourages the students to look for topics that really interest them. By listening and questioning, she helps focus and deepen the students' understanding of the topic. And finally, she provides the mechanics of writing—letter formation, written conventions, spelling—which the students are not yet fully able to control.

Gradually, the focus and teacher support are altered. The students begin to produce stories with other readers in mind, at the same time becoming readers of the experience stories of others. As the children write with others in mind, they develop a concern for the experiences and language which a reader might bring to the material. When they read the writing of others, they begin to predict the material on the basis of the way they know the author thinks and writes.

At the same time, the teacher begins removing aspects of her support as a scribe. The students will become responsible for getting the first rough draft on paper. They can dictate the story onto a tape recorder so that it can be played back in sections as they concentrate on writing mechanics without the fear of losing their thoughts. They can be encouraged to use an initial letter and a blank as placeholders for words they cannot spell.

Tom c_____ the dog down the street.

The one scribe function which the teacher can retain is that of editor. When the material is intended to be formally reproduced for others to read, the teacher can edit the rough draft, limiting herself to inserting writing conventions—capitals, paragraphing, punctuation, spelling—but not changing the authors' organization, word selection, or grammar.

Implications for the Teacher

Any kind of instructional program for children must take place in an environment in which the student feels respected and accepted. This must include the acceptance and respect for the child's language, culture, and learning style. School should be a place where the teacher as well as the student is willing to learn. A teacher who shows an interest in learning from the students will give the students reasons for sharing their experiences with the teacher and the rest of the children. Through this open give and take, the teacher can learn a great deal about how children learn, about their language and their culture.

The following six psycholinguistic principles are the ones we believe deserve the greatest attention from teachers, since they may have the most significance for the development of reading programs in the classroom. With each principle, we suggest specific classroom applications.

Principle *Language communication involves the transmission of meaning from a language producer to a language receiver.*

Reading is language. Therefore, any reading program which is used in the classroom must show readers that searching for meaning is their main concern. The major criterion that a teacher uses to screen reading materials or programs must be: *Does this program help my students focus on understanding the meaning of what they read?* Many of the programs now used in schools would pass such a criterion. Language experience programs, for example, concentrate on the students' gaining meaning. Suggestions in the teacher's manuals of basal reading programs emphasize comprehension. Individualized or personalized reading programs (Veach, 1966) which permit the students to select their own reading materials are also based on the notion that what students read must concern them personally and make sense to them. A teacher who understands the significance of readers' search for meaning can incorporate all aspects of the above programs to develop a comprehension-centered or meaning-centered reading program.

Principle *Reading is a receptive but* very active *language process.*

Too many instructional programs are designed to provide readers with the notion that reading is telling exactly and carefully what is on the printed page, or that reading is dramatic oral presentation of what an author has written. The first view will only impede the development of readers' efficiency. The second view makes one seldom-used purpose of reading into a primary goal. But reading is a receptive process, and readers must be concerned primarily with constructing a message from their reading. This can happen only in independent reading.

Only silent, independent reading should be called reading. A third-grade teacher recently instituted an individualized reading program. By the fourth week of the program, most of the children were reading independently and silently from thirty to forty-five minutes a day. Many of these children would come up to Ms. Curtis, the teacher, and ask, "Why aren't we having reading today?" Joan's mother came to school one day and asked Ms. Curtis why she was not having reading in school any more. Joan had come home and said that there was no reading going on. Ms. Curtis began to realize that most of the children thought reading was the time spent in a twenty-minute reading group, where everyone reads orally two or three minutes with the teacher and then does exercises of some sort.

Reading instruction activities should be called seat work, follow-up activities, or reading instruction. Oral reading should be called interpretive or dramatic reading. Group discussions to interpret a story should be called group activity or discussion time. All activities which surround the reading experience should be called other things—*only the time for independent silent reading should be called reading.*

Principle *What is read is language. Reading materials must always involve the interaction of the three language systems: graphophonic, syntactic, and semantic.*

Since what is read is language, reading should be taught using "real" or "natural" language as its medium of instruction. Reading must be a means to an end for the learner, not an end in itself. It might be best not to relegate reading to a separate reading class but instead to incorporate it within the wide range of activities and subject matter which students explore during the school day. As readers use materials written for social studies, science, math, music, and so on, they will have to develop a range of reading strategies which are appropriate to the particular syntactic, semantic, and graphophonic systems used to express the differences within these various fields.

Teachers in content areas must realize that many of the concepts from their particular fields take on appropriate meaning only in the context of the language of that field. A vocabulary item like the word *axis* is not the same in math as it is in social studies. Even within the field of social studies the term can refer either to the pole around which the earth turns or the powers that fought the Allies during the Second World War. Only within the "natural" context can the reader reconstruct meaning.

Attempts to separate the graphophonic system from the syntactic system or meaning system provide readers with artificial language. Artificial language is too abstract for children, who use language for knowledge and social interaction. Reading material must be presented in a form that readers recognize as language, so that they will treat it as something they know and can read.

Principle *People can understand what they read when the material is expressed in language with which they are familiar.*

The closer the written language is to the oral language of the reader, the more easily the material will be understood. The written language does not have to represent exactly the oral language of the student, however. It can also represent the oral language of the people around him. Children can understand a wider range of dialects than they can speak. But the teacher must become aware of the language the students speak and hear in order to provide appropriate beginning language materials, as well as to expand the students' receptive control of a variety of written styles. In beginning reading, the dictated experience stories of the individual child are an appropriate place to start. Later, the students can read group- or teacher-written stories based on common experiences. This will provide varied language forms for readers to handle.

At the same time, the teacher should expand the receptive language of the students by reading to them daily from the rich variety of literature for children and youth. Writers of such literature use a variety of literary styles (Huck and Kuhn, 1968; Reid, 1972), and their syntax and vocabulary often represent a variety of oral dialects. Some authors are now using dialects which were not previously expressed in written language (Steptoe, 1969; Graham, 1970). There are also books, magazines, and comics which use print variations to indicate dialect differences. These give students many opportunities to deal with variations in written language.

Principle *People can best understand what they read when the material is related to their own background and experience.*

It is very difficult, if not impossible, to read something which is totally foreign to one's own background. Reading a legal contract is a common example. The solution to the problem is to consult a lawyer; but this does not provide the reader with appropriate strategies for reading future legal contracts on his own. Only an appropriate background can help the student deal with many new concepts in reading.

All written materials contain words or phrases which authors do not explain because they assume that the reading audience is familiar with the ideas expressed or the words used. It is, therefore, the teacher's responsibility to make sure the students have a variety of pre-reading experiences to prepare them for any unfamiliar concepts which they may read about. Such experiences will take on more meaning if the activities involve the learners in a concrete and active manner and permit the learners to think and talk about what is happening. These kinds of pre-reading experiences may be more necessary for the reading of informational material than for fiction. However, sometimes a piece of fiction that was written at a different time in history or in a unique culture can be quite foreign to the students. In these situations, the teacher may need to help the students bridge the cultural or time gap.

In some cases authors build the concepts related to the words, phrases, or ideas through their story or article. For the teacher to explain such terms or concepts prior to reading would interfere with the interaction between the reader and writer. *One of the purposes of reading is, in fact, the extension of knowledge through new learning.* It will take teachers who are sensitive to the language as well as the background and experience of their students to know which concepts need to be presented prior to reading and which concepts should be left to the readers' own strategies.

Principle *People can best understand what they read when the material is interesting.*

When students are interested in what they read, all aspects of their reading become a great deal easier. Motivation is built in. Since students' interests vary, a wide variety of reading material must be available in the classroom. Readers must be involved in planning their own reading experiences and in selecting appropriate materials. In addition to paperback and hardback books, newspapers, magazines, comics, and so on should be available. There should be opportunities for students to read and follow directions—for construction of various kinds, for cooking, sewing, knitting, or crocheting. Song sheets of popular music which students can follow as they listen to records or sing, science corners with written directions for experimentation, or mathematics tables with suggestions for problems are all a legitimate part of such a program.

In Conclusion

Linguists, psycholinguists, and sociolinguists have studied language and thinking and their effect on learning and on society. Only teachers, however, can apply this knowledge to the classroom. Not only must they be aware of the most up-to-date information from the scientists who study children, their language, and how they learn, but teachers must build a framework or a philosophy to understand the implications for classrooms of the emerging knowledge and ideas. It becomes their responsibility to decide the best ways in which to develop this knowledge into instructional programs for children. This is, indeed, the most significant part of the teacher's professional role.

References

Britton, J. *Language and Learning*. Florida: University of Miami Press, 1970.

Brown, R., ed. *Psycholinguistics*. New York: The Free Press, Macmillan, 1970.

Chomsky, N. *Aspects of a Theory of Syntax*. Cambridge, Mass.: Massachusetts Institute of Technology Press, 1965.

Flavell, J. H. *The Developmental Psychology of Jean Piaget*. New York: Van Nostrand, 1964.

Gleason, H. A. *Linguistics and English Grammar*. New York: Holt, Rinehart and Winston, 1965.

Goodman, K. "Let's Dump the Up-tight Model in English." *Elementary School Journal*, October 1969.

Goodman, K., and Buck, C. "Dialect Barriers to Reading Comprehension: Revisited." *The Reading Teacher*, October 1973.

Goodman, K., and Burke, C. *A Study of Oral Reading Miscues That Result in Grammatical Re-transformations.* Health, Education, and Welfare: Project No. 7-#-219, Contract No. OEG-0-8-070219-2806 (010), June 1969.

Goodman, K., and Burke, C. *Theoretically Based Studies of Patterns of Miscues in Oral Reading Performance.* Final Report, Project No. 9-0775, Grant No. OEG-0-9-320375-4269. U.S. Department of Health, Education, and Welfare, Office of Education, Bureau of Research, May 1973.

Goodman, K., and Niles, O. *Reading: Process and Program.* Champaign, Ill.: National Council of Teachers of English, 1970.

Graham, L. *David He No Fear.* New York: Thomas Y. Crowell, 1970.

Graham, L. *Every Man Heart Lay Down.* New York: Thomas Y. Crowell, 1970.

Hodges, R., and Rudorf, H., eds. *Language and Learning to Read: What Teachers Should Know About Language.* New York: Houghton Mifflin, 1972.

Hormann, H. *Psycholinguistics.* Translated by H. H. Stern. New York: Sprenger-Verlag, 1971.

Huck, C. S., and Kuhn, D. Y. *Children's Literature in Elementary School.* New York: Holt, Rinehart and Winston, 1968.

Huey, E. B. *Psychology and Pedagogy of Reading.* Cambridge, Mass.: Massachusetts Institute of Technology Press, 1968.

Laffey, J., and Shuy, R., eds. *Language Differences: Do They Interfere?* Newark, Del.: International Reading Association, 1973.

Lee, D., and Van Allen, R. *Learning to Read Through Experience.* New York: Appleton-Century-Crofts, 1963.

Lindsay, P. H., and Norman, D. *Human Information Processing: An Introduction to Psychology.* New York: Academic Press, 1972.

Malmstrom, J., and Weaver, C. *Transgrammar: English Structure, Style, and Dialects.* Glenview, Ill.: Scott, Foresman, 1973.

Reid, V. M. *Reading Ladders for Human Relations.* Washington, D.C.: American Council on Education, 1972.

Robinson, H., ed. *Coordinating Reading Instruction.* Glenview, Ill.: Scott, Foresman, 1971.

Shuy, R. *Understanding American Dialects.* Urbana, Ill.: National Council of Teachers of English, 1968.

Smith, E. B.; Goodman, K. S.; and Meredith, R. *Language and Thinking in the Elementary School.* New York: Holt, Rinehart and Winston, 1970.

Smith, F. *Psycholinguistics and Reading.* New York: Holt, Rinehart and Winston, 1972.

Smith, F., and Miller, G., eds. *The Genesis of Language.* Cambridge, Mass.: Massachusetts Institute of Technology Press, 1966.

Stauffer, R. *The Language-Experience Approach to the Teaching of Reading.* New York: Harper and Row, 1970.

Steptoe, J. *Stevie.* New York: Harper and Row, 1969.

Veach, J. *Reading in the Elementary School.* New York: Ronald Press, 1966.

Vygotsky, L. *Thought and Language.* Cambridge, Mass.: Massachusetts Institute of Technology Press, 1962.

Wardhaugh, R. *Introduction to Linguistics.* New York: McGraw-Hill, 1972.

Winkeljohann, Sister Rosemary, ed. *The Politics of Reading: Point Counterpoint.* Newark, Del., and Urbana, Ill.: International Reading Association and National Council of Teachers of English, 1973.

Chapter
Five

Preview

The preceding chapters have dealt with theoretical, psychological, and sociocultural aspects of the reading process. This chapter, changing the focus somewhat, deals with the *teaching* of reading in the context of the school. Professor Ransom first describes the characteristics of the mature reader—the goal of all reading instruction—and then outlines a comprehensive curriculum with guidelines for establishing long- and short-term objectives. She discusses the role of teachers, paraprofessionals, and others who are often involved in the reading program, and, while allowing for individual differences in teaching style and programs, she emphasizes that the reading program as a whole must have direction and focus. This issue is controversial and the discussion herein should provide the impetus for further reading and discussion.

Reading:
Curriculum and Objectives

Peggy Ransom, Ball State University

Objectives

After you have read this chapter, you should be able to:

1. List three specific aspects of self-actualization in reading. For each of these, suggest at least one teaching strategy which should encourage self-actualization in general and reading achievement specifically.
2. Work in small groups with fellow students and supply specific data about the current "Right to Read" efforts.
3. List three of the most significant characteristics of a mature reader.
4. Suggest a teaching procedure which should help develop each of the characteristics you listed in number three.
5. List similarities and differences among the four types of reading programs presented in the chapter: developmental, functional, recreational, and corrective-remedial.

Reading instruction is one of the most important parts of the school curriculum. Through it teachers influence not only their students' ability to read but also their ability to achieve their full potential as individuals and as members of society (Merton, 1948). One way teachers exert this influence is through expectations they have for their students.

"I really like to read," says Betty, a fourth-grade pupil. "My teachers tell me I'm an excellent reader, and they help me find interesting books in the library. I hope some day I can be a teacher and help children to read, too!" This enthusiastic reader has obviously encountered success in reading throughout her school years, and her reading skills have been supported by teachers. She is an example of a successful reader.

Jim, however, says, "I can't read." When asked, "Why can't you read, Jim?" he is apt to answer, "Because the teacher told me I can't read." The teacher's expectations—whether for the success or failure of the students —are likely to be fulfilled.

Teacher Expectations

Because teachers have different expectations for children from the middle and lower socioeconomic levels, it is not surprising that these children are often low in academic performance and are frequently classified as discipline problems (Rosenthal and Jacobson, 1968). The teachers' expectations for mastery in reading can and should be high, regardless of the social class of the students. Children who go to school where teachers expect them to master the material do indeed succeed. "It is difficult to estimate precisely the value of a positive teacher attitude or the damage of a negative one; however, the value and damage are real" (Wilson, 1972).

Teachers' responses to the question, "How well do you think your pupils should be reading?" reveal a great variety of expectations. A first-level teacher in a school enrolling pupils classified in the middle socioeconomic range answered this way: "I expect most of the students to be reading at the end of the school year. However, some of them who have scored low on tests might not be able to read until the end of first reading level or beginning second reading level. You understand, I don't expect them all to be at the same place, for children progress at different rates."

Another first-level reading teacher responded to the same question as follows: "Most of these children will not be able to do much reading at the end of the first year in my room, but when they reach a stage of wanting to read, I will teach them." This teacher must search for specific indications that a child wants to read and is "ready" to do so.

Still another first-level reading teacher gave this response to the question: "I expect every child to read to the best of his abilities. When they start school with me, I try to continually assess their reading abilities and needs in order to provide a teaching program adjusted to each individual. Some children need more help than others, but with my additional aid and guidance, they will become both effective and efficient readers. I try to keep in mind that reading can be fun, and help children to enjoy it."

Stop and think about yourself: Where did you go to school? What were your teachers like? Were you given rewards by teachers for succeeding academically? Did you like school better some years than others because of the teachers you encountered? Why are you preparing to be a teacher, or to improve your teaching skills? Did you have teachers who led you to self-actualization in reading?

Then ask yourself: What will I expect from children? Do I have plans for helping them reach their potential? Am I (or will I be) giving them all the help I can, enabling them to learn to the best of their abilities? It is to be hoped that you will become a teacher of reading who helps students meet their own goals and those which society has set for them.

Meeting Society's Needs

In 1968, Dr. James E. Allen, Jr., then U.S. Commissioner of Education, made the following discomfiting disclosures:

1. One out of every four students nationwide had significant reading deficiencies.
2. In large city school systems, up to half of the students read below expectation.
3. There were more than three million functional illiterates in our adult population.
4. About half of the unemployed youth in New York City, ages 16–21, were functionally illiterate.
5. Three-quarters of the juvenile offenders in New York City were two or more years retarded in reading.
6. In a recent U.S. Armed Forces program called Project 100,000, 68.2 percent of the young men fell below grade seven in reading and academic ability.

Dr. Allen stated: "The tragedy of these statistics is that they represent a barrier to success that for many young adults produces the misery of a life marked by poverty, unemployment, alienation, and, in many cases, crime" (Allen, 1969, p. 2). Allen was so concerned over these results that he set a goal: by the beginning of the 1980s no one would leave school without the skill and the desire necessary to read to the full limits of his capabilities. Dr. Allen left office soon after this proclamation, but the total national commitment to the Right to Read Effort is being implemented to some degree throughout the United States.

Right to Read is designed to coordinate all reading-related efforts now being made at the federal, state, and local levels into a united attack on the nation's reading problems. The Right to Read Effort has (1) identified some of the most effective reading programs in the nation and packaged information about them, (2) shared these packages with Right to Read sites, so they can use components from the models to build their own effective programs, and (3) retrained teachers and community leaders so they can cope with a variety of reading problems, rather than just a few. The basic principles of Right to Read are:

1. With the exception of the small portion of the population which is considered uneducable, all people can learn to read if they are provided with programs designed to meet their needs.
2. Teachers will adopt new methods of teaching reading if they are convinced that these will help them teach more effectively.
3. The United States has the resources necessary to at least ease, if not solve the reading crisis.

These principles remain to be translated into better teacher training, as well as innovative and effective educational programs.

All classroom teachers are part of the Right to Read Effort, for every time a teacher helps a child in reading, he has helped him realize his right to read. Teachers can further assist the effort by making a personal commitment to find and implement better ways of teaching reading.

To be an effective citizen today, one must be able to read at least minimally. Applying for a job, obtaining a driver's license, and even buying groceries all require functional literacy. The Adult Basic Education Act of 1965 established programs to aid adults in reading and other areas. As the teaching of reading in elementary school classrooms improves, however, the need for programs to counteract adult illiteracy should diminish.

The School's Accountability

Increasingly, educators are being held accountable for the literacy of their students. They are accepting responsibility for the results of their teaching. Some school districts have accepted this accountability by establishing systems analysis. They review student data from standardized tests and informal reading inventories, gather data regarding students' attitudes and interests, and survey standardized test scores. With this information, school personnel can more adequately assess the reading achievement of the pupils. They can compare test scores from pupil to pupil within individual schools (districtwide comparison is probably unfair because of the differences among schools), and the resulting analysis helps teachers improve their reading programs. Faculties and administrators can then compare changes which result from systems analysis.

Each day, the effective teacher of reading diagnoses children's weaknesses, strengths, and needs, and adjusts teaching plans, materials, and procedures in terms of these diagnoses. This process represents acceptance of the principle of accountability. It is important that teachers decide at the beginning of the year how they will demonstrate their accountability for the teaching of reading. The school and community will not question teaching techniques when they can see the results of an evaluation of diagnostic-prescriptive procedures of teaching reading for each individual pupil.

Reading and Language Arts

The child's language facility, much of it developed in pre-school years, contributes to the development of skills in reading, listening, speaking, writing, spelling, and literature. What facilitates and fosters growth in one area also facilitates and fosters growth in the others. The teacher's responsibilities, therefore, include the following:

1. Being flexible enough to allow for the range of language abilities children have when they come to school.
2. Understanding the language of the community from which the children come.
3. Valuing and appreciating the language of every child.
4. Developing widening experiences with children, thereby fostering language development (Smith, Goodman, and Meredith, 1970, p. 165).

Language-related instruction has progressed far beyond that offered under the headings of reading, spelling, written composition, and speech only a few years ago. Reading is seen as a facet of communication, not as an isolated fragment of the language arts. Teachers who attempt to teach listening, speaking, writing, spelling, reading, grammar, and literature as isolated elements appear to be ignoring natural relationships that exist among these areas of the language arts.

The medium through which teaching and learning take place is language. When a child comes to school, he has already learned much about the grammar and vocabulary of the language spoken in his home. Teachers, therefore, can "use the oral efficiency that children bring to school as the means of developing a complementary efficiency in reading and writing" (Burrows, 1972, p. 96).

Courses relating the language arts to one another will help pupils improve their ability and flexibility in communication. Listening and reading, for example, involve related skills, as do writing and speaking. When students work in small groups on activities related to the reading program, there is more opportunity for speaking and listening than there is if pupils are called upon individually. These communication skills are an important initial step toward skill in reading.

For the same reason, a listening center is an important part of the classroom. Materials in the listening center can include taped stories with questions to be answered at the end. The answers to the questions could become the basis for dramatizing a story using puppets, or for preparing a tape recording to be heard by other pupils. The result will be an integration of the various aspects of the language arts, including reading. This kind of integration should be the classroom teacher's goal.

Characteristics of the Mature Reader

One of the major goals of a reading program is to help students develop into mature readers. The mature reader (1) reflects on what he is reading; (2) effectively organizes and utilizes materials; (3) thinks critically about the *content* of what he reads; (4) tries to determine the qualifications of authorities consulted; and (5) selects authors who fulfill his own immediate needs (Bond and Wagner, 1966).

Gray and Rogers[1] add the following characteristics to the list:

1. A genuine enthusiasm for reading.
2. A tendency to read
   a. a wide variety of materials that contribute pleasure, widen horizons, and stimulate creative thinking.
   b. serious materials which promote a growing understanding of one's self, of others, and problems of social, moral, and ethical nature.
   c. intensively in a particular field or materials relating to a central core.
3. Ability to translate words into meanings, to secure a clear grasp and understanding of the ideas presented, and to sense clearly the mood and feelings intended.
4. Capacity for and habit of making use of all that one knows or can find out in interpreting or construing the meaning of the ideas read.
5. Ability to perceive strengths and weaknesses in what is read, to detect bias and propaganda, and to think critically concerning the validity and values of the ideas presented and the adequacy and soundness of the author's presentation, views, and conclusions. This involves an emotional apprehension, either favorable or unfavorable, as well as a penetrating intellectual grasp of what is read.
6. Tendency to fuse the new ideas acquired through reading with previous experience, thus acquiring new or clearer understandings, broadened interests, rational attitudes, improved patterns of thinking and behaving and richer and more stable personalities.

---

[1] Reprinted from *Maturity, Its Nature and Appraisal* by William S. Gray and Bernice Rogers by permission of the University of Chicago Press. © 1956, The University of Chicago.

7. Capacity to adjust one's reading pace to the needs of the occasion and to the demands of adequate interpretation (pp. 54–55).

Few readers ever achieve full maturity in reading, but many make continuous progress toward the achievement of each of the stated characteristics. The teacher's role is to assist and encourage this progress.

Each student's progress toward maturity in reading should be evaluated in terms of his potential. A teacher must try to develop the potential of each individual so that his lifetime reading habits may be made more worthwhile and personally satisfying.

The Reading Curriculum

The reading curriculum must encompass specific reading programs which will help pupils develop into mature readers. We use a somewhat technical language when discussing reading curriculum or programs. Some of the terms used are *developmental reading, functional reading, recreational reading,* and *corrective-remedial reading.* In comprehensive reading programs, instruction, guidance, and media are provided in all these areas. What do these terms mean, and how do they relate to an effective instructional reading program?

The most important goal of the *developmental reading* progam is learning to read. Developmental reading programs teach (1) skill in the mechanics of reading, and (2) skill in reading comprehension. The mechanics of reading include developing sight vocabulary; developing skills in identifying unfamiliar words through structural analysis, context clues, dictionary work, and phonics; developing efficient eye movements; developing speed in silent reading; adjusting to the types of material one reads; developing oral reading skills such as phrasing, expression, pitch, and enunciation.

Reading comprehension skills include development of a more extensive reading vocabulary; development of the ability to remember, evaluate, and generalize from what one has read; the ability to note and recall details; and the ability to understand the author's ideas and point of view.

The primary objective of *functional reading* programs is to enable a reader to obtain information from various types of reading, or just to read to learn. It sometimes is called study-type reading as well as functional reading. The skills important in functional reading include the following:

1. ability to locate needed reading material by means of an index, table of contents, encyclopedia, library card file, or other bibliographic aid;
2. ability to skim or scan material in search of information;
3. ability to comprehend informational materials which require the applica-

tion of the comprehension skills for developmental reading, and development of specific skills required by special subject areas, such as reading for social studies content, reading arithmetic problems, reading maps, charts, and graphs;

4. ability to select the materials needed to gain specific information;
5. ability to organize what is read—to summarize, for example, or to outline chapters within books.

The major purpose of *recreational reading* or free reading is enjoyment or appreciation. The skills involved in this kind of reading are (1) developing and raising the level of interest in reading, and (2) developing literary judgment and taste (Harris, 1970). The teacher can develop students' interest in reading by demonstrating his own enjoyment of reading as a leisure-time activity. He can also help pupils select reading materials for themselves. To help them develop deeper literary judgment and taste, the teacher must establish different learning strategies for fiction and nonfiction, prose, poetry, and drama, and also develop an appreciation for the style and beauty of language.

Developmental, functional, and recreational reading cannot be completely separated. Developmental reading will often be taught with a recreational reading activity or a functional reading assignment. Programs which are truly comprehensive include all these types of reading, and also provide for pupils who need corrective-remedial help.

Corrective-remedial reading programs are usually planned as supplements to the regular developmental program. Whereas the other three types of programs described are group oriented, the corrective-remedial program operates on an individual or small group basis. It usually involves skills in the mechanics of reading and in reading comprehension, for the students are usually weak in one or both of these. The teacher frequently must develop new ways of teaching the basic skills in order to help the students learn to read. As much as possible, the teacher should also provide remedial students with functional and recreational reading; but since these students lack the basic reading skills, the emphasis is placed on the developmental program, adjusted to individual differences.

Even though corrective-remedial reading is related to developmental, functional, and recreational reading, there are some differences. The goals of a corrective-remedial program and of a regular program are the same: (1) teach every child to read to the best of his abilities; (2) permit a more open atmosphere for learning; (3) diagnose students for specific learning difficulties; (4) give daily individualized instruction; (5) motivate children to want to read. But in a regular classroom, with thirty or more students, these are often only verbalized, while in a corrective-remedial program, where teaching is on a one-to-one basis, they become an actuality (Heilman, 1972).

Curricular Determinants

Teachers and administrators often differ from each other in attitudes and philosophy. Controversies exist over such issues as teaching the child at his own reading level, permissiveness in individual instruction, and emphasizing interest in reading. Other areas of controversy concern the appropriate number of conferences with parents, the need for diagnosing the child more thoroughly, and techniques for allowing him to set non-competitive reading goals.

The school's position on such issues will influence the curriculum. For this reason, teachers should be familiar with the philosophy of schools where they apply for teaching positions. What the teacher believes should, ideally, be in general agreement with established school policies. When teachers see the need for a change of philosophy or practice, however, they have a professional obligation to try to effect such a change.

The way the teacher organizes the reading program will depend on the materials and techniques he or she uses and on the structure of the classroom—whether it is a self-contained, non-graded, or team-teaching situation. The first step in setting up the program is to set long range goals, such as, "The child will be able to read to the best of his ability during this year." The next step is to diagnose the children's reading skills, and, according to the results, select the techniques and materials to be used and set specific objectives for each child, either daily, weekly, or monthly. The most effective diagnosis makes use of as many sources of information as possible. Standardized tests, teacher observations, informal reading tests, and cumulative cards can all be valuable.

It is often helpful to organize an individual reading folder for each student. Table 1 shows one system for recording skill development data. Teachers may modify this to suit their own teaching situations.

A completed table will indicate what reading skills the child possesses, and which ones yet need to be taught or practiced. The teacher can develop specific teaching objectives from this information. He can decide how to group pupils, determine which pupils need individual instruction, and select appropriate materials and teaching techniques.

Table 2 shows one teacher's plan for a day's reading program. This teacher has grouped the students into four reading groups. She tries to work with three groups each day. She has a tutor and a paraprofessional to help her. The same type of daily program could be used in a team teaching situation.

Table 2 represents only one type of lesson plan. Each teacher must adjust his lesson plans to meet the needs of his students. Effective reading instruction is based on careful planning. The plans suggested in the guides

Table 1   Individual Reading Folder for Students

Name _____   Grade Level _____

Teacher _____

Reading levels   Standardized   Reading
                                                       test scores   capacity

Informal reading inventory

Independent   _____   _____   _____

Instructional   _____   _____   _____

Frustration   _____   _____   _____

	Introduced	*Practiced*	*Applied*
I. Pre-reading skills			
A. Letter names			
B. Listening			
C. Speaking vocabulary			
D. Visual discrimination			
E. Auditory discrimination			
F. Left-to-right orientation			
II. Word analysis skills			
A. Sight vocabulary (level)			
B. Phonic analysis			
1. Initial consonants			
2. Final consonants			
3. Blends			
4. Digraphs			
5. "Long" vowels			
6. "Short" vowels			
7. Vowel generalizations			
8. Contractions			
C. Structural analysis			
1. Prefixes			
2. Suffixes and endings			
3. Compound words			
4. Syllabication			
III. Comprehension and study skills			
A. Vocabulary			
B. Details			
C. Main ideas			
D. Sequence			
E. Inference			
F. Dictionary			
G. Book parts			
H. Other			

Table 2   Plan for a Daily Reading Program

	Group 1	Group 2	Group 3	Group 4
9:00–9:30	(With Teacher) Introduce new story and read silently.	(With Tutor) Practice on vocabulary phrases and sentences. Oral reading from science textbook.	(Alone) Pupil goes to kdg. to read a story to them, or reads independently.	(Alone) At listening center. Tape with a practice story prepared by the teacher, who has already taught the story.
9:30–10:00	(Alone) Listening center. Tape with a reading (mystery) story that has the ending omitted.	(With Teacher) Individualized reading. Teacher works with 5 students individually.	(With Tutor) Play games on initial consonants since the students need to practice this skill.	(With Paraprofessional) Work on writing sentences with new vocabulary presented by teacher on previous days.
10:00–10:30	(With Teacher) Each write his own ending to the taped mystery story.	(With Teacher) Listening center. Tape on spelling worksheet to follow. Writing spelling words in sentences.	(With Teacher) Read a story from a linguistic series.	(Alone) Record the written sentences on tape recorder or read independently.

which accompany basal readers, while helpful, can never accommodate all the needs represented in a typical reading group.

Objectives of the Reading Curriculum

Since reading is highly complex and involves the learning of many specific skills, very specific objectives should be planned for the reading program. Vague objectives will yield poor results. A good set of objectives indicates the reading skills that children should demonstrate as a result of the reading program, and thus guides the teacher in the types of learning activities and evaluation procedures he uses (Barrett, 1969).

The *major objective* of a reading program might be, "At the end of the school year, each pupil will read to the best of his reading ability." A *specific objective,* however, is related to the teacher's diagnosis of the pupil's strengths and weaknesses and the day-by-day activities which follow the diagnostic and prescriptive analysis. One specific objective, for example, might be, "Today this pupil will read a paragraph at his instructional level, missing only one word and answering questions about content with 75 percent accuracy." The specific objective helps the teacher know when a student has mastered a particular skill.

The major goal of the developmental program is learning to read; for the functional program the goal is reading to learn; for the recreational program the goal is reading for enjoyment or appreciation. Under each of those goals some specific objectives can be listed, and these objectives (or behaviors) will be the specific plans for reading lessons. Table 3 shows an example of a comprehensive goal, a major objective resulting from that goal, and the specific objectives established for lessons.

When the objectives of the reading program are stated concretely and specifically, progress can be made and assessed. Pupils as well as teachers can see where they are going and what they have accomplished.

Pupils will frequently set up their own objectives. Pupils' objectives, however, are more likely to be specific skills and knowledge and less likely to involve the development of positive attitudes, interests, and appreciations. Since students often do not see the applications of reading to real situations in school and life, it is important that they, as well as the teacher, be aware of and work toward specific objectives.

To encourage pupils to develop initiative in making choices, teachers may want to suggest rather than prescribe goals. Pupils can be led to develop their own objectives, perhaps in this way: Have the pupil make a study of his own reading needs and achievement; then ask him to select the goals most appropriate for him from a comprehensive list. Each goal should be accompanied by specific objectives, so that the student can see exactly what he will be working on. The pupil should mark the objectives he wants to work toward and identify those specific objectives on which he thinks the most progress can be made. This not only helps the pupil, but adds focus to the pupil-teacher conference on reading.

In order to develop effective objectives, the teacher should answer the following important questions: (1) What is it that must be taught? (2) How can the teacher know when it has been taught? (3) What materials and procedures will work best in teaching what is to be taught? If further guidelines are needed, those listed by Mager (1962), including steps to follow in the development and use of behavioral objectives, might be helpful:

1. A statement of instructional objectives is a collection of words or symbols describing one of your educational intents.
2. An objective will communicate your intent to the degree you have described what the learner will be doing when demonstrating his achievement, and how you will know when he is doing it.
3. To describe terminal behavior (what the learner will be doing):
   a. identify and name the overall behavior act.
   b. define the important conditions under which the behavior is to occur.
   c. write a separate statement for each objective; the more you have, the better the chance you have of making clear your intent.
   d. if you give each learner a copy of your objectives, you may not have to do much else (Mager, 1962, p. 52).

If an objective is not stated in behavioral terms, the teacher and pupil will have no way of telling whether or not the objective has been attained. "A student can follow written directions" is a non-behavioral objective. It does not identify the specific behavior that is expected of the student: With what degree of accuracy can he follow directions? What materials will he use? How will the teacher and the pupil know when this objective has been accomplished? A good behavioral objective will answer questions like these.

The Author's Viewpoint

It is important for teachers to establish both major objectives and specific behavioral objectives in order to understand what is to be taught and the direction the learning process should take. When a teacher has established behavioral objectives, it will be easier to develop learning activities to meet students' needs and to evaluate their performance. Teachers should not rely

Table 3 Goals, Objectives, and Behaviors of a Reading Program

This is an example of a page that could be given to students. Other goals and objectives could be added according to the teaching situation and the needs of the individual students. Teachers could benefit by keeping records of the reading achievements of individual students.

Student _____   Teacher _____

Level _____   School _____

Goal	Major Objectives	Specific Objectives and Behaviors
I. Development of vocabulary skills	A. To use many different kinds of firsthand experiences to gain understanding of words.	1. Read a newspaper, locate new words and write them with meanings. 2. Be able to write ten new words and their meanings every two weeks for six weeks.
	B. To learn key words in studying other school subjects.	1. Listen to three TV programs and write unknown words. Locate meanings in the dictionary. Try for 5 new words in two weeks. 2. Write a story after six weeks using all new words for this time. 3. Read three library books in six weeks and locate new words and their meanings.
	C. To consult dictionary for exact meanings of words.	1. Start a pupil dictionary to enter new words of the six weeks. 2. In six weeks the dictionary should contain 50 new words and their meanings.
	D. To learn word origins and the different meanings of the same word in different contexts.	1. After six weeks take a test of 50 new words and be able to give the meanings of 45 words. Also write the 45 words in sentences.

II. Development of word recognition skills

A. To identify words through context clues.

1. Be able to identify new words through context clues four out of five times.

B. To identify words through phonics.

1. Be able to identify orally the initial consonant letters and sounds of selected words.
2. Be able to identify all the final consonant letters and sounds of these same words.
3. Be able to identify blends and digraphs in words selected.

C. To use the dictionary efficiently.

1. Be able to locate ten new words and write their meanings in fifteen minutes.
2. Be able to use three different types of dictionaries.
3. Be able to write ten new words correctly in sentences after locating them within twenty minutes.

D. To identify words through structural analysis.

1. Be able to locate prefixes and suffixes in five stories.
2. When given four stories, be able to identify the compound words in all five of them.
3. Be able to tell why words are divided into syllables (or divide them correctly ten out of ten times).

III. Development of comprehension skills

A. To use a variety of comprehension strategies.

1. Be able to identify new word meanings in ten stories, using the dictionary.
2. State main ideas and supporting details.
3. Be able to follow written directions ten out of ten times.
4. Be able to give a sequence of events for all stories read in a six-week period.

B. To comprehend sentences accurately.

1. Be able to recall the ideas of sentences ten out of ten times.
2. Be able to identify word meanings in sentences ten out of ten times.
3. Be able to sequence a set of sentences into a story at least five times.

IV. Development through reading

A. To read for personal growth and enjoyment.

1. Be able to select many different types of materials related to ideas to be read about (maintain a written list of these).
2. Read for appreciation and enjoyment when given extra time (observation by teacher). Make a list of books read with a short summary of each.

on only one learning activity for all students before a performance is given. When students do not understand a behavioral objective after one learning activity, there should be two, three, even four other activities they can do to achieve a successful performance. Students build on successes, and repeated failure to meet a behavioral objective can be devastating. Therefore teachers need to have, for each objective, many learning activities and different types of performances.

Teachers have often failed to understand the sequence in which reading skills should be taught throughout the elementary grades. Having to set goals and define expected behaviors forces them to recognize and follow this sequence.

Clear objectives can also assist pupils' self-actualization. If teachers understand what they want pupils to achieve in a reading lesson, then they are better able to predict what each individual child will successfully achieve. Success will raise pupils' self-esteem and allow them to proceed to the next reading skill in the program.

If teachers are to be accountable for the results of their teaching, then they must develop goals and objectives which delineate specific behaviors, so they can demonstrate that their objectives have been met. Goals and objectives should also be established for each school, and these should closely relate to the philosophy of that school. This will give the teacher insight into the school's entire reading program.

Organizing a Reading Program

Most reading curricula consist of developmental, functional, recreational, and corrective-remedial teaching procedures. Within each of these areas the teacher establishes objectives and specifies behaviors for obtaining those objectives. Then he selects the materials best suited to his program.

Basal readers with workbooks are frequently used in developmental reading programs, because they are built upon the sequential learning-to-read process. Publishers of these readers usually list the objectives and outline the scope and sequence of their programs. They also provide tests and suggestions for supplemental reading. Other materials, however—such as programmed learning materials—are also designed sequentially and can be used for developmental reading. The teacher can make his own materials, too, as long as they are prepared according to the correct developmental sequence. Work on basic sight words, for example, should come at the beginning levels of reading and throughout the first year of reading instruction. Developmental programs organized on an individualized basis depend for success on the teacher's awareness of appropriate sequences for the pupils.

One way of using a developmental reading program is to follow carefully four basic steps in teaching a lesson: readiness, silent reading, oral re-reading, and reaction to and application of what has been read. This sequence can be adapted to any type of material used in the classroom and can be used with small groups or with the whole class.

Each major publisher's basal reading program presents a sequence of steps to be followed in teaching a reading lesson. An outline of steps in a reading lesson, including readiness, reading, and response, is presented in Table 4. All steps need not be accomplished in one reading lesson, but setting the purpose for reading is very important and should be done before pupils read. The remaining steps can occur within a day, two days, or even a week.

The functional reading program is the application of the developmental program. The materials used in functional reading are usually content area books, maps, charts, and teacher-prepared materials, especially those designed to promote study skills. The same approaches are recommended for content area reading as are appropriate for the developmental reading program. The lesson consists of a readiness stage, a reading stage, and re-reading and application stages. It is a teach, practice, and apply process. The program can be organized for whole classes, interest groups, tutorial groups, or research groups.

A list and description of reading materials to be used with a developmental, functional, or corrective-remedial reading program can be found in *Learning to Read: The Great Debate* (Chall, 1967). Chall also presents a classification chart of twenty-two reading programs, which can be helpful to teachers looking for programs to meet particular needs. A selected bibliography of materials for teaching comprehension, useful for developmental and functional reading programs, is given in *Reading Instruction for Classroom and Clinic* (Fry, 1972).

Most of the materials in the recreational program will be trade books—paperbacks especially, which tend to excite pupils about reading. Books the pupils prepare themselves can also be included. Teachers and pupils talk together about the books the pupils have read. Recreational reading programs usually do not include direct reading instruction unless the developmental reading program is individualized, in which case the two programs become one. Time should be allotted for recreational reading in every teaching day. Too often, recreational reading is neglected, and this is unfortunate; few things are more exciting than to read books that provide important experiences and information.

In many schools, the corrective-remedial program is organized and managed by the classroom teacher. In some schools, however, special reading teachers are available. When this is the case, coordination between

Table 4   Steps in Teaching a Reading Lesson

Readiness	Reading	Response
1. Motivation (Build interest)	5. Silent/Oral Reading (Always silent first unless in a diagnostic situation)	6. Discussions (Comprehension)
2. Background (Build associations)		7. Skill Development (Follow-up activities)
3. Vocabulary (Teach new words)		8. Transfer-Application (Use in other areas)
4. Purpose for reading (Set stage for reading; always done just before silent reading)		

Source: William Powell, University of Florida.

the classroom and the remedial programs is important. Too frequently, the remedial teacher loses contact with classroom teachers. Some authorities believe that a remedial reading specialist can best work with individuals or small groups *within* a classroom, where the classroom teacher can observe the teaching situation and use it to the advantage of the pupils during the day. Occasionally, the reading specialist might meet with pupils separately, individually or in groups. The classroom teacher, too, should work with small groups of pupils who need additional corrective-remedial reading instruction.

Table 5 provides a comprehensive organizational pattern including all the types of programs discussed so far.

Paraprofessionals and Volunteers in the Reading Program

Paraprofessional and volunteer help can be valuable in all of these types of reading programs. When students need additional practice, the supervision of such practice can be assigned to paraprofessionals, aides, parents, or older students in the school. The professional teacher becomes the one who plans and selects appropriate methods and materials, initiates the lessons or exercises, and evaluates the degree to which the learner has advanced in his reading skills. The teacher formulates all assignments given to aides, basing them on specific objectives set for individual pupils, so that each aide understands what he is to do and what the end result should be. At the end of each session, the teacher confers with the aides in order to understand problems they encountered or to adjust assignments for future days.

The teacher should keep in mind that aides and volunteers do not have the professional expertise of a teacher. Therefore, they should not be expected to make decisions for which they are not equipped. The materials they will use must be carefully evaluated. Are the directions too complicated for them to deal with? Do the materials require direct instruction which should be done by the teacher? Has the aide or volunteer been given sufficient on-the-job training to carry out certain specific instructional tasks?

With proper guidance, aides and volunteers can be a vital part of the school reading program (Cooper & Ransom, 1973). Such differentiated staffing is becoming more and more common in our school districts. Helpful materials on the subject can be found in the *Handbooks for the Volunteer Tutor* (International Reading Association, 1969).

The following are some of the advantages of additional personnel within a school:

Table 5 *Organization for a Reading Program*

	Developmental	Functional	Recreational	Corrective-Remedial
Curriculum	To learn to read	To read to learn	To learn to enjoy reading	To try to balance skills needed in reading.
Materials	Basal readers Programmed reading Linguistic reading Language-experience Teacher-made materials Individualized reading	Content text Maps, charts Teacher-made materials Supplementary books	Library books Microfiche Paperback novels Newspapers Magazines Student-made books	All the materials mentioned, but many high interest, low vocabulary books. Materials adjusted to individual needs.
Method	Steps in teaching a lesson	Steps in teaching a lesson: 1. Survey 2. Question 3. Read 4. Recite 5. Respond	Independent teacher-pupil cooperation	Steps in teaching a lesson, but geared to meet the needs of individual pupils.
Personnel	Teacher: Professional leader, planner, decision-maker Aided by : Paraprofessionals, cross-age tutoring, volunteer tutors, parents			Special cases: Reading specialists

1. Additional help is provided for pupils.
2. The pupil-teacher ratio is reduced.
3. Better public relations are established when parents and neighborhood people assist in the classroom.
4. Such personnel are less expensive than additional hired teachers.

There are some disadvantages, too, however:

1. Teachers are given additional responsibilities.
2. In-service training may not be provided for aides and teachers.
3. The administration may enlarge classes, assuming the aides perform the same job as teachers.
4. A professional teaching position may be filled by an aide, who can be paid a lower salary.
5. Because of large class assignments, teachers are sometimes forced to behave as though their additional personnel had professional preparation.

Only when in-service training for teachers and paraprofessionals is provided and the roles and responsibilities of teachers and aides are carefully defined can pupils gain the full benefit of differentiated staffing.

Summary

Schools today offer a variety of organizational patterns, additional personnel to assist the teacher, and a flexible reading curriculum, adjusted to the individual needs and interests of the pupils. This variety and flexibility is necessary for meeting pupils' differing needs; but variety alone does not ensure a successful reading program. Research has generally shown that the single most important factor contributing to the success of a reading program is the teacher—the trained and experienced teacher who is open to new designs in reading instruction and who is willing to implement these approaches in the classroom. Such a teacher—whether in a self-contained classroom, a non-graded classroom, or an open classroom, with or without additional personnel—will be most likely to achieve the major goal: to teach every child to read to the best of his ability.

References

Allen, James E., Jr. "The Right to Read—Target for the 70's." Washington, D.C.: U.S. Department of Health, Education, and Welfare, Office of Education, 1969.

Barrett, T. C. "Goals of the Reading Program: The Basis for Evaluation." In *Elementary Reading Instruction*, edited by A. Berry, T. C. Barrett, and W. R. Powell. Boston: Allyn and Bacon, 1969.

Behavioral Objectives. Bloomington, Ind.: ERIC/CRIER Clearing House on Reading, Indiana University, 1971.

Betts, E. A. *Foundations of Reading Instruction.* New York: American Book Company, 1957.

Bond, G., and Wagner, E. B. *Teaching the Child to Read.* 4th ed. New York: Macmillan, 1966.

Burrows, A. T. "Children's Language: New Insights for the Language Arts." In *Language Arts Concepts for Elementary School Teachers*, edited by P. C. Burns, J. E. Alexander, and A. R. Davis. Itasca, Ill.: F. E. Peacock Publishers, 1972.

Chall, J. *Learning to Read: The Great Debate.* New York: McGraw-Hill, 1967.

Cooper, J. D., and Ransom, P. *Local Concerns.* Unpublished manuscript. Ball State University, 1973.

Fry, E. *Reading Instruction for Classroom and Clinic.* New York: McGraw-Hill, 1972.

Gray, W. S., and Rogers, B. *Maturity, Its Nature and Appraisal.* Chicago: The University of Chicago Press, 1956.

Hafner, L. E., and Joy, H. B. *Patterns of Teaching Reading in the Elementary School.* New York: Macmillan, 1971.

Harris, A. J. *How to Increase Reading Ability.* 5th ed. New York: David McKay, 1970.

Heilman, A. W. *Principles and Practices of Teaching Reading.* 3rd ed. Columbus, Ohio: Charles E. Merrill, 1972.

Lapp, D. *The Use of Behavioral Objectives in Education.* Newark, Del.: ERIC/CRIER and the International Reading Association, 1972.

Lavatelli, C. S. "An Approach to Language Learning." In *Language Arts Concepts for Elementary School Teachers*, edited by P. C. Burns, J. E. Alexander, and A. R. Davis. Itasca, Ill.: F. E. Peacock Publishers, 1972.

Mager, R. F. *Preparing Instructional Objectives.* Palo Alto, Calif.: Fearon Publishers, 1962.

Merton, R. K. "The Self-fulfilling Prophecy." *The Antioch Review*, Summer 1948.

Popham, W. J.; McNeil, J. D.; Baker, E. L.; and Millman, J. "Measurable Objectives Collections." Los Angeles, Calif.: Instructional Objectives Exchange, 1970.

Rauch, S., ed. *Handbook for the Volunteer Tutor.* Newark, Del.: International Reading Association, 1969.

Rosenthal, R., and Jacobson, L. *Pygmalion in the Classroom.* New York: Holt, Rinehart and Winston, 1968.

Sebesta, S. L., and Wallen, C. J. *Readings on Teaching Reading.* Chicago, Ill.: Science Research Associates, 1972.

Shane, H. G.; Redder, M. E.; and Gillespie, M. C. *Beginning Language Arts Instruction with Children.* Columbus, Ohio: Charles E. Merrill, 1961.

Smith, E. B.; Goodman, K. S.; and Meredith, R. *Language and Thinking in the Elementary School.* New York: Holt, Rinehart and Winston, 1970.

Smith, J. A. *Creative Teaching of Language Arts in the Elementary School.* Boston: Allyn and Bacon, 1967.

Smith, J. A. *Creative Teaching of Reading and Literature in the Elementary School.* Boston: Allyn and Bacon, 1967.

Strang. R. "The Reading Process and Its Ramifications." Invitational Addresses, Tenth Annual Convention. Newark, Del.: International Reading Association, 1965, pp. 49–52.

Strang, R., et al. *The Improvement of Reading.* Newark, Del.: International Reading Association, 1961.

Whipple, G. "Characteristics of a Sound Reading Program." In *Reading in the Elementary School,* 48th Yearbook of the National Society for the Study of Education, Part II. Chicago, Ill.: University of Chicago Press, 1949.

Wilson, R. M., and Hall, Maryanne. *Reading and the Elementary Child.* New York: D. Van Nostrand, 1972.

Chapter
Six

Preview

The problems of assessment in reading have become more critical for teachers in this era of accountability in education.

This chapter presents a framework of assessment procedures and describes their application to the reading program at several levels. Included in the chapter are practical suggestions for the use of tests and manuals and the interpretation of data.

We hope that this chapter will not only increase teachers' knowledge about reading assessment, but also help them synthesize the content of the chapters that follow.

Karlsen believes that reading teachers are often poorly prepared to deal with the problems of testing and evaluation. This chapter should help to remedy that situation.

Reading: Assessment and Diagnosis of Abilities

Bjorn Karlsen, California State College, Sonoma

Objectives

After you have read this chapter, you should be able to:

1. Describe the diagnostic teaching of reading and demonstrate this approach with pupils.
2. Name five common types of reading tests and describe all in some detail.
3. Describe the difference in diagnostic usefulness between a standardized survey test and a standardized diagnostic test.
4. Make correct judgments about the appropriateness of answer sheets for a group of pupils.
5. Explain the three most common types of norms and explain, in general, how they are derived.
6. After administering and scoring a standardized test, demonstrate the use and interpretation of the appropriate norm tables.
7. With respect to reading readiness assessment, delineate the main differences between the prognostic and the diagnostic approach.
8. List at least ten different situations in which one of the assessment techniques described in this chapter will help a teacher of reading.

Reading instruction is most efficient when it is aimed toward the needs of each individual student in a classroom. But before reading instruction can be individualized, it is necessary to determine how each student reads, what skills he needs help with, and what new skills he is ready to learn. This process is generally referred to as *diagnosis,* and the systematized diagnose-teach-diagnose-teach approach to reading instruction has been called the *diagnostic-prescriptive* approach. Diagnosis, then, is not simply analysis of the basic causes of reading problems. It is oriented toward the future and is most effective when it helps the teacher arrange meaningful

147

and efficient learning experiences that will help each student become a skillful reader.

When it is part of an intensive case study of each child, diagnosis precedes instruction. But the classroom teacher has one big advantage over the clinical diagnostician: he can observe the child every day, so that diagnosis becomes an ongoing process, interacting at all times with instruction. When a child makes a mistake, the teacher notices the nature of this mistake and decides what remediation is necessary. When it is time to teach the next skill in the reading program, the teacher has already had many opportunities to observe how a child functions with respect to that skill. As a result, he can decide how intensively the new skill should be taught. This is *diagnostic teaching*—an approach in which instruction and diagnosis interact continually.

There are times when the teacher will need to stop and analyze the reading abilities of an individual, or a group, or the entire class. At that point, he will need to know some specific techniques with which to test for such abilities. We will refer to this process as *assessment*. The techniques of assessment chosen will depend on the purposes for which the results will be used. Some techniques are appropriate for the evaluation of individual students' needs; the assessment of the overall growth of a class calls for an entirely different approach. Reading materials which are specifically designed to make assessments are generally referred to as reading *tests*.

A Diagnostic Viewpoint for Teachers

The need for diagnosis in a broad sense is stressed throughout this chapter, since teaching is most efficient when the pupils are being taught what they need to know in order to develop. Assessment techniques are necessary for effective diagnosis.

Teachers often have difficulty going from assessment to instruction—deciding what to teach and what not to teach. For example, a child reveals low test scores in comprehension, decoding, and speed. The teacher gives the pupil instruction designed to improve speed. Another student, having difficulty with the /o͞o/ sound (as in *pool*) as well as problems with both the long and short o sound (as in *pole* and *pot*), is grouped with others who have difficulty with the /o͞o/ sound. These are two examples of correct assessment but incorrect teaching. The child should master the prerequisite skills before going on to the more advanced skills.

The fundamental viewpoint, then, is that we must determine where a child is and then teach him from that point at a rate which is sufficiently comfortable to give him a feeling of success and self-confidence. Poor readers are not challenged by reading material that is very difficult for them; they are frustrated by it. This is often a problem in testing, where we are trying to determine what a student knows and what he doesn't know; a difficult test can be very frustrating. Instructional material, however, need not elicit this reaction.

Student Attitudes toward Testing

Many teachers have created unhealthy attitudes toward tests among their pupils. Sometimes, when these pupils grow up and become teachers, they are reluctant to subject their own pupils to the "ordeal of being tested." They blame the tests for these attitudes rather than their teachers, who have perceived testing as something done *to* children rather than *for* them. Teachers should explain assessment techniques to children before administering tests, and they should explain the results afterwards. Eventually, the pupils themselves might administer and score some of the tests, so that they can become involved in self-diagnosis. It is natural for children to want to improve; this is as true of reading and school achievement in general as it is of physical and social activities. If they don't, we must deal with their attitudes and their self-concepts.

Some Common Types of Reading Tests

A great many approaches to the testing of reading are currently being used. These assessment techniques range all the way from simply having teachers sit and listen to the child read out loud to very elaborate diagnostic tests. No attempt will be made here to cover every possible technique; instead, we will concentrate on what are probably the seven most common approaches to reading testing in a typical school setting. This section will deal with the types of tests, and the following section will deal with their most common applications.

Teacher-made Tests

The main advantage of a teacher-made test is that it is specific; it covers exactly what has been taught in the classroom, using the vocabulary and the specific content of the reading lessons, including even the teacher's particular style and emphasis. The main drawback of such tests is that they are often poorly constructed. They may contain items that are ambiguous and simply do not work for a given group; multiple choice questions may include distractors that are also correct; or, for some questions, there may be no clearly correct answer at all. Also, there are times when pupils have difficulty understanding the directions. It is useful, therefore, after administering such a test, for the teacher to find out exactly which children had difficulty with what items. The best teacher-made tests are generally those designed for specific groups within the classroom, rather than tests which are given to everybody. Students should be tested on what specifically has been taught through group-individualized instruction (Wood, 1960; Nelson, 1970; Educational Testing Service, 1961b). The instructional technique generally referred to as "individualized reading" particularly requires a great deal of teacher testing (Harris and Smith, 1972). Since the children work so much on their own, the teacher will need to plan an instructional program for each child, which necessitates periodic re-evaluation of the students' abilities and instructional needs.

Basal Reader Tests

The vast majority of American children are taught from a basal reader or by some sort of reading instructional system (Auckerman, 1971). These systems generally include printed tests which are used mainly to determine how well the students have learned the content of a specific unit of instruction. Such tests are generally more carefully constructed than teacher-made tests, but they are specific to each reader, and norms are ordinarily not supplied. Occasionally, a basal reader test will be accompanied by a set of "tentative norms," which have often been obtained from a few relatively small school districts within a narrow geographical area rather than from a national sample, as is the case with a standardized test. Basal reader tests have a definite place in the assessment program, since they can help teachers determine if students have actually learned the content of a specific unit. The teacher can then determine who needs specific remediation, who can be advanced at the usual pace, and who might be accelerated somewhat.

Since the basal reader test is generally given immediately following a unit of instruction and covers the basic objectives of that unit, such tests tend to be fairly easy for the students, a fact which makes for ease of test administration but inadequate assessment of the very high achievers. However, the tests do show up the problems of those children who have not achieved well in a particular unit.

Some basal readers have tests built into their workbooks. These tests are sometimes limited to a specific skill, and they can serve some very useful diagnostic purposes. The teacher will also find that analyzing a student's workbook is another way of getting good insights into the kinds of problems the student has. However, a word of caution is necessary about using workbook performance to diagnose reading problems. Because the difficulty of workbooks is often not carefully controlled, the teacher should determine if a particular exercise was especially difficult for all students before jumping to conclusions about one student's specific problem. There are two main determiners of student performance on a reading test—reading ability and item difficulty. Only standardized tests control and publish the difficulty of each individual item, the index of difficulty being the percentage of students who pass each item.

Criterion-referenced Tests

In recent years we have seen the advent of the so-called "criterion-referenced tests," also referred to as "objectives based" tests because they attempt to determine the extent to which the pupils have reached specific objectives or certain performance criteria in reading (Wrightstone, 1971). Behavioral objectives state the behaviors pupils should exhibit after they have reached a particular objective. See, for example, the behavioral objectives at the beginning of this chapter. The criterion-referenced test simply attempts to determine if each child or class has reached a given objective (Kibler, 1970). Part of this approach consists in stating exactly at what point a child has reached a certain level of behavior or a class has reached a certain level of proficiency in a given skill. One can say, for example, that a class has reached a certain objective if 80 percent of the class can perform a given task, this percentage being the criterion of achievement mastery. (These tests are also called "mastery tests.")

These tests are used to determine if a given child has reached a certain level of performance in a given skill. For this purpose, attempts are being made to specify each individual skill and subskill in every single subject. Needless to say, in order to determine whether students have learned these hundreds if not thousands of skills, we need tests which can determine the extent to which each objective has been achieved. The criterion-referenced test often determines whether a child has reached a certain criterion by means of a single item, sometimes a couple of items. From a measurement point of view, this is not a good practice, because children's performances on a task which they have just learned are not stable enough to warrant making decisions about their accomplishments on the basis of one or two test items. Also, it has been found in measurement studies that the percentage of children who can perform correctly on a given task will vary, depending on the particular words that are being used to measure the particular skill in question (Madden, 1972). The 80 percent criterion, then, can be reached either because children perform well on that task or because easy words have been chosen with which to test that task.

Maybe an example will help illustrate this point. For the author's own research, a national tryout was made of several thousand test items. One of the subtests was a decoding test containing an item designed to determine the knowledge of the /oi/ diphthong. One would expect sixth graders to know this, but that depends on one's criterion. These three test words were used, yielding the following percents passing: *joy*—90 percent, *toy*—86 percent, and *point*—78 percent. With an 80 percent criterion level, the students have passed if either of the first two items is used, but only the use of *joy* as a test word enables them to reach the 90 percent criterion level. On specific skills like this, there were variations within one grade of as much as 30 percent and even occasionally 40 percent, demonstrating time and again the need for many items to assess a specific educational attribute.

There is a further problem associated with the criterion-referenced test. It has often been assumed that children at a given grade level ought to perform at the 80 percent level of proficiency in those tasks which are being taught at that grade level. If one looks at the data on standardized achievement tests, however, ordinarily given in a "technical supplement" to an achievement test battery, one will readily find data which indicate that what is ordinarily taught for the first time at any given grade level is rarely learned by as many as 80 percent of the children in a given class. Hence, if the 80 percent criterion were really to be taken seriously, there would result a rather drastic downgrading of material in American schools, even to the point where, for example, the material now being taught in grade four would be taught in grade six or some point where one could reasonably expect the children to achieve at the 80 percent level. The 80 percent criterion is actually an arbitrarily chosen figure for which there appears to be no particular scientific basis. Some people use other percentages, but 80 percent appears to be the most common figure quoted in the professional literature.

The criterion-referenced test has been embraced as a replacement for the "norm-referenced" test. This is a meaningless dichotomy, since a normed test is simply a test for which norms have been obtained. There is no reason at all why we could not have a criterion-referenced, normed test; all we would have to do would be to standardize a criterion-referenced test. One often hears a teacher say, "Now that I have found out what my students can do, what does it mean? How do they compare with those in other schools and in other classes like mine?" Such questions indicate a continuing need for some kind of comparison information, some sort of norm.

A compromise position is being sought by both the *Iowa Test of Basic Skills* (1973 edition) and the 1973 *Stanford Achievement Test.* These tests are designed along the lines of criterion-referenced tests, but they have been normed. They both speak of criterion-referenced interpretation of norm-referenced tests.

The entire issue of criterion-referenced tests is very current and controversial; we will hear a great deal of discussion about it in the next few years. And, in all likelihood, these tests will find their place among the many different kinds of evaluation instruments at the teacher's disposal.

Informal Reading Inventory

The informal reading inventory is a versatile and useful instrument. It is a way of determining the child's ability to handle the instructional material being used with a class and is often used for a quick evaluation of children new to a school or class, or as a periodic re-evaluation of children's reading abilities. Ordinarily, the teacher will have the child read silently and orally from the instructional material, having picked selections of varying degrees of difficulty to determine the level at which the child functions for instructional purposes. The process has been worked out in great detail, and there are extensive references on how to make up informal inventories (Johnson and Kress, 1965), the different uses of the informal reading inventory, and so on, which are covered in detail in Chapter Twelve.

The informal reading inventory usually covers a wide range of skills, from rather easy material to rather difficult. But the main advantage is that the child is reading the actual material from which he is going to be instructed. This avoids the problem of determining the relationship between a separate test and the specific set of instructional material to be used with the student. Since this is an individual test, it also offers the teacher many opportunities to observe the student's lip movements, eye movements, problems with comprehension, handling of words he is unable to decode, and so on. The procedure is somewhat difficult to handle at first, but most teachers have found it very useful to learn. The observational techniques involved with the informal reading inventory are described in considerable detail in the section of this chapter called *The Individual Diagnostic Conference.*

Standardized Survey Tests

Of all the formal, printed reading tests taken in the United States, the standardized survey test is by far the most common. There are over thirty such tests on the market, although those most frequently used tend to be part of an achievement test battery. These batteries include such well-known tests as the *California Achievement Test, Comprehensive Test of*

Basic Skills, Iowa Tests of Basic Skills, Metropolitan Achievement Tests, SRA Achievement Series, and *Stanford Achievement Test.*

Survey tests usually assess two or three relatively broad reading objectives, such as comprehension, word study skills, and vocabulary. The tests are typically developed from lists of instructional objectives, which the test items sample. After the tests have been written, they are tried out to determine the adequacy of each individual item. The final test is then assembled and *standardized* (Burrill, 1972). This means that it is given to a sample of American children which is representative of the country as a whole. Information from this process is used in establishing national *norms,* making it possible to compare the scores of an individual child with children in general. For this reason, these tests are sometimes said to be "norm-referenced."

Standardized tests are generally used once a year as a periodic check on the educational growth of each child and of a class as a whole. The norms of different levels of the same test battery are comparable. One will, however, find some variation in norms from one test battery to another. This variation is the result of different samples being used for standardization, different content, and variations in the year of standardization. Within the last several decades we have seen considerable fluctuation in the scholastic achievement of American children, so that the date when a test was standardized is a crucial piece of information for those evaluating test results (Kelley, 1966; Stanford Research Report, 1974).

Since a major purpose of giving a survey test is to determine the reading level of each individual student, such a test must of necessity cover a rather wide span of reading ability, individual differences in reading within a single grade being rather extensive. It is important for teachers to realize that the survey test is probably the most difficult test children will take. Most of the students' test-taking experiences have been with easy tests, and to those who are used to obtaining perfect or near perfect scores, the survey test can be a frustrating experience. Hence the need for the teacher to explain the purposes of such a test. The 1973 *Stanford Achievement Test* alleviates this problem by providing practice tests.

One of the controversies surrounding survey tests has to do with their diagnostic usefulness. Since the items generally sample the main objectives of reading instruction, would it not be possible to look at each item to find out which skills a student has learned and which ones he has not? Most measurement specialists are of the opinion that more than one or two items are needed to make a diagnosis which can be used as a basis for remediation of an individual student (Mehrens and Lehmann, 1973). But the procedure can be used for an entire class; that is, one can find out which specific skills a class as a whole seems to have a great deal of difficulty with. Obviously, every bit of information we can gather about a student is useful in gaining a better understanding of his reading characteristics and instructional needs. But if we are going to place a lot of weight on reading test results for educational planning, we will have to use a test which evaluates all major aspects of reading thoroughly. Since such a test is used to "diagnose" reading instructional needs, it is referred to as a diagnostic reading test.

Standardized Diagnostic Reading Tests

The main purpose of the diagnostic test is to assess a student's strengths and weaknesses in the major aspects of reading, so the teacher may plan an instructional program for him. However, such tests do not diagnose the basic causes of reading handicaps in students. Instead they are a tool for the "diagnostic-prescriptive" approach to reading, described earlier in this chapter. They are used to diagnose each individual student's reading characteristics, and the results lead to a prescription for his main instructional needs.

There are two main types of diagnostic reading test: those which require individual administration and those which can be given to an entire class simultaneously. The individual test has the obvious disadvantage of being time consuming, requiring up to one and a half hours of testing time, but also has the advantage of not subjecting the very poor reader to extensive testing with items which are much too difficult for him. This problem is minimized if the group test emphasizes mainly those areas in which a student shows weaknesses, which also means that the test is relatively easy.

The two main individual diagnostic tests are the *Durell Analysis of Reading Difficulty* and the *Gates-McKillop Reading Diagnostic Tests.* These tests are so technically difficult to administer and interpret that they are used primarily by reading specialists who have been trained in their application.

There are about a dozen group diagnostic reading tests in use at present. Perhaps the best known are the *Diagnostic Reading Scales, Silent Reading Diagnostic Tests*, and *Stanford Diagnostic Reading Test.* These tests are relatively easy for a classroom teacher to administer, but their interpretations present some rather persistent problems. The teacher must have a good enough grasp of the hierarchy of reading skills to be able to assign instructional priority to the skills problems which have been diagnosed, and must know enough about these skills to be able to develop or to find in the existing instructional materials the kinds of exercises from which each student can benefit the most. Such a service is currently being offered in conjunction with the machine scoring of the *Stanford Diagnostic*

Reading Test; a computer analyzes the profile of each individual student, sending instructional suggestions for each student back to the teacher. This service is called Instructional Placement Report.

The norms of a standardized diagnostic reading test are used somewhat differently from those of a survey test. With the diagnostic test, the teacher makes inter-test comparisons to determine the student's relative strengths in the various subskills. Both kinds of tests can be used to measure growth, but for instructional grouping they are used quite differently. Survey tests are often used to group students by reading *level* (high, middle, low), while diagnostic tests are used for grouping according to *needs* (phonics, comprehension, speed, vocabulary). Because diagnostic tests are used for inter-test comparisons, the subtests must be long enough to provide a stable assessment of each skill (test reliability). This makes the tests rather lengthy—a problem that is perhaps the most commonly criticized aspect of diagnostic tests. Such tests require two to three hours for administration and, in cases where teachers hand score the tests for an entire class, several hours for scoring and interpretation.

Accountability Tests

The early 1970s saw the advent of the accountability trend in education (Lessinger, 1970). Because of the extreme importance of reading, much of the discussion of accountability centered around reading instruction. How well are the children reading? How much better do they read as the result of additional federal funding? How well do the children in this state read as compared to children in other parts of the country? These questions inevitably led to the initiation of large-scale testing programs, which are costly and time consuming since they require the administration of fairly lengthy tests to enormous numbers of children.

As we mentioned earlier, the accuracy of measurement for a single child (test reliability) is directly related to the number of items in a test. An accurate group *average,* however, can be obtained with fewer items. Since the politicians and school board members who wanted testing for accountability purposes were only interested in averages, they could get this information by sampling the test; that is, they could give only part of a test (item sampling). An equally stable average could be obtained by giving the entire test to only some of the students (student sampling). These two approaches could be combined by giving, say, every fifth student one-fifth of the test (matrix sampling), thus giving good group data on an entire school population, but requiring relatively little testing time. The main drawback, of course, is the lack of individual pupil data.

The late 1970s will see extensive experimentation with this approach, on both a district and a statewide basis. At present, somehow, many school districts feel that their schools must be at least average for the country as a whole. But it is in the nature of averaging that about half be above and about half below a national average. When children advance more than they have in the past, more than half will be above average on the old norms; but as soon as new norms are established, we will be back to a fifty-fifty situation again, because of the nature of norms (Mehrens and Lehmann, 1973).

Some Common Uses of Reading Tests

Any one of the tests described in the preceding section could be used for a great many purposes. But many of them would be inefficient for certain uses, and so the teacher is faced with the job of selecting the most suitable test for each of a variety of purposes. This section will describe six common situations for which teachers will need some type of test and make suggestions as to which type of test will do the job. The main idea is, of course, to get the most useful information with the least expenditure of time and money.

In many phases of education, one can see examples of false economy, and testing is no exception. One will find teachers making up their own tests because the school can't afford to spend five dollars to buy them. So the teacher spends one weekend, ten ditto masters, and two hundred sheets of ditto paper to develop his own. The writer once reviewed a "diagnostic notebook" which a teacher had made up; she wanted to show him the test and how she analyzed and applied the test results. When asked how much of her spare time she had used to develop this material, she said, "About one month." That service could have been purchased for twenty-five cents per student. There are some advantages in having teachers score tests if they do item analyses (Ahmann and Glock, 1971), but this also can now be done very quickly by computer. And, incidentally, there are some teachers' organizations which have policies against their members doing clerical tasks, including test scoring.

Organizing the Class into Reading Groups

The most usual scheme for grouping within the classroom is based on the reading levels of the students. Typically, there is a high, a middle, and a low group. Such grouping is global, and is ordinarily not based on any kind of diagnostic study. In its simplest form, this grouping requires that the students be ranked from highest to lowest, then split into groups. The teacher can make some readjustments later, based on observations.

The standardized survey test is often used for grouping purposes. If the students have taken such a test at the end of the preceding year, and if there is not a great deal of mobility in the school, the teacher can have a tentative grouping on the first day of school.

Another rather common approach is to give a pretest or placement test which is part of the basal reader, and place the students in the readers indicated by the test results. This approach can result in more than three reading groups.

Organizing the Class by Instructional Needs

This approach to grouping is used either for the basic reading instruction or as part of a supplementary reading program. Some schools will have one reading period in which the class is divided into the typical groups and another session in which the class is divided according to needs.

This approach requires that the teacher make a rather careful study of the reading needs of each student. The standardized, diagnostic group test is perhaps the most efficient way of doing this. It will cover the main skills which the students need to know to develop adequately in reading and will help teachers pick suitable instructional materials. One problem to be alert to is the possibility of such a test being too difficult. When teachers feel that something must be done to deal with the students individually, it is typically because many of them are having problems with reading. It is probably safer to select a test according to a student's approximate reading level than his grade level (Educational Testing Service, 1961a).

If the class is to be grouped according to need, a criterion-referenced test could also be used. This requires that the teacher have a good grasp of the skills needed at different grade levels because, after the testing, the teacher will need to make decisions as to which specific needs of each student have instructional priority.

The informal reading inventory can also be used in this situation, although it is more appropriate when instruction according to needs is to be entirely individualized. This technique requires a good deal of background and is rather time consuming.

Evaluating Individuals and Small Groups

Periodically, the need arises to evaluate one student, or maybe a small group. A transfer student might suddenly arrive, or the teacher may feel that one specific student belongs in a different group or needs to have his problems re-evaluated. Here the informal reading inventory, or what is described later in this chapter as the individual diagnostic conference, is an appropriate assessment technique. It will tell the teacher whether what has recently been taught has actually been learned, and also how to plan subsequent educational experiences for the student.

When the time comes to re-evaluate a small group, a criterion-referenced test, covering the specific skills that the teacher has been trying to teach, is appropriate. Some people also give such a test for the next skill to be learned, to determine the need for such instruction. The criterion-referenced test should be reviewed carefully to ascertain that it indeed does cover the skills it claims to cover, and to make certain that the number of items is sufficient for diagnosis.

Teacher-made tests of a great variety can be used for this type of evaluation. In many instances the teacher will have accumulated enough observations to make a formal test unnecessary.

Correcting Specific Difficulties

There are times when the teacher needs to study an individual child in more depth than usual—a child who is not responding to classroom instruction, for example. If the school has a school psychologist who is knowledgeable about reading diagnosis (many of them are not) or a reading consultant, a referral to one of these specialists would be appropriate. An individual diagnostic reading test would be helpful in planning remedial instruction, although many reading specialists are now administering group diagnostic reading tests to individuals. Such individual administration works well and it can be accomplished in much less time than group administration. This is a procedure which the classroom teacher can also carry out.

Criterion-referenced tests can also be used in this situation, if the teacher knows which one to use to determine the most pressing instructional needs of a student. But workbooks could probably be used with as much success. The teacher has the child do those pages designed to teach the specific skills the child seems deficient in. It will be necessary to go into the workbooks for the grades below the student's own grade level, but pages can be reproduced by means of a sheet of acetate and a transparency marker, which avoids marking up a workbook just for a few pages.

The biggest problem in this area is knowing which skills to analyze and test for. The most common mistake is not going low enough in the skills hierarchy. Just because a child does not know a specific skill does not necessarily mean that it should be taught to him at that time. A child who has difficulty with vowel digraphs, for example, should be tested on long and short vowels, then consonants, then auditory discrimination. Children must be able to hear sounds before they are taught to associate sounds with the letters representing them.

Every teacher will encounter children with very severe reading problems, intermediate grade pupils whose general reading level is two or more years below their grade placement. One can even find students in the secondary school whose reading level is below fourth grade level. These students need an intensive clinical diagnosis, followed by lengthy individualized remedial reading instruction. Their problems are typically of such a complex nature as to take more skills and time than the classroom teacher has. A referral through the school principal is recommended.

Assessing the Instructional Program

When it comes to trying to assess the effects of a reading program, the standardized survey test remains the main instrument. In fact, over half the schools with a testing program use the tests primarily to measure the results of schooling. They do this by administering a survey test in the month of May. Many have argued that this is not a particularly good time to test because such testing is almost completely retrospective; by May nothing can be done to rectify problems, and there is often so much shifting and moving among the pupil population during the summer that the May data might not be very useful the next year. Some test people have argued that testing should be done about two-thirds of the way through the year in order to leave some time available to remedy problems of the instructional program.

It has often been said that the survey test should not be used to evaluate teachers because of the great many variables which affect school learning. But teachers certainly ought to use test data, along with everything else they know about their students, to evaluate their own reading programs. Such evaluation is particularly critical when there has been a change in methods or materials and is most useful if the testing is done annually, giving the teacher some basis for comparing the results from one year with those from preceding years.

Recently, a great many schools have begun giving standardized diagnostic tests in the fall and often again in the spring. This gives much more information about the effects of a particular program on a great many skills, rather than just one or two. Other schools follow up fall diagnostic testing with a spring survey test. In either case, they are interested in educational growth. From a measurement point of view, this is a particularly difficult problem to deal with; a separate section of this chapter has been devoted to it.

Some schools use basal reader tests to evaluate the effects of their reading program. Such an assessment is all right for determining if the material in a specific reader has been learned. But most educators prefer to evaluate with a test that is completely separate from the instructional material. They want to know how their students, going through the particular reading program they have chosen, compare with other students throughout the country. In some experimental programs, the sponsoring agencies insist not only on the use of an independent test but also on a program evaluation made by an independent, outside organization. Such an assessment program is called an "external audit" (Lessinger, 1970).

School-wide Reading Assessment

In recent years we have seen a great increase in school-wide, system-wide, and even state-wide reading assessment programs. In fact, there is also a nationwide systematic testing program called National Assessment of Educational Progress (Womer, 1970). This latter program has developed its own tests. In practically all other large-scale programs, however, the standardized survey test is the common approach. Much of this testing has not proved to be of direct benefit to the students (NAEP, 1972); results have been used mostly for accountability purposes. Therefore a great deal of controversy has arisen over this type of testing program. It is fairly easy to determine how well a system is performing in comparison to the state or national norms, but how does one evaluate the results? There is no test made to tell administrators and politicians how children *ought* to perform. And what does it mean for a system to be below the national average in reading? It could be a result of poor teaching, but it is also possible that this district spends less time or money on reading and more on other activities. Improving reading usually means spending more time doing it. Since the length of the school day is fixed, that time must come from somewhere. Should it be taken from art, music, social studies, physical education?

In the wake of accountability testing we are seeing a new process coming to the fore, that of *priority setting*, which is an attempt to decide where a school should place its emphasis in effort and finances. For example, if tests reveal low average scores, school boards may decide that since reading achievement is their first priority, resources must be taken from other school efforts such as art, music, athletics, and other activities to pay for special reading programs. A danger with such an approach is that the school may overemphasize those educational objectives for which pupil achievement can be readily measured. Such assessment over time is an important aspect of a school testing program in order for all concerned to make intelligent decisions. The section in this chapter dealing with the assessment of growth should help develop an appreciation of some of the difficulties entailed by that process.

Large-scale testing programs tend to be time-consuming, expensive, and cumbersome. The accountability test is specifically designed for exactly this type of reading assessment. At the time of this writing, no such test is commercially available, but it is safe to assume that by the time this is being read accountability tests will be in use in some state-wide testing programs.

Administration and Scoring of Tests

The term *assessment* has been used here in a broad sense. When a teacher asks a student to read a paragraph out loud to determine if a book he has selected is of suitable difficulty, the teacher is engaged in assessment. It is informal, and is approached casually both by teacher and student. But these day-by-day observations are very useful in studying student behavior over a long period of time. They are also a way of communicating to the child that assessment is an integral part of education and that it is done to help the student advance; it is oriented toward the future. So it is important that the teacher spend some time explaining to each child how the results of all assessments, formal and informal, are being used to help him. The teacher should make some effort to communicate to the students that "this test will help us plan what you should learn next," rather than give the students the impression that "this is a test to find out how smart (or dumb) you are."

A few specific problems of testing will be discussed in this section. These pertain, in part, to all sorts of tests, but the main emphasis is on the standardized test. The reader who has never reviewed a standardized reading test would find it beneficial to do so before proceeding with this chapter.

Test Administration

Most of the questions teachers have about test administration are answered in the test manual. It is imperative that the teacher study this manual carefully before giving a test. This is particularly crucial for a standardized test, since part of the standardization process is the standardization of the directions. It is only when the standardized directions are being followed that the norms are applicable. Deviating from the directions to the point of allowing additional time for completion of a timed test or giving help with the answers invalidates a standardized test.

The teacher should try to maintain as normal a class situation as possible in order to ensure valid results. And he should keep in mind that the purpose of a reading test is to determine the students' reading ability, not their skill at following directions. It is appropriate, therefore, to explain the directions again to those who do not understand how to take the test. If they fail to turn the page, they can be told to do so, and if they mark the answer in a wrong way, this can be rectified while they take the test. It should not be counted as a mistake if it is not discovered until the test is scored. The teacher should keep extra pencils handy in case a student needs one.

When a particularly difficult test format is encountered, the directions should be followed rigidly. In all likelihood, the author has experimented with different sets of directions, and the test has been standardized with those directions which appear in the manual.

The biggest test administration problem arises when answer sheets are being used, but this problem will be discussed in the next section.

Test Scoring

It is exceedingly difficult to score a batch of tests with one hundred percent accuracy either by hand or by machine. The sources of error are numerous. For example, the erasures of one student might be heavier than the regular marks of another student, a fact which some test scoring machines adapt to by having a mechanism which first determines the density of each pupil's handwriting and then adjusts the machine to that particular marking. Some children will mark two options; some will actually write answers onto the answer sheet. The teacher can do several things to improve the validity of test scoring.

1. Inspect the answer document for obvious and gross problems such as writing out the answers, crossing out wrong answers rather than erasing them, and so on. Verify the marking of name grids, etc.
2. When hand scoring, score twice.
3. Score only one subtest at a time for the whole class.
4. When several forms of a test are available, make sure the form of the scoring key matches the form of the test.
5. Rescore all near perfect and near zero scores; rescore the tests of those students whose scores are grossly at variance with their classroom performances.

One comment should be made about the "chance score" concept (Fry, 1971). This score is obtained by dividing the number of items in a test by the number of options per item. A 36-item test of four-choice multiple choice items would give a "chance score" of 9; that is, if a student took the test by simply guessing rather than reading the items, he should obtain a score of 9 on the average. Most students do not behave this way. The typical pattern is a series of correct answers at the beginning of the test, then some items which are mixed correct and incorrect, then a few incorrect answers in a row, and then stop. But a few students guess throughout; they tend to have low achievement. One can easily discern their test-taking pattern after scoring their test booklets, because the items they answer correctly are scattered rather evenly throughout the test, their total scores being fairly close to the "chance score." Such tests should be considered invalid.

Record Keeping

The evaluation of a pupil's growth in reading is particularly meaningful when it is done on the basis of a large variety of data over time. The elementary school teacher has the necessary material for such an evaluation. But it is important that data collected over a period of time be gathered in such a way as to be maximally useful.

The simplest form of assessment is the informal observation. Its main strength is that it can be used to gather information regularly. After listening to a child read one day, the teacher might make a note that "John is still having trouble with final *e* making the preceding vowel long, as in *mad* and *made*." Such an observation should be verified from time to time to determine if the same problem occurs in spelling and other written work. The persistence of the problem over several months is cause for remedial action.

Student performance in workbooks and on worksheets is also a potent source of evaluative information, and it is useful to save worksheets periodically. Worksheets often provide the best evidence a teacher has that a child is making progress—proof that he can do something now which he couldn't do before. They can also show a teacher when a student has a unique problem which has persisted over a period of months despite rather specific teaching; such evidence suggests that the student might possibly have a specific learning disability.

Perhaps the single most useful piece of information in a cumulative folder is the results of a standardized reading test. In fact, many schools purchase pregummed labels with each child's test results in conjunction with the machine scoring of the tests. These are then pasted directly into the child's folder. It is important that the recording of test results be made in such a way as to facilitate interpretation. One such record is the "class analysis chart." This chart tabulates the scores of the students in one class in all subtests onto a single one-page chart.

Another approach to record keeping is the "bivariate distribution." This can now be purchased along with machine scoring in the cases where both an achievement test and an intelligence (scholastic aptitude) test have been administered. Such charts, worked out and printed by a computer, permit the comparison between aptitude and achievement in all achievement areas tested. The most recent development is the use of a measure of children's language competency as a basis on which to compare achievement (Madden, 1972). This approach is promising since it should assist educators in making the kind of diagnosis which will most readily lead to remedial instruction.

Test Norms

The "raw score" on a test, usually the number of items marked correctly, carries little meaning in and of itself. Converting it to a percentage is not very meaningful either, since the percentage score obtained on a test is as closely related to the difficulty of the questions as to how well the students perform. The fact that a student received a 90 percent on a test could mean either that he did quite well or that the test was very easy. The 90 percent could have been the highest or the lowest score in the class. The solution to making a score more meaningful has been to provide norms whereby the performance of each student is compared to the performance of a national sample of students.

There are two basic approaches to the development of test norms. First, we can have a kind of growth scale where the raw scores are compared to the norms for successive grade levels. A *grade norm* of 5.4 on such a scale means that a given child's raw score is the same as the average score for students who are in the fourth month of the fifth grade, regardless of the student's present grade level. There are some problems, however, with the grade norm, particularly with students at the extreme ends of the distribution of scores. If, for example, a test is designed primarily for second grade, it lacks meaning to say that a pupil has done as well as an average fifth grader because we don't know that the fifth-grade curriculum was sampled. A second type of norm avoids this difficulty by comparing the child's performance only to that of a national sample of students who are at the same grade level. For many years, this *percentile norm* was used extensively.

Percentiles are points in a distribution of raw scores. At or below each point, one will find the percent of students indicated by the given percentile. For example, if Sally had sixteen items correct on a test and the percentile table showed this to have a percentile rank of 45, we would know that 45 percent of American children score 16 or less, while the remaining 55 percent would score 16 or higher. (Those scoring 16 are usually divided in half.) In addition to national norms, some tests have norms for a given state or for a local school district, all generally referred to as *local norms*.

As was the case with grade norms, percentile norms were used because they seemed easy to interpret. But these norms were deceptive and cumbersome in some ways. Because children tend to be about average, the scores would pile up in the middle and so would the percentiles. Percentiles of 45 and 55 were quite close together on the distribution, while 5 and 15 were separated by quite a margin. The farther from the mean (average) we went, the farther apart were the percentile points. The scale is divided into one hundred unequal percentile units, meaning that inter-test comparisons are very difficult to make and scores cannot be averaged (Anastasi, 1968). To solve this problem, several scales have been devised that are relative to the mean but in equal units of deviation from the mean. They are based on the *standard deviation,* a commonly used unit of variability, and are generally referred to as *standard scores.* The most common standard score in use with reading tests is a relatively brief, nine-point scale called stanines, an abbreviation of "standard nine."

The relationship between stanines and percentiles is shown in Table 6. Remember that we are comparing the test performance of one child with that of all children enrolled at the same grade level, without regard for any other variable such as location of school, type of school, or method of reading instruction used. Ordinarily, special norms for such groups as "inner-city" school children or bilingual students are not available. But special editions of tests are sometimes available, such as tests which have been transliterated into the initial teaching alphabet (i.t.a.) or the braille and large print editions of the *Stanford Achievement Test* available from the American Printing House for the Blind. In such cases, the regular norms are usually applied.

Norms have sometimes been criticized for not telling exactly how well a child reads; they merely tell how his reading scores compare with those of other children. The criterion-referenced tests were designed to meet this criticism. But they, in turn, are being criticized for not relating reading performance to some sort of standard or norm (Mehrens and Lehmann, 1973).

The question of standards of performance is a difficult one. While norms tell us how well a child is doing, standards specify how well he ought to be doing. Whether it is beneficial to set standards is still an unresolved issue among American educators. It is closely related to the issue of *expectancy,* which has often been determined by means of IQ tests and, more recently, by a measure of language competency. This problem is discussed in a later section of this chapter.

Table 6   The Relationship between Stanines and Percentiles

Stanines	Percentiles	Percent per stanine	
9	97–99	Highest 4%	
8	90–96	Next highest 7%	Above average 23%
7	78–89	Next 12%	
6	61–77	Above middle 17%	
5	41–60	Middle 20%	Average 54%
4	24–40	Below middle 17%	
3	12–23	Next 12%	
2	5–11	Next lowest 7%	Below average 23%
1	1–4	Lowest 4%	

How to Read a Test Manual

The typical standardized reading test consists of the test itself, the manual, and auxiliaries such as scoring keys, charts, and lists for recording scores. The test manual will cover the details of test administration, interpretation, and a variety of technical information. When the reading test is part of an achievement test battery, there might be separate manuals for administration and interpretation, as well as a "technical supplement." These manuals are virtual gold mines of factual information often overlooked by educators. They answer most questions commonly asked about tests. The main problem appears to be that most educators have a great deal of difficulty reading and interpreting the manuals, particularly the more technical ones. In this section, therefore, we will provide some background for understanding these manuals, including some practical suggestions as to how to interpret the information they ordinarily contain.

Test and Item Format

The degree of difficulty a student has with a test is influenced by the particular item format the test uses. This is especially true in the primary grades. Some test publishers provide a practice booklet in order to familiarize the students with the particular item formats used. In achievement test batteries, one will sometimes find a change in item format from one subtest to the next, which slows down the testing and is potentially confusing to the student.

Generally speaking, the more a student has to switch around in order to respond to a test, the more difficulty he will have. The biggest contributor to low test scores resulting from the test format is the separate answer sheet. Below grade four, most students have some difficulty with answer sheets; but even in grades four, five, and six the poor readers have difficulty with some answer sheets (Clark, 1968). Then why are answer sheets used if they tend to lower some students' scores? There are two main reasons: economy and scorability. The use of answer sheets makes it possible to reuse the test booklet and, since answer sheets are generally single sheets of paper while the test booklets may have eight to thirty-two pages, the use of answer sheets can reduce the cost of a testing program by as much as 50 percent. Also, even if a test is hand scored, it is much easier to score a single-page answer sheet than a test booklet. And answer sheets can be filed much more readily. Further, all answer sheets available for standardized reading tests can be scored by a test scoring machine; many school districts even have their own machines.

Around 1970 we had a new development in test scoring which greatly benefits those students who have difficulty with an answer sheet. It is called the machine-scorable test booklet. There is a machine that can score the test booklet itself by cutting off the spine of the booklet and then running each page through an optical scanner. If this scoring system is tied in to a computer, the computer can tabulate data, calculate group statistics, plot charts, interpret the data to the teacher, and even send back sets of instructional suggestions for each student in the class. The computer performs this analysis with such incredible speed as to make the entire process economically feasible.

Test Validity

The most important question to ask oneself when evaluating a reading test is, "Does this test measure what is being taught as reading?" Or, in test terminology, "Is this a valid test?" One must determine what instructional objectives the test covers and if these objectives coincide with the major objectives of the reading program used with the students. This can be done by reviewing the test's objectives or by a direct analysis of the test items.

There are also some statistical ways of determining the validity of a reading test; one of these is to correlate it with other reading tests. Before going into that problem, we will briefly discuss the concept of correlation. The *correlation coefficient* is a number which indicates the degree of relationship between two variables. It can range from -1.00 to $+1.00$. Zero correlation indicates that two variables have no relationship whatever. The farther from zero, the higher the correlation. The sign shows the direction of the correlation. A negative number reveals a negative correlation; that is, a high score on one variable tends to be associated with a low score on the other. For example, the score on a reading test and the number of errors on a spelling test might correlate $-.70$. But if the spelling test were scored by counting the number of words spelled correctly, the correlation would be $+.70$. The two coefficients are of the same magnitude, but in different directions. Most correlation coefficients found in test manuals are positive. One way of deciding on the significance of a correlation coefficient is to make a rough estimate of what percentage the two variables have in common. This is done by simply squaring the coefficient. For example, a correlation of .70 would give $.70 \times .70 = .49$, or about 50 percent commonality between two variables. It would be considered a fairly substantial relationship (Ahmann and Glock, 1971).

Two tests of reading comprehension should correlate on the order of about .80. If the correlation is substantially less than that, one might suspect that the two tests measure somewhat different aspects of reading. When looking at the intercorrelations among several subtests, a good rule of thumb is to assume that intercorrelations among tests of different aspects of reading should be within the .40 to .70 range, showing that they do measure different aspects of reading but are still positively correlated.

The intercorrelations among the subtests of the *Stanford Diagnostic Reading Test, Level I,* are given for grade three in Table 7. The table shows, for example, that Reading Comprehension correlates .64 with Vocabulary (second number in the top line in the matrix). But it is interesting to note that the correlation between Reading Comprehension and several decoding skills tends to be higher than the correlation with Vocabulary. The scores on the phonics test called Sound Discrimination, for example, tend to correlate higher with other phonics tests than with Vocabulary, which is as it should be. The opposite situation would have made us a bit suspicious of the Sound Discrimination test. Now, what is Auditory Discrimination correlated with? It seems to have moderate correlations with all the other subtests, none of them very high, leading us to believe that this is a characteristic which is not covered in other subtests. Test 5, however, shows rather substantial correlations with tests 6 and 7 and, since all of these relate to phonics, omitting test 5 would do the least harm in arriving at a valid diagnosis.

Test Reliability

If a teacher were to give the same test twice, he or she would want some assurance of getting rather consistent results. This consistency is referred

Table 7   Intercorrelations among SDRT Subtests for Grade 3

Subtest	1	2	3	4	5	6	7
1. Reading Comprehension	(.95)	.64	.65	.63	.72	.71	.68
2. Vocabulary		(.88)	.59	.30	.45	.50	.54
3. Auditory Discrimination			(.96)	.52	.61	.60	.61
4. Syllabication				(.79)	.61	.63	.58
5. Beginning and Ending Sounds					(.87)	.81	.78
6. Blending						(.94)	.76
7. Sound Discrimination							(.94)

Source: *Manual for Administering and Interpreting Stanford Diagnostic Reading Test, Level I.* Reprinted with permission of Harcourt Brace Jovanovich, Inc.

to as *reliability* and can be determined by actually administering the same test twice. The correlation coefficient between these two sets of scores is referred to as the *reliability coefficient*. Examples of these are found in Table 7, the coefficients appearing in parentheses. As a general rule, reliability coefficients of .90 or better are considered highly adequate. If they are less than .85, one should assume that the scores obtained on that subtest are subject to more chance fluctuation than the rest (Madden, 1972). For example, among the subtests shown in Table 7, one would have less faith in the precision of the Syllabication test than the others, its reliability being .79.

These generalizations about reliability pertain only to the scores of individual students. Group averages will show much higher reliability than individual scores, since individual chance fluctuations tend to wash out in the means. Also, it should be understood that the single most important factor in reliability is the number of items in a test. The longer the test, the more reliable (Anastasi, 1968). Note that the Syllabication test mentioned above is the shortest of all the subtests listed, having only twenty items. The problem of reliability is one of the main reasons why many test experts reject the idea of measuring the achievement of specific objectives with one or two criterion-referenced test items.

When studying a test manual, one should also make sure that the reliability coefficients reported were obtained for a single grade level. Pooling the data for several grade levels will yield inflated values. In most manuals, one will also find, next to the reliability coefficients, a statistic called the *standard error of measurement*. This is a measure of the degree of precision of each test; it provides an exact basis for evaluating changes in test scores. It tells us something about the magnitude of such chance fluctuations (Mehrens and Lehmann, 1973). As an example from everyday life we can use the reading of a thermometer. Many outdoor thermometers lack precision, so if one were to say that it is 30.5° outside, one's certainty would be quite low, since there are no marks between 30 and 32, and those two numbers are quite close together on the scale. However, the certainty with which one could say that it is between 30 and 32° outside would be much greater than for 30.5°. And one could state with even greater confidence that the temperature is between 28 and 34 degrees. In educational testing we have actually gone one step further and specified in probabilistic terms the degree of precision of a test score or the extent to which a score is subject to chance fluctuations from one day to the next. Two examples from educational testing are shown in Table 8. First, in grade five, the standard error of measurement in grade scores is 0.5. The table shows the magnitude of the chance fluctuations as we encompass, successively, one, two, and three standard errors of measurement on each side of the mean. As we increase the certainty (probability) of our statements, the range increases considerably. The test upon which this is based had a reliability of .93. The second example, shown in the last three lines in Table 8, pertains to an IQ test with a reliability of .90, a fairly typical situation.

Table 8   Interpretation of Standard Error of Measurement

If standard error of measurement is	the probability is about	that a score of	could fluctuate by chance from
.4 years	68%	grade 5.5	5.1 to 5.9
.4 years	95%	grade 5.5	4.7 to 6.3
.4 years	99%	grade 5.5	4.3 to 6.7
5 points	68%	IQ 90	85 to 95
5 points	95%	IQ 90	80 to 100
5 points	99%	IQ 90	75 to 105

Reliability is certainly an important concept in interpreting individual scores and changes in such scores, but, again, these are individual data. If we look at the mean for a typical class, the error of measurement is reduced to about half of that shown in Table 8. If a student was tested in the middle of grade five (5.5) and again in the middle of grade six (6.5), and in that year had "grown" only 0.2 year, one could easily ascribe this change to chance.

The same holds if he had "regressed" 0.2 year in that time, since such minor fluctuation could easily occur from one day to the next. But suppose he had gained 1.0 year in this time. The probabilities that this has occurred by chance are so small that it could safely be ascribed to "growth." The probability of a mean changing 1.0 year because of pure chance fluctuations is extremely remote.

It is the responsibility of those who use tests to understand that test scores are subject to chance fluctuation, and that of the test author to report in the manual the exact magnitude of this fluctuation.

Norm Tables

Test manuals contain norm tables which are used to convert one kind of score to another; for example, they permit conversion from raw scores to scaled scores to percentiles to stanines. But they also contain a wealth of very interesting and useful information. For example, a large school system decided that a certain standard of reading proficiency should be required for their entering (grade ten) high school students. One member of the board of education, having heard something about eighth grade proficiency being a kind of minimum level of "functional literacy," proposed that students scoring below 8.0 grade score on a standardized reading test should enroll in a course called "Remedial English." This became a regulation; in each high school they set up such a class and the students were tested at the end of grade nine. The selection was to take place during the summer so that the students could be enrolled in Remedial English upon entering the tenth grade.

A look at the table of norms for the test they were using reveals that a grade score of 8.0 in reading has a percentile equivalent of 32 at 9.9; that is, in a national sample, about 32 percent of the population will, at the end of grade nine, score 8.0 or lower. Since nobody had taken a look at these tables beforehand, one can well imagine the amazement of the school administrators when they discovered that, as one of them put it, "about one-third of the students entering high school lack functional literacy." The fact of the matter was that the students were doing about average.

Table 9 is a reproduction of the norm table for the 1964 *Stanford Achievement Test*, Intermediate II Battery, for the end of grade six.[1] One will see that the fiftieth percentile for all subtests coincided with a grade score of 6.9 for all subtests, by definition. If we look at the grade scores under the reading test called "Paragraph Meaning," we can make a number of interesting observations. Many who write about reading problems say

[1] The 1964 S.A.T. table was used because it provided a direct comparison between grade scores and percentile ranks, a procedure now rarely used.

Table 9   Stanines and Selected Percentile Ranks Corresponding to Grade Scores

End of Grade 6 (May-June)

Sta-nine	%ile Rank	Word Mean.	Para. Mean.	Spell.	Lang.	Arith. Comp.	Arith. Concepts	Arith. Appl.	Social Studies	Science	%ile Rank	Sta-nine
9	99	121	120	122	118	117	118	119	121	121	99	9
	98	115	117	118	115	112		115	119	116	98	
	96	105	112	115	113	105	111	111	114	113	96	
8	94	100	109	112	110	100	103	106	112	110	94	8
	92	96	106	108	107				110	107	92	
	90	93	104	105	105	96	95	101	107	104	90	
	89				104						89	
7	88	90	100	102	102	91	88		104	100	88	7
	86			97	100			96	100		86	
	84	88	96	92	98	86	85			96	84	
	82		92	88	97			91	96		82	
	80	85	87		95	84	82		90	92	80	
	78			85	93			86			78	
	77	83	84		90				86	88	77	
6	76			82	88	82	80				76	6
	74	80	82		86			83	83	85	74	
	72			80	84		78				72	
	70	78	80	78	82	79		80	81	81	70	
	68		78		80				79		68	
	66	76		76	79		76			78	66	
	64		77		77	77		77	77		64	
	62	75	75	75	76				76	75	62	
	60			73	75	74	73	74	74		60	
5	58	73	73		74					72	58	5
	56		72	71	73	71	70		72		56	
	54	71			72			71	70		54	
	52			70	70	71					52	
	50	69	69	69	69	69	69	69	69	69	50	
	48	67	67	68	67	68	68	68	68	67	48	
	46			67	66	66		66	66		46	
	44	66	66	66	65		66		65	66	44	
	42		65		64	65		65	64		42	
	40	64	64	64	63		65			64	40	
4	38		62	63	62	63		63	63	62	38	4
	36	62			61				62		36	
	34		61	62	60	62	63	61	61	60	34	
	32	60	60	60	59					58	32	
	30	59	59	59	58	60	61	59	60		30	
	28		57		56				59	57	28	
	26	57	56	57	55	59	59	57	58	56	26	
	24		54	56	54				56	54	24	
	23	56			53	58	56	56			23	
3	22		53	54	52				55	52	22	3
	20	54	52	53	51	56		54	54		20	
	18	52	50	51	49		54		53	50	18	
	16		49		48	54		51	52	49	16	
	14	51	48	50	46		52	49	51	47	14	
	12	49	47	48	44	52			50	46	12	
	11	47	46	47	43		49	46	49	44	11	
2	10	46	44	45	42	50			48	43	10	2
	8	44	43	44	39	48	46	44	46	42	8	
	6	42	41	41	37	46	43	42	44	41	6	
	4	39	38	40	34	44	40	38	42	38	4	
1	2	36	32	36	30	38	36	36	39	35	2	1
	1	33	29	33	28	36	31	34	36	33	1	

Source: Adapted from Truman L. Kelley, et al., *Directions for Administering Stanford Achievement Test, Intermediate II Battery.* New York: Harcourt, Brace and World, 1964, p. 22.

that those students who score a year or more below grade level are having reading difficulties. In this case, that would mean a grade score of 5.9. The table reveals that 30 percent of a normal population will qualify. If we use a year and a half as our criterion, taking us down to 5.4, we find that about one-fourth of the population will score that low.

What is the range of reading scores among sixth graders in a typical school district? The table shows that the range of individual differences in such a group would be eight to nine grades, from the beginning of third to about the beginning of twelfth grade. Admittedly, the scores at the extremes of the distribution are difficult to interpret, but there seems little doubt that the sixth grade teacher is going to have to deal with rather extreme variations in reading. Actually, the typical elementary teacher handles these variations quite well in reading, but less well in the other subjects. One need not be very persuasive to convince teachers of the need for individualization in all subject areas after they have studied the data in Table 9 or, better yet, the data from their own classrooms.

The Individual Diagnostic Conference

The more a teacher knows about the procedures for teaching reading at many levels and how to pick appropriate instructional techniques and materials, the less he needs to rely on periodic evaluation with highly detailed, standardized reading tests. A perceptive teacher can get a great deal of insight into a child's reading characteristics through an individual diagnostic conference. A great many techniques can be applied in this situation; some of them, however, require extensive practice.

There are several observational systems and checklists available commercially which are generally designed to help teachers cover all major skills. The *Barbe Reading Skills Check List* (Barbe, 1961) contains the main objectives for grades one through six, which teachers can check off as they listen to children read and recall what was read. A much more formal and systematic analysis of children's oral reading characteristics is the *Reading Miscue Inventory* (Goodman and Burke, 1972); it is a very complex observational system, although it is not norm referenced.

The individual diagnostic conference to be described here is loosely structured and is considered an adjunct to other assessment techniques. Its purpose is the analysis of an individual child's reading characteristics. The following paragraphs describe some techniques for observing the major aspects of reading. The material used is ordinarily the book which is being used for reading instruction, or it could be a book the student has selected to read on his own. The teacher may have worked out a form, dittoed, which is filled out and filed in each child's folder, or may simply take notes, as with the individual reading inventory. The former procedure will ensure more systematic coverage, of course. The teacher can have the child read silently, then orally. Under both circumstances, the teacher can time the child to determine silent and oral reading speeds.

The Student's Behavior While Reading

During the silent reading part of the diagnostic conference, the teacher should sit across from the child. It is helpful to have the student hold up the book so that his eyes can be observed across the top.

Start timing the child when he starts to read silently. At the outset, it is important to observe the student's eyes (Wilson, 1971). When he first looks at the page, are both eyes together? If not, or if one leads, the other following perceptibly behind, the student might have eye coordination problems. Make note of characteristics such as lip movements, finger-pointing, whispering, and so on. If the reading material is fairly simple for him, there should be little such extraneous behavior; but nearly all children exhibit some of these behaviors when the material is difficult or if they are under stress.

It takes a lot of practice to be able to count eye movements, but some problems can be observed readily. Of particular interest is the student's eye behavior when he is unable to decode a specific word. Some will keep looking at the same word, trying to "sound it out," often with accompanying sound effects. Others will look around for picture clues. Those who start the sentence over again, or who try to read farther, are generally searching for context clues.

Two kinds of fingerpointing can be observed: the student may follow along as he reads, or he may use his finger as a line holder to make sure that his eyes will hit the next line after the return sweep from the previous one. These are often found in pupils in the primary grades; if this occurs in the intermediate grades, it might indicate problems of eye coordination. Ordinarily, children who have persisted with fingerpointing will discontinue it by the end of third grade; the same holds true for whispering. Lip movements might persist a bit longer.

Comprehension

After a student has read silently for three to five minutes, he should be stopped when there is a natural break. At this point, the teacher should ask a few questions to determine the child's comprehension of what was read. It is important that this questioning go beyond the very obvious and superficially literal content of the material. (See Chapter Eleven by Guszak for a detailed discussion of teacher questioning techniques.) When the child cannot answer a question, the teacher might ask him to find the answer in the book. It is useful to find out what it was he did not understand. Questions of inference should be asked for all pupils, although for younger pupils they should be fairly simple.

The teacher must be sure to ask comprehension questions that the student cannot answer unless he has read the story. It is necessary, therefore, that the teacher be well acquainted with what the child has been reading and see to it that questioning goes beyond a superficial "What was this story about?"

Vocabulary

Lack of comprehension is sometimes caused by vocabulary problems, of which there are several kinds. First, the child might not have previously encountered a specific word like *beneficial, inflammable,* or *perquisite.* Many teachers limit their vocabulary instruction to this level. But children also have problems understanding the multiple meanings of words. To test for this, the teacher might point to a word in the story just read and ask what meaning of the word was used in that particular sentence.

A third type of vocabulary problem to consider is the ability to deduce the meaning from context. When a student does not know the meaning of a word, the teacher should ask, "What do you think it means?" Such questioning will encourage the use of context. A related set of skills pertains to the meanings of affixes and root words. The meaning of a word can often be deduced from a combination of context and knowledge of word parts. For example, if you did not know the word *affixes,* but you did know the meaning of the prefix *a-,* the root *fix,* and the suffix *-es,* you would probably be able to figure the word out.

This illustrates another aspect of vocabulary teaching—the morphemic unit. The student should know from the final *-s* or *-es* that the word *affixes* might be either a plural or the present tense of a verb. When testing for vocabulary, it is useful to determine if the student understands common morphemes such as *-er* (a person who), *-ed* (past tense), *-less* (without), and so on.

Bright students are often interested in words, their derivations, and their origins. With the less able student, one should probably be quite specific when diagnosing and remedying deficiencies in vocabulary.

Decoding

We now come to the oral reading phase of the individual diagnostic conference, where problems of decoding can most easily be diagnosed. When the student encounters an unknown word, exactly what does he do? What he should be doing depends on his level of reading ability; primary pupils may try letter-by-letter sounding, while intermediate students will often try syllabication first. The decoding process has been analyzed in many ways, none of which is completely satisfactory because of the interaction of several simultaneous processes. One analysis says that a student must go through three processes. First, the word must be divided visually into units such as letters, digraphs, and syllables. Second, each unit must be pronounced. Third, these pronunciations must be blended together.

When a child is reading orally, the teacher has many opportunities to observe the kinds of errors he makes, but it takes quite a bit of experience to translate this information into remedial action. A review of the scope and sequence chart found in most teacher's editions of basal readers will help in determining the hierarchy of the phonics skills taught.

The oral reading situation is also a good place to determine the student's ability to transfer recently taught skills to his independent reading. This will also give the teacher feedback as to the effectiveness with which the skills were taught.

Asking the student comprehension questions after his oral reading will sometimes reveal rather limited understanding of what was read. This is particularly true when the student has a tendency to become self-conscious or nervous in an oral reading situation. If this is the case, it is usually the attitude rather than reading skills which requires remediation.

Reading Rate and Efficiency

The student should be timed during both the silent and oral reading. The easiest way to do this is to note how far he has read at the exact minute you stop him; that is, if he is close to finishing after four minutes, note the exact word he is reading at that time and divide the number of words read by four. The longer the student reads, the more reliable this rate measure will be. The same procedure should be followed with both the silent and oral reading. This will give a comparison between the two.

Typically, the two rates coincide until about the end of third grade, at which time the rate is close to 140 words per minute. The oral reading rate might level off at 130 words per minute and increase little from then on. But the silent reading rate will increase about fifteen words per minute each year up to junior high school. From then on, the increase is about ten words per year; the average high school senior is reading about 250 words per minute (Taylor, 1963).

Many people feel that a measure of reading rate is not much help in diagnosing the reading of primary graders. But reading rate becomes a significant bit of information if viewed not just as a measure of speed but as a measure of *decoding efficiency.* Some children can decode practically every book put in front of them, but at a rate so slow as to make the reading deficient. By the end of second grade, the typical pupil will read about two words per second. Less than one word per second is considered inefficient. Clinical experience with children with extreme reading disabilities has also revealed that the most stubborn cases were the word-by-word readers. These children, when confronted with repetitions of the same word on the same line of print, would read it the second or even the third time just as slowly as the first. Extremely laborious reading, even if mostly correct, is generally symptomatic of a reading deficiency.

The Assessment of Reading Readiness

The assessment of a child at the pre-reading level presents certain unique problems, many of which have been discussed in the earlier chapter on reading readiness. This chapter will concern itself only with the specific problem of readiness testing and not with the assessment of the many physical, social, and other maturational characteristics relating to readiness.

At one time, reading readiness was thought of as a rather specific stage of development, a point in a child's life when he was ready to be taught to read. Some researchers in the 1930s tried to determine that crucial moment, and some school administrators worked out schedules showing when each child would reach a certain mental age as determined by an intelligence test. Later on, readiness testing was used to predict success in beginning reading instruction; one could call it prognostic testing. And it was found that both intelligence tests and reading readiness tests were good tests for predicting school success of a group of children, although individual prediction was subject to some fluctuation (Mehrens and Lehmann, 1973).

By the early 1970s, however, teachers became increasingly impatient with the prognostic approach. As teachers, they wanted to know what to do. If a child made a low score on a readiness test, how could they negate the prediction of low achievement? In other words, the teachers wanted a diagnostic approach to readiness testing. But what should be diagnosed? Scholastic aptitude? Or some of the skills and abilities which are necessary for learning to read? Both approaches are currently in use and will be discussed in some detail.

Scholastic Aptitude

The main purpose of most intelligence tests is to determine the student's probability of success in school. This is particularly important at the time of school entry, since we do not have any past scholastic records with which we can predict later success. Some schools, therefore, use group intelligence tests in the first grade for purposes of prognostication. There are many such tests on the market; two of the more commonly used are the *Cognitive Abilities Test* and the *Otis-Lennon Mental Ability Test,* group intelligence tests which contain several batteries extending from kindergarten through high school. Such tests are generally administered to small groups and depend rather heavily upon the comprehension of language, a factor which is a particularly good predictor of success in school.

Attempts have also been made to assess the particular cognitive abilities which are required for success in school. A good example of a test for this purpose is the *Analysis of Learning Potential,* which yields prognostic scores for both reading and arithmetic.

Most aptitude testing in kindergarten and first grade is done with the readiness tests, since they tend to show a higher correlation with later reading ability than do the more general intelligence tests. The readiness tests include the measurement of such abilities as matching symbols and other visual discrimination skills, auditory discrimination, aural comprehension, letter recognition, and other reading-related abilities. A very commonly used readiness test is the *Metropolitan Readiness Test.*

The prognostic approach to readiness testing has been criticized by teachers who feel that the results do not tell them what to do for the students. Some first grade teachers, however, use the results of prognostic tests to group the children by level, providing prolonged readiness instruction for the low scorers, a normal period of readiness instruction for those with about average scores, and little if any such instruction for the high scorers. Such differentiated instruction from the beginning has been shown to be beneficial to the children at all levels of reading readiness (Spache, 1966).

Readiness Diagnosis

The diagnostic approach to readiness instruction is similar to the behavioral objectives approach in that the teacher first lists all those abilities which are necessary for learning to read, then determines (with a diagnostic readiness test) if each student has those skills and abilities to a sufficient degree, and finally teaches those skills which each student is lacking by means of an individualized readiness program. It is an orderly scheme which obviously makes a lot of sense. It has only one drawback: we don't know exactly all of the skills and abilities which are prerequisites for learning to read, even though the major factors have been studied extensively (Harris, 1970).

Some research and a great deal of rhetoric can be found on this topic, the two often being contradictory. For example, learning to read obviously requires visual acuity; certainly the child must be able to see the print. However, research with visually handicapped children has shown that children with equal degrees of measured visual handicap differ greatly in their ability to utilize their vision (Jones, 1961); they range from function-ally sighted to functionally blind. There are even some "legally blind" children, whose visual acuity is so limited as to be unmeasurable with a Snellen Chart, who can actually read large print. Since many "legally blind" children can learn to read from basal readers, visual acuity is probably grossly overrated as a problem in learning to read (Benton, 1970).

Visual acuity is a relatively simple concept, and certainly an attribute we can all agree on as being a prerequisite to learning to read. A great many others—such as attention, auditory discrimination, and language develop-ment—also enter into the act of learning to read. It seems safe to conclude, therefore, that a comprehensive diagnostic readiness test is a long time in the future. Some tests are approaching this type of diagnosis, but on a very limited scale. Examples of such tests are the *Murphy-Durrell Reading Readiness Analysis* and the *Stanford Early School Achievement Test.*

Even if we could test for all of the prerequisite abilities, we would still not have a complete picture. We must also take into account the child's ability to compensate for his deficiencies and the degree to which his motivation will override some of his poorly developed skills. Many experts feel that, while the teacher should employ many techniques, it is just as important that he approach the job of diagnosis with a flexible and imaginative attitude.

Teacher Evaluation of Readiness

Several studies of readiness tests have shown that teacher prognostication correlates as highly with later reading ability as do scores on readiness tests (Karlin, 1971). The data have often been cited as evidence that teachers' judgment is really quite good. They can also be used as evidence in favor of the tests, however, since the teacher needs a couple of months of experience with the children to make such a prediction, and the test can do it in about one hour of testing time. But, as has been pointed out earlier in this chapter, the teacher is in the unique position of being able to use those testing techniques we have described, observe how the students respond to the instruction designed for them, alter this instruction as the need arises, diagnose again, and so forth. In fact, this possibility is perhaps the strongest argument we have in favor of the self-contained classroom.

The Assessment of Growth

Teachers have always been interested in growth and improvement; in a way, that is what education is all about. But in the past most educators have been satisfied when they thought a student was improving. Assessment of the student's improvement was based on teacher judgment not only of how much each student had improved, but also of how much improvement each student was capable of making. Along with the accountability trend have come demands for more quantitative measures of growth. Statisticians are pointing out some of the difficulties of measuring growth, giving the general impression that the measurement of growth might not be particularly reliable or valid as a single measure of status (Wrightstone, 1971). For example, it was pointed out earlier that tests are not perfectly reliable. When we then calculate the difference between two not perfectly reliable measures, the difference (growth) has lower reliability than either of the two individual test scores. But these are problems beyond the scope of this chapter. What will be discussed here are some of the very specific curriculum problems relating to the assessment of growth in reading. More detailed discussions of these measurement issues can be found in Farr (1970).

The Reading Growth Curve

Children grow at different rates with regard to a great many variables. If we plot a specific measurement against the child's age, we get his growth curve. Such growth curves have been plotted for height, weight, strength of grip, head circumference, and so on. When we plot averages, say every six months, for a large, randomly chosen group of children, we get a norm, or normal growth curve. These normal growth curves often show that growth is not even; for example, in most areas we often find the familiar "adolescent growth spurt." Plotting such curves is a fairly easy task when dealing with inches and pounds, but how can it be accomplished in reading?

The unit of measurement most commonly used to determine growth in reading is the reading grade equivalent norm. This norm has been worked out as part of the standardization process. The average score for, say, the end of grade four is set equal to 4.9, the same for grade five. The in-between points are interpolated, assuming this growth to be linear. It is also assumed that the growth from 3.9 to 4.9 is the same as from 4.9 to 5.9. The whole scale is based on the assumption that growth in reading is linear. Further, the scale implies that children grow on the average 1.0 units per year—that is, for example, that growth from 2.9 to 3.9 is the same as from 10.9 to 11.9. The scale also has the advantage of being decimalized and easy to handle statistically.

Many reading experts believe, however, that this assumption of a linear growth curve is wrong, that there is a levelling off in the secondary school. In fact, there are many variables which make the plotting of a reading growth curve difficult. Different aspects of reading develop differently; there is disagreement as to which characteristics to include on a growth curve; and we have not had the proper scale with which to measure reading in terms of units which represent equal steps in "functional reading ability." Various statisticians have attempted, however, to develop a continuous scale which measures achievement in approximately equal units. Such a procedure was applied to the 1973 *Stanford Achievement Test* (Madden, 1972). This scaled score, as it is called, can be used to measure growth and also to plot a reading growth curve. The author has done so for reading comprehension by consulting the various *Norms Booklets* for this test, plotting the mean grade level against the mean scaled score obtained by pupils of various grades. The result is shown in Figure 6.1.

According to this growth curve, the greatest amount of gain in functional reading occurs in grades two, three, and four. The growth tapers off in junior high school and even more in senior high school, but it does continue. In other words, more growth takes place in second grade than in tenth, on the average. Therefore, when attempts are made to evaluate the amount of growth achieved by a group of pupils, one needs to know not only the amount of growth, but the group's mean score. The class whose average has gone from 2.0 to 3.0 has gained more than one which has gone from 8.0 to 9.0. In scaled score units, the former has gained fourteen points, the latter has gained six. (It should be pointed out that the material presented here is in many respects original, representing the author's thinking about this issue. It is presented here in the belief that we now have a technique which can resolve one major problem in the measurement of growth and that this will become a common approach in the future.)

In the past, we have used the linear measuring scale—the grade equivalent—to measure growth in reading, which is curvilinear. The grade equivalent score was introduced because of its apparent simplicity; we are now saying that it is deceptively simple, leading to many erroneous conclusions. We hope that the scaled score will replace grade equivalents

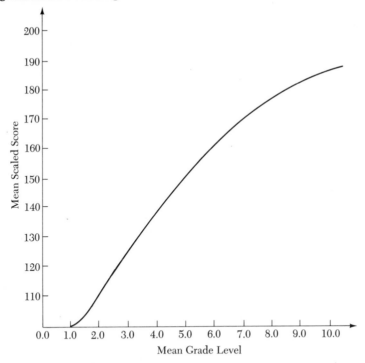

Figure 6.1   The Scaled Score Growth Curve for Reading Comprehension.

as a measure of growth, though this is not likely to happen in the near future.

Growth According to Capacity

Growth in reading is usually evaluated by comparing the amount of growth that *has* taken place against the amount of growth that *ought to have* taken place, or against what educators have usually referred to as *expectancy*. This gets us into the very difficult problem of prediction. We can actually make fairly good *group predictions*—that is, we can predict how well a class average will come out at the end of the year. There are several factors which influence the outcome of education, such as the socioeconomic background of the students, the educational level of their parents, the extent of bilingualism in a school, and the average IQ level. Actually, the single best predictor is the mean reading score which the group obtained the year before, assuming that they will continue at the same rate. But it is very difficult to make *individual* predictions—that is, to be able to predict how well each child will do. And to use this prediction as a determiner of what he ought to be doing is going a bit beyond our data.

The single most common predictor of reading success is a measure of capacity, ordinarily determined with an IQ test. To say that a student must read at a level commensurate with his IQ is to say that there ought to be a correlation of $+1.00$ between IQ and reading ability. In reality, that correlation turns out to be around .70. Obviously, the two factors go together, but there is also a great deal of individual variation. There is too much variation to warrant making this type of one-to-one prediction; there are too many variables entering into the picture. The teacher needs to look at each child in totality and then try to estimate what would be a "reasonable" expectancy. This issue is an exceedingly complex one (Madden, 1972), much beyond the scope of this book, but the beginning teacher should know enough about the concept of "learning capacity" to realize that there are many factors in addition to the IQ which relate to school achievement.

Even though we cannot specify exactly how well students at different IQ levels should do, there is a great deal of empirical data available which specify how students at different IQ levels actually do perform in reading. Such a table has been compiled to show how well the bottom fourth, the top fourth, and the total of a national sample on an IQ test perform in reading.

Table 10 shows that, as a group, the bottom fourth of the population will gain, on the average, about 0.7 year per year in grades four through eight, while the top fourth averages 1.3 years per year. (These figures were compiled from Kelley, 1966.) Since we are talking about a growth rate, the differences between the average group and these extreme groups will increase with age. It might appear that the lower IQ students are getting farther behind the longer they stay in school. But the fact is that they are improving every year.

The main reason for testing and evaluating students is not to classify them but to help plan the best possible educational experiences for all students. To do so, we must know them well, and IQ tests add one more dimension to our understanding. But we must realize that there are students whose reading is quite different from the predictions made from IQ tests. If a child performs better, he is not an "overachiever"; we made the error of "underprediction." If he does more poorly, we should not label him an "underachiever," but see it as an error of "overprediction" (Thorndike, 1963). But, in either case, tests will help because we know that all students can improve with time. That is the nature of a child's development. Therefore, testing must be done with an eye toward the future.

Table 10   Normative Growth in Reading Grade Scores by IQ Levels

Grade	Low 25%	Total	Top 25%
4	3.2	4.6	6.2
5	4.1	5.6	7.2
6	4.7	6.6	8.7
7	5.4	7.6	10.3
8	6.2	8.6	11.4
Mean Gain	0.7	1.0	1.3

Source: Adapted from *Stanford Achievement Test*, Technical Supplement. New York: Harcourt Brace Jovanovich, Inc., 1966.

A Year's Growth in a Year?

The average American child gains a year in reading ability each year, by definition. That is the way grade equivalent norms are made. This fact has led some school administrators to the erroneous conclusion that not only should the average go up a year each year, but each child should gain at least a year per year.

Again, we are back to talking about what children *ought* to do, which is essentially a philosophical issue, and, again, we are back to the problem of prediction. It is a well-known principle of educational psychology that past performance is the best single predictor. If one wishes to predict a student's success in a particular subject, the simplest approach is to look at how he is doing in that subject at the present time. There is an abundance of such data in the various test manuals.

Table 11 was constructed from the various manuals of the 1973 *Stanford Achievement Test*, but it would be essentially the same if it had been taken from another achievement test battery. It shows normal growth in the total population for grades one through seven, as well as for the lowest fourth of the class, in terms of reading ability, and for the highest fourth. One can see that, on the average, the lowest quarter gains only 0.6 year per year as a group; the highest quarter gains 1.5. Again, it must be kept in mind that these are averages and that there is much individual variation within each of these groups. But the data give us some idea of how children do develop with respect to reading.

The top and bottom 25 percent were chosen arbitrarily. Had more extreme groups been picked, deviations from the average gain of 1.0 would

Table 11   Normative Growth in Reading Grade Score by Reading Level

Grade	Low 25%	Total	Top 25%
1	1.1	1.9	3.0
2	1.7	2.9	4.4
3	2.3	3.9	6.2
4	2.9	4.9	7.4
5	3.5	5.9	9.3
6	4.2	6.9	10.5
7	4.5	7.9	11.8
Mean Gain	0.6	1.0	1.5

Source: Adapted from Stanford Achievement Test Manuals. New York: Harcourt Brace Jovanovich, Inc., 1973.

have been greater. For example, had we chosen to use the top and bottom 8 percent, the data at the end of grade five in Table 11 would read: 3.0, 5.9, 10.5.

To expect every class to gain at least one year on the average on a reading test is often unreasonable. Many will gain more, many gain less. There are simply too many variables which affect reading. And to hold teachers *accountable* for an average gain of this magnitude is often unfair, besides creating unnecessary anxiety in teachers and a poor relationship between teachers and administrators. But, even though standardized test results should not be used to evaluate teachers, the teacher should use these data, along with other forms of evaluation, to make some judgments about the adequacy and appropriateness of his or her methods and materials. Again, the emphasis should be upon the future. It is for the purposes of educational planning and individualization of instruction that the many forms of evaluation described in this chapter should be most helpful.

The Student and Behavioral Objectives

A list of behavioral objectives was provided at the beginning of this chapter. The reader should now re-read these objectives to determine, as a form of self-diagnosis, if he can exhibit the behaviors called for. Should there be some about which the reader is uncertain, he should study further the appropriate sections of this chapter. Some of the items in the list of references might be helpful in case the reader wishes to study a given topic in more depth.

Major Publishers of Reading Tests

Information about current reading tests can be gotten free by writing to the test publishers for catalogs. A list of the major publishers of reading tests is given below:

1. Bobbs-Merrill Co., Inc.
   4300 West 62nd Street
   Indianapolis, Ind. 46268

2. California Test Bureau
   Del Monte Research Park
   Monterey, Calif. 93940

3. Educational Testing Service
   Cooperative Tests and Services
   Princeton, N.J. 08540

4. Follett Educational Corporation
   1010 West Washington Boulevard
   Chicago, Ill. 60607

5. Harcourt Brace Jovanovich, Inc.
   757 Third Avenue
   New York, N.Y. 10017

6. Houghton Mifflin Company
   110 Tremont St.
   Boston, Mass. 02107

7. Lyons & Carnahan
   407 East 25th Street
   Chicago, Ill. 60616

8. Personnel Press, Inc.
   20 Nassau Street
   Princeton, N.J. 08540

9. Science Research Associates, Inc.
   259 East Erie Street
   Chicago, Ill. 60611

All tests published are reviewed in Buros (1972), *Mental Measurements Yearbooks*; every standardized reading test is described and reviewed by at least one authority in one of the yearbooks. They are extremely valuable resource books which are published every three or four years, the latest, the seventh, having been published in 1972, the next being slated for 1976 publication. When a test is published, it is usually reviewed in the next *Yearbook* in some detail, but may not be reviewed in subsequent books unless the test is revised. In these *Yearbooks* one will find a description and a critical review by at least one authority of every standardized test published.

Below is a bibliography of the tests mentioned in this chapter and of some additional reading tests which are commonly used in American schools.

Test References

Adult Basic Learning Examination. Adults achieving at grades 1–12. B. Karlsen, R. Madden and E. Gardner. New York: Harcourt Brace Jovanovich, 1967, 1970.

Analysis of Learning Potential. Grades 1–12. W. N. Durost, E. F. Gardner, R. Madden. New York: Harcourt Brace Jovanovich, 1970.

California Achievement Test. Grades 1–12. E. W. Tiegs and W. W. Clark. Monterey, Cal.: California Test Bureau, 1970.

Cognitive Abilities Test. Grades K–13. R. L. Thorndike, E. Hagen, I. Lorge. Boston: Houghton Mifflin, 1968.

Comprehensive Test of Basic Skills. Grades 2–12. CTB. Monterey, Cal.: California Test Bureau, 1968–70.

Cooperative Primary Tests. Grades 1–3. Cooperative Tests and Services. Princeton, N.J.: Educational Testing Service, 1965–67.

Diagnostic Reading Scales. Grades 1–8. George D. Spache. Monterey, Cal.: California Test Bureau, 1963.

Durrell Analysis of Reading Difficulty. Grades 1–6. D. D. Durrell. New York: Harcourt Brace Jovanovich, 1955.

Gates-MacGinitie Reading Tests. Grades K–12. A. I. Gates and W. H. MacGinitie. New York: Teachers College Press, Columbia University, 1970.

Gates-McKillop Reading Diagnostic Tests. Grades 2–6. A. I. Gates and A. S. McKillop. New York: Teachers College Press, Columbia University, 1962.

Gilmore Oral Reading Test. Grades 1–8. J. V. Gilmore and E. C. Gilmore. New York: Harcourt Brace Jovanovich, 1968.

Iowa Silent Reading Tests. Grades 6–12. R. Farr, ed. New York: Harcourt Brace Jovanovich, 1973.

Iowa Test of Basic Skills. Grades 3–9. A. N. Hieronymus, et al. Boston: Houghton Mifflin, 1973.

Metropolitan Achievement Test. Grades K–9. W. N. Durost, H. H. Bixler, J. W. Wrightstone, G. A. Prescott, and I. H. Balow. New York: Harcourt Brace Jovanovich, 1970.

Metropolitan Readiness Test. Grades K–1. G. H. Hildreth, N. L. Griffiths, and M. E. McGauvan. New York: Harcourt Brace Jovanovich, 1964–65.

Murphy-Durrell Reading Readiness Analysis. Grades K–1. H. D. Murphy and D. D. Durrell. New York: Harcourt Brace Jovanovich, 1964–65.

Otis-Lennon Mental Ability Test. Grades K–College. A. S. Otis and R. T. Lennon. New York: Harcourt Brace Jovanovich, 1967.

SRA Achievement Series. Grades 1–9. L. P. Thorpe, D. W. Lefever, and R. A. Naslund. Chicago: Science Research Associates, 1954–69.

Silent Reading Diagnostic Tests. Grades 2–6. G. L. Bond, B. Balow, and C. J. Hoyt. Chicago: Lyons and Carnahan, 1970.

Stanford Achievement Test. Grades 1–9. R. Madden, E. F. Gardner, H. C. Rudman, B. Karlsen, and J. C. Merwin. New York: Harcourt Brace Jovanovich, 1973.

Stanford Diagnostic Reading Test. Grades 2–13. B. Karlsen, R. Madden, and E. F. Gardner. New York: Harcourt Brace Jovanovich, 1966–74.

Stanford Early School Achievement Test. Grades K–1. R. Madden and E. F. Gardner. New York: Harcourt Brace Jovanovich, 1969–70.

References

Ahmann, J. Stanley, and Glock, Marvin D. *Evaluating Pupil Growth.* Boston: Allyn and Bacon, 1971.

Anastasi, Anne. *Psychological Testing.* 3rd ed. New York: Macmillan, 1968.

Auckerman, Robert C. *Approaches to Beginning Reading.* New York: John Wiley and Sons, 1971.

Barbe, Walter B. *Educator's Guide to Personalized Reading Instruction.* Englewood Cliffs, N.J.: Prentice-Hall, 1961.

Benton, Curtis D., Jr. "Ophthalmologists Recommend Less Emphasis on the Eyes in Learning Disorders." *Journal of Learning Disabilities* 3 (1970): 54–56.

Bloom, Benjamin S., Hastings, J. Thomas, and Madaus, George F. *Handbook on Formative and Summative Evaluation of Student Learning.* New York: McGraw-Hill, 1971.

Buros, Oscar K., ed. *The Seventh Mental Measurements Yearbook.* Highland Park, N.J.: Gryphon Press, 1972.

Burrill, Lois E. "How a Standardized Achievement Test Is Built." *Test Service Notebook* #125. New York: Harcourt Brace Jovanovich, 1972.

Clark, Carl A. "The Use of Separate Answer Sheets in Testing Slow-learning Pupils." *Journal of Educational Measurement* 5 (1968): 61–64.

Educational Testing Service. *Making the Classroom Test: A Guide for Teachers.* Evaluation and Advisory Service Series No. 4. Princeton: E.T.S., 1961(b).

Educational Testing Service, *Selecting an Achievement Test.* Evaluation and Advisory Service Series No. 3. Princeton: E.T.S., 1961(a).

Farr, Roger, ed. *Measurement and Evaluation of Reading.* New York: Harcourt Brace Jovanovich, 1970.

Fry, Edward. "The Orangoutan Score." *The Reading Teacher* 24 (1971): 360–362.

Goodman, Yetta M., and Burke, Carolyn L. *Reading Miscue Inventory.* New York: Macmillan, 1972.

Harris, Albert J. *How to Increase Reading Ability.* 5th ed. New York: David McKay, 1970.

Johnson, Marjorie S., and Kress, Roy A. *Informal Reading Inventories.* Reading Aids Series. Newark, Del.: International Reading Association, 1965.

Jones, John W. *Blind Children, Degree of Vision, Mode of Reading.* Bulletin 24. Washington, D.C.: U.S. Office of Education, 1961.

Karlin, Robert. *Teaching Elementary Reading.* New York: Harcourt Brace Jovanovich, 1971.

Kelley, Truman L., et al. *Stanford Achievement Test: Technical Supplement.* New York: Harcourt Brace Jovanovich, 1966.

Kibler, Robert J., et al. *Behavioral Objectives and Instruction.* Boston: Allyn and Bacon, 1970.

Lessinger, Leon M. *Every Kid a Winner: Accountability in Education.* Palo Alto, Calif.: Science Research Associates College Division, 1970.

Madden, Richard. "Assessing the Total Reading Program." In *Administrators and Reading*, edited by Thorsten R. Carlson. New York: Harcourt Brace Jovanovich, 1972, pp. 110–134.

Mehrens, William A., and Lehmann, Irvin J. *Measurement and Evaluation in Education and Psychology.* New York: Holt, Rinehart and Winston, 1973.

National Assessment of Educational Progress. *Reading: Summary.* Report 02-R-00. Denver: NAEP, 1972.

Nelson, Clarence H. *Measurement and Evaluation in the Classroom.* Toronto, Canada: Macmillan, 1970.

Silvaroli, Nicholas J. *Classroom Reading Inventory.* Dubuque, Iowa: Wm. C. Brown, 1973.

Spache, George D. *A Study of a Longitudinal First Grade Reading Readiness Program.* Research Project 2742. Washington, D.C.: U.S. Office of Education, 1966.

Stanford Research Report. *Equivalent Scores for the 1973 Edition of Stanford Achievement Test and the 1964 Edition of Stanford Achievement Test in Terms of Grade Equivalents.* #5. New York: Harcourt Brace Jovanovich, 1974.

Taylor, Sanford. *Eye Movements and Reading.* Reading Newsletter 30. Huntington, New York: Educational Developmental Laboratories, 1963.

Thorndike, Robert L. *The Concepts of Over and Underachievement.* New York: Bureau of Publications, Teachers College, Columbia University, 1963.

Wilson, John A. R., ed. *Diagnosis of Learning Difficulties.* New York: McGraw-Hill, 1971.

Womer, Frank B. *What Is National Assessment?* Denver: NAEP, 1972.

Wood, Dorothy Atkins. *Test Construction.* Columbus, Ohio: Charles E. Merrill, 1960.

Wrightstone, J. Wayne, et al. "Accountability in Education and Associated Measurement Problems." *Test Service Notebook* #33. New York: Harcourt Brace Jovanovich, 1971.

Part Two:
Instructional Strategies

Chapter Seven

Preview

Reading methodology receives thorough treatment in the next two chapters. In this chapter Dale Johnson provides some background with a brief history of reading instruction, designed to put the topic in perspective. Then he describes in detail three widely used approaches to teaching reading: the language-experience approach, individualized reading—including some variations such as I.P.I., C.A.I., and I.G.E.—and basal readers. It will be clear to the reader that Johnson endorses the first two approaches. Recognizing that basal readers are used in the vast majority of classrooms, however, he also discusses the organization and teaching strategies for using this approach effectively.

In conclusion, he describes a variety of other organizational arrangements and reminds us that no method guarantees success for all learners; it is the *teacher* who makes a difference!

Reading:
Current Approaches,
Part One

Dale Johnson, University of Wisconsin

Objectives

After you have read this chapter, you should be able to:

1. State some of the historical antecedents of current practices in reading instruction.
2. Describe the similarities and differences among three current instructional approaches in reading: the language-experience, the individualized, and the basal.
3. Recognize specific instructional practices appropriate to each of the three approaches.
4. Cite research evidence about teacher versus method.
5. State the major strengths and weaknesses of each of the three approaches.
6. Recognize three intra-school organizational arrangements.

And so to completely analyze what we do when we read would almost be the acme of a psychologist's achievements, for it would be to describe very many of the most intricate workings of the human mind, as well as to unravel the tangled story of the most remarkable specific performance that civilization has learned in all its history (Huey, 1908, p. 6).

Although teachers, researchers, and scholars have been studying the reading process for years, they still do not fully understand it. Nonetheless, virtually every American elementary school has an instructional reading program, and the great majority of American children learn to read during their early years in school. Inevitably, a question arises: "How do we teach that which we do not fully understand?" And two further questions present themselves: "Where are we currently in reading instruction?" and "Where have we been?"

This chapter will examine several aspects of reading methodology, briefly summarizing the history of reading instruction so that current practices can be viewed in an historical perspective. Then three major reading methodologies in wide use today will be described and specific suggestions given for implementing each approach. The chapter ends with an explanation of some additional organizational arrangements and the author's viewpoint about approaches to teaching reading.

A Brief History of Reading Instruction

Several thousand years ago the Greeks, coming in contact with Phoenician traders in their economic dealings, learned that the Phoenicians had developed a writing system for their Semitic language. Greek scholars began to devise a graphic system for their own language and borrowed freely from Semitic. Since the two languages, Greek and Semitic, belonged to different linguistic families, some Greek sounds were not represented in the Semitic system, so it was necessary to devise unique graphic symbols. Eventually the Greeks produced a system of written symbols with which they could represent each phoneme in their language. Each letter had a name *(nomen)*, an appearance *(figura)*, and a "power" *(potestas)* or sound. By the fifth century B.C. the Greeks had achieved a uniform phonemic alphabet and had established the left-to-right, top-to-bottom direction in writing.[1] Other peoples had used various pictographic writing systems long before the Greeks established their alphabet. The Greeks, however, were quick to comprehend that words are combinations of sounds and all speech sounds, therefore, must be accounted for in writing.

> Other peoples, such as the Babylonians and the Egyptians, had caught glimpses of the desirability of having signs represent *sounds,* not *things,* but were never able to break with convention to the extent of setting aside picture writing in favor of letter writing. The fundamental defect of picture writing was that it was not based upon sounds at all. The Greeks saw this basic weakness and by avoiding it achieved everlasting distinction (Mathews, 1966, pp. 7–8).

[1] See I. J. Gelb, *A Study of Writing* (Chicago, 1952), and Martin Sprengling, *The Alphabet* (Chicago, 1931) for a complete discussion of the development of the Greek alphabet.

So, several centuries before Christ, the necessity arose for reading instruction. First instruction in reading was in names and forms of letters. Though the printing press would not be invented for centuries—so written symbols were in no way standardized—the task was not as difficult as it may seem, since all letters were capitals. Students learned them in alphabetical order and practiced by searching through written materials for occurrences of letters they had mastered. They recited the alphabet backward and forward, sang alphabet songs, and drilled at length on meaningless but pronounceable syllables *(ab, ob, ub, eb)*. Mathews cites a statement made by a Greek school boy as reported by W. Rhys Roberts:

> When we are taught to read, first we learn all the names of the letters, then their forms and their values, then in due course syllables and their modifications, and finally words and their properties, viz., lengthenings and shortenings, accents, and the like. After acquiring these things we begin to write and read, syllable by syllable and slowly at first . . . (Mathews, p. 6).

These early methods were to reappear many times in later days and in other societies.

The Romans borrowed the Greek letters from the Etruscans. Instead of using the Greek letter names, however, they named the vowels after their sounds and the consonants from close approximations of their sounds. Their method of instruction was basically oral and leaned heavily upon syllabication.

As a result of more than three centuries of Roman rule, many people in England learned the Latin language. When the English language was first put into writing in the seventh century A.D., Latin letters were naturally selected to represent English sounds. Since new letters had to be added, the English alphabet used today is quite different from its ancestor. Little is known about reading instruction in the first several hundred years after a writing system was developed for English. One of the earliest discussions of the English writing system was Alexander Hume's *Of the Orthographic and Congruities of the Britain Tongue* (1617). Hume concerned himself with spelling patterns and sounds of Latin and English.

Earliest records of reading methodology in fourteenth- through seventeenth-century England indicate that the methods used originally by the Greeks and Romans—learning letter names, then sounds, then combinations and syllables—were still in use. After extended drill children would begin to read by first spelling and then pronouncing *each* word—before moving on to the next.

This "alphabetic" method of reading instruction, which dates back thousands of years, was no doubt the *initial* means of reading instruction once alphabets were developed. It was brought to the new world in the 1600s, along with the famous "hornbook," which was mentioned in a poem written in the 1400s (Wright and Halliwell, 1841, p. 63):

> *When a child to school shall sent be*
> *A book him is brought*
> *Nailed on a board of tree*
> *That men call abc.*

The hornbook was a small wooden paddle with a protective sheath of cow horn covering a piece of paper on which the ABCs were written (often in the form of a cross), as well as some syllables and the Lord's Prayer or some other religious selection. Hornbooks were widely used for reading instruction in England and colonial America.

The *New England Primer* was the first published book designed for American schools. It went through more than twenty editions in the mid-1700s. According to Smith (1965) the book was called a *primer* because of the primary essentials of religious knowledge it contained (Psalms, Commandments, the Creed) rather than from the fact that it was the child's first book. The approach to reading instruction found in the Primer was essentially alphabetic, as described earlier.

The "whole-word" method, developed in Germany during the eighteenth and nineteenth centuries, began to receive attention in America and elsewhere. The whole-word approach—also referred to as "Normal-Word" and "Analytic-Synthetic Method"—involved the following basic steps:

1. Presentation of an object or picture of an object denoted by the word to be taught.
2. Presentation of the written word.
3. Analysis of the sounds and syllables within the word (letter *names* were not mentioned).
4. Reformation of the complete word.
5. Finger-tracing the word shape.
6. Writing the word on a slate.
7. Reading the word orally.

The first American book utilizing the whole-word method was *My Little Primer*, written by Josiah Bumstead in 1840. With the advent of the graded school, the development of graded series of reading books was encouraged. One of the most popular series was *The McGuffey Readers*, published and reissued between 1836 and the early 1900s, which sold over 122 million copies.

Many heated debates developed between proponents of the alphabetic method and the whole-word method—forerunners of the methodology arguments heard throughout the past 100 years. Horace Mann was probably the most eloquent American proponent of the whole-word or "look-say" approach to teaching reading. In a series of noted lectures he scathingly deplored the alphabetic approach. In supporting the whole-word method he said,

> The acquisition of the language, even from its elements, becomes an intelligible process. The knowledge of new things is introduced through the knowledge of familiar things. At the age of three or four years, every child has command of a considerable vocabulary consisting of the names of persons, of animals, articles of dress, food, furniture, etc. The sounds of these names are familiar to the ear and the organs of speech, and the ideas they represent are familiar to the mind. All that is to be done, therefore, is to lead the eye to the like familiarity with their printed signs. But the alphabet, on the other hand, is wholly foreign to a child's existing knowledge . . . (Mathews, p. 80).

A third method of reading instruction began to gain popularity in the late nineteenth and early twentieth centuries—the phonic method. In this method attention was called to letter *sounds,* not *names,* and the children's task was to "sound out" or pronounce words by applying the rules they had learned. This ability was encouraged by presenting "regularly spelled" words first *(rat, cat, hat, pat).* The phonic method was sometimes used concurrently with the whole-word method.

In summary, reading instruction in America has gone through five rather distinct but overlapping periods:

1. About 1600 to 1840—the alphabetic or "spelling" approach.
2. About 1840 to 1880—the whole-word approach.
3. About 1880 to 1920—the phonics approach, which, unlike the alphabetic approach, stressed letter *sounds* rather than names.
4. About 1920 to 1960—the "Basal" Era. This was principally a whole-word approach with an emphasis on meaningful reading. Research studies during the phonics period showed children could pronounce words, but could not read well silently. Language experience charts, discussed later, came to be widely used. The alphabetic method virtually disappeared and supplementary phonics instruction was minimal.
5. About 1960 to the present—basal reading with an increased emphasis on "decoding." The basal reader is discussed in detail later in this chapter, and decoding programs are described in the next chapter.

More than ever before, reading methodology is based upon research findings in child development (language acquisition), human learning, psycholinguistics, and reading pedagogy. Dozens of reading "approaches" and countless published programs are in use today. Three of the most

widely used reading methods, the language-experience approach, individualized reading, and the basal reading approach, will be examined in the
remainder of the chapter.

The Language-Experience Approach

The label *language-experience* is, in itself, a hint as to what this approach
entails. In essence the term implies that reading should be based on the
language and experiences of the learner. In her book *Teacher* (1963), Sylvia
Ashton-Warner describes her work with the Maori people of New Zealand.
She entitles her method "Organic Reading" and considers it a bridge
between non-reading and reading. In defining the "Key Vocabulary," the
first words a child learns to read, Ashton-Warner articulates a fundamental
tenet of the language-experience approach. She states: "First words must
have an intense meaning. First words must be already part of the dynamic
life. First words must be made of the stuff of the child himself, whatever
and wherever the child" (p. 32). The language-experience approach is a
method in which the reading materials are developed by recording the
spoken language of the child, so that what the child reads reflects his
experiences as well as his language patterns. The four language arts—listening, speaking, reading, and writing—are integrated.

The language-experience method is, at least *at the outset,* a whole-
word approach. Further, it is a whole-word approach in which the words
are obtained from the child. But it is much more than that. Mary Anne Hall
(1972) discusses the relationship between oral language and reading, and
cites four implications for reading instruction based on the relationship
between oral and written language.

1. The language of initial reading material should represent the child's
   speech patterns.
2. Reading instruction should build upon the relationship between spoken
   and written language.
3. Reading experiences should be taught as communication experiences,
   even in the beginning stages.
4. Reading instruction must be related to the total language program (p.
   28).

Children come to school with highly developed language facility. They
can use and understand thousands of words in conversation. They have
command of most syntactical structures and can understand and generate
countless utterances new to their experience. With the language-experi-

ence approach each child is given the opportunity to use his private storehouse of linguistic ability. The language-experience approach has been viewed as both a *group* and an *individualized* method. When used most effectively, it is really both. Individual interests, needs, and experiences are accommodated and group processes are developed.

Procedures

The language-experience method is most often used in *beginning* reading, commencing in either kindergarten or first grade. In some schools the approach is used for a few months only, while in others it is the basic program throughout first and into second grade. It may also be used with older children needing remedial instruction. Some of the comments in this section, though primarily pertaining to initial instruction, may also apply to older children.

Vocabulary Proponents of the language-experience approach believe that children learn to read more easily if the initial vocabulary is important and interesting to them. They believe that "first words" should come from the child, not from some external source. In this they disagree with the phonics enthusiasts, who believe first words should be highly patterned and have consistent letter-sound correspondences to make decoding easier. They also differ with the approach taken by many basal readers (discussed later in this chapter), which build vocabulary according to frequency: those words that are thought to occur most often in the pupil's speaking and understanding vocabularies are taught first.

With the language-experience approach, the teacher regularly asks the children to tell her words that they would like to learn to read. This may be done daily, twice daily, or more often. When the child tells the teacher a word, she writes it on a blank piece of paper or a card and gives it to the child, who then practices reading the word, tracing it with his finger, and perhaps writing it.

Many teachers have each child develop an alphabetized vocabulary book. As each new word is learned the child copies it into the vocabulary book. This becomes a personal list of words he can use when writing sentences or stories of his own. Others have the child keep the word cards in a "word bank," usually a sturdy file box. As words accumulate, the child can be tested informally. Sylvia Ashton-Warner believes that if a child cannot remember one of his words, the card should be destroyed because the word was apparently not important to him. In pairs or small groups, children can take turns reading their words to the other children and can then try to read the other children's words. Some children may wish to draw pictures or do other artwork to illustrate their words. They can label their pictures and display them about the room.

Individual Dictation As time permits, children should be given the opportunity to dictate short stories, observations, poems, beliefs, questions, or the like to the teacher or teacher's aide. The teacher or aide serves as "secretary" or "recorder" and writes the child's dictation, legibly, on a sheet of paper or newsprint with a marker, pen, or crayon. The child may then read the story to the teacher, who can help with unlearned words, if necessary. The child can practice reading the story at his desk, or illustrate it, or record words in the vocabulary book while others in the class are dictating their stories. When all the children in the group have finished the dictations, some children may want to read their stories to each other or to the group, and they may also want to read someone else's story.

There is disagreement about vocabulary and syntactic control in these stories. Psycholinguists generally believe that the stories should be recorded in the language patterns of the child, whether grammatically "correct" or not. Some reading specialists, on the other hand, believe sentences, no matter how dictated, should be simplified and rendered grammatically correct. Heilman contends that the difficulty of controlling vocabulary is a weakness in dictated stories. He believes that too many words may be introduced at one time and basic sight words may not be repeated frequently enough to ensure mastery (Heilman, 1972, p. 210). Few people would advocate altering the spelling of words to match the dialectal pronunciation of the child. For example, if the child says "hep" for *help,* it should still be spelled *help.*

It is this writer's contention that dictated stories should be recorded, as closely as possible, in the syntactic structures of the child. This means a teacher must be acutely aware of the dialects of her pupils. Nothing is more frustrating to a child, or potentially injurious to his self-concept, than to have his language "corrected" when, in his social milieu, it is perfectly acceptable. On the other hand, since all of us talk in thought clusters that contain run-on sentences and repetitions, it will be necessary for the teacher to determine sentence boundaries and punctuate accordingly.

One of the greatest advantages of the language-experience approach is its ability to match printed with oral language to facilitate interest and comprehension. It would be an error to destroy this advantage by being overly concerned with vocabulary control and repetition.

Many children will need motivation for dictating stories. The following short list of topics can be used for individual or group dictation. These topics can be mentioned in class, listed on a bulletin board marked "Topics for the Day" (or week), displayed about the room, or posed as questions.

Some Topics for Dictation

animals	toys	mother	father
sister	brother	home	friends
church	synagogue	parades	teacher
ghosts	rainy days	lazy days	games
vacations	school room	summer	our principal
winter fun	night time	airplanes	seasonal holidays
trains	boats	sledding	favorite books
basketball	school work	policemen	the grocery store
Yom Kippur	Christmas	Easter	the family car
Valentine's Day	monsters	TV shows	other countries
magazines	dreams	submarines	school programs

Teachers can easily expand this list by discovering the interests of their pupils and by being attuned to timely topics and events. While many children will be able to select their own topics, others will need suggestions to get started.

Group Experience Stories Though individually dictated stories are generally preferable to group stories, the teacher cannot be available to twenty or more children individually very often. As an alternative to individual stories, group experience stories are often very successful. Some children respond better in a group situation and may contribute more freely. Developing group stories is often a good way to introduce reading on the first day of school.

Construction of group experience stories develops from group discussion about meaningful *shared* experiences or interests. Some examples follow.

Experiences for Group Stories

a class pet or animal
plans for a class trip
a recurring activity:
   coming to school
   recess time
   the hot lunch menu
a TV show the group has seen
a recent field trip

favorite food

grandmothers

If I could go to the moon . . .

If we sailed across the ocean . . .

If it was always night time . . .

If Pooh Bear visited our classroom . . .

Discussion topics can be in the realm of reality or fancy. The main concern for the teacher is to discover topics interesting to the *children*. The constraints of time and interest will determine how long and involved the discussions become.

The group stories can be written as the discussion is under way or as a summary to a completed discussion. The latter is often preferable, since discussions can deteriorate when frequently interrupted for recording sentences. It is useful, though, to keep an abbreviated record, either on the chalkboard or on note paper, of the main points being discussed. The disadvantage to writing stories summarizing discussions is that the spontaneity and originality of the children's thoughts and language may be lost.

After a certain period of discussion, the teacher might say, "Now, let's write about what we've been discussing. Let's write a story about what we've said. Who can think of a good title for our story?" After an agreement is reached, the title can be recorded. While some teachers write group experience stories on the chalkboard, many others prefer to write them on large newsprint, tag board, or poster paper so they can be saved and perhaps illustrated.

The following dialogue from a first-grade class shows the procedure followed in writing a group story about a discussion of "favorite foods."

Teacher: Do we all agree that "Hamburgers and Malts" will be the title of our story?

Class: Yes.

(Teacher writes "Hamburgers and Malts" on a large piece of paper, using a felt-tipped pen.)

Teacher: How shall we begin our story?

Lisa: Let's say, "Some food tastes *icky*." (Class giggles)

Teacher: Shall we begin "Some food tastes *icky*"?

Class: Yes.

Kirk: No, let's start, "Down with gravy!" (Class giggles)

Julie: I like "Some food tastes *icky*."

Others: Me too. Let's begin that way.

(Teacher writes "Some food tastes *icky*.")

This group experience story session continued for about fifteen minutes—after an earlier fifteen-minute discussion of favorite foods. The final product was:

Hamburgers and Malts

Some food tastes icky.
Prunes, potatoes, beets and corn.
Pizza is good.
Breakfast cereal, too.
Also hot dogs, coke, and steak.
But, we could eat hamburgers and
   malts every single day.

The teacher's role, in addition to writing the story, is to ask questions and interject comments to help the children recall their discussion. The story is written in the children's own language.

Once the story is written, the teacher reads it to the class, pointing to each word. Children are then asked to read the story in unison along with the teacher. Finally, children can volunteer to read different lines or the entire story by themselves.

In one elementary school, four first-grade classes discussed the same topic, a field trip they had all been on. Each class constructed its own experience story and then shared it with the other classes. The stories were so different that a reader might have wondered if the children had been on the same trip!

Many teachers who use the language-experience approach like to prepare mimeographed books for each child. After each story has been completed, the teacher writes or types it on a ditto master and duplicates a copy for each child, leaving space for illustrations. Each child can make a cover of heavy construction paper and write a title on it—"Our Stories" or "Words of Wisdom from Wilson School" or something else. In addition to the individual duplicated books, a class "big book" will grow as each story is completed on large paper. Some teachers make an additional copy of the large experience story, which can be marked or cut up for use in developing word identification and comprehension skills.

Thus at the end of the first day of school a child may take home a story he has helped write and read it to his family—often with a great deal of excitement and pride.

Developing Reading Comprehension An effective means of developing reading comprehension is by asking questions. In his "Taxonomy of Comprehension," [2] T. C. Barrett describes four levels of comprehension questions: Literal, Inferential, Evaluative, and Appreciative. Too often teachers (and test makers) ask only literal questions, which simply require the recognition or recall of specific facts and details from a story. Asking questions *beyond* the literal level (such as, "What would have happened if . . . ?" "Do you think this could really happen?" "Have you ever had a bad dream? What was it?") can provoke much more thought and generate far greater interest than using such questions as "What color was the hat?" The suggestions about reading comprehension in Chapter Eleven are particularly pertinent to the use of group experience stories. In any approach, considerable attention must be devoted to the development of reading comprehension. Since Chapter Eleven rather thoroughly discusses this most important aspect of reading, this chapter will treat it only briefly.

Word Recognition Skills The language-experience approach is often criticized for being too "whole-word" oriented and for neglecting the development of needed word recognition skills. Most beginning readers need practice in auditory and visual discrimination and with the basic decoding skills of phonic, structural, and contextual analysis (all are examined in detail in Chapters Nine and Ten. In the language-experience approach these skills are taught *as the child needs them* and as the experience stories provide opportunities for teaching them, rather than in the arbitrary sequences found in basal reading programs.

The teacher can develop students' visual discrimination by asking them to find a word in the story that begins, or ends, or has the same medial letters as a word the teacher writes on a flashcard or on the chalkboard. One way to increase auditory discrimination is to say and repeat a word, for example *dog.* Then read a group story in unison and ask children to raise their hands when they hear words that begin (or end) like *dog.* The procedure can be repeated with other words.

In describing the word recognition development in her first-grade language-experience class, Dahl (1971, p. 16) said:

In the Language-Experience approach, the number of words and sentences in beginning stories lends itself to presenting many skills in an incidental manner. For instance:

    [2] In Richard J. Smith and T. C. Barrett, *Teaching Reading in the Middle Grades.* Reading, Mass.: Addison-Wesley, 1974, pp. 53–56.

1. Example of a Group Skill

   After we recorded stories about our gerbils, students were asked to locate the word *gerbil.* When some of the children pointed to the word gerbil*s,* a lesson in forming simple plurals was a natural thing and was easy for the class to understand. We then made plurals of many known words:

rat	bed	carrot	tail	cage
rats	beds	carrots	tails	cages

2. Example of an Individual Skill

   A little girl dictated the sentence—"Harriet can drink from a bottle." As *drink* was printed, the little girl said, "*D*rink, *d*ream, *d*rive—they all start the same, don't they?" Thus, our first lesson on blends was taught to an individual early in October.

3. Example of an Individual Skill

   Student (dictating): "The rat didn't like her, so he went away."
   Teacher (printing): "The rat did not. . . ."
   Student: "Not *did not,* I said *didn't.*"
   This provided a perfect opportunity to present contractions!

can not	did not	is not	have not

Through similar experiences and activities nearly all phonics generalizations (letter-sound correspondence), structural components, and syntactic and semantic contextual clues can be taught. Since there is no research evidence supporting any *particular* sequence of word recognition features, and since children often learn best those things that have immediate application, there is no reason why the language-experience approach cannot be an effective vehicle for developing decoding ability. It will be imperative, however, for the *teacher* to have a thorough understanding of word identification skills and techniques so they can be introduced when opportunities arise.

Creative Writing Creative writing is an integral part of this method of reading instruction. Children begin to write by copying words from their vocabulary cards and by copying individual or group experience stories. Some children will write two or more words and combine words into thought units (which may or may not be grammatically "correct") about themselves or their experiences. Handwriting, spelling, punctuation, and grammatical accuracy should not be criticized during the first several months of writing, since this can stifle creativity. But the teacher can give help and suggestions while the children are writing. Often children will ask the teacher to help them spell words or to suggest alternate words. Many teachers provide the children with desk copies of the alphabet for reference.

Since story building and language usage are inherent to this approach, children begin to write very early. Before long children will be writing their own small books, often with the help of the teacher or a classmate. Soon after beginning to write and illustrate short books, children may become interested in sharing their books with other pupils and in reading books written by their classmates. Reading and writing thus reinforce each other again. The teacher's role is to be a resource person—answering questions and providing suggestions—and a listener. As children increase their writing efforts and read more works of their classmates, they will feel the need for accuracy in capitalization, punctuation, and spelling. The list of topics presented earlier (p. 203) provides possibilities for creative writing as well as story dictation. Other topics are presented in the next section, "Individualized Reading" (p. 212).

Printed Materials

Children cannot go through life reading only materials written by themselves, their teacher, or their fellow pupils. The ability to read published printed matter is as important in school as it is useful in life, and it opens countless doorways to knowledge and pleasure.

Teachers using the language-experience approach see to it that large numbers of magazines, paperback books, school newspapers, trade books, pre-primers, primers, and early readers are available in the classroom. These materials afford the children an opportunity to reinforce skills they have learned, locate words from their experience stories, and develop wider interests. Children should be encouraged to visit the school library if there is one, and urged to get a library card for the nearest public library, to which most language-experience teachers arrange an early field trip. Usually by the end of the first grade most children are reading widely in published materials within the framework of an individualized reading program, which naturally follows a beginning language-experience approach.

One criticism levelled at the language-experience approach is that it makes evaluation difficult. Although there are relevant evaluation and record keeping techniques (discussed in the next section), end of chapter tests are unavailable, and with individualized vocabularies, standardized achievement tests are not really applicable. In this author's opinion, however, the *development* of reading ability should take precedence over the *measurement* of it.

Summary

The language-experience approach to reading instruction is based on the belief that children will learn best when they are *interested* and when reading material originates with children themselves and reflects their own experience and language. Though this approach is most often used as a beginning reading method in kindergarten or first grade, it can also be used successfully with older children needing remedial help and with children of culturally or linguistically diverse backgrounds.

Individualized Reading

An individualized reading program is a natural extension of the language-experience approach to beginning reading. The essential difference between the two is that most of the reading material in an individualized program is published—books, magazines, newspapers—while most of the materials in the language-experience method are prepared by the children. Individualized reading with prepared materials is rarely used as an *initial* reading method. Teachers usually begin individualized reading *after* children have achieved a certain independence in reading—that is, when they possess a reasonable sight vocabulary and basic word recognition skills. So most schools do not begin using this method until late in first grade or in second or third grade. It can follow virtually any initial program: basal, modified alphabet, programmed, linguistic, or language-experience.

The term *individualized reading* means many things to many people and is consequently hard to define. Most elementary teachers individualize their reading instruction to some degree. Many proponents of individualized reading view it more as a belief about reading than a method.

In an individualized reading program, the child starts where he is and moves at his own rate in the directions of his interests. He searches for and selects his own reading material according to his interests and ability, and he reads at his own pace. During reading time in an individualized classroom, children will be reading alone, not in groups with the teacher, and each child will probably be reading from a different self-selected book. The teacher is free to provide skill instruction as it is needed, to help with words, and, very importantly, to engage in private conferences with each child as often as possible. Sharing periods will be held occasionally, and special skill groups will be formed when more than one child shows the same need. Interest groups are sometimes formed, but all grouping is flexible, and groups are dissolved when no longer needed.

Individualized reading is not new; its origins can probably be traced to the very beginning of teaching to read prior to the advent of mass education. During the past decades, interest in individualized reading instruction has greatly increased. Several books, countless journal articles, a variety of conferences, topics, and seminars at professional meetings, and a number of research studies have resulted from this renewed interest. Terms such as *Individually Prescribed Instruction, Individually Guided Education*, and *Computer-Assisted Instruction* have been the most recent manifestations; their application to reading instruction will be discussed later in this section.

Individualized reading is based on the recognition that children differ greatly in many ways: each child has his own ability, motivation, wishes, drives, thoughts, and interests. Reading is recognized as a very personal, individual, often private experience. It is common knowledge that most children (and adults) work long and hard when they have the opportunity to choose their own tasks and set their own goals. Similarly, children enjoy reading more and can sustain their interest longer when they select their own materials.

This section will present suggestions for conducting an individualized program, cite some of the commonly stated advantages and disadvantages of such a program, and examine research and recent developments.

Procedures

Some individualized programs in reading are highly prescriptive and teacher directed; others are more *laissez-faire*. We will describe here an individualized program that is not totally prescriptive.

Materials An individualized program thrives on materials. No ideal number of books or other printed materials has been empirically verified, but estimates of the number of different books needed for each child range from ten to thirty to a hundred. Remember there are many printed materials other than books. If children are going to be free to read, a large quantity of materials must be available. Where will these materials come from?

Begin in the classroom and in the old closets, workrooms, and offices of the school. Multiple copies of outdated reading books, magazines, newsletters, and supplementary materials are probably around. Remember that even if materials are old, were written for older (or younger) children, or are not of interest to you, they may still be of interest to a child in the class. Teachers will probably want to exert some selection control over materials furnished by parents and children; but "self-selected" materials are basic to individualized reading, and the child's judgment must be trusted. This is not the occasion for rigid censorship.

Many school libraries and public libraries will make available rotating collections. A group of twenty-five to fifty books, exchanged for another group every two or three weeks, adds another supply of reading material.

Teachers of individualized reading often become great scavengers. The attics, garages, storerooms, basements, and bookshelves of their friends, co-workers, and themselves can be good sources of suitable printed matter. Some teachers send notes home to the parents of their pupils asking for the donation or loan of books and materials belonging to older brothers and sisters, which may be seldom read anymore. Children feel great pride when they bring a box of books from home to share with their classmates.

There are many paperback book clubs for children. Such books are relatively inexpensive, and some clubs give free books in proportion to the number purchased—which adds to the class collection.

In addition to books, current magazines, and newspapers, teachers may subscribe to children's magazines and newspapers. Travel literature, advertising matter, maps and globes, encyclopedias and dictionaries, phone books, musical scores, airline flight schedules, cookbooks, driver education manuals, filmstrips—all these and many more add to the quantity and variety of printed material for the classroom. While some teachers do not permit them, many members of the "over-thirty" generation developed their reading interest and ability with comic books!

Organization Reading materials can be organized according to topic, level of difficulty, or type. Grouping materials by reading level may be more time-consuming and potentially harmful than worthwhile. Children tend to seek materials they can handle, and they may feel a stigma associated with materials labelled at given levels.

Organizing by type may be the most useful method. Placing books borrowed from the school library in one area, those borrowed from the public library in another, and those borrowed from pupils or friends in a third will facilitate accounting procedures. Donated books could be in another area, and magazines and newspapers on a table or rack. Materials should be arranged in ways that encourage browsing. Occasionally grouping materials by topic can help children select according to their interests.

Room arrangements will vary according to classroom size and type, available furniture, and other considerations. A relaxed, informal class-room lends itself best to individualized reading. Carpet remnants, cushions, and old living room furniture are more conducive to reading than nailed-down desks. As adults, how often do we read for pleasure while sitting in a straight-backed chair?

Hammerstrom (1972) describes a number of interest centers she used in her individualized program. Depending on room size and furniture availability, some or all of the following may be possible.

Book Nook: This is the area of the room where most of the reading material is located. Colorful carpet samples sewn together, mats, pillows, easy chairs, and other pleasant furnishings will enhance the attractiveness of the area. Some teachers have used pup tents, boxes, and old bathtubs filled with pillows to attract children to reading.

Creative Corner: This area is designed to stimulate creative writing and expression. It should be provided with tables, extra desks and chairs, and a supply of paper, pencils, and dictionaries. A chart or bulletin board entitled "What Should I Write About?" can contain suggestions, which should be changed periodically. The following is a list of suggestions for creative writing topics:

What is red?

If I were a snowball, I'd . . .

What color is happiness? Why?

Which room in your home do you like best? Why?

Write about a dream you have had.

Use all of the following words in a story—*role, press, hard, squeeze, throw, apple, balloon.*

I'm happy today because . . .

Why does a banana have a peel?

If you were a witch, what would you be like?

How does it feel to be blue?

How would it feel to be a pumpkin on Halloween?

If you were a Christmas present, what would you like to be? Who would you like to be given to?

What is spring fever?

What will you do when spring comes that you couldn't do before?

What would it be like to own an elephant?

How would it feel to be an astronaut?

Why do cats have whiskers?

Write a story about "The Robot Who Cried."

What would you do if you were President?

How would it feel to be a bubble?

Poet's Pad: This area is set aside for reading, writing, sharing, and discussing poetry. Books of poetry should be available and children's work displayed. Colorful posters of poems can decorate the walls.

Art Cart: There are days when people do not feel like reading. This area provides an alternative. It contains a table or desks covered with newspaper or oilcloth. Boxes of string, yarn, buttons, scraps of cloth, stones, paper, cardboard, crayons, glue or paste, pipe cleaners, paint, clay, brushes, chalk, and junk will provide ample materials for creative expression. Children can create art work as a way of sharing a favorite book or character with others in the class.

Listening Center: This area could contain a tape recorder, headphones and a jack, a record player, and records. Activities carried on here include (1) making tape recordings to share with others, (2) listening to records and tapes of stories, (3) listening to music, and (4) working on listening skills. Several children at a time—as many as there are headsets—can listen to popular tapes or records.

Patterns and Puzzles Place: The materials in this area encourage reading, thinking, and following directions, as well as adding interest and variety. Items included are crossword puzzles, brainteasers, books of riddles, patterns for making toys, instructions for knitting, blueprints and model kits for constructing airplanes, ships, or cars.

Skill Center: Labelled files of practice exercises, games, and lists for improving word recognition, comprehension, and study skills are found in this area. Permanent practice exercises can easily be made by removing workbook pages, mounting them on tag board, and covering them with plastic or transparent paper.

Beginning a Program Some teachers interested in individualized reading begin with the whole class while others start with one group. Some begin gradually—for part of the reading period or only once or twice a week. So that none of the students feel confused or left out, however, it is probably preferable to begin with the whole class and for the entire reading period each day. Before beginning, the teacher should discuss individualized reading with the children, so that they understand how the program will differ from their current or previous program. This discussion should consider roles and responsibilities as well as rewards. Classroom guidelines can be developed and explanations of the various learning centers should be clearly given. Children need to understand the nature of conferences, skill groups, and sharing. Some teachers suggest including only reading and conferences the first week and later starting to develop group activities. In the beginning some children may need a good deal of help in selecting a book. In addition to giving aid and encouragement, the teacher will sometimes need to select a book for a child. If the children are older and have had a year or more in some other program such as a basal reader, it may be difficult to convince them that they really are free to read what they want for interest, information, and personal enjoyment.

Conferences Integral to the success of an individualized reading program is the pupil-teacher conference. The conferences have both diagnostic and instructional value.

Ideally conferences should be held with each child at least once a week. Some children will require more frequent conferences, while others will be happy to read independently, conferring with the teacher as infrequently as once a month. Conference time may range from two to ten minutes, or more. Perhaps the best way for the teacher to determine *who* to confer with is to have children sign on a chalkboard or some other place if they desire a conference that day. The teacher can then meet with each child wherever and whenever seems best. A semi-private area of the room, off-limits to other children during conferences, can be designated. The teacher should also allow time to stroll about the room looking for children who may need help.

The child should be prepared for a conference. He should be ready to read portions of his latest book, or one that he especially enjoyed, to answer questions about it, and to describe his feelings and opinions. He should also bring his folder of up-to-date records. Specific activities within each conference will vary depending on the needs of the child and the purposes of the teacher. By listening to the child's reading, the teacher may diagnose skill needs and involve the child in a skill group or direct him to self-instructional activities in the skill center. Noting the child's interests will help the teacher to recommend particular materials.

There are many questions a teacher can ask about materials read, even if the teacher herself has not read the materials. Among them are the following:

1. What was the setting? Where did the story take place?
2. Describe the characters you liked most or least.
3. Briefly summarize the story.
4. What did you learn from it?
5. How did you feel as you read it—frightened, happy, worried?
6. Could it have ended differently?
7. Could this really have happened?

Children should not be questioned about or held accountable for everything they read. As adults, how often would we read a book, article, or news story if we had to answer questions or write a book report about it?

The conference not only allows the teacher to diagnose skill needs, determine comprehension ability, and ascertain interests, it also enables teacher and student to get to know each other better. It is invaluable to an individualized reading program.

Sharing Individualized reading is sometimes criticized for being *too* individualistic and for not providing enough opportunity for peer-group interaction. Children—like adults—are social creatures who develop through human contact. Sharing time can be arranged to provide this needed interaction.

Sharing activities can be arranged in a number of ways. A short time each day or perhaps two or three times a week can be set aside for sharing. Attendance can be mandatory or optional. The sharing group might consist of the full class, sharing teams (small groups), or pairs. Temporary sharing groups might be established according to common interests (monsters, model cars, horse stories, and so on), with each child reporting on his favorite reading within the topic.

Sharing time should be worthwhile, interesting, and enjoyable for all involved. Formal oral book reports, which can be very boring, should be avoided. There are many other ways to share a book or story and at the same time exchange ideas and experiences. The following list contains some ways of sharing a book:

1. Try to sell the book or story to the class by arousing their interest in it.
2. Read some parts orally to the group.
3. Show an illustration from the book and explain it.
4. Tell about an interesting, exciting, or amusing part.
5. Explain new and unfamiliar words from the story.
6. Pantomime characters or events.
7. Make puppets and give a puppet show.
8. Demonstrate how to do something you read about.
9. Make a shadow box.
10. Make clay models of some characters.
11. Draw and color a map or a floor-plan.
12. Dress a doll as a character.
13. Write a different ending and read it to the group.
14. Make a book jacket and write the "blurb."
15. Draw a picture of some event.
16. Give a TV show dramatizing parts of the book.
17. Report on interviews with others who have read it.
18. Design a bulletin board portraying several things you have read.
19. Write a simpler version for younger children.
20. Make a diorama of a scene.

Skill Development Skill needs can be diagnosed during pupil-teacher conferences and through formal or informal testing procedures. Once these needs are determined, instruction can be specifically matched to them.

Most students will direct their own instruction, using materials that are self-scored.

Workbooks, textbooks, and other materials can be disassembled by the teacher, aide, or pupils and reassembled as self-directed exercise cards with answer keys. File boxes for vocabulary, phonics, structural analysis, and context and study skills may be constructed to contain these self-directed cards. Each file box may be subdivided (initial consonants, short vowels, and syllabication for a phonics box, for example; prefixes, compound words, and suffixes for a structural analysis box) and each exercise card code-numbered.

In addition to the self-directed exercise cards, an assortment of teaching games, kits, and instructional materials can be included in the skill center. They may be both commercially prepared and teacher or pupil made. Three excellent sources of materials, games, and activities are *Individualized Reading—Self-Pacing Activities* by Evangeline L. Garrison (1970), *Improving Reading through Individualized Correction* by Delwyn G. Schubert (1968), and *Locating and Correcting Reading Difficulties* by Eldon Ekwall (1970).

When more than one child needs work in the same skill area, it is frequently useful to form groups. Depending on the activities and the availability of materials, the teacher's presence with the group may or may not be required.

Record Keeping With each child reading different materials, participating in varying activities, and practicing individually needed skills, record keeping becomes very important. Children can profit from recording their progress; teachers can use records to make instructional decisions and to clear up parents' misconceptions about the reading program.

Some teachers require pupils to keep a daily log of titles and number of pages read. Others ask that students make and organize a vocabulary book, making new entries as they encounter and learn new words. Records can be kept of each sharing activity, indicating the title of the book and the method of presentation. Reading wheels can be made and marked indicating the type of written material read (book, pamphlet, magazine article, newspaper story) or the topic (careers, animals, mystery, "how to"). Some teachers use dittoed formats, which have places for descriptions, summaries, and impressions. If pupil record keeping becomes too cumbersome, however, it can have a negative effect on reading growth. In one program observed by this writer, children appeared to spend more time on record keeping than reading.

Teacher-kept records note comprehension and skill strengths and weaknesses (formally or informally measured), reading interests, accomplishments, and perhaps summaries of pupil-teacher conferences. Skill group assignments and skill pre- and post-test scores may be needed for

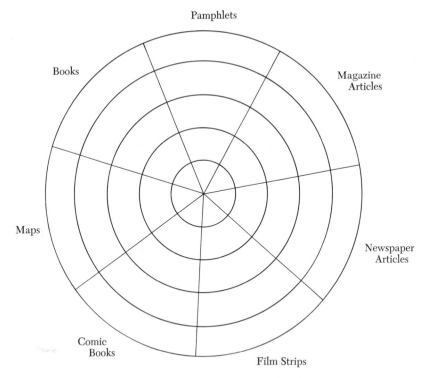

Figure 7.1   A Reading Wheel.

As the child completes a reading in a category, he shades in part of the appropriate space.

children who are not yet accomplished readers. Teachers' record keeping, however, should not use time that could be more beneficially spent with children.

Evaluation   Evaluation of reading growth in an individualized program (or a language-experience approach) is of necessity more personal and informal than in other types of programs. There are no end-of-book tests, and standardized measurement instruments may not match the skills being learned. Many of the greatest advantages of this approach are not very easy to measure—there are no grade-level norms for a love of reading.

The most useful evaluation is done through informal observation, diagnostic conferences, examination of exercises and activities completed, and pupil- and teacher-made records. Attitude inventories can reveal interest in reading, and short assessment tests can be given following specific skill instruction. In addition, most schools administer yearly standardized tests of overall reading comprehension and vocabulary.

Teacher Role

Wendell Johnson (1956) has said,

> Reading is something we do, not so much with our eyes, as such, as with our knowledge and interests and enthusiasm, our hatred and fondnesses and fears, our evaluations in all their forms and aspects. Because this is so, a fondness for reading is something that a child acquires in much the same way as he catches a cold—by being effectively exposed to someone who already has it (p. 123).

Teachers serve as models in many ways. If a teacher believes there is value in reading and wishes her pupils to value reading, a good beginning is to do a lot of reading, to be seen reading, and to discuss her reading interests and experiences with the class. Lyman Hunt (1970) has proposed an idea called "uninterrupted sustained silent reading" (USSR). In essence, the idea calls for a time each day, perhaps the thirty minutes before lunch, when everything else in a school stops and everyone reads: the pupils, the teachers, the principal, the aides and secretaries, the cooks and custodians. Phones go unanswered and teachers *do not* use the time to grade papers or write letters. The writer knows of several schools in which USSR is being used, and it has become the most popular part of the school day. Children read because everyone is reading. This is modeling at its peak.

Another role of the teacher is to read to children. Boys and girls of all abilities, interests, and ages in elementary school enjoy being read to. The unruliest classes become quiet when a story is being read. Any school librarian can tell you what book or story has been read to a class on a given day because of the demands for the book from the children who have just heard it.

Seeing the teacher as a reader and being read to by the teacher are not uniquely advantageous to an individualized reading program, of course; any program can profit from them. Specific to individualized reading is the teacher as a classroom organizer, a gatherer of materials, an arranger of learning centers, an advisor, a diagnostician, a prescriber, a listener, and a friend.

Advantages of Individualized Reading

Proponents of individualized reading state that it heightens and sustains children's interest. Teachers report that many children who seem "turned off" to reading become interested again when allowed to choose what they wish to read. Enjoyment encourages children to read more and consequently gain skill. Some children reportedly read voraciously when allowed the freedom to choose.

Individualized reading programs can reduce the harmfulness of over-sized classes. Boredom, anxieties, and frustrations tend to be eliminated, and discipline problems diminish. Careful organization is required; children and teacher alike must understand their roles and establish parameters.

In an individualized program, the teacher who recognizes individual differences and needs more readily can often design more relevant instruction than in a group program. Skills are taught individually or in small groups when they are needed rather than in a sequence prescribed by a published program. This requires that *the teacher have a thorough understanding* of the various aspects of reading development as well as the ability to diagnose reading needs.

Umans (1963) suggests that the conferences between child and teacher help develop close personal relationships and better understanding. Most children greatly value having some time of their own with their teacher. The better the teacher knows each of her pupils as individuals, the more useful she can be as a consultant, advisor, teacher, and friend.

In many programs, average and advanced readers are held back by the pace of the group, the class, or the reading book. There are no external "brakes" applied in an individualized program, and better readers tend to advance rapidly.

Slower readers can receive a greater amount of personalized help because the teacher need not spend as much time with good readers. Children are not subjected to the stigma attached to placement in the "slow group." They are not compared to each other as often, and "mistakes" remain private between teacher and child. There may still be competition, but it has to do with amount of reading rather than ability, and the sense of failure many children experience is diminished. Self-respect and self-confidence are increased.

Independence, self-direction, and personal responsibility tend to be fostered by individualized reading. Children are permitted to make many decisions and are "told" less often.

Disadvantages of Individualized Reading

Robinson (1965) believes that an individualized reading program is difficult to organize and places giant demands on the teacher. Such a program requires unusual teaching ability and a thorough knowledge of reading. This cannot be disputed; but teachers in any kind of program, to be successful, must meet those requirements. First-year teachers may have difficulty with an individualized program. Since teachers must learn a great deal about children, the reading process, and teaching methods during their initial years of teaching, the structure provided by sequential (published) programs may be advantageous for beginners. After gaining some experience, however, teachers may find that individualized reading makes no greater demands than other approaches.

Critics point out that individualized reading programs lack vocabulary control and a predetermined sequence of word recognition and comprehension skills. Proponents of this approach, however, feel that skills should be taught when they are needed so they become more meaningful. Students in individualized classes are often motivated to learn new words by their high interest in reading.

Spache and Spache (1969) believe teachers must be familiar with all materials read by the children in order to assess comprehension adequately. The teacher who accepts this idea will have a hard time with an individualized reading program. The older children become and the better they read, the more widely they will read. Thousands of books and countless magazine articles, newspapers, pamphlets, and filmstrips will be read. It would be impossible for any teacher to keep up with the wide reading of her class.

Complexity and time-consumption of necessary record keeping has been criticized by Frost (1967), and many teachers say that the large quantities of reading materials required can be prohibitively costly.

Research Findings

Much of the reported research shows that individualized reading makes no overwhelming difference in increasing reading progress. However, interest in reading and quantity of reading is often greater with children who have been in an individualized program.

A three-year study reported by Rodney Johnson (1965) showed that children in such programs can achieve just as well as children taught with basals, in the aspects of reading measured by standardized tests. An analysis of the results of seven controlled studies comparing individualized reading with basal reading showed that the individualized children did better in four of the studies while the basal pupils performed better in the other three (Vite, 1961). Abbott (1972) found that basal and individualized reading groups did equally well on a test of basic reading skills but that the individualized group had a higher commitment to independent reading. In a study with fourth-, fifth-, and sixth-grade pupils, Karlin (1957) found that the individualized groups showed more interest in reading and read more than the basal group.

Thus there seems to be neither clear-cut evidence favoring individualized reading nor any empirical base for attacking it. Children's ability seems to develop in this kind of program about as well as in other kinds. The 1964–1965 U.S. Office of Education studies showed that there is no *one method* of reading instruction that is superior to all others. There is often more variability in growth *within* a method than *between* methods. This finding further verifies the belief that the key factor in any learning situation is the *teacher*, not the method or material. Proponents of individualized instruction assert that this approach offers a good chance to increase interest in reading and create lifetime readers—*without* loss of achievement.

Recent Developments

In recent years some new instructional approaches related to individualization have been developed. All have been used to prescriptively individualize reading instruction, particularly "skill" aspects of reading. Three of them are briefly discussed here.

Individually Prescribed Instruction The Learning Research and Development Center at the University of Pittsburgh developed individually prescribed instruction (IPI). Individual lessons are assigned to each child on the basis of pretest information and teacher observations. Following printed instructions, the child obtains his lessons from catalogued files or shelves. The lessons are selected principally from commercially produced reading textbooks, workbooks, programmed materials, and the like. After the child completes the lesson, it is scored by the teacher, who determines which lesson the child should complete next. Further assignments are made on the basis of continuous evaluation.

IPI emphasizes skills more than the previously described approach to individualized reading, but the major difference is that lessons are prescribed by the teacher rather than selected by the child.

Computer-Assisted Instruction Very similar in concept to IPI is computer-assisted instruction. The major difference is that the child relates to a computer instead of a teacher. Sequential instruction is determined in advance and programmed for a computer. Most computer-assisted instructional systems use audio and visual presentations to which the child responds. For example, three words may appear on a cathode ray tube *(too, for, tub),* and the child may be asked to indicate the word which begins differently from the others. A recorded voice might read the words while they appear visually. Then the computer would "instruct" the child as to the next step, which might be to try again or to move to another frame, depending on the child's answer.

Most computer-assisted instruction in reading has, to date, been in the area of basic word recognition skills. Conceivably more complex aspects of reading could be programmed. Criticism of this system centers on its impersonality (shades of 1984) and its high cost. But ours is a technological society, and it is highly likely that many schools of the future will take advantage of the efficiency of computer-assisted instruction. Computer-assisted instruction will be discussed in greater detail in Chapter Eight.

Individually Guided Education The University of Wisconsin Research and Development Center for Cognitive Learning has directed its research and development activities toward individually guided instruction. Related to IGE are the multi-unit school, intern-in-team teaching, and individualized programs in various areas.

The aim of the IGE reading program is to provide a framework by which a skill development program can be worked out locally. The Wisconsin Design for Reading Skill Development, an integral part of IGE, consists of six skill areas: word attack, comprehension, study skills, self-directed reading, interpretive reading, and creative reading. Explicit behavioral objectives are stated for the first three and general guidelines for the latter three. The purposes of the reading component of IGE are: (1) to provide a means of assessing individual skill development; (2) to provide a management system for grouping children and planning skill development instruction; and (3) to provide a plan for monitoring pupils' progress in skill development.

Through an elaborate system of skill testing and coding, pupils are grouped according to skill needs. Resource files keyed to commercially available reading materials are provided so that teachers may use whatever materials are available in their basic reading program. No instructional materials are included in the Wisconsin Design. IGE is similar to IPI in that teachers make decisions about materials and lessons through which each child may follow a unique route. The major difference between the two is IGE's emphasis on variability of local selection of appropriate procedures. Pupil self-selection is not a feature of this individually guided skills program. Some schools use it as an adjunct to a more typical individualized reading program, but the majority of schools use it in conjunction with a basal reading program (Wisconsin Design, 1971).

IPI, CAI, and IGE programs have been soundly criticized for their fragmented view of the reading process and their over-emphasis of "skilling" and "drilling" (Johnson and Pearson, 1975).

Summary

There are many degrees of individualization and many kinds of individualized reading programs. Despite vast differences, the thread common to them is the recognition that all children are unique individuals who have different abilities, interests, and potentials. While most teachers individualize in some ways, only a minority of them would classify theirs as a totally "individualized reading" approach. By far the majority of American children are taught to read using the basal reading approach, discussed next.

The Basal Reading Approach

The most common approach to reading instruction, the basal reader program, is used in an estimated 80 to 95 percent of American schools (Chall, 1967; Staiger, 1969). In a sense, basal reading materials and programs have been with us since the days of the hornbook, which contained what was considered to be basic (essential) content. Since those early days basal programs have greatly expanded and contain many components. A number of publishing houses publish basal programs, which have both common features and differences.

The basal reader approach was until recently referred to as the "look-say," "controlled vocabulary," or "whole-word" method. None of these terms is totally accurate or comprehensive enough to include the many features of basal reading programs. With the evolution of the graded school in the middle of the last century, a need arose for grade-levelled reading materials. Through the years basal programs expanded from one book to several and further expanded by adding workbooks, teacher's manuals, supplementary materials, and more recently audio-visual aids such as tapes, cassettes, and transparencies. Generally, though, the overall purpose has not changed: to provide a *total, comprehensive, sequential* program aimed at teaching reading to all children.

Basal reading programs introduce vocabulary gradually and usually include words that various researchers have identified as occurring frequently in children's vocabularies. Words are repeated often to assure mastery. Word analysis skills are introduced gradually and sequentially. Each aspect of the total scope and sequence of the program is tightly controlled and interwoven so that children progress through a learning-refining-broadening continuum.

During the past decade, basal reading programs have undergone rather sweeping changes, and many of the criticisms previously levelled at them are no longer valid. Throughout the 1940s and 1950s basal reading programs tended to be very much alike, but today they vary considerably. Before examining the components of basal programs and their related instructional strategies, we will cite some early and recurring criticisms and show how basal reader authors and publishers have responded.

Traditional Criticisms of Basal Materials

1. Story content and illustrations portray an all-white, middle-class world in which minority groups do not exist except in service roles.

This scathing criticism was true until the past decade. Virtually all characters were white and lived in rural or suburban areas. They were clean, well-fed, and well-clothed, and children possessed only unbroken toys. Father usually worked in an office or in some occupation requiring a white shirt and necktie. Mother never worked outside of the home but was always well-dressed and usually found in the kitchen. Black, American Indian, and Chicano families were not included.

Early in the 1960s this began to change. At first light tan faces began to appear, but the environments remained the same. The Bank Street Readers (1965) and the Chandler Language-Experience Readers (1966) were more realistic. Urban environments replaced suburban, and blacks as well as other ethnic groups came to be represented. However, in a study of environmental settings, multi-ethnicity, and success-failure outcomes reported by Waite (1968), it was found that of seven basal reading series published in 1965 and 1966 only *two* had more than 19 percent of the stories located in urban settings, four contained 40 percent or more "white-only" stories, and in three series, 30 percent or more of the stories ended in failure rather than success for the characters.

Today nearly all of the recently published basal reading series have multi-ethnic characters and a variety of environmental settings. With respect to race and ethnicity, *basal reader content is much more realistic* and representative of life in America than in previous years. This is not true with regard to women. Sex-role stereotyping continues to be prevalent. A study of sex stereotyping in children's readers (*Dick and Jane as Victims*, 1972), revealed the following facts. Of the 2,760 stories from 134 books, boy-centered stories outnumbered girl-centered stories 5 to 2, male biographies outnumbered female 6 to 1, and men were shown in 146 occupations compared to 25 for women. Females were generally more docile, passive, and dependent. Clearly, content of basal reading materials needs considerable overhauling to eliminate sexism.

2. Syntactic structures in basal reader stories do not closely match language usage of children.

This continues to be something of a problem. Basal readers, with their emphasis on vocabulary control and the heavy repetition of words, have often ignored linguistic structures. What we know about language development in children is still not being applied in books. For example, Shuy (1971) points out that one basal used the construction, "Over the fence went the ball," though few if any children use sentences which begin with a prepositional phrase followed by a predicate. It is encouraging to note that some of the most recently published programs show improvement in the inclusion and manipulation of varying syntactic structures.

3. Insufficient attention is paid to the development of letter-sound relationships in beginning materials.

Since basal readers take a "whole-word" approach, phonics materials have tended to be supplementary and have been introduced late and treated lightly. However, the most recent basal program authors and publishers have sought the advice of teachers and linguists and have considered research findings, resulting in *a much increased treatment* of the decoding skills. Though most programs still begin by teaching sight words, attention is given very early to the development of letter-sound correspondence strategies.

4. Story content is repetitive, dull, and insipid.

Efforts have recently been made to include a wider variety of stories both in terms of realism and fantasy. Illustrations, photographs, and drawings are more varied today and even the use of print has become more innovative. Various sizes and types of print as well as modifications of left-to-right sequence (for example, in one program print goes up the stairs and down in one story and around in a circle in another) are found in the newest books.

In general, then, authors and publishers of basal reading programs have made many changes in the content and format of the material. Though further improvements are needed, the materials of the seventies appear to be far better and more diverse than those of a decade ago.

What Is the Basal Program?

As comprehensive reading programs designed to introduce non-readers to beginning reading skills and then facilitate their development into mature

readers, the programs typically consist of the several components described below.

Reading Readiness Books and Materials Readiness materials usually consist of workbooks, kits, games, charts, and activities designed to improve
visual and auditory discrimination, language and experiential background,
directionality, and story development. Visual discrimination activities give
practice in visually perceiving similarities and differences in graphic
shapes: pictures, geometric designs, letters, real and nonsense words, and
longer units. A typical exercise might be: "Circle the letter that is not the
same as the others."

1.	o	o	e	o
2.	t	f	t	t

Auditory discrimination exercises are included to develop ability to perceive auditory similarities and differences. Typical exercises require identifying pairs of words which begin or end with the same sound (such as
books and *bat*). Other readiness components include picture books without
words, from which the child is to tell the story, activities (such as "show
and tell") for developing oral language, and objects for categorizing and
classifying.

Pre-primers Pre-primers are the pupils' first books. They are very thin and
usually have paperback covers. Very few words are introduced—perhaps
twenty or twenty-five in each pre-primer—and the words are frequently
repeated. Many illustrations are included, and the characters are usually
the same ones the children "met" in the readiness program. Because of the
tightly controlled vocabulary, the stories lack any kind of literary merit.
However, few authors or teachers could compose anything resembling a
literary masterpiece with a vocabulary of two or three dozen words.
Furthermore, the purpose of these books is to expose children to a limited
number of words and to repeat these words frequently so the children will
master them. Development of literary appreciation is not the goal.

Primers Following a series of two to four pre-primers, children begin to
read the primer—usually the first hardback book in the series. One of the
newest basal programs, however, uses small paperback books throughout
the series. The primer is built on the vocabularies, and sometimes the story
line, of the pre-primers. Typically one hundred or more new words are
introduced.

The Readers After completing the primer, children advance to the readers.
In some series they are tightly grade-levelled. For example, the two

first-grade books are labelled "one^1" and "one^2"; the second grade books are "two^1" and "two^2," and so on. After third grade there is usually one reading book per year in these series. The newest basal series have abandoned these tight grade-level notations, primarily because of the stigma attached to them. It is often embarrassing for the slow reading fourth-grade child to be seen with a book marked "two^1." However, even in the newer series the materials are gradated. In one series there are at least thirteen books intended for the first four grades—each expanding and building on the vocabulary and skills presented in the previous one. In another series, a number of thin paperbacks are coded at varying levels of difficulty. These series of small books are based on the belief that some children are frustrated by the thickness of a hardback book and are motivated to read a small paperback because they feel they can finish it.

Until recently most basal readers did not introduce more than 400 words by the end of first grade, but vocabulary size has greatly increased in some of the newer series.

Workbooks Workbooks usually accompany each reading book in the series, including the readiness materials. Contained in the workbook are decoding activities in phonics, syllabication, structural analysis, and contextual analysis, as well as comprehension activities related to the stories in the readers. Vocabulary building exercises and work with dictionaries and other reference materials are sometimes provided. The workbooks in some series are not related to the reading books and can be used as separate supplementary programs.

Proponents of basal reading programs believe that children need sequential introduction to the basic word recognition and comprehension skills and that workbooks are a sensible vehicle for assuring that none of the essential skills is missed. Teachers are sometimes cautioned that not all pupils need to do every workbook page. Pre-tests or checkpoints are sometimes provided to help determine which children would profit from the workbook exercises. Workbooks have received considerable criticism both from pupils and reading authorities. Children have been heard to say, "I like to read, but I hate reading," meaning they particularly dislike completing workbook pages. Many reading authorities feel that the term *work* should be removed from the activity books to make them less foreboding.

Teacher Manuals These guide books contain numerous suggestions to teachers for using the materials. Some are so detailed that they list specific questions for each of the stories. They also explain how teachers may use the materials diagnostically and indicate particular workbook pages to be prescribed when a student makes certain errors in oral reading. Typically there is a separate manual for each of the reader-workbook pairs. An acquaintance of this writer who is a teacher in New Zealand complains that American teachers are "spoiled" by the teacher's manuals. She believes there are so many suggested activities, questions, games, and the like that the teacher really does not have to think for herself. Whether or not this is the case, beginning teachers are usually most grateful for the manuals as a thorough resource for instructional planning.

Supplementary Materials Type, amount, and quality of supplementary materials vary greatly among the published basal reading programs. Supplementary story books built on the vocabulary and skills presented, filmstrips, charts, posters, kits, audio tapes, and games are included to some degree with most current programs. They are intended to add interest and variety.

Tests Most basal reading programs include an assortment of pre- and post-tests for assessing students' mastery of the materials and skills covered and for diagnosing students' reading weaknesses in order to place them within components of the program.

Using the Basal Approach

After a certain period of readiness work—its length depends on the needs of the children—instruction with the reading materials begins. With most basal reading programs a four-step instructional format is followed each day, or with each lesson or story: (1) background development, (2) prescribed reading, (3) skill development, and (4) extended reading.

The teacher begins the lesson by developing background. This usually includes a discussion of the story's topic in relation to the lives of the children in the group. If the story is about subways, the teacher might ask, "How many of you have been on a subway?" "Who will tell us about it?" and other related questions. New vocabulary is introduced during this discussion. If three new words (subway, tunnel, turnstile) are presented in the story, they might be written on the chalkboard within context:

> The *subway* train is fast
> a *tunnel* under the city
> a *turnstile* gate . . .

In addition to sharing experiences and introducing new vocabulary, the discussion establishes purposes for reading. The teacher asks questions or gives directions related to the story: "When you read the story, see if you can learn why Tom's friend wasn't with him."

Prescribed reading takes a variety of forms. Most often the teacher asks the group to read the story silently. Then a discussion is held and the teacher asks comprehension questions. These discussions can be very interesting if questions are asked beyond the literal level. It is certainly more fun to respond to an inferential question like, "Do you think Tom will ever ride a subway alone again?" than to, "How big was Tom's ticket?" Following the discussion the teacher may have the children read the story orally. There are usually two purposes for this oral re-reading. One is simply that most children enjoy reading aloud. The other is that the oral reading allows the teacher to diagnose problems children might be having.

Basal reading instruction is often criticized for this "round-robin" reading, in which children in a small group of six to twelve take turns reading orally, with everyone focused on the same line. Some children read slower and some faster than others, which can cause boredom or confusion. Likewise it can be embarrassing for the child who reads poorly. One remedy to this legitimate criticism is to divide the group into "reading pairs" for oral reading. The two paired children can alternate reading each paragraph or page. In this way every child will have more opportunities to read. The teacher can move from pair to pair to listen and give assistance if needed. The two children can help one another with words and check with the teacher if both are stumped. There may be a louder noise level in the room, with four or five children reading aloud instead of one, but it need not be a problem.

For skill development, teachers may use both the reading book story and the accompanying workbook exercise. Letter-sound correspondences are taught or reinforced by calling attention to words within the story that have identical letter-sound relationships. Structural analysis (play, play*ed*, play*ing*), contextual analysis, and comprehension strategies are presented.

The teacher can encourage further reading by calling attention to books or records within the classroom or library which relate to the content, theme, location, or some other aspect of the story just read. Many children are interested in doing related reading but need suggestions as to what is available and where to find it.

Classroom Organization in a Basal Program

According to information gained from pretesting and observation, the teacher forms a number of groups consisting of children reading at approximately the same level. The range of children's abilities will be wide. In one class of fourth graders, for example, there may be both non-readers and children who read at a high school level. Forming groups based on reading ability reduces the range within any one group—though it is important to remember that there will still be a range. The number of groups may range from one to six or more, though for some reason, most basal reader teachers form three reading groups. Each group, the high, the middle, and the low, works with a different set of materials. Some school systems use three separate basal series—a different series for each group. In other schools, different levels of the same series are used with each group.

The three-group plan has been often criticized for its rigidity. It has been found that there is little mobility between groups within a school year or even within a child's several years in an elementary school. Once a child is assigned to the low group in grade one he may continue in the low group for many years. Bosman (1972) found that 80 percent of the children in fifth grade in her school were in the same reading group level (high, middle, or low) they had been in since first grade. The three-group plan is also criticized for the potential psychological damage it can do to children who are labelled "dummies" and are daily identified with the low group. Many teachers attempt to camouflage the groups by using neutral names like "red, blue, and green" groups or "Bill's, Mary's, and Sandy's" groups or euphemistic terms like "bluebirds, sunbursts, and twinkle-stars." But children are not fooled by labels; everyone knows who is in the low group.

Smith and Barrett (1974) have proposed forming flexible groups. Interest groups would form and dissolve frequently during the year, skill groups would be formed as needed and then disbanded, and basic groups could continue. Different types of groups would meet on different days. In this way no one would be continuously affiliated with only one group. During a typical reading period of about one hour, the teacher spends fifteen or twenty minutes with each group. In the meantime other children, individually or as groups, do workbook exercises, read independently, prepare for the session with the teacher, or work on projects.

Summary

The basal reading approach encompasses a number of series or programs, commercially produced, which provide continuous reading instruction throughout the elementary grades. Vocabulary is controlled and introduced gradually, and skills are presented sequentially. Children progress from the familiar to the unfamiliar, ever broadening their reading ability. Reading materials are grade-levelled; each new book builds on vocabulary, concepts, and skills presented earlier. Children are usually grouped according to reading ability, and small group instruction prevails.

Research and the Basal Approach

One of the major research studies of instructional approaches in reading was the one sponsored by the U.S. Office of Education and coordinated by Bond and Dykstra (1967). It is generally referred to as the "first grade studies." In analyzing twenty-seven different comparative studies, many of which compared a basal reading program with some other approach (language-experience, i.t.a., and so on), the researchers came to the following major conclusions:

1. Children learn to read by a variety of materials and methods. . . . Pupils become successful readers in . . . vastly different programs. . . . Furthermore, pupils experience difficulty in each of the programs utilized. No one approach is so distinctly better in all situations and respects than the others that it should be considered the one best method and the one to be used exclusively.
2. Combinations of programs, such as a basal program with supplementary phonics materials, often are superior to single approaches. . . .

In their chapter in *The First Grade Reading Studies: Findings of Individual Investigations*, edited by Stauffer (1967), Bond and Dykstra have this to say about comparisons of the basal reading approach to a variety of other approaches and combinations:

> . . . the basal reader approach was somewhat less often in a position of superiority. This is especially true in the area of word recognition. The basal reader approach fared better when it was coupled with a strong word-recognition program than it did without such an increased emphasis. It also held up better in the areas of comprehension and spelling, but still did not have a superior position (p. 6).

It is very difficult to compare the basal reading approach with other approaches because there are so many different published series. As indicated earlier in this chapter, a great deal depends on the teacher. Some excellent teachers use a basal approach, and others, equally excellent, use a different approach. Unfortunately some teachers teach poorly regardless of method or material. It seems safe to say that the basal reader approach is no poorer or better than other methods—though it is improved when supplemented with additional decoding materials. The newest basal programs have heeded the recommendations of Bond and Dykstra and have strengthened the word recognition components.

In considering the future of the basal reading approach—the approach used by perhaps four out of five elementary teachers—it is worth recalling the words of Ralph Staiger (1969):

> The change of the past was an evolutionary one, in which gradual acceptance could be waited for. Will gradualism in the adoption of new ideas in basal readers be possible in the era in which we now live? Will the knowledge of the high speed technology which surrounds us—computer-assisted instruction and television, for instance—permit the gradual adoption of new ideas into basal readers? Time alone will tell. At present, the educational market provides adequate profits for investments in major projects, such as basal readers. Will this policy also hold in five years?
>
> The future will be disquieting to those who abhor change, but it will be interesting (pp. 293–294).

Other Organizational Arrangements

We have examined the language-experience approach and the individualized approach with their individualization and their flexible short-term grouping arrangements. We have also mentioned the within-class ability grouping particularly found in basal reading programs. Three other developments should be mentioned before we conclude this chapter.

The Joplin Plan

So far, we have considered reading programs in relation to the self-contained classroom. A modification of within-class (intraclass) ability grouping is the across-class (interclass) ability group plan known as the Joplin Plan.[3] In this scheme children remain in a self-contained classroom with one teacher for most instruction but are grouped across classes for reading instruction. For example, if there are two fourth-, two fifth-, and two sixth-grade classes in a building, six interage reading classes would be formed—based on ability. The very top group might contain mostly sixth graders, some fifth graders, and a few fourth graders, while the reverse might be true for the very bottom group. At a certain time each day children leave their regular classroom and go to their reading class. The method of instruction is usually basal, but other approaches to reading are

---

[3] The arrangement was tried in many schools but became best known after its inception in the Joplin, Missouri, public schools.

also found in Joplin Plan schools. Each reading group theoretically has a range of achievement, which is smaller than would be found in any one of the self-contained classrooms. Ranges of ability will still exist, however, as well as varying interests and maturity levels. The stigma of being in the low group may be even greater with this plan since it will become public knowledge to children from other classes. Among others, one recurring criticism of the Joplin Plan is that it deprives classroom teachers of intimate knowledge of their pupils' reading abilities and interests, since many children from one teacher's classroom may be instructed in reading by a different teacher. It might also be noted that Joplin Plan organizational patterns tend to isolate instruction of reading from other areas of the curriculum, the other language arts particularly.

Departmentalized Reading

Like most high schools and middle schools, some elementary schools have done away with the self-contained classroom in favor of subject matter groups. This is often done informally. Mrs. Smith does not like to teach science but enjoys reading. Mr. Jones likes science best, and Mrs. Mott's favorite subject is mathematics. So at the third-grade level Mrs. Smith teaches reading to all three classes, Mr. Jones teaches science, and Mrs. Mott teaches mathematics. They each keep their own class for the remainder of the school day for language arts, social studies, and other areas. While this approach allows teachers "to do their own thing" and therefore, presumably, do it better than the others on the "team," there are some potential problems. Some teachers will not have reading-instructional contact with their homeroom pupils, or for that matter, with any other pupils. This lack of reading contact can have detrimental effects on the teacher's ability to help children in other subjects—nearly all of which require reading ability.

Team Teaching

In schools employing team teaching, two or more teachers generally combine their classes to form one large group of sixty or more pupils. This is sometimes done within a grade, but in the multi-unit, or non-graded, school (increasing in popularity) it is done across grades. The teaching team, usually with the help of paraprofessionals and perhaps student teachers or interns from a nearby university, plans the instructional program. It is possible for them to offer differentiated instruction in the framework of a number of different-sized groups. Any number of reading groups might be formed (as with other curricular areas), and teaching assignments are cooperatively determined.

These three are but a few of the many and varied organizational arrangements currently in use. Although they can all be used successfully, teachers should remember that no organizational plan can ever guarantee success with reading. As we know, the teacher makes the difference.

The Author's Viewpoint

In presenting brief descriptions of some of the many ways of teaching children to read, one attempts to remain relatively objective and dispassionate. I hope it is clear that none of the approaches examined is a panacea. All approaches to reading can work, and all can fail to work depending on the particular mix of individuals and environment. Despite the lack of research evidence supporting any particular method, however, and though I recognize that the teacher makes the difference, I do have a bias. *Teachers will perform best when allowed to select the method and materials that suit them and their pupils best.* Yet continuity is important. It can be quite damaging to children, their ability to read, and their interest in reading if they bounce from one approach to another year after year. So it is important for elementary school staffs to meet and plan and try to develop some agreement on desirable instructional procedures so that the child is not caught in the middle. It is also important for principals and those who hire and place teachers to be aware of teachers' varying philosophies. I am by no means suggesting that everyone act and think alike. But permit an example from a school whose faculty members I know fairly well. Two of four first-grade teachers preferred to use a programmed linguistic series, but all of the second- and third-grade teachers favored a multi-basal approach and *refused* to accept children from the "deviant" classes. How do you resolve this? What is more important, continuity or teacher preference?

So I will describe what I consider the ideal approach, recognizing that it will not suit every teacher or every school. I believe the language-experience approach to beginning reading is the most sensible and the most exciting to young children. Nearly all diversities of language and dialect can be accommodated, and reading is intensely meaningful from the start. Since I view the language-experience approach primarily as an *initial* method (except in remedial cases), I would follow it with an individualized program as described in this chapter. Thus somewhere between early first and perhaps early second grade, children would shift from the reading of stories written by themselves and their classmates to the world of published print. The ideal setting for such a program would be an elementary school in which all teachers are proponents of language-experience and individualized reading, and these methods—however individually executed—would permeate all grades and classrooms. Classrooms would be self-contained. I believe it is hard enough to get to know twenty-five children well enough to be of maximal help, let alone fifty or a hundred. Skills would be taught as they were needed. A multitude of groups would form and disappear, but from the start—and throughout the five or six years—children would read freely, independently, and as widely as they wished, beginning with those first few words they asked the teacher to write for them.

References

Abbott, J. "Fifteen Reasons Why Personalized Reading Instruction Does Not Work." *Elementary English* 49 (January 1972): 33–36.

Ashton-Warner, S. *Teacher.* New York: Simon and Schuster, 1963.

Bond, G. L., and Dykstra, R. "The Cooperative Research Program in First Grade Reading." *Reading Research Quarterly* 2 (Summer, 1967): 5–142.

Bond, G. L., and Dykstra, R. "Interpreting the First Grade Studies." In *The First Grade Reading Studies: Findings of Individual Investigations*, edited by R. G. Stauffer. Newark, Del.: International Reading Association, 1967.

Bosman, D. R. *Mobility in Basal Reading Groups.* Unpublished paper, University of Wisconsin, 1972.

Chall, J. S. *Learning to Read: The Great Debate.* New York: McGraw-Hill, 1967.

Dahl, S. S. *The Language Experience Approach: A Study and Implementation of the Method.* Unpublished paper, University of Wisconsin, 1971.

Dick and Jane as Victims (Sex Stereotyping in Children's Readers). Princeton, N.J.: Women on Words and Images, 1972.

Ekwall, E. *Locating and Correcting Reading Difficulties.* Columbus, Ohio: Charles E. Merrill, 1970.

Fries, C. C. *Linguistics and Reading.* New York: Holt, Rinehart and Winston, 1962.

Frost, J. L. *Issues and Innovations in the Teaching of Reading.* Glenview, Ill.: Scott, Foresman, 1967.

Garrison, E. L. *Individualized Reading—Self-Pacing Activities.* New York: The Instructor Publications, 1970.

Gelb, I. J. *A Study of Writing.* Chicago: University of Chicago Press, 1952.

Hall, Mary Anne. *The Language Experience Approach for the Culturally Disadvantaged.* Newark, Del.: International Reading Association, 1972.

Hammerstrom, K. H. *Individualized Reading Instruction: A Third Grade Program.* Unpublished master's paper, University of Wisconsin, 1972.

Heilman, A. W. *Principles and Practices of Teaching Reading.* 3rd ed. Columbus, Ohio: Charles E. Merrill, 1972.

Huey, E. B. *The Psychology and Pedagogy of Reading.* New York: Macmillan, 1908.

Hunt, L. "The Effect of Self-Selection, Interest and Motivation upon Independent, Instructional and Frustrational Levels." *Reading Teacher* 24 (November 1970): 146–151.

Johnson, D. D. and P. D. Pearson. "Skills Management Systems—A Critique." *Reading Teacher* 28 (May 1975): 757–764.

Johnson, R. H. "Individualized and Basal Primary Reading Programs." *Elementary English* 42 (December 1965): 902–904, 915.

Johnson, W. *Your Most Enchanted Listener.* New York: Harper and Row, 1956.

Karlin, R. "Some Reactions to Individualized Reading." *Reading Teacher* 11 (December 1957): 95–98.

Lee, D. M., and Allen, R. V. *Learning to Read through Experience.* 2nd ed. New York: Appleton-Century-Crofts, 1963.

Mathews, M. M. *Teaching to Read, Historically Considered.* Chicago: University of Chicago Press, 1966.

Robinson, H. A., ed. "Recent Developments in Reading." *Proceedings of the Annual Conference on Reading.* Chicago, 1965.

Schubert, D. G., and Torgerson, T. L. *Improving Reading through Individualized Correction.* 2nd ed. Dubuque, Iowa: Wm. C. Brown, 1968.

Shuy, R. W. "Some Things That Reading Teachers Need to Know About Language." Paper presented at IRA Conference, Atlantic City, April 1971.

Smith, N. B. *American Reading Instruction.* Newark, Del.: International Reading Association, 1965.

Smith, R. J., and Barrett, T. C. *Teaching Reading in the Middle Grades.* Reading, Mass.: Addison-Wesley, 1974.

Spache, G. D., and Spache, E. B. *Reading in the Elementary School.* Boston: Allyn and Bacon, 1969.

Sprengling, M. *The Alphabet.* Chicago: University of Chicago Press, 1931.

Staiger, R. C. "Basal Reading Programs: How Do They Stand Today?" In *Current Issues in Reading,* edited by N. B. Smith. Newark, Del.: International Reading Association, 1969, pp. 283–293.

Stauffer, R. G. *The Language Experience Approach to Reading.* New York: Harper and Row, 1970.

Umans, S. *New Trends in Reading Instruction.* New York: Teacher's College Press, 1963.

Veatch, J. *Individualizing Your Reading Program.* New York: G. P. Putnam's Sons, 1959.

Vite, I. W. "Grouping Practices in Individualized Reading." *Elementary English* 38 (February 1961): 91–98.

Waite, R. R. "Further Attempts to Integrate and Urbanize First Grade Textbooks: A Research Study." *Journal of Negro Education* 7 (Winter 1968): 62–69.

Wisconsin Design for Reading Skill Development. University of Wisconsin Research and Development Center for Cognitive Learning, 1971.

Wright, T., and Halliwell, J. O., eds. *Reliquiae Antiquae.* London: 1841, p. 63.

Chapter
Eight

Preview

The author of this chapter discusses some important approaches to reading instruction. Although these approaches are not as commonly used as those discussed in the previous chapter, they merit serious attention. Their impact has been significant, particularly at the beginning levels.

Moe examines linguistic approaches available from several publishers, pointing out their general strengths and weaknesses and comparing the more popular programs. He reviews programmed materials, computer-assisted instruction, and two general types of phonics instruction: synthetic and analytic. In addition, he describes orthographic variations such as i.t.a. UNIFON, and Fry's Diacritical Marking System. Words in Color, Rebus, and Multi-Media approaches are also discussed.

The chapter concludes with the author's viewpoint as to the value of the several approaches he has presented for different types of children (for example, the culturally different pupil). The author offers suggestions for integrating these approaches to teaching reading with the approaches more commonly used.

Reading: Current Approaches, Part Two

Alden J. Moe, Purdue University

Objectives

After you read this chapter, you should be able to:

1. Trace the evolution and development of each approach.
2. Restructure the rationale behind each approach.
3. List the characteristics which typify each approach.
4. Apply and modify a variety of approaches and corresponding materials as options for the teacher to use in meeting each student's needs.
5. Identify characteristics which may be used in conjunction with or in place of other approaches even though each approach is considered independent of others.

The previous chapter dealt with the more commonly used approaches to the teaching of reading. The focus of this chapter will be on several other approaches which—though perhaps not as common as those described previously—deserve serious attention since they are used to teach reading in many classrooms. Some of these have had a major influence on reading instruction, particularly at the lower grade levels.

Specifically, five current instructional approaches and their respective materials will be considered in this chapter. They are (1) linguistic approaches, (2) programmed and computer-assisted reading, (3) phonic approaches, (4) orthographic variations, and (5) multi-media approaches. Finally, the author will identify what he considers to be the salient features of each of these approaches.

Linguistic Approaches

As background for considering the linguistic approaches to the teaching of reading, it is helpful to know the characteristics of language as viewed by the linguist.[1] Bishop (1971) offers the following principles as representing the current attitude among linguists:

1. Language changes constantly.
2. Change is normal.
3. Spoken language is *the* language.
4. Correctness rests upon usage.
5. All usage is relative.

As we shall soon see, it is the third principle, that spoken language is primary, which has been most emphatically stressed in the development of published linguistic reading materials.

Readers who desire an overview of linguistic applications in reading and other language arts are referred to *Linguistics in Proper Perspective* (Lamb, 1967) for a thorough but non-technical treatment of the subject.

A Brief History of Linguistics and Reading

Although Mathews (1966) reports that a book which presented what might now be called a linguistic approach to the teaching of reading was published in 1913, he states that this book "appears to have failed utterly in arousing either interest or understanding" (p. 153). Credit for presenting the first linguistic approach to the teaching of reading has generally been given to Leonard Bloomfield, a well-known linguist (Heilman, 1972; Ives and Ives, 1970; Lamb, 1967).

Bloomfield became interested in reading instruction in the 1930s, when his son was about to begin school. Bloomfield reasoned that since his son could understand and speak several thousand words he knew the language; therefore, he saw reading as decoding—transferring the printed symbols into speech sounds which were already familiar to the reader.

In two articles Bloomfield (1942) outlined procedures which he believed should be followed in teaching children how to read. Although Bloomfield and his colleague, Clarence Barnhart, experimented throughout the 1940s and 1950s with materials they had devised, it was not until 1961 that their reading program was published as *Let's Read: A Linguistic Approach.* Two other notable publications appeared at about the same time

[1] See Chapter Four for a more complete discussion of the issues briefly noted here.

representing similar philosophies: *Sound and Spelling in English* by Robert A. Hall, Jr. (1961), and *Linguistics and Reading* by Charles C. Fries (1962). Bloomfield, Hall, and Fries all viewed reading as essentially a decoding process, and it is this view that has become known as the linguistic method of teaching reading.

Another book, *Linguistics and the Teaching of Reading* by C. A. Lefevre (1964), took a much broader approach to reading instruction. Whereas Bloomfield and Fries were concerned primarily with the decoding of words, Lefevre points out that "it is not enough to consider only phonemic-graphemic correspondences and the ordering of difficulties of spelling patterns" (Wardhaugh, 1969, p. 27). Lefevre's concern was with structures and patterns, particularly sentence patterns. His views consider more complex aspects of language than either Bloomfield's or Fries's, and have only recently appeared in published reading materials.

Other writers have written extensively on various aspects of linguistics and reading; among the more notable are Goodman (1967, 1968), Goodman and Burke (1970), Shuy (1969a, 1969b), and Wardhaugh (1969), all of whom discussed the complexities of language and reading.

Since 1961, when the first linguistic materials appeared on the market, the emphasis has been largely on decoding; only recently has a different linguistic approach become apparent. Therefore, our discussion of published linguistic materials will examine two general types: (1) the more traditional linguistic approaches, which emphasize decoding—particularly the decoding of words, and (2) linguistic approaches which consider syntactic structure—phrases and sentences.

Decoding Emphasis Linguistic Programs

Bloomfield and Fries advocate a linguistic approach which defines reading as essentially a decoding process. Their approach relies primarily on only one aspect of linguistic science, phonology, the study of the sounds of a language. Hence, they view reading as the ability to make the proper phonemic-graphemic matches—that is, saying [cat] for the word which appears in print as *cat*. They claim further that, since the child has already mastered oral language by the time he comes to school, his main task is learning to break the coded relationships between sound and symbol.

An examination of four published decoding emphasis linguistic programs will show, however, that while they are grouped here under a common heading, there are a number of differences among them.

Let's Read was published in 1961 as one large 465-page volume by the Wayne State University Press and had a very limited distribution (Aukerman, 1971). In an effort to market the program, Clarence L. Barnhart formed his own company and divided the large volume into nine smaller, more easily handled books which were first published in this form in 1963.

Examples of the *Let's Read* materials are found in Figures 8.1 and 8.2. The following are the major characteristics and special features of the program:

1. There are nine books in the program.
2. It is intended for grades one to three.
3. Reading instruction begins with the teaching of letter names.
4. Reading is viewed as a process of decoding from print to sound.
5. Emphasis is placed on mastery of the alphabetical code—whereby each letter of the alphabet possesses but one phonemic value.
6. There is stress on learning phonemic-graphemic relationships with individual words.
7. Words are always pronounced as wholes, never letter by letter.
8. Sound-letter correspondences are established by phonemic contrasts, as with *hat–cat, rip–zip, kid–kit.*
9. Mastery of spelling patterns is stressed.
10. Motivation for student learning is provided by the act of decoding.
11. No pictures are used in any of the texts.
12. Nonsense words such as *din, dib, jin, lin, nin,* and *zin* are used.
13. Word length is controlled.
14. No sight words are presented in the initial reading.
15. There is little story content with which the reader can identify.

The *Merrill Linguistic Readers* (Fries, Wilson, and Rudolph, 1966) have probably been the most widely used of the published linguistic approaches. Like Bloomfield, Fries views reading as a decoding activity and puts little emphasis on comprehension. During the course of the development of the *Merrill Linguistic Readers*, however, Fries became somewhat more concerned with reading for meaning than he had formerly indicated (perhaps because of the influence of his co-author, Rosemary Wilson). The words and sentences in the *Merrill Linguistic Readers* do form stories, whereas the Bloomfield content often does not; this is especially apparent in the books prepared for the very early stages of reading. Furthermore, Fries does not employ nonsense words and does introduce several function words *(is, a, the)* at the very beginning of the program. The major characteristics of the program are as follows:

1. There are six books in the program.
2. It is intended for grades one and two, and possibly grade three.
3. Reading is viewed primarily as decoding, although some emphasis is placed on reading for meaning.
4. Letters and letter names are learned prior to the introduction of first words.
5. Stress is placed on the learning of phonemic-graphemic relationships with individual words and words in sentences.

A pig had a wig.

Dan had a big map.

Sal had a big pig.

A cat ran. A rat ran.

Pal can dig. Dig, Pal, dig!

Pam had a big fig.

Nat had fig jam.

Can Nan jig? Can a cat jig?

Can a big, fat pig jig?

Figure 8.1   Let's Read, Part 2, *Experimental Edition.*

6. Sound-letter correspondence is established by minimal phonemic contrasts, as with *cat–fat, man–fan,* and *sad–bad.*
7. Mastery of a very limited number of spelling patterns is expected.
8. A few irregularly spelled structure words are introduced early (*the, to,* and so on) as sight words.
9. No illustrations are used in any of the texts.
10. Word length is controlled.
11. Stories are generally set in a familiar background.

The Linguistic Readers (formerly Harper and Row Linguistic Readers, 1965) are now published by Benziger, Inc., a subsidiary of Crowell Collier and Macmillan. This program looks like the traditional basal reader, since pictures are used and the sentence construction is like that found in the usual reader. However, Aukerman (1971) states that "there *is* a significant difference. It is to be found in the consistency with which new words are introduced" (p. 174).

Although the early materials stress the use of words which fit a very limited number of spelling patterns, the story content is more interesting than that found in the Bloomfield or Fries materials. Major characteristics of the program are as follows:

1. Materials include three pre-primers, one primer, one first reader, one second reader, and one third reader.
2. Reading is decoding, but there is emphasis on meaning also.

Playing Gold Rush Days

Lizzie and Willie, who live in an
apartment, have a game they play on
rainy days. It is called Gold Rush Days.
They are settlers going West to seek gold.
Willie makes a wagon from old boxes and
blankets, and Lizzie gets several of Mom's
dented tin pots and plates to eat from. If
they are lucky Mom lends them a milk
bottle to keep water in and gives them a
tin box to keep cookies in.

They have six oxen to haul their wagon
along over the dusty trail and across
rivers. They are bold and brave, going
West in terrible rain and cold.

When Mom calls both of them in to
lunch, they crawl away from their wagon
and hunt bear on their way to the kitchen.

Figure 8.2   Let's Read, Part 8, *Experimental Edition.*

Source: Reprinted by special permission from *Let's Read 8* by Leonard
Bloomfield and Clarence L. Barnhart, © 1965 by Clarence L. Barnhart, Inc. All
rights reserved.

3. Stress is on phonemic-graphemic relationships with individual words
   and words in sentences.
4. Whole-word recognition of initial sight vocabulary is stressed.
5. Illustrations in earlier editions were one color, but in later editions are
   multi-color.
6. Content of pre-primers is concerned completely with familiar animals.
7. Vocabulary is introduced more rapidly than in the usual basal reader.

The Miami Linguistic Readers (Robinett, Rojas, and Bell, D. C. Heath,
1964–1966) were developed during the early 1960s in an effort to meet the
need of the many refugees who left Castro's Cuba. In his description of

the program, Robinett (1965) states that it is a language program and not just a reading program. Aukerman (1971) summarizes well:

> The rationale for the Miami Linguistic Readers was, consequently, twofold: (1) to develop books which were "culture-free," and which would have themes with which children of any background could relate; (2) to develop books which would provide an approach to American English with the least amount of phonemic irregularity—this being necessary, especially for children who already had some knowledge of a relatively regular phonemic language: Cuban-Spanish (p. 209).

Characteristics of this program are as follows:

1. It consists of twenty-one small paperback booklets and sixteen workbooks.
2. It is intended to be used for the first two years of school.
3. Decoding is preceded by language experience activities.
4. Reading is reinforced by writing.
5. There is some emphasis on spelling patterns.
6. The program emphasizes the learning of letter names in the initial stages.
7. Content of stories is familiar to children.
8. Initial regular words are introduced as sight words until the child gains insight into spelling patterns.
9. Word length is generally not controlled.
10. Illustrations are black and white cartoon-type drawings.

Summary of Decoding Emphasis Linguistic Programs It should be apparent that while the four programs are all described as decoding emphasis programs, they are not the same. Some authors are concerned exclusively with decoding, while others emphasize comprehension as well. Nevertheless, we can list the distinguishing characteristics of the decoding emphasis linguistic approach in general:

1. Pupils are taught a systematic decoding system at the beginning of their reading experience rather than after they have acquired a sight vocabulary.
2. Letters and letter names are introduced early.
3. Sound-letter relationships are established by repetition of known words and through the use of minimal contrasts *(fat–cat),* but sounds which make up a word are never presented in isolation.
4. The introduction and patterning of consonant and vowel combinations are systematically controlled through the use of common spelling patterns.
5. Pictures and context clues are not considered part of the decoding system, although some programs introduce them as separate skills.

For those who have reservations about the linguistic programs just described, Lamb (1972) provides this caution:

> To criticize the authors and publishers of these materials because they obviously do not emphasize meaning is to accuse them of not achieving an objective they never had. If one considers meaning an important factor in reading at the beginning levels, then one selects different materials or supplements these more narrowly conceived reading materials, choosing ones designed to achieve broader goals (p. 15).

Linguistic Approaches That Emphasize Sentence Structures

Whereas most linguistic approaches have been concerned with words and their systematic presentation in orderly spelling patterns, other linguists have argued for an emphasis on meaning and an examination of units of language larger than the word. Perhaps the earliest case for such an examination was presented by Lefevre (1964). In the preface to his book, *Linguistics and the Teaching of Reading*, he states that the method he proposes "is a whole-sentence method that applies a scientific description of American English utterances to the problems of teaching reading. No one can get meaning from the printed page without taking in whole language patterns at the sentence level, because these are the minimal meaning-bearing structures of most written communications" (p. vii). In agreement with other linguists, he rejects the teaching of the sounds of letters in isolation and advocates that only complete words be pronounced.

Lefevre's approach develops reading comprehension by building students' ability to understand sentence sense. He stresses that readers must be able to translate written language back into its primary form, the spoken language. For Lefevre, therefore, intonation is more important than other aspects of the reading process. While Bloomfield and Fries emphasized the importance of word identification, Lefevre emphasizes the importance of word comprehension.

In contrast to Bloomfield and Fries, Lefevre argues strongly that the single word is not a principal language unit, and that most English words "are 'chameleon' in both structure and meaning" (p. 5). He explains that a concrete noun may be used in a sentence as a noun, a verb, an adjective, or an adverb. So he concludes that "each 'word' discovers its meaning and use in every sentence where it occurs" (p. 5). Following this premise, he provides the following observations:

1. The basic fault in poor reading is poor sentence sense, which is often demonstrated orally in word-calling.

2. True reading requires that isolated words be brought back into the larger patterns that function linguistically and carry meaning.
3. Reading should be taught by language patterns that carry meaning. Intonation and word order provide reliable clues to the total meaning-bearing pattern.
4. The most significant structures in English are syntactical word groups, intonation patterns, grammatical word groups, clauses and sentences (Lefevre, 1964, pp. 5–6).

In agreement with Lefevre, Goodman (1963) states "that at all levels reading materials should have meaning, that words should have meaning, that words should never be introduced in isolation unless they are individually communicative, that the child must be provided opportunities to learn the signals of structural meaning, and the child must be taught to utilize these signals in obtaining meaning from his reading" (pp. 295–296).

Although we now see the influence of Lefevre and Goodman and others (Shuy, Bormuth, Ruddell, and Wardhaugh, most notably) in many of the newer basal materials, the first effort in this direction was made in the *Harper and Row Basic Reading Program* (O'Donnell and Van Roekel, 1966). While the program was similar in format to a typical basal program, the authors emphasized the following linguistic exercises:

1. Exercises dealing with pitch, stress, and juncture to help the child bridge the gap between spoken and written language.
2. Activities focusing attention on noun phrases, verb phrases, and prepositional phrases in order to promote the reading of groups of words.
3. Exercises dealing with word substitution in sentence patterns.
4. Sentence building exercises stressing the function of word types such as descriptive words, noun markers, and so on.

Among the newer basal programs the influence of recent linguistic thought is evident. For example, in the *Scott Foresman Reading Systems* (Monroe et al., 1971) the vocabulary controls typically found at the primary levels have been eased considerably, and the stories are composed of much longer sentences. An excellent example of a beginning story is *The Bus Ride* (Monroe, et al., 1971), Level 2, Book A.

To what extent other publishers will emphasize sentence structure in addition to word structures in the materials for beginning readers is not certain. It does appear, however, that the materials for the 1970s are concerned with larger units of language than the word and that sentences found in basal readers are now much more representative of the sentences children speak.

For their interest in reading instruction and their tenacity in encouraging educators to learn about language and language learning, the linguists deserve much credit.

Programmed and Computer-Assisted Reading Instruction

It is actually redundant to refer to programmed *and* computer-assisted reading instruction, since all computer-assisted reading instruction is in fact highly programmed. Here, however, for descriptive purposes, *programmed reading* will refer to that type of instruction which employs only software (books) as opposed to hardware (computers).

Programmed instruction teaches by means of carefully sequenced steps. Each step leads to increased mastery of the subject with minimum error. Each step is constructed so that the student can confirm the correctness of his response before he progresses to more complex materials.

Programmed instruction differs from the conventional methods in several respects. It is an individual learning process in which the student accepts a far wider responsibility for his own learning and progresses at his own pace; it requires an active response with immediate confirmation of results; and the subject matter is so programmed that the student's learning behavior is shaped in a particular manner (Hughes, 1962).

A Brief History

As early as 1912, Edward L. Thorndike advocated a form of programmed instruction. He said that although students needed to learn by discovery, the content of reading materials should be controlled so that careful reading and understanding preceded the reading of hints or further explanation. In 1925 Sidney L. Pressey demonstrated the first teaching machine to provide an automated feedback to each student in a conventional classroom setting. The same type of questions and examinations used by classroom teachers were written in multiple-choice format for a machine presentation. Since only correct responses permitted the viewing of the following question, students knew immediately whether or not their answers were right. Recently the major proponent of programmed instruction has been B. F. Skinner; a programmed book (Holland and Skinner, 1961) in psychology which he co-authored has now been used for many years.

Programmed reading came about largely through the efforts of Cynthia Dee Buchanan and her former teacher, M. W. Sullivan. Although they began the development of their program in 1957, it was not until after much experimentation and revision that their materials were finally published by McGraw-Hill in 1963.

Although programmed instruction may be presented by a teaching machine or a computer, it is most often presented in a book. The two major kinds of organization for programmed materials are: *linear,* where the items come one after the other; and *branching,* where items may be skipped or repeated. The linear type of programming is most often employed in programmed textbooks, whereas the branching type is used in computer programming.

Programmed Reading

The Buchanan-Sullivan (1963) materials, *Programmed Reading,* have become synonymous with programmed reading in general, although the materials have also been described as being representative of "linguistic" materials. The program consists of a sequence of twenty-one colorfully illustrated workbooks in which the student writes his response to each item and then checks the correctness of his answer before progressing to the next item.

One of the major advantages of this type of program is that if the material is properly arranged, success is maximized and failure is minimized. Another advantage is that the student is free to work at his own pace. Among the disadvantages, however, is that while repetition and "short steps" from one item to another do, in fact, guarantee success for most students, these things can also be tedious, and the need for a lockstep program through which all students must progress may well be questioned.

An important element of the program is the series of small hard-cover *Storybooks* which the student may read after the completion of the appropriate workbooks. These *Storybooks* are appealing both in content and format; the stories are excellent and the colorful illustrations are delightful. These books provide excellent reading for children regardless of whether the programmed workbooks are used.

It must be emphasized that first grade children do not simply start on page one of the *Programmed Reading* workbooks and begin to learn to read. They must first master a number of skills in what the publisher calls the programmed pre-reading stage. Heilman (1972) claims that children must have mastered the following skills:

1. The names of the letters of the alphabet (capital and small).
2. How to print all the capital and small letters.
3. That letters stand for sounds.
4. What sounds to associate with the letters *a, f, m, n, p, t, th,* and *i,* which are used as the points of departure for the programmed readers.
5. That letters are read from left to right.
6. That groups of letters form words.

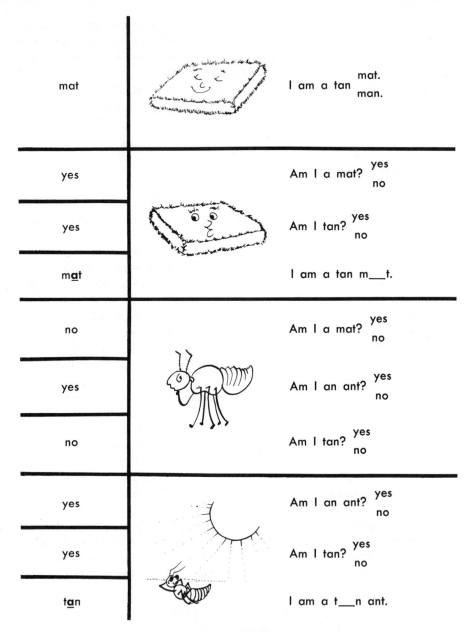

Figure 8.3   Programmed Reading Book 1, *Rev. Ed.*

Source: From *Programmed Reading Book I*, p. 4, 1968. Reprinted by permission of Behavioral Research Laboratories.

7. The words *yes* and *no* by sight, how to discriminate the words *ant, man,* and *mat* from each other, and how to read the sentences, *I am an ant, I am a man, I am a mat, I am a pin, I am a pan, I am tan, I am thin, I am fat* (pp. 189–190).

Intended for students in grades one through three, the Buchanan-Sullivan workbooks are now also published by Behavioral Research Laboratories in essentially the same format as the McGraw-Hill program.

While admitting that children do learn to read through the use of programmed materials, several reading authorities (Spache and Spache, 1973; Heilman, 1965) have expressed reservations about widespread adoption of programmed reading as the basic program. The teacher who is considering such a program may wish to ask the following questions:

1. Does this program provide for instruction in the skills I consider essential for my class?
2. Will my students accept the structure of this program?
3. Are the repetitions provided in the program necessary for all of my students?
4. Is pupil-book interaction sufficient, or is pupil-teacher-book interaction necessary?

Computer-Assisted Reading Instruction

Only a few years ago computer-assisted instruction was in its experimental stages. However, with the advent of computer time sharing, which allows for the simultaneous operation of many remote terminals,[2] the use of a computer as the primary instructional aid—rather than a teacher or a book—has become more common, particularly on college campuses where computer terminals are generally more accessible. The branching type of programming described earlier provides for a much greater range of individual differences than the linear format of programmed books.

A distinction should be made between computer-based, computer-assisted and computer-managed instruction, although the terms are sometimes used synonymously. In computer-based instruction, the computer is the primary source of instruction, whereas in computer-assisted instruction, the teacher provides most of the instruction, and the computer assists with practice exercises. With computer-managed instruction, the computer is used for diagnosis and provides the teacher with recommendations for instruction.

[2] A remote terminal may be miles away from the main computer facility; messages to and from the computer are usually sent over telephone wires.

A good computerized instructional program must make available a great many alternate routes through which the student may be routed to the subsequent phase. It must also have the capacity to assess and use the student's achievement at each stage of the instructional program.

As the student receives his instruction from the computer, he is seated at a terminal called a teletypewriter, which looks much like a regular typewriter. This teletypewriter provides instructions and sends student responses to the computer.

The use of computers to teach reading came about largely through the efforts of Richard Atkinson and his associates at Stanford University. With the resources of the Carnegie Foundation and the IBM Corporation, they were able to construct and equip a building adjacent to an elementary school near Stanford University. This endeavor soon took on the name of the school (Brentwood Elementary School, East Palo Alto, California) and became known as the Brentwood Project (Atkinson, 1968) and more recently in reading circles as the Stanford Project in Computer-Assisted Instruction in Reading.

The initial objective of the Stanford Project was to implement a system for teaching initial reading completely through the use of computers (Atkinson and Hansen, 1966; Atkinson and Fletcher, 1972). While Atkinson reports success in achieving this objective (Atkinson, 1968), he has more recently stated that "it became clear that the cost of such a program was prohibitive. Economically and pedagogically, some aspects of initial reading seemed better left to the classroom teacher" (Atkinson and Fletcher, 1972, p. 319).

Recently the Stanford researchers have designed a low-cost computer-assisted instruction (CAI) program that supplements normal classroom instruction. This program is concerned with reading instruction from kindergarten through grade three and has emphasized decoding. The Stanford CAI program is divided into six basic parts, or strands, as Atkinson calls them. A brief description of each strand follows:

Strand I.   The readiness strand. Gives basic instructions on manual operation of the program; provides exercises on some aspects of reading readiness.

Strand II.   The letter strand. Concerned with the recognition and copying of the letters of the alphabet.

Strand III. The word strand. Presents a sight vocabulary, particularly those words which do not have a regular phoneme-grapheme correspondence.

Strand IV.   The spelling strand. Teaches recognition of monosyllabic words according to spelling pattern groups *(fan, man, ran)*.

Strand V. The phonics strand. Continues the exercises on spelling patterns, but provides more practice on the substitution of word elements such as the substitution of consonants and consonant clusters.

Strand VI. The comprehension strand. Provides practice on word and sentence meaning.

It should be emphasized that the student does not have to complete one strand before moving into the next (as he would in linear programming); a minimum level of proficiency in one strand enables the student to begin work in the next strand. It is possible that a student's lesson may include exercises from as many as five strands.

In its most recent use, the Stanford Project provided for approximately twelve minutes of supplementary instruction per student each day. The program was marketed commercially for several years; now, however, no computer-assisted reading program is available commercially—although experimentation continues.

The earliest reports of teaching children to read by computer (Atkinson and Hansen, 1966) were greeted with dismay by many educators (Spache, 1967) who felt that computers threatened to replace the normal human interaction of classroom instruction. But computer-assisted instruction in reading is not intended to replace the teacher (although the teacher who *can* be replaced by a computer probably *should* be). Atkinson and Fletcher (1972) state that "on the contrary, it is a tool that can free the teacher for more creative forms of instruction" (pp. 326–327).

The Future of Computers and Reading Instruction

The prohibitive cost and the shortage of well-developed programs presently make computer-assisted reading instruction unavailable to most elementary students. Computer-managed reading instruction, however, holds promise for greater use, especially for corrective and remedial diagnosis and instruction. For several reasons, it seems likely that the use of computers to teach reading will increase. First, there is now a better understanding of the potential of computer-assisted and computer-managed instruction in reading; though the awe may still be present, the fear is gone. Second, some school systems now use remote terminals (though unfortunately more for record keeping than for instruction). Third, present experimentation is providing new and better computer programs. And fourth, observations have shown that computer instruction is efficient, feasible, and humane for at least some of our students during a portion of the daily instruction.

The Intensive Phonics Approach

Since all—or almost all—approaches to the teaching of reading employ the use of phonics to some degree, this discussion will be restricted to those methods and materials which advocate intensive training in phonics; this approach is often referred to as the *total* or *intensive phonics approach* to the teaching of reading. Advocates of this approach believe that phonics should be introduced either before a sight vocabulary is established or concurrent with the introduction of sight words in the beginning reader. The approach requires much work with isolated words and phonic elements, and such work is usually begun at the initial stages of reading instruction. Word recognition skills are taught in a variety of sequences. The order in which the various phonic elements are introduced varies from one publisher's program to another's; some begin with short vowels, others with long vowels, others with consonants.

Programs which take the linguistic (decoding emphasis) approach and those which take the intensive phonics approach are not always easily distinguished from each other. We will briefly discuss, therefore, some of their similarities and differences.

Phonics and Linguistics: Some Comparisons

There are more similarities between the phonics and linguistics approaches than differences. (The reader must continue to bear in mind that *linguistic approaches* here refers to those that emphasize decoding.) Indeed, several years ago, Chall (1967) stated that materials appearing with the "linguistics" label were advocating methods identical to materials with the "phonics" label and that a number of current materials could be classified as either phonic or linguistic. The characteristic the approaches hold in common is that they both emphasize decoding from the initial stages of instruction. The means by which they teach the decoding system, however, differs markedly.

Linguistic approaches emphasize the primacy of oral language. Proponents of phonics approaches, however, have never completely agreed; while viewing competency in oral language as necessary for success in beginning reading, the proponents of phonics view the *printed word* as their primary concern. It is how this printed word is decoded into familiar speech that brings out the differences in the two approaches.

1. Many phonics proponents would teach the student to break up a word into parts. The word *cat* may be broken up in the decoding process as

c-at, ca-t, or *c-a-t.* The linguist, however, would view this breaking up of words into isolated parts as a corruption of our language.

2. While both approaches emphasize the learning of letter-sound relationships, the linguist would have the child compare known words with unknown whole words. For example, the unknown word *mat* might be compared with the known words, *fat* and *man,* and through the use of such minimal contrasts, the student would learn new sound-letter relationships and subsequently be able to decode new words. The phonics approach, however, may emphasize individual letter-sound relationships. The teacher might state, for example, that the letter *b* stands for the sound you hear at the beginning of *boy, bounce,* and *bird* (which a linguist would support) or the letter *b* stands for the [buh] sound, the letter *d* stands for the [duh] sound (which a linguist would not support).

Analytic vs. Synthetic Phonics

The analytic method of teaching phonics begins with the introduction of sight words before the student begins to learn letter-sound relationships. For example, after the words *run, rabbit, real, red,* and *ride* have been learned as sight words, the student is guided to realize that (1) the words all begin with the same sound when spoken, (2) they all begin with the same letter, and (3) the same written letter represents the same sound at the beginning of each word. It is probably safe to say that in many respects the linguistic approach leads children to learn letter-sound relationships in the same manner as the analytic approach.

The synthetic approach establishes letter-sound correspondence by drill on individual letters and letter combinations. For example, after the student has learned the letter-sound relationship for *m, a,* and *t,* the sounds may then be blended together to form the word *mat.*

For a more detailed description of analytic and synthetic phonics, see Chapter Ten.

Intensive Phonics Materials

Teachers may purchase a number of different workbooks which teach children to use phonics in decoding new words. Such workbooks are rarely used as total programs, however; they are generally used to present information the teacher may find lacking in the basic program. Examples of such phonics workbooks are the following:

1. *The Phonics We Use Series,*
   Lyons and Carnahan, 1972.

2. *Phonics Is Fun,*
   Modern Curriculum Press, 1970, 1971.
3. *Merrill Phonics Skilltexts,*
   Charles E. Merrill, 1973.

There are also several basal reading programs which employ an intensive phonics approach. Some representative samples of those basal series follow:

1. *Keys to Reading,*
   The Economy Company, 1972.
2. *Lippincott's Basic Reading Program,*
   J. B. Lippincott Company, 1969.
3. *Open Court Basic Readers,*
   Open Court Publishing Company, 1971.

Phonics materials are neither inherently good nor inherently bad. But if the materials are used to teach phonics to the exclusion of other word recognition techniques, children may not learn other important word recognition techniques. For this reason, approaches which emphasize only phonics must be carefully examined and discriminatingly used.

Orthographic Variations

The traditional orthography of the English language has been much criticized because of the inconsistencies with which it represents spoken English. A number of attempts have been made to change the traditional orthography in order to help beginning readers acquire a rapid mastery of sound-symbol correspondence. In some cases the changes have been relatively minor; in others the changes have resulted in sets of symbols which bear little resemblance to the twenty-six letters of our regular alphabet. Such changes are referred to here as orthographic variations.

Initial Teaching Alphabet

The Initial Teaching Alphabet, or i.t.a., is an attempt to establish a one-to-one relationship between grapheme and phoneme. Instead of the twenty-six letters of traditional orthography (T.O.), i.t.a. uses forty-four characters to represent the sounds of our language. While i.t.a. is presented here as an approach to the teaching of reading, strictly speaking, it is not;

the proponents of its use are quick to state that it is simply a new alphabet which regularizes the sound-letter correspondence and as such may be used with a variety of approaches.

Figure 8.4   Initial Teaching Alphabet.

Source: *i.t.a. bulletin* 4, 1 (Fall 1966), p. 12.

The Development of i.t.a. Credit for the development of i.t.a. is generally given to Sir James Pitman, an Englishman, although his grandfather, Sir Isaac Pitman (inventor of the Pitman Shorthand System) actually began work on an alphabet in 1842. And though James Pitman had been interested in a new alphabet for many years, it appears that the support he received from George Bernard Shaw in 1947 provided the impetus he needed to complete the project (Pitman and St. John, 1969, pp. 111–114). It was not until 1960, however, that Pitman convinced school officials in England that an experiment should be conducted whereby i.t.a. could be compared with T.O. (traditional orthography) in the initial stage of reading. With some difficulty he found twenty schools willing to try i.t.a. There was no problem in finding schools to provide control groups. Thus, the first experiment began in September 1961.

The early experiments provided highly satisfactory results for the students who learned to read with i.t.a. (Harrison, 1964, Chapters IV, XV, and XVI, pp. 127–161), and the alphabet became quite widely adopted in other English schools during the 1960s. During this early period John Downing became the chief spokesman for i.t.a.; he is now its major international proponent.

How It Is Used The i.t.a. is a writing system—not a system for teaching writing, but a "system of ink marks on paper to represent the primary system of sounds in air which is the spoken language" (Downing, 1968). It is a forty-four-character alphabet with an almost one-to-one correspondence between sound and symbol. Of the forty-four characters, twenty-four are borrowed directly from the traditional alphabet. The letters *q* and *x* are omitted; the sounds usually associated with them in T.O. are represented by *kw* and *ks,* respectively, in i.t.a. spellings. Fourteen of the i.t.a. characters are combinations of familiar letters:

æ ɛɛ ie ue ꞔh ʈh ᵵh ʃh ŋ au ou wh œ oi

and six are peculiar to i.t.a.:

ſ ꟙ ʒ ɑ ꞷ ꞷ

Woodcock (1966) offers the following additional principles as a guide to understanding the i.t.a. approach:

1. A capital letter is indicated in i.t.a. by writing the sound-symbol approximately one and one-half times the size of the lower-case symbol.
2. The abbreviations *Mr.* and *Mrs.* are spelled out in i.t.a.:

mister missis

3. Foreign words and names retain traditional spellings in i.t.a. material.
4. Consonants are doubled in i.t.a. spellings if the corresponding letters in T.O. are also doubled *(ball, better, stuff).*
5. Short vowel sounds are represented by traditional letter forms in i.t.a. *(a, e, i, o, u).*
6. Long vowel sounds are represented by special double characters:

æ ɛɛ ie œ ue

Proponents maintain that the consistency of i.t.a. makes it possible to introduce letter sounds and letter combinations earlier than with T.O. An example of i.t.a. consistency between sound and symbol is provided here:

T.O.	i.t.a.
I	ie
eye	ie
by	bie
buy	bie
bye	bie
hide	hied
high	hie
tie	tie

Basically, once a child learns the i.t.a. symbols, he is ready to read any word written with these symbols. If he sees an unfamiliar word, he "spells" the word, an operation of pronouncing every sound in the new word. Therefore, the reader reads exactly what is written.

Several different programs using the i.t.a. approach have been developed in America and England since 1961, which allows a teacher of i.t.a. some freedom of choice. There are four basic types of i.t.a. programs as described by Downing (1968):

1. The most familiar is a transliterated i.t.a. version of T.O. basal readers. In this program the methods and content remain the same as in the T.O. edition. Only the alphabet used to print the words is changed from T.O. to i.t.a. One benefit of this program is that it is ideal for basic research comparing i.t.a. with T.O.
2. Another program easily converted to i.t.a. is the language-experience approach. Again, the only modification needed is the use of i.t.a. instead of T.O. in the teacher's and pupil's writing and reading of experience charts and booklets.
3. The Creativity-Discovery Approach is designed especially for use with i.t.a. The materials are written only in i.t.a. and emphasize a child's need for self-expression in creative writing. The Downing Readers provide an example of an i.t.a. basal series that uses the creativity-discovery approach.
4. There is a more formal expository approach, written specifically for i.t.a. as a teaching method. An example of this formal teaching approach is the *Early-to-Read* i.t.a. series by Albert Mazurkiewicz and Harold Tanyzer. The *Early-to-Read* series emphasizes the learning of individual sounds and corresponding i.t.a. symbols. It is based on the premise that children should first learn the individual sound symbols before being taught to synthesize them into words, sentences, paragraphs, and eventually stories.

lemonæd, lemonæd, fiev sents a glass!

ωun dæ polly, molly and jack wer
plæiŋ in ʃhe frunt yard.

up ʃhe street cæm a big truck. ʃhær
woꞅ a sien on ʃhe truck ʃhat sed "**sircus**."

mueꞅic cæm from ʃhe truck.

ʃhær wer ʃhree clounꞅ on ʃhe back
ov ʃhe truck.

"ʃhe sircus iꞅ in toun!" ·caulld ʃhe
first cloun.

"ωun week œnly!" caulld out
ʃhe second cloun.

"cum wun, cum aull!" caulld ·out
ʃhe ʃhird cloun.

Figure 8.5   Early-to-Read, Book 4, *Rev. Ed.*

Source: *Find A Way*, Book 4, Early-to-Read i.t.a. Program by Albert J. Mazurkiewicz and Harold J. Tanyzer. Copyright © 1966 by Initial Teaching Publications. Reprinted by permission of Pitman Publishing Corp.

The i.t.a. approach, when used by a school system, is introduced in kindergarten or first grade. Pitman's i.t.a. design is intended to encourage early reading without frustration. It is not meant to be a panacea for all reading problems.

UNIFON

Like the initial teaching alphabet, UNIFON is an attempt to establish a one-to-one correspondence between sound and letter. The UNIFON system, also called the single-sound alphabet, consists of forty characters with which the child learns to read and spell in his initial school experiences.

Origins The developer of UNIFON, John R. Malone, was an advocate of radical spelling reform both for faster mastery of the writing system and also for simplification of electronic data processing of language (Malone, 1962). By 1960 Malone had the system developed, and it was used experimentally with pre-school children. Most of the experimental studies involving the use of UNIFON appear to have taken place in the period 1963–1966; there is little recent mention of the method in the literature.

The Method The forty characters of the UNIFON include twenty-two upper-case letters from the traditional English orthography plus eighteen additional characters which in most cases appear to be modifications of traditional letters. The letters are large block type (no upper- and lower-case), and all words are spelled exactly as they sound with no silent or double letters used. All words which sound the same are spelled the same; therefore context must determine the meaning of many words.

DMS

The diacritical marking system, usually referred to as DMS, is another attempt to eliminate the problem of inconsistency in the letter-sound relationships of English. With DMS, traditional orthography is maintained although modified somewhat by slashes, lines, dots, and asterisks. Edward Fry, who devised DMS, stated that its purpose is to "regularize orthography for beginning reading instruction by adding marks to regular letters. The marks are used because basic word form is preserved. They can later be vanished as the reading habit is established" (Fry, 1964, p. 528).

The basic rules for modifying the traditional orthography with DMS are as follows:

1. Regular consonants and short vowels are unchanged.
2. "Silent" letters have a slash mark *(wrīte, rīght)*.
3. Long vowels have a bar-over mark *(māde, māid)*.
4. Schwa vowels have a dot-over mark *(ȧgo, lemȯn)*.
5. Other consistent sounds than those above are indicated by the bar under *(i̱s, au̱tō)*.
6. Digraphs have a bar under both letters *(s̲h̲ut, c̲h̲at)*.
7. Exceptions to the above basic rules have an asterisk above the letter *(o̊f, o̊n̲c̲e)* (Fry, 1964, p. 528).

The major advantage of the DMS over other modified alphabet systems like i.t.a. and UNIFON is that the regular letters of our alphabet are maintained. DMS has not become widely used, however, and Fry (1967) himself has reported that his method was no better than the traditional orthography.

Words in Color

Another method devised to overcome the inconsistencies of letter-sound relationship is one devised by Caleb Gattegno. Called *Words in Color*, it is an attempt to simplify the English language for the beginning reader (Gattegno, 1968).

Origins In 1957, while working for UNESCO in Ethiopia, Gattegno devised this method for teaching illiterate adults to read and write. In 1958 Dr. Gattegno's experimentation with English came to the United States, first in Texas with kindergarten children and later in California (Gattegno and Hinman, 1966).

In studying the English language, Gattegno identified forty-seven distinctive phonemes. He divided these forty-seven phonemes into twenty vowel sounds and twenty-seven consonant sounds. As a way to make the language more phonetic, he introduced the aspect of color into the program. Each of the forty-seven vowel and consonant sounds was coded to a different color shade so that each phoneme could be distinguished from the others on the basis of color alone. *Words in Color* does not change the traditional spelling of words or introduce any new graphic symbols into the language.

The Method Classroom materials consist of twenty-one charts which progress from the regular to the irregular spelling of words, eight phonic code color charts which present a systematic organization of vowels and consonants and their varied spellings, and a set of word cards which introduce words of different parts of speech.

The eight colored phonic wall charts are hung around the classroom to be used as a constant reference for the children. The charts are divided into forty-seven columns, each representing one of the unique phoneme sounds. Under each vowel or consonant heading is a vertical listing of all the different ways that particular phoneme sound can be spelled. For example under the [f] phoneme sound (coded in mauve) are listed *f, ff, fe, ph, lf, gh, ffe, pph,* and *ft* also color coded in mauve (Gattegno, 1968). The child learns that the sound [f] can be spelled in at least nine different ways. A distinctive sound is always represented by the same color regardless of its spelling. The short sound of [a], for example, is white whether it is in *pat* or *laugh*. It is Gattegno's belief that children use these color clues to help fix the image of the sound in their mind.

Advantages Bentley (1966) states that there is no problem with reversals (such as *on* for *no*) "since the criteria of spoken speech (in which we do not reverse words) are connected to written speech from the beginning" (p. 517). *Words in Color* may also have some value as a motivational device for teaching children who have experienced difficulty by another method. The introduction of color and the novelty of the presentation may provide motivation for slow learners and less interested students. *Words in Color* may also be more suited for slower children because initially all the words presented are regular and the students are not confused by spelling irregularities. However, this spelling regularity can be maintained *without* the use of color.

Disadvantages Because of the similarity in hues, some children may have trouble discriminating one color from another. Another disadvantage is that initial reading instruction must be restricted to the classroom, where the child has access to the phonic color-code charts. The child never reads words printed in color outside of the classroom charts and the few words a teacher may write with colored chalk on the blackboard. Furthermore, there is no evidence to indicate that learning to read with color is superior to any other method of learning to read.

Peabody Rebus Program

The *Peabody Rebus Reading Program* is a beginning reading program which uses pictures—the rebuses—in place of words in teaching children how to read. The development of the program began in 1964 as a method of teaching reading to mentally retarded children. Authors of the program, which is published by American Guidance Service, Inc., are Richard W. Woodcock, Charlotte R. Clarke, and Cornelia Oakes Davies.

The first characters the child "reads" are almost exclusively pictures with the exception of a few symbols which stand for common function words; for example, the symbol + represents the word *and*. As the child reads, he reads pictures rather than words; as he learns to comprehend the rebuses, words are introduced which gradually replace the rebuses.

The basic materials consist of three paperback workbooks and two paperback readers. By the time the child completes the program he should have a sight vocabulary of approximately 120 words and should be able to read primer materials from most published basal reading series.

Multi-Media Approaches

Up through the 1950s the materials used for reading instruction were almost exclusively books and workbooks. Recently a number of programs which employ machines for teaching reading have become popular. In this section such approaches will be described as multi-media approaches, and the discussion will be limited to those multi-media approaches which use machines to a major or minor degree for teaching reading.

The EDL Program

The Educational Development Laboratories, better known as EDL, market several machines to be used for reading instruction. Among the most widely used of the EDL machines is the *Tach-X* tachistoscope, a sophisticated filmstrip projector which can be used to project images on a screen for as long as $1\frac{1}{2}$ seconds or as briefly as $\frac{1}{100}$ of a second. The *Tach-X* is intended for group use; a smaller hand-held tachistoscope, the *Flash-X,* is designed for individual use.

Perhaps the most popular EDL machine is the *Controlled Reader,* which is also an elaborate filmstrip projector. For use with the *Controlled Reader* there is a variety of filmstrips which range in difficulty from pre-reading activities to college level instruction.

EDL also markets what it intends to be a total reading program, which includes filmstrip projectors, filmstrips, audio tapes, workbooks, and books. While some teachers have expressed reluctance to use mechanical devices in the classroom because they are difficult to operate, it has generally been the contention of EDL that most first-grade children can be taught to use their machines, thus freeing the teacher for other teaching responsibilities. At the pre-reading and beginning reading stages, however, many teachers prefer not to use such devices until students have a mastery of essential word recognition and comprehension skills.

Responsive Environment

The responsive environment began as an approach to teach reading to pre-kindergarten children through the use of a special typewriter. This typewriter became popularly known as the "talking typewriter" and received much attention among educators and child psychologists. Its inventor, O. K. Moore, developed the machine in order to provide the learner with an environment in which to explore and interact freely in problem-solving situations.

According to Moore, a responsive environment meets the following conditions:

1. It permits the learner to explore freely.
2. It informs the learner immediately about the consequences of his actions.
3. It is self-pacing—that is, events happen within the environment at a rate determined by the learner.
4. It permits the learner to make full use of his capacity for discovering relations of various kinds.
5. Its structure is such that the learner is likely to make a series of interconnected discoveries about the physical, cultural, and social world (Aukerman, 1971, pp. 424–425).

As the child operates in Moore's "responsive environment" he is seated in front of a typewriter and—in the initial stages—is encouraged to freely explore the keyboard. Free exploration is followed by matching exercises and later by word construction, reading, and writing.

The approach is now being used with elementary students at all grade levels in developmental, corrective, and remedial programs. Though it is expensive to implement, it has proven to be an efficient means of teaching reading.

Other Machines for Reading Instruction

Several machines have been marketed as supplementary aids for the teacher. Perhaps the most widely used is the *Language Master* by Bell and Howell, which allows the student to see a word on a card and then hear that word pronounced. The child may then record his pronunciation of the same word and compare it to the pre-recorded voice. The *Language Master* is easy to use and has applications at all achievement levels.

The *Craig Reader*, which presents a filmstrip on a small screen, has been a popular addition in situations where students experienced difficulty with other methods. Its use, however, is by no means limited to remedial students.

Machines have been designed to increase speed of reading, to combine audio instruction with the printed word, and to improve word recognition skills in a variety of ways. Although they are more costly than software and may occasionally break down, they have the decided advantage of having unlimited patience. Furthermore, they give the teacher more time for doing the things that only a human being can do.

The Author's Viewpoint

In this chapter and in the previous chapter we have described a number of approaches that have been used to teach children how to read. While these approaches all have some merit in that they *do* succeed in teaching children to read, it is this writer's contention that two critical factors determine which approaches are most effective. These two factors relate to teacher competencies in two areas: the first is the extent to which the teacher understands language, particularly as linguistic knowledge relates to the reading process, and the second is the degree to which the teacher understands the students and *their* language.

Does this mean that methods and approaches are of little consequence? No, but the employment of method and approach must be based on an understanding of the child's needs—his language, his interests, his environment—and this cannot be done unless the teacher is competent in the two areas mentioned.

For teachers who know language and their students, there are many alternatives available in teaching reading. Teachers who are limited in their knowledge of language and their students have fewer options. Such teachers may become slaves to a manual, a guide, or an approach. The purpose of this book, of course, is to develop competencies that will enable teachers to make intelligent decisions concerning reading instruction.

Assured of teacher competencies in the aforementioned areas, what would this writer recommend? In general, the best method uses the language-experience, the individualized, or the basal approach, either individually or, more likely, in some combination that will include aspects of all three approaches. Phonics workbooks should be used when necessary and, of course, trade books should always be included.

This writer would not use an orthographic variation in teaching reading because he feels that these systems are based on a faulty premise—that the problem in learning to read can be attributed to our alphabet. Any approach that directs attention to anything but the learner should be rejected.

Reading programs will vary depending on the children being taught. Slightly different approaches are appropriate for each of the following:

1. The middle-class beginning reader.
2. The culturally different beginning reader.
3. The middle-class child at later levels.
4. The culturally different child at later levels.

The Middle-Class Beginning Reader

The typical middle-class child enters first grade with an immense knowledge of his language. While his oral language is not exactly the same language he encounters in books, he usually adapts to the "book language" quickly. For this child the teacher might use a basal approach, an individualized approach, or a language-experience approach. Phonics materials might or might not be included. This writer would probably use a basal approach and supplement it with the language-experience approach in a self-contained classroom. (The language-experience approach could be used exclusively, but with the middle-class child it may be as easy and as effective to use a published program.) He would attempt to individualize as much as possible, and have an abundance of trade books available in the classroom. He would systematically teach decoding strategies, using selected phonics materials where necessary, but he would always emphasize the meaning of the printed words. If computer-based instruction were available, he would consider it as a supplement.

The Culturally Different Beginning Reader

For the culturally different beginning reader, whose language and experience are often different from those of middle-class children, this writer advocates the use of the language-experience approach, since the words and sentences the child learns to read will be determined by his language and his experience. Supplementary materials for developing word recognition skills may be employed. A variety of easy trade books would be desirable. After the child learns how to read about *his* experiences in *his* language, he will be able to learn the language of the trade books. For many culturally different children, this transition into "book language" can take place in grade one.

The Middle-Class Child at Later Levels

For children who have become somewhat independent in reading (the third-grade child and up), this writer advocates the use of an individualized approach for the more able and the basal approach for the less able. Teachers might also use a basal series as the core program and individualize within that program by providing individual help when needed. Again, many good trade books should be available in the classroom. And where the interests of the students so dictated the basal readers would be replaced—usually for only short periods—by the language-experience approach.

The Culturally Different Child at Later Levels

If the culturally different child has made the transition to "book language" this writer would use a basal approach combined with the individualized approach and the language-experience approach. The degree to which one approach predominates is determined by the language and interests of the child. Many trade books of interest to the students would be available in the classroom. Individual skills exercises in word recognition or comprehension may be provided by supplementary workbooks, and machines may be employed for those motivated by such devices.

Summary

It is important to emphasize that the approaches to the teaching of reading discussed here need not be mutually exclusive—with one approach used to the exclusion of all others. It is this writer's hope that all teachers will understand the reading process and their students so well that the approach or approaches selected for instruction will provide the maximum in reading achievement for each student.

References

Atkinson, R. C. "Computer-based Instruction in Initial Reading." *Proceedings of the 1967 Invitational Conference on Testing Problems.* Princeton, N.J.: Educational Testing Services, 1968, pp. 55–66.

Atkinson, R. C., and Fletcher, J. D. "Teaching Children to Read with a Computer." *The Reading Teacher* 25 (1972): 319–327.

Atkinson, R. C., and Hansen, D. N. "Computer-assisted Instruction in Initial Reading: The Stanford Project." *Reading Research Quarterly* 2 (1966): 5–25.

Aukerman, R. C. *Approaches to Beginning Reading.* New York: John Wiley and Sons, 1971.

Bentley, H. "Words in Color." *Elementary English* 43 (1966): 515–517.

Bishop, M. "Good Usage, Bad Usage, and Usage." In *The American Heritage Dictionary of the English Language,* edited by W. Morris.

Boston: American Heritage Publishing Co., and Houghton Mifflin, 1971, p. xxiii.

Bloomfield, L. "Linguistics and Reading." *Elementary English Review* 19 (April 1942): 125–130; (May 1942): 183–186.

Bloomfield, L., and Barnhart, C. L. *Let's Read: A Linguistic Approach.* Detroit: Wayne State University Press, 1961.

Bloomfield, L., and Barnhart, C. L. *Let's Read*, Levels 1–9. Bronxville, N.Y.: Clarence L. Barnhart, 1966.

Buchanan, C. D., and Sullivan Associates. *Programmed Reading.* New York: McGraw-Hill Book Company, 1963.

Chall, J. S. *Learning to Read: The Great Debate.* New York: McGraw-Hill Book Company, 1967.

Downing, J. "Alternative Teaching Methods in i.t.a." *Elementary English* 45 (1968): 942–951.

Fries, C. C. *Linguistics and Reading.* New York: Holt, Rinehart and Winston, 1962.

Fries, C. C.; Wilson, R. G.; and Rudolph, M. K. *Merrill Linguistic Readers.* Columbus, Ohio: Charles E. Merrill Books, 1966.

Fry, E. "A Diacritical Marking System to Aid Beginning Reading Instruction." *Elementary English* 41 (1964): 526–529.

Fry, E. "First Grade Reading Instruction Using Diacritical Marking System, Initial Teaching Alphabet and Basal Reading System—Extended to Second Grade." *The Reading Teacher* 20 (1967): 687–693.

Gattegno, C. *Teaching Reading with Words in Color.* New York: Educational Solutions, 1968.

Gattegno, C., and Hinman, D. "Words in Color—The Morphologico-algebraic Approach to Teaching Reading." In *The Disabled Reader: Education of the Dyslexic Child*, edited by J. Money. Baltimore: Johns Hopkins Press, 1966.

Goodman, K. "A Communicative Theory of the Reading Curriculum." *Elementary English* 40 (1963): 290–298.

Goodman, K. *The Psycholinguistic Nature of the Reading Act.* Detroit: Wayne State University Press, 1968.

Goodman, K. "Reading: A Psycholinguistic Guessing Game." *Journal of the Reading Specialist* 4 (1967): 126–135.

Goodman, K., and Burke, C. "When a Child Learns to Read: A Psychological Analysis." *Elementary English* 48 (1970): 121–129.

Hall, R. A. *Sound and Spelling in English.* Philadelphia: Chilton Books, 1961.

Harrison, M. *Instant Reading: The Story of the Initial Teaching Alphabet.* London: Pitman, 1964.

Heilman, A. W. "Phonics Emphasis Approaches." In *First Grade Reading Programs*, edited by J. F. Kerfoot. Newark, Del.: International Reading Association, 1965, pp. 65–71.

Heilman, A. W. *Principles and Practices of Teaching Reading.* 3rd ed. Columbus, Ohio: Charles E. Merrill Publishing Co., 1972.

Holland, J. G., and Skinner, B. F. *The Analysis of Behavior: A Program for Self-instruction.* New York: McGraw-Hill Book Company, 1961.

Hughes, J. L. *Programmed Instruction for Schools and Industry.* Chicago: Science Research Associates, 1962, pp. 8–11.

Ives, S., and Ives, J. P. "Contributions of Linguistics to Reading and Spelling, Part 1: Linguistics and Reading." In *Linguistics in School Programs,* edited by A. H. Marckwardt. The Sixty-Ninth Yearbook of the National Society for the Study of Education. Chicago: University of Chicago Press, 1970.

Lamb, P. *Linguistics in Proper Perspective.* Columbus: Charles E. Merrill Publishing Co., 1967.

Lamb, P. "Linguistics and the Teaching of Reading." *Indiana Reading Quarterly* 4 (1972): 14–16.

Lefevre, C. A. *Linguistics and the Teaching of Reading.* New York: McGraw-Hill Book Co., 1964.

Malone, J. R. "The Larger Aspects of Spelling Reform." *Elementary English* 39 (1962): 435–445.

Mathews, M. M. *Teaching to Read, Historically Considered.* Chicago: University of Chicago Press, 1966, pp. 153–154.

Monroe, M., et al. *Scott, Foresman Reading Systems.* Glenview, Ill.: Scott, Foresman and Company, 1971.

O'Donnell, M., and Van Roekel, B. H. *The Harper and Row Basic Reading Program.* Evanston, Ill.: Harper and Row, 1966.

Pitman, J., and St. John, J. R. *Alphabets and Reading: The Initial Teaching Alphabet.* New York: Pitman, 1969.

Robinett, R. F. "A Linguistic Approach to Beginning Reading for Bilingual Children." In *First Grade Reading Programs, Perspectives in Reading No. 5.* Newark, Del.: International Reading Association, 1965, pp. 132–149.

Robinett, R. F., Rojas, P., and Bell, P. W. *Miami Linguistic Series.* New York: D. C. Heath and Co., 1964–1966.

Shuy, R. W. "A Linguistic Background for Developing Beginning Reading Materials for Black Children." In *Teaching Black Children to Read,* edited by J. C. Baratz and R. W. Shuy. Washington, D.C.: Center for Applied Linguistics, 1969(a).

Shuy, R. W. "Some Language and Cultural Differences in a Theory of Reading." In *Psycholinguistics and the Teaching of Reading,* edited by K. S. Goodman and J. T. Fleming. Newark, Del.: International Reading Association, 1969(b).

Skinner, B. F. "The Experimental Analysis of Behavior." *American Scientist* 45 (1957): 343–371.

Spache, G. D. "A Reaction to Computer-assisted Instruction in Initial

Reading Instruction: The Stanford Project." *Reading Research Quarterly* 3 (1967): 101–109.

Spache, G. D., and Spache, E. B. *Reading in the Elementary School.* 3rd ed. Boston: Allyn and Bacon, 1973.

Wardhaugh, R. *Reading: A Linguistic Perspective.* New York: Harcourt, Brace and World, 1969.

Woodcock, R. *ITA for Teachers.* New York: ITA, 1966.

Chapter Nine

Preview

This is the first of a series of chapters concerned directly with the teaching of reading. Ollila focuses on young children and their initial reading experiences. He deals with a question that has concerned parents and educators for many years: When is a child ready to read?

The author explains the factors associated with reading readiness and provides a valuable checklist to help teachers assess the reading readiness of their students. He offers many concrete teaching suggestions in such areas as attention, language training, left-to-right orientation, letters and words, and auditory and visual discrimination. He concludes the chapter with a brief review of pre-school and kindergarten training programs and the role of parents and paraprofessionals at these levels.

Ollila emphasizes that children bring a wide range of abilities and skills to the initial processes of learning to read. This chapter should help teachers to understand and deal with children's varying needs. It deals with all aspects of preparing children to read—a complex and controversial topic.

Reading:
Preparing the Child

Lloyd Ollila, University of Victoria

Objectives

After you have read this chapter, you should be able to:

1. Define both *readiness* in the broadest sense and beginning or initial reading readiness.
2. List and explain the factors that determine a child's readiness for reading and describe how you would evaluate them.
3. Describe the importance of the teacher's diagnosis in preparing children for reading, and give some examples of diagnostic "tools."
4. Explain some of the pros and cons of using commercial readiness materials in a classroom.
5. Locate in this chapter or elsewhere readiness skills that can be developed and give some examples of activities to develop them.
6. Develop a rationale for involving parents in pre-schools, and give five examples of what pre-schools are doing to get parents involved in the education of their children.

After an exciting, hectic first week, Ms. Lane, the teacher at Sunnydale School, is reflecting on the children in her class. They will be quite a group to work with. Some seemed shy, hesitant, and a bit frightened. Others made themselves right at home, chatting happily and enjoying the games and activities. Ted brought his model dinosaur collection to Show and Tell and rambled on in a detailed discussion of his favorite, the allosaurus. Joey had trouble cutting with his scissors and cried out his frustration. Joan's consuming interest seemed to be painting at the easel. Bobby kept moving from activity to activity, never lingering longer than five minutes. They were all different in background, skills, and abilities. Some seemed very ready for reading. One girl, Mary, even brought her favorite story, *Peter Rabbit*, and read several pages to the teacher. Others seemed totally unable to settle down to any task. Most, thank goodness, seemed to fall away from that extreme. Most were neither completely ready nor completely unready to read. How could the teacher help prepare these children for reading? How would she know who was ready to read?

When Is a Child Ready to Read?

Each child's readiness to read gradually develops over a long period of time. As the baby grows from infant to toddler through ages three, four, and five he accumulates a wealth of background experiences and concepts. His auditory, tactile, visual, perceptual-motor, and speech skills are being formed and sharpened. He is gradually introduced to the world of objects, symbols, and words. All these various kinds of knowledge and skills help prepare the child for the act of reading. Further preparation may be done at school, but the groundwork begins at home. Since a child's readiness to read is built gradually, we cannot say, "Yesterday this child was not ready to read, but today he is."

A Definition of Beginning Reading Readiness

Reading educators tend to view reading readiness as a match between the child and his instructional program. This view is stated by Durkin in *Teaching Them to Read* (1974):

> The question of a child's readiness for reading has a twofold focus: (a) his capacity (a product of an interplay among genetic endowment, maturation, experiences and learnings) in relation to (b) the particular instruction that will be available (p. 123).

This definition takes into account both the child and the school that he attends. In other words, the teacher determines whether or not a child is ready to read by asking, "What does this child have to know and do in order to succeed in this particular reading program?" If, for example, the beginning program puts a premium on phonics, he will make sure that the children have sufficient auditory discrimination skills.

Much of the preparation for reading is done at home prior to formal school. But any teacher who just waited around for readiness to occur in the classroom would be negligent. It is the teacher's responsibility to provide activities and experiences that prepare the child for initial reading. Numerous studies have shown that children can be directly trained in different readiness skills and that this training will contribute to their readiness to read (Spache et al., 1965; Blakely and Shadle, 1961). The teacher should not only prepare the child for a particular beginning reading program but also look for ways to adapt the beginning reading program to the individual differences in the class. If the program is modified, some children may be ready to read sooner. The teacher's goal is to discover the best way of fitting the child to the program and the program to the child.

A General Concept of Reading Readiness

Although we seem to place more emphasis on readiness in the first years of school, this concept is important to the entire reading program. The sixth-grade teacher asks, "Are these children ready to learn dictionary skills?" The high school teacher wonders, "Does this class have the background of understanding necessary to comprehend the chapter in this physics text?" Every teacher has to continually assess the readiness of his class and prepare them for new, more difficult learning. Readiness in the broadest sense is basic to any new learning at any level.

Factors Associated with Reading Readiness

Research studies have indicated that a number of pre-reading skills and abilities contribute to a child's success in beginning reading. However, because of the uniqueness of each child and of the school reading program in which the child is placed, the importance of these abilities and skills will vary from child to child. Reading success is not guaranteed by the presence of all the skills or precluded if some are missing. Our discussion will be limited to a few factors, which are generally regarded as important to the child's learning to read. These factors are grouped arbitrarily into broad categories: physiological, intellectual, environmental, social and emotional, and instructional factors. They are summarized in the chart below. The reader will note that these factors are not only important at the readiness level, but also at other reading levels. To answer the question, "Is this particular child ready to read?" the teacher will observe the child, collect evidence, and assess his readiness according to these factors:

The Child	*The Instructional Program*
Physical Factors	Expectations of the Teacher
general health	Knowledge of Skills of the Teacher
vision	Beginning Reading Program
hearing	Size of Class
speech	Classroom Organization
sex of child	School Policies
Environmental Factors	
experiential background	
cultural	
socioeconomic	
Language Development	
Intellectual Factors	
general intelligence	
reasoning abilities	
Desire to Read and Persistence	
Social and Emotional Factors	
motivation	
social and emotional maturity	

Physiological Factors

Physical Health, Neurological Considerations, and Sex General good health is important for learning to read. A fatigued and listless child is at a disadvantage in any learning situation. Some researchers have pointed out that neurological limitations (various brain defects, mixed dominance, etc.) and lack of physical maturity are related to failure in learning to read. Most teachers, however, will not get much practical help from looking for signs of these in their classes.

Generally girls in North America are ready to read earlier than boys. Differences on readiness tests often seem to favor girls slightly (Anderson, Hughes, and Dixon, 1957). Although the teacher can probably expect a few more boys than girls to be immature in reading tasks, most boys and girls will score similarly on readiness tests. Therefore most schools have not felt it necessary to offer separate readiness or reading programs to boys and girls. However, the teacher should be sensitive to the special needs of those boys lacking in readiness. For instance, Downing and Thackray (1971) feel that the female teacher should find ways of letting boys know that reading is important to men.

Speech, Vision, and Hearing Defects Poor speech, hearing, and vision can slow a child's progress in learning to read. For instance, phonic analysis may be hard for a child with a speech or hearing problem. Teachers should be alert for significant signs—constant rubbing of eyes, squinting to see words, needing to have directions repeated again and again—and be ready to refer a child to the proper medical specialist. Most children with one of these handicaps will learn to read quite well if the teacher recognizes the problem and adjusts his instruction accordingly.

Some children's eyes are not fully developed until the age of eight (Getman, 1962). These visually immature children tend to be farsighted. Those who are opposed to early readiness and reading activities often call attention to this fact. They contend that the school is expecting too much from a child physiologically by requiring long periods of close work. Other researchers, however, refute these claims. Eames (1962) found five-year-old children to have more accommodative power than children possess at any subsequent age. He also found that even the most nearsighted child in his investigation had sufficient vision to read commonly used textbooks. The controversy over the effects of reading on young children's eyes is yet to be resolved, but each teacher should be continually sensitive to signs of possible visual problems in the early stages of reading. Each child, especially those at the kindergarten and nursery school levels, should have an eye examination before beginning close pre-reading tasks. Obviously a thorough test of vision can be done only by professionals.

The teacher should recognize that the commercial vision screening tests available to schools will provide an incomplete picture of the child's vision. Take, for instance, the Snellen test, which has been widely used in schools for years. This test measures visual acuity at a twenty-foot distance. When a child reads books the distance between his eyes and print is much shorter. The child may easily pass the Snellen test, but still have undetected visual problems, which could hinder his reading growth. Testing kindergarten children in New Haven, first with the Snellen test and then with more thorough tests, researchers (Peters, 1961) reported that 46 percent had visual problems that had been missed by the Snellen.

Visual Discrimination Some children who can see adequately in most situations may have trouble learning to read because they have not fully developed their abilities to discriminate between printed symbols such as letters, numerals, and words. For instance, in reading, a child is called upon to see the similarities and differences between letters like *b, p,* and *d.* He is asked to notice that the word *dog* is different in length from *something* and different in shape from *pretty.* He is also called on to discriminate between *dog* and words similar to it, like *dig* and *god.* Children who lack these fine visual discrimination skills probably will profit from special training prior to beginning reading.

Auditory Discrimination Auditory discrimination—the ability to hear likenesses and differences in letter sounds—is often considered a more important factor than adequate hearing in determining a child's reading readiness. Most children hear adequately and distinguish between different sounds on coming to school. Many children, however, have not developed this power to the fine degree needed for learning to read. They cannot isolate beginning, middle, or ending sounds, distinguish rhyming elements, or blend a number of speech sounds into words. These five discrimination abilities enable a child to recognize a word in print, such as *cat*, by "sounding out" its elements *(c-a-t)*. Children who lack this skill probably will need special training, especially if phonics is stressed in the beginning reading program.

Intellectual Factors

General Intelligence and Mental Age All things being equal (an unlikely situation), the teacher can expect bright children to learn to read faster than slower children. Numerous researchers contemplating this positive relationship between reading and intelligence have suggested that there is a certain level of intelligence, or minimum mental age, necessary before a child can succeed in learning to read. The influential Morphett and Washburne study (1931) proposed a mental age of six and one-half years. However, most recent studies conclude that it is impossible to say that children must attain a definite mental age before they can learn to read. There are far too many other factors to be considered. Studies such as Davidson's (1931) on teaching dull five-year-olds to read and Durkin's study (1963) of three-, four-, and five-year-olds who learned to read early show that some children with mental ages below six and one-half can learn to read successfully under the right conditions.

The relationship between intelligence and beginning reading success varies from one reading program to another. Gates (1937), in his now famous readiness factor research, concluded that the minimal age concept is meaningless without qualifying information as to the methods, procedures, and materials used in the beginning program plus information on the teacher's ability to individualize the instruction to meet pupils' needs. Two writers, Spache and Spache (1973), expand upon this view, observing, "It is the stereotyped, inflexible, and mass-oriented reading program that demands a higher mental age, and makes intelligence so important a factor in reading success in our primary classrooms" (p. 64).

Conceptual Development and Specific Reasoning Ability While the general intelligence of a child determines beginning reading success to a certain extent, those facets of general intelligence that are related specifically to reading are an even better predictor. Downing (1971) contends that the cognitive factors involving the development of reasoning abilities and concepts of reading "may be the most important of all the foundations of readiness for learning to read." He cites as research evidence several studies, including the extensive review of the research on poor readers by Vernon (1962). Vernon found that the common characteristics of children who failed in reading were "cognitive confusion" and "lack of system about the whole reading process." She felt that the main problem of disabled readers was a failure in developing "a particular type of reasoning process." This reasoning process was necessary in understanding such important concepts as the relationship of written language to speech.

Reid (1958) and Downing (1971), in interviews with five-year-olds in their first year of primary school, found the children confused about the nature of reading and the problem-solving tasks they were required to do. Reid observed that the children showed "a general lack of any specific expectancies of what reading was going to be like, of what the activity consisted, of the purpose and the use of it." Furthermore, the children had trouble understanding abstract technical terms such as "word," "number," "letter," and "sound." Downing reports that at the end of the school year a minority of children remained confused about the reading process while others made "varying degrees of progress towards developing the concept of reading and developing the specific abilities in learning to read." Downing's description of the development of cognitive clarity about the reading process indicates five features: children grow in understanding the communication purpose of written language; their conception of the functions of symbols becomes clearer; their concepts of linguistic segments, such as "word" and "sound," approach those of the teacher; their corresponding spontaneous command of the abstract technical terminology of language increases; their understanding of the process of decoding alphabetic letters to speech sounds and vice versa improves.

Reid's and Downing's studies have an important implication for teachers of young children. Downing points out, "It would be a grave error to assume that the young child's perception of the process of reading and writing is the same as that of the adult who desires to teach him these useful skills."

Environmental Factors

Home Background and Experience A number of environmental factors both subtle and obvious are at work in shaping the child's personality, experiences, attitudes, values, and language abilities. Conditions in the home influence a child's personal and social adjustment, which in turn may help or hinder that child's learning to read. A child with a stable home life and parents who love and understand him and provide him with a sense of individual worth will have one less stumbling block between him and reading.

The home also influences the child's attitudes towards books and reading. Parents who read and own books and who appreciate reading themselves and enjoy reading stories to their children usually produce children who want to read. Parents who take an interest in the school, in what the child is learning and doing there, reinforce this positive attitude.

The quality and extent of a child's experiences at home are also important to his progress in reading. Reading should be a meaningful act, and children's past experiences enable them to comprehend what they read. Probably most school beginners have the background of information and experience necessary to handle most beginning reading material. It is, of course, important to remember that the teacher's instruction should be based on the child's previous experiences.

Socioeconomic Class and Culture There is a tendency for middle- and upper-class children to be ready earlier for beginning reading instruction. However, as Harris (1961) observes, "What counts for child development is not the wealth of the home but the intellectual and social environment with which the child is surrounded" (p. 38). Time rather than money is needed. Parents should spend time talking with their children, enjoying and sharing story books with them, and sharing and broadening their experiences. Children from low socioeconomic homes where parents pursue such activities have an excellent chance to become good readers.

Recently there has been much interest in cultural environment and its effect on a child's readiness. In our North American culture there are several subcultures (black, Mexican-American, rural mountain, urban disadvantaged, Indian, and so on). These subcultures to some extent determine children's speech, their experiences and concepts, their attitudes, and their values (Mickelson and Galloway, 1973). Some children from these subcultures are not ready for middle-class schools and their reading instruction. Reading and other intellectual activities are not highly valued in some subcultures (Deutsch, 1960). Stories may seem foreign to some children's previous experiences. Some of these children come from homes where a foreign language is spoken. Others speak variations of English which may be quite dissimilar to the English used in most schools. So teacher expectancies for behavior in school may seem alien to some children.

Language Abilities Most school beginners will have the language readiness necessary to make good progress in reading. The richness of their vocabulary and complexity of their spoken sentences are likely to surpass the common words and simple sentences that they are taught in their beginning readers. Some children, however, have immature language development and faulty habits such as "baby talk." Some come from foreign speaking homes and are relatively unfamiliar with English. Others are members of culturally isolated groups where non-standard English is spoken. Differences in grammar, language structures, and sounds may make these children's variations of English different from the English in the average reading program. These small groups will need some special accommodating instruction so they will not be handicapped in learning to read.

Social and Emotional Factors

Motivation Motivation is a key factor in learning to read. It helps to explain why some children who are deficient in a number of readiness abilities make good progress in beginning reading, while other children with the same deficiencies are slow to read. Fortunately, most five- or six-year-olds are excited about going to school and want to learn how to read. Teachers should do everything in their power to sustain this enthusiasm and desire. However, some children would rather play games, climb, run, wrestle—anything but sit still and learn to read. Others would rather be read to by their parents or the teacher than have to read for themselves. The teacher must work hard to arouse these children's interest in learning to read. But there is little reason to delay reading simply because a child is not showing a desire to read. This motivation can and should be nurtured and encouraged during actual instruction.

Social and Emotional Maturity and Adjustment A child's social and emotional adjustment and maturity may be a barrier or a help in learning to read. Harris (1961) emphasizes three aspects of emotional and social maturity—emotional stability, self-reliance, and ability to participate in groups—as particularly important for school or reading readiness.

A child should have a certain degree of emotional control. Boys and girls who have temper tantrums, cry and over-react when they cannot get their own way, or withdraw or sulk when they have trouble with a lesson will be less likely to make normal reading progress than children who do not.

Children need to be sufficiently self-reliant in a classroom. If the teacher hands out worksheets (suited to the child's ability level) and explains how to do them, each child should be able to continue working on his own. Boys and girls who have grown too dependent may not be able to do independent activities by themselves and may make unreasonable demands on the teacher's attention. They may be less likely to make normal progress in reading than others.

As much of the instruction in the average classroom is done in groups, the ability to participate actively and cooperatively is important. Boys and girls should be able to listen well, pay attention to the teacher's explanation, and follow the teacher's directions. They should be able to take turns with the other group members and respect their rights. Children who cannot learn in group situations will be at a disadvantage in the average school.

Fortunately most children will come to school with personal and social adjustments sufficient for them to make normal progress in reading. A few children, however, may be emotionally and socially immature and show this immaturity in many ways. They may be relatively self-centered, inattentive, unwilling to cooperate with their teacher, and shy. Past pre-school experiences may have given them marked feelings of insecurity, inferiority, or hostility that can inhibit learning. Sometimes their behavior disrupts not only their learning but that of their classmates. If the teacher suspects real emotional disturbance, she should refer the child to the school psychologist or other appropriate authority or agency.

On the other hand, immature behavior does not necessarily signal maladjustment. Time and familiarity with the teacher and classroom procedures are allies in working with immature children. One of the most important things a teacher can do is to help the child with social and emotional problems to achieve numerous successful experiences with reading.

Instructional Factors

So far we have focused on the child—how experience and his physical, emotional, social, and intellectual development influence his readiness for reading. We must now turn to the school's instructional program.

Kindergarten Many studies stress the importance of kindergarten in helping children do well in first-grade reading programs. We would expect kindergartens which teach special readiness programs tailored to the needs of the children to be especially helpful. However, just the kindergarten experiences of becoming acquainted with the school, working with the teacher in groups and alone, and socializing with other children make school adjustment easier (Spache and Spache, 1973). Learning to listen and pay attention to the teacher, following directions to play games, even finding out how to use scissors, paste, and crayons all help develop a child's readiness for reading.

The Teacher Researchers (Bond and Dykstra, 1967) continually point to the teacher as the key factor in the instructional program. The teacher influences the child's readiness in a number of subtle and direct ways. His concept of reading readiness and his expectancies will guide him in deciding who is ready to read and when reading should be begun. One teacher may decide who is ready to read by judging each individual child's maturity. Another teacher may decide that the children who have completed their readiness workbooks successfully are the ones ready for reading. A child labelled "ready to read" by one teacher may not be "ready to read" in another classroom.

How and when children are given readiness instruction will also depend on the teacher's competency and abilities. Some teachers have a broader knowledge of basic reading and readiness skills, methods, and materials than others. Some have better organizational skills and can more successfully provide individualized reading readiness instruction. These teachers may be able to handle several readiness and reading groups and keep track and stimulate various subgroups and individual activities without confusion and wasted effort. Children in these rooms will be more likely to acquire the skills needed for reading earlier. Other teachers may feel that two or three boys and girls in a class are ready for reading at the beginning of school, but also feel that they will not be able to teach them effectively in the class. These children may have to wait until others are ready and the teacher can deal with the logistics of instruction.

Basic knowledge is important, but so is the teacher's interest in the children, the warm learning atmosphere he develops and the enthusiasm that he brings to his readiness and reading instruction. He may know each child's readiness needs, have at his disposal colorful and comprehensive material to teach them, be able to maintain five readiness groups successfully, and still unknowingly turn children away from learning. Other teachers provide an atmosphere where it is fun to learn. Even an abstract and potentially dull concept such as understanding the relationship between sounds and letters can be taught in interesting and meaningful ways. Teachers who are interested and enthusiastic will spark the same attitudes in their students. And these children in a happy learning atmosphere will in all likelihood develop readiness and reading skills sooner than their bored and disinterested peers.

The School's Beginning Reading Program Many schools follow a set policy that prescribes a certain reading program or series. This reading program may influence the child's readiness to read. Some programs require more refined skills; a child may not be ready for such a program until age seven. Other programs may be modified and adapted so five-year-olds will be ready for them. Each teacher must know what skills and abilities are necessary for children to succeed in the adopted program.

Classroom Conditions Conditions such as class size and classroom resources and facilities may be factors in the teacher's readiness instruction.
Teachers who have class loads of thirty to forty pupils will not be able to
teach each child as effectively as those who have twenty to thirty children
(Frymier, 1964). Some schools provide teacher aides (salaried or volunteer
assistants for teachers in the classroom) or volunteer helpers. Such help
allows the teacher to devote more time to individualizing instruction.
Well-equipped classrooms, well-planned resource centers with varieties of
audio-visual aids and books, and special services such as a psychometrist
(a person in charge of school testing) and a reading coordinator are big
assets in the teacher's instructional program.

Determining Reading Readiness and Instructional Level

Although our teacher at Sunnydale School has only known and worked
with her group one week, she has already begun to evaluate and decide who
is ready for reading and who needs further preparation. This is a *most
important* step in good teaching and must be given the thought, time, and
effort it deserves. A doctor does not prescribe treatment without a
thorough diagnosis. Neither should a teacher.

A good evaluation answers two questions. First, it gives the teacher a
global assessment. It tells her who is ready to begin reading and who needs
further preparation. Second, it points out fairly specifically what instruction is needed by each child. This is most important because children not
only vary among themselves but within themselves. Not every child
develops the various abilities that comprise reading readiness simultaneously. For instance, a child's oral language abilities may be well developed,
but at the same time he may have trouble detecting likenesses and
differences between words he sees. Because of the varied abilities in each
individual, one writer (Durkin, 1972) suggests that teachers talk in terms of
child "readiness*es*" rather than the all-encompassing "readiness." Therefore the teacher asks specific questions such as: Can the child match
letters? Can he participate well in group instruction? The teacher must also
consider the beginning reading program that each child has to be ready to
undertake. All this knowledge will provide the raw material for designing
an effective and more individualized pre-reading and reading program.

Determining Where the Child Is Now

Techniques to determine the child's pre-reading strengths and capabilities include both formal tests and teacher judgments. The teacher will want to know if the child has any physical conditions that might hinder his success in beginning reading. Ideally each child will have a physical check-up, including an eye and ear examination, prior to school entrance. The teacher should be liberal in referrals if she thinks anything is amiss. Readiness tests, valuable to many teachers, especially inexperienced ones, serve to support and reaffirm the teacher's judgments and provide a quick assessment. The subtests may also be a source of ideas for readiness training activities. Some teachers also use intelligence tests. However, there is a danger of too much reliance on formal tests. Their results may influence the teacher's expectations for her students.

Some factors, such as interest in reading, attention span, and social adjustment, cannot be easily measured by tests. These can be better measured informally. Teachers can use "homemade" tools such as checklists, anecdotal records, and teacher-made specific skills tests. The first-grade teacher can tap the previous kindergarten teacher's knowledge about the child. The experience charts that are used to prepare children to read can also serve as a test of children's progress. Simply trying the child out on a sample of the beginning reading task may provide an excellent basis for evaluation. For instance, the teacher may print the vocabulary of the first pre-primer on cards and have the child learn the words. If he learns the words quickly, he is more apt to be ready for the task. Downing (1971) reports that this practice is used by many teachers in Great Britain for grouping beginning readers.

Teachers also can form judgments from observing children in and out of the classroom. Is the child interested in the stories that the teacher reads? Can he work by himself? The knowledge of each child's pre-reading strengths and weaknesses can be summed up on individual checklists. An example of a checklist is shown on pp. 286–287. The teacher may wish to modify this one or develop one of his own to suit his particular situation.

Determining What the Program Requires

Next the teacher will want to have a knowledge of the beginning reading program to be used. Both kindergarten and first-grade teachers should become acquainted with the method, materials, content, and principles of instruction used in the program. Each teacher will ask herself, "What skills does this particular child need to succeed in this program? Does this program stress any particular method of teaching reading?" We know that

Reading Readiness Checklist

Name of Child _____

Date _____

Write *yes* or *no* or other appropriate answer for each of the following questions:

Physical Considerations

What is the sex of the child?
Have the child's general health, vision, and hearing been examined?
If so, has any special restriction been imposed or has any special treatment
    been prescribed?
Are there any signs of visual, auditory, or speech problems?
Is his attendance in school regular?
Is he alert and responsive to instruction?

Social and Emotional Adjustment in the Classroom

Is the child overdependent on the teacher?
Does he interact well with other members of the class?
Does he adapt himself easily to new situations?
Can he assume responsibility and work independently?
Does he complete assigned tasks?
Does he know when to talk and when to listen to the teacher?
Does he participate well and take turns in group activities?
How well does he cope with minor frustrations?
Does he have patience and show persistence in completing activities?

Desire to Read and Reading Concepts

Does the child enjoy hearing stories?
Can the child listen to a story with sustained interest for ten minutes?
Does he voluntarily look at school books in the library?
Does he seem to have established a sense of left-to-right, top-to-bottom
    orientation in experience chart activities?
Does he show interest in words and messages in the classroom?
Does he bring books from home to school?
Does he handle books with reasonable care?
Can the child write his own name?
Does he seem to understand that reading is talk written down?

Intellectual Factors

Has the child had an intelligence test? If so, what were the results?

Does the child seem to be mentally alert?

Does the child interpret pictures effectively, seem to contribute pertinent ideas to class discussions?

Does the child have a good memory for past experiences? Can he memorize simple rhymes or remember simple messages?

Does he show originality in his ideas and classwork?

Does he understand and follow directions with a minimum of assistance?

Does he seem to reason well and pick up new learnings quickly?

Does he show some ability in problem solving?

Background of Experience and Language Abilities

Is the child able to recite common nursery rhymes and is he acquainted with well-known fairy tales?

Has the child attended nursery school and/or kindergarten?

Does the child have knowledge about common concepts—food, family, house, animals, etc.? Are the child's concepts reasonably accurate?

Is English spoken in the child's home?

If not English, what language is spoken?

Can the child speak with reasonable fluency?

Does he seem to have a reasonable vocabulary to communicate his experiences?

Can the child use more complex language structures in addition to so-called simple sentences?

Does the child use and/or understand standard English?

Does he use a non-standard form of English?

Does the child understand the school's language of instruction?

Visual and Auditory Perception

Can the child see differences in pictures and geometric shapes?

Can the child recognize his own name?

Can the child match letters and discriminate words that have gross differences (O and x; see and hello)?

Can the child discriminate between words that have only minor detail differences (wear, were)?

Can the child recognize words that have been repeatedly presented to him?

Can the child rhyme words?

Can the child add to a list of words beginning with the same initial sounds?

Can the child discriminate between words that sound very similar (watch and witch)?

Does the child demonstrate knowledge of the sound-letter relationship? (That is d. It makes the first sound in dog.)

language-experience programs, phonic programs, and linguistic programs, to use some examples, may emphasize some pre-reading skills and place less importance on others. For instance, an individualized beginning reading program may put a greater premium on independent work habits and a lesser emphasis on group work.

Planning the Assessment of Reading Readiness

Teaching reading readiness involves a commitment to instruction at the child's level. Therefore, the assessment of reading readiness should begin in the first weeks of kindergarten and first grade, or even with parent interviews prior to kindergarten. Assessment at this early stage involves informal measures. As children change rapidly in pre-reading skills and abilities, evaluation should be done continuously. Durkin (1974) suggests that each teacher ask himself over and over again, "Why am I doing what I'm doing?" (p. 96). Formal assessments—reading readiness tests—are usually conducted at the end of kindergarten and after the second or third week of first grade, often determined by school policy.

Developing Readiness Skills

Although children will learn some readiness skills incidentally, readiness training should not be left to chance. Neither should it be concentrated entirely in isolated drills. A good training program is well organized and carefully thought out. The teacher should have a sense of where he is going—why he is doing a particular activity with a child. The diagnosis of each child's skills and abilities in relationship to the school's beginning reading program reveals the child's particular readiness needs. These needs determine the content and emphasis of the readiness program.

Evaluating the class at Sunnydale School, Ms. Lane found that two children were reading at second-grade level. She also noticed that a few children scored very well on teacher-made and published texts of reading readiness. They seemed to have the maturity, intelligence, language abilities, and conceptual background needed for the beginning reading program. She decided to begin their formal reading as soon as was practical because they had no need for a readiness training period. After her best effort at assessment, the teacher was still not sure about three children's readiness to read, so she decided it was probably better to wait. A child who has been pushed into reading before he is ready is more likely to fail than one who has been delayed a short period of time.

Most of the children in Ms. Lane's class would profit from readiness training. Some children in this group were strong in some readiness skills but needed training to bolster other skills. Her job was to strengthen the skills in which pupils had demonstrated weakness. A few children would require an extended time of training. They seemed to have deficits in almost every area. It is not uncommon to see one or two first graders from each class spend a half year in preparation. These very late starters are a real challenge to a teacher. She must try to keep the children from being discouraged as they see everyone else beginning to read. The teacher must also frequently contend with parents who come to school wondering, "Why isn't my child reading yet?"

Organizing and Individualizing a Readiness Program

There are a number of ways to organize and individualize a readiness program. Some schools have adopted unusual organizations, such as transition rooms, a sort of half step after kindergarten for those who are not ready for first grade. Some teachers in open area schools team teach, dividing their classes to arrive at groups of closer abilities. Some teachers have teacher aides. Most teachers, however, work in self-contained classrooms, and the readiness program must conform to this situation. Two useful aids in organizing readiness programs—flexible groupings and learning centers—are presented below. Other ideas for organization will be found in books listed at the end of this chapter.

Flexible Grouping Many teachers organize their classes into flexible groups, formed around special needs and interests, and later disbanded when they have served their purpose. These represent one method of individualizing instruction. Ms. Lane established such groups on the basis of a global assessment of each child's present achievement. Her three basic groups were (1) readers, (2) children who were ready to read, and (3) children who needed further preparation before reading. She then went through each child's reading readiness inventory and placed individuals in special needs and interest groups. For instance, two children in the "ready to read" group needed further preparation in beginning consonant sounds, as did fourteen children in the "further preparation" group. Seven children had expressed an enthusiastic interest in trucks, so a special group was formed including both reader and non-reader members. A diagram of Ms. Lane's grouping appears on p. 290.

Notice that children in both "reading" and "ready to read" groups may also be involved in some readiness activities. This is because readiness and reading subtly blend into each other. Many of the readiness activities will probably be continued into initial reading, providing the child with

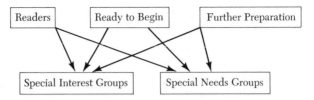

Figure 9.1   Readiness Grouping.

added practice and review. There is no clear dividing line. The readiness program should provide a smooth transition between non-reading and reading.

Learning Centers To facilitate all types of readiness experiences, learning centers can be established in the classroom. The centers consist of designated areas of the room in which a child can do different readiness activities. Centers can be listed pictorially on a magnetic chalkboard. Each child can be given two or three name cards with which he can choose centers. Teachers can reserve two or three cards per child, and put them at the centers to which they wish to assign children, according to skill weaknesses. Children can remove the card as they complete the work at the center. Learning centers might include one or more of the following:

1. a writing and word center
2. a book center
3. a play or game center
4. a story center
5. a phonics center
6. a building and block center
7. a printing center

There are many more. Types of centers are limited only by the creativity of the teacher and the special needs of the class.

The teacher introduces each center to the children and discusses the different activities that can be done in each. The activities or centers may be changed from time to time and each new addition discussed. Not all these centers will appeal to every pre-reader. However, many teachers have found learning stations effective in coping with individual differences and providing activities for free play or independent work periods.

The *writing and word center* is for children who want to learn a "special" word. There is a large pocket-chart in which each child has his own pocket for storing his words. The teacher prints the child's word on a card. On succeeding visits to the word center, the teacher may review the child's old words with him. No pressure should be applied. If the child does not remember the word after being told it several times, it should be unobtrusively destroyed. The center can also be used in writing captions for pictures. Other children may have a special message or story they want to have written down. For instance, a child may draw a front cover for his mother's birthday card and dictate a message which the teacher copies on the inside of the card.

A *printing center* contains samples of letters that children can copy and practice.

A *book center* or library is set up in a corner of the room. This area can be made quite cozy and inviting with a *small area rug,* book shelves, some little chairs, or a small table with books displayed on it. Children may come here when they are through with their work or at playtime to look at the books. This book corner can contain a variety of books—both published children's books and class-made diaries or illustrated short stories dictated by members of the class to the teacher.

A *play or game center* provides a variety of individual and group readiness games. The games might include puzzles, flannel board story kits, lotto, a magnetic board with magnetic letters, picture or shape dominoes, sequence puzzles, and so on. The teacher should introduce each game to the children, showing them how each can be played.

Activities to Improve Readiness Skills

There are vast numbers of activities that the teacher can use to prepare children for reading. The author has included a few examples for each skill. (The reader will notice that one activity may develop a number of readiness skills.) At the end of the chapter and in the section on the current readiness programs, sources for other activities are presented. Also, much of value can be learned through visits to different classrooms and schools in the area.

Teachers should choose activities that can be made interesting and meaningful. For example, the teacher should not say, "What words begin with the same sound as *moon*?" when there is a Mary in the class. She should use Mary's name, which makes the lesson more interesting to the children.

Adjusting to Physical Deficiencies How can the teacher help a child with poor vision, speech, and hearing in the pre-reading period? There are a number of ways. She may modify the pre-reading program to adapt to the child's deficiencies, keep a sharp eye out for signs of physical problems, and make referrals when necessary. Important, too, is a good cooperating relationship between teacher and parent. For instance, if the child comes to school each day looking tired, the teacher should feel free to suggest to the parents that perhaps the child may need more sleep.

Improving Personal and Social Adjustment to School It is very important for reading and other learning as well that a child's first experiences with the school be happy and successful ones. During the pre-reading period, the teacher should watch each child's personal and social adjustment carefully. Often, work in small groups, group games, praise, encouragement, and success in learning activities will help children who are having adjustment problems. Parents and teachers should feel free to discuss and enlist each other's aid in improving the child's emotional and social development. Many helpful suggestions may be found in books included at the end of this chapter.

Developing Backgrounds of Experience Many children have a background of experiences which enables them to understand what they will read about in the beginning reading program. However, a small group of children, including those from culturally different or culturally disadvantaged backgrounds, may not. For all children a stimulating classroom environment, rich in firsthand experiences, is beneficial. However, with children of limited and meager concepts and experiences, this rich and varied background building program becomes even more important. Such a program must be carefully structured. Some ideas for building backgrounds are listed here. Other ideas may be found in the discussion of pre-reading programs for the culturally disadvantaged.

1. Look at the beginning reading program. What are the stories about? The background of experience and concepts needed to understand the stories should be introduced in the pre-reading program as well as other concepts.
2. Active, firsthand experiences are very valuable. Children might plan and care for a school garden, care for classroom pets, prepare a rhythm band, and make a play store, house, or post office. Field trips are good for enlarging concepts and knowledge about the community. They can include excursions to places like the zoo, the neighborhood fire station, the post office, and a farm. Science experiments also are useful in providing firsthand experiences.
3. Audio and visual aids are useful. Records, motion pictures, models, pictures, television, photographs, and slides can be looked at, handled, or heard and then discussed with the teacher. Classroom discussion is very important. It broadens the child's understandings and provides the teacher with some feedback on the children's thinking. Mere exposure to the audio-visual aid is not enough.

Developing Attention and Persistence Goals for improving attention and persistence should be included as a part of all other lessons in preparing a child for reading. Attention and persistence will improve if the teacher remembers to:

1. Capture the child's interest with the lesson. It should be meaningful to him. Children who have notoriously short attention spans in the classroom often sit and play with favorite toys or watch cartoons for lengthy periods at home.
2. Keep the room as free of distractions as possible.
3. Ensure that each child experiences success. Then he is apt to be more interested. His attention span and persistence with the lesson will increase.
4. For children who have extremely short attention spans, begin with brief activities. The length of the activities may be gradually extended.

To develop persistence, the teacher should require the child to complete what he has begun. Children should be given classroom responsibilities such as taking care of the library or of outside play equipment (balls, jump rope) and feeding fish or gerbils. The teacher should check to see that these are well done to encourage habits of persistence. If a child has not completed an activity that is at his instructional level, he should be encouraged to finish it. A number of teachers also recommend behavior modification techniques as helpful in improving attention in their class.

Developing the Desire to Read An essential goal of the teacher during the readiness training program is to develop and maintain a desire to read. There are many ways of doing this. First, the child should feel that to learn to read is something important to himself personally. The teacher can make reading meaningful for the child by:

1. Writing the schedule for the day on the chalkboard and reading it with the children. The class will be interested in what they are going to do, especially if something special is happening (someone has a birthday, a visitor is coming). The chalkboard can also be used to write shorter messages of interest to the children. For instance, some days the teacher may go to the board and say "Good morning" while writing it on the chalkboard. Other phrases such as "Happy Birthday, Sally," "John, pass out the papers," "Harry, put on your coat" can be used.
2. Having the children help compose experience charts about field trips they have taken, new people in the class, special messages for parents, and so on.
3. At story time frequently giving different children a chance to pick a story they like to hear. The teacher can let children bring stories from home for her to read. She can let them pick from three available stories. When reading a story, she can let the children discuss some of the pictures.

The teacher's interest in books can be a model for the child. Children like to imitate their teacher. Many love to play school. By reading to the class, with expression and enthusiasm, a teacher is building a foundation for a lifetime love of reading in students. Visitors can be invited to read stories to the class. The school principal can also give valuable help in this way. Boys will be quite impressed also when an older fourth, fifth or sixth grade boy reads a story to them.

Teachers also influence a child's desire to read by the negative and positive comments they make during pre-reading instruction. Browne (1972) studied this teacher-pupil verbal interaction during first-grade reading periods. She found that the high achieving groups were able to respond more successfully to the reading tasks and were met with much praise from their teachers. On the other hand, children in the low achieving groups had much more difficulty with their reading tasks and received for their effort more corrective statements from their teachers. Browne also found that the teachers spent more time with the lower achieving children. Thus, the lower achieving children, who needed praise and encouragement, received a longer period of continuous negative comments.

Children need praise and success with the various pre-reading activities if they are to develop and maintain a desire to read. If a child is not succeeding in some pre-reading activity, the teacher should muster some encouraging words and lower the level of difficulty of the activity so that the child can succeed and receive positive reinforcement. Then learning can start from that level.

Developing Concepts about Reading We as adults have already learned to read. Having accomplished this task, we often take for granted certain basic concepts about reading that children may not know. These basic concepts and words should be presented clearly in the classroom. They include ideas such as "reading is talk written down" and the meanings of reading instruction words such as *letter*, *word*, and *sentence*. Teach the children how to handle books and read from top to bottom, left to right. Remember also to share with the children the ideas of reading as adventure, escape, mystery, and excitement. We not only want children to learn to read, but also to become lifelong readers.

A readiness program should be rich in experiences with words. Vocabulary skills and concepts can be emphasized indirectly and informally through experience charts, reading readiness books, and other meaningful and relevant activities with letters and words. Repeated informal mention of these concepts is helpful. Long, detailed explanations of words and letters will most likely be wasted effort. Vocabulary can be taught well by pointing out examples when the child shows interest or by using the right term at the right time.

Developing Language Abilities—
Speaking and Listening

Speaking and *listening* are two of the major building blocks for beginning reading. Armstrong (1967) explains the importance of oral language:

> Oral language is needed to relate the child's background to the story, to enlarge concepts necessary to an understanding of the story, to relate concepts to vocabulary, to build interest, to build familiarity with unfamiliar language structures, and to enhance the functioning of the higher mental processes used in reading. Discussion, skillfully guided, does these things (p. 57).

Most children will have a vocabulary and store of concepts that are more than adequate for getting meaning from the beginning readers. In many classrooms, then, the major emphasis will be on improving other language abilities. Some children may need to develop a greater range or fluency of oral expression. When the teacher asks a child something, he may answer only with gestures or monosyllables. At the other extreme are the children who reply with a long-winded answer plus a few extra bits of information that are not really needed.

Some children will also need help in developing more complex sentence structures—for example, "I like dogs when they let me pet them," rather than simply, "I like dogs." They need to be familiar with language patterns similar to those used in the stories so that they will read to get meaning from the stories. They also need to be familiar with the language of instruction used by the teacher. This similarity of language patterns can be developed by: (1) planning oral language training for the child, (2) writing down the child's language for him to read as in the language-experience approach, and (3) helping children participate effectively in class and group activities. Some children need help in overcoming shyness in a group. Some children need to learn how to ask questions.

Language Training: A Part of All Activities The majority of training in language is done indirectly outside the isolated "language training sessions." Language training involves the total time that the teacher is with the child in school. The first step is providing many chances for the child to express himself. He should talk to and listen to the teacher, talk to and listen to other children. The teacher can provide an atmosphere where children feel free and are encouraged to express themselves within classroom limits.

Communication skills can be developed during art, music, free play, science, and other times. Conversation is often easier for children with poorer language development when they are actively involved in an activity. The teacher should make a point of talking individually to each student. This is especially important with children who need extensive improvement. The teacher "models" her language for each child to copy.

Besides serving as a model for language development, the teacher must take time to listen to what the class has to say. Although this sounds very obvious, researchers have found that teachers do almost all of the talking in the class. Children spend far too much of their time sitting and listening. Improving language abilities requires that classroom communication be a two-way street.

Direct Language Training Activities. Although language training should be seen as a part of every school activity, there are a number of games and activities which develop language skills directly. They may be used with the whole class or smaller groups. Smaller groups are often more effective with timid and less verbal children. Several examples of "teacher tested" activities are listed below:

1. Take polaroid pictures of a class field trip, classroom activities, free play, or lunchroom happenings. Ask children questions about them. Use a toy telephone or tin can telephone, puppets, child-made imaginary paper animals, and so on to stimulate conversation.
2. Have a show and tell period where children tell about objects, share interesting events, or tell a story they made up to the other children in the class. For a variation, try "choose and tell." In this activity the teacher provides various objects or pictures, and children pick one and talk about it.
3. Take advantage of children's imagination and love of make-believe. Children can take various roles in dramatic play. They can pretend to be a teacher, a mother, a father, a storekeeper, and so on.
4. Develop grammatical drills using models or miniatures. The children or teacher can move these around and make up sentences about them to develop proficiency in verb forms, comparative terms, prepositions, and singular and plural forms. Example: The cow is eating grass. The cow is bigger than the chicken.
5. Ask the child to draw a picture and then give a verbal description of it. Draw some pictures yourself and have the children give verbal descriptions of them.

Listening Comprehension Children need training in listening comprehension skills—understanding what other people are saying. This type of training is the preliminary step in comprehending stories in the readers. It enables children to go beyond just parroting words in a book. The child needs to understand what the words say so he can react to them. This includes both knowing the meaning of specific words such as *boy* and *bathtub* and comprehending sentences, paragraphs, and stories. Children also need skill in listening to benefit from reading instruction. They must listen to and understand what the teacher is teaching them. They must learn how to follow directions. Below are a few suggestions for developing listening comprehension:

1. To provide practice in understanding and recalling facts: Read a story to the children and ask them specific questions about it.
2. To provide practice in putting events in a sequence: Ask the children to draw pictures illustrating a story and then have them line up the pictures in the right order for showing on the class-made cardboard television set.
3. To provide practice in following directions: Demonstrate how to make a simple art project before the class. Then let each child do the project. Ask a child who has trouble in following directions to explain what he did to make the project.
4. To provide practice in interpreting and evaluating ideas and stories: When discussing a story read to the children, go beyond asking factual questions and develop some of the following questions: "Could this story really happen?" "Why?" "Why did you think George was nice to his little sister?" "Why did you or why didn't you like this story?" "What do you think will happen next?" and "What would you do in this situation?"

Auditory Discrimination Children must be able to hear likenesses and differences in sounds in order to recognize words by a phonics method. Activities to develop this skill should follow in a sequence from gross to finer discriminations. They can be taught in games, in rhymes, and as drills. Most children will need very few lessons with the more basic discriminations, such as hearing the difference between the *moo* of a cow and the *quack* of a duck. For many children these basic lessons can be skipped altogether. Some children will need frequent practice in hearing sounds in words, so teachers often use commercial materials designed for this purpose. Types of training activities that develop skill in auditory discrimination include the following:

1. Ask the children to be silent for a moment. Then they can discuss the sounds they heard.
2. Play short records with different but familiar sounds. Children can identify each sound as it is played. Sometimes pictures of the objects making the sound are used. Children can take turns finding the right picture from a group on the bulletin board.
3. Have children guess the sources of sound as one child hides from view and does the following things: (a) claps hands softly; (b) shakes a rattle; (c) crumples a piece of paper; (d) bangs on a drum.

4. Introduce the concept that words are made up of sounds. Have children listen to different common long and short words. Pronounce the words slowly and see if the children can tell how many separate sounds they hear.

5. Recite or play records of nursery rhymes. Point out which words rhyme. Have children complete rhymes such as "I know a mouse. He lives in my _____." Have children pick out from a group of four words the one that does not rhyme. Ask children to say a word that rhymes with another word.

6. Introduce initial consonants in a word context. Say that *b* is the first sound of *balloon* rather than that *b* says "buh." Start with easy to learn and common consonants such as *m, b, f,* and *p* and then continue with others, *g, c, t, l, d, h, j, k, r, n, w, s, y, v, x,* and *z.* Vowels are frequently introduced later, although for a few basal programs the opposite is the case. It is a good idea to gear the auditory discrimination training program to what will be taught in the children's beginning reading program.

Some teachers like to introduce initial consonants with worksheets which include activities such as circling or coloring all the pictures that begin with a certain sound. Others prefer to use scrapbooks with pages to be filled with pictures of words starting with the various consonant sounds. Some teachers combine both formal and informal approaches. Games provide good practice. For instance, the teacher reads a list of words and requires each child to stand up or clap when she says a word beginning with a certain sound.

7. Teach initial consonants in a story context. Say, for example, "Charlie put _____ on his hands so he could make snowballs." She explains that what he put on begins with the same sound as *Mary.*

Developing Visual Discrimination

Visual discrimination exercises follow a sequence from gross discrimination of non-letter forms to fine discrimination in letters and words. The amount of visual discrimination training necessary will vary from child to child. Training should start at each child's level of skill as determined by readiness and teacher-made tests. Children who recognize most letters but have difficulty in discriminating between *b, p, q,* and *d* should not have to begin their training with low-level activities such as matching pictures or geometric forms. For some children weakness in visual discrimination is a problem of short attention span or lack of interest in words. When these problems are solved, visual discrimination will improve. Frequently finer auditory and visual discrimination skills are taught together so that children will learn the sound-letter relationship in words.

Perception and Discrimination of Non-Letter Forms Some children are not able to see differences in letters and words. With these children, visual discrimination training begins with activities stressing likenesses and differences in objects, pictures, and geometric forms. When the child shows some skill in these basic discriminations, the teacher should begin discrimination training with words and letters. The value of exercises with non-letter forms may be rather limited. Robinson (1972), in a recent review of research findings, says, "The research shows no conclusive answers to the question of the effectiveness of perceptual training to improve reading. While some programs appear to improve perceptual performance in the areas trained, the long-term effect on reading is uncertain" (p. 145). In general, the more visual discrimination training resembles reading tasks, the more effective it will be in developing reading readiness. Exercises with non-letter forms may, however, help some children who have short attention spans, have trouble following directions, and have no background of looking at words or books (Durrell, 1956). They are also fun for many children to do and can be made easy enough to give almost any child a successful pre-reading experience.

Activities to develop general perceptual skills are found in many basal readiness books, children's magazines, and commercially produced activities books. There are even whole commercial programs devoted to developing visual perception. As noted before, the value of using these *whole* programs in readiness training is questionable (Paradis, 1974). Some activities with non-letter forms include:

1. Matching of objects, pictures, and geometric forms. A child is given a miniature cow. He must pick out an identical cow from a group of animals. Matching with pictures and geometric forms is done in the same manner. The activity can be made more difficult by increasing the alternative choices or making the alternative choices very similar.
2. Lotto and bingo type games with pictures and shapes. A child holds up the master picture and the other children cover the same picture on their individual card with the master picture or a marker. The first child to have all the pictures covered or, in bingo, a straight row marked, wins the game.
3. Toys and puzzles where children have to fit a certain shape in the right place may be useful.
4. Pictures containing hidden pictures can be found in some basal readiness books. The children have to find and color the hidden pictures. In other exercises the children must discover what is missing (picture of a dog minus one ear) and draw it in.

Visual Discrimination of Letters and Words Activities for seeing likenesses and differences in letters and words start from gross discrimination of letters, such as telling *x* from *o*, and proceed to fine discrimination between words, such as *mat* and *met*. Much of the teaching in fine discrimination of words will be done during beginning reading instruction as sight vocabulary is introduced. Isolated drills and worksheets should not be overstressed, since children quickly lose interest in simply matching or copying words and letters. Suggested activities are listed below:

1. Worksheets using the following types of exercises may be developed by the teacher or ordered from commercial publishers. The difficulty of each worksheet can be increased by (a) increasing alternatives to choose from; (b) increasing the number of right answers; and (c) choosing alternatives that are very similar to one another.

    a. Circle the letter that is different.

o	w	o

    b. Underline the word in the big box that is the same as the one in the little box.

be	rain	to	be	see
wet	Mary	wet	see	here

    c. Underline the word in the big box that begins with the letter in the little box.

h	school	me	from	hunt
l	love	three	sun	peace

    d. Circle the two words that have the same beginning and ending letter.

went	wheat	where

    (Although children should be able to see likenesses and differences in all parts of words, the teacher should provide more exercises that stress differences in beginnings of words. This helps to develop the habit of looking at a word from left to right.)

2. Develop small group activities and games similar to the above worksheet exercises. As examples:

    a. Each child in the group is given three letters (words). The teacher prints one of three letters on the chalkboard and each child must hold up the same letter card.

    b. Lotto and bingo type games can be made with letters and words.

3. Have the children trace various words or letters. Variations of this activity include finger tracing of letters or words made from sandpaper, tracing words with a pencil or crayon, or forming letters and words from clay. Example:

4. Activities which develop writing skills can be useful in developing visual discrimination. As the child copies a short message to take home, he must look very closely at each word so that he can reproduce it.

5. Develop discrimination in words and letters in other situations:
   a. Point out various differences in words on experience charts by saying, "Can anyone find another word in the chart that is exactly the same as this one I've printed on this card? Look at this word. It's really long."
   b. Say, "All boys whose names begin with the first letter of Bobby's name (already printed on the chalkboard with first letter underlined) may get their coats."
   (This last exercise also develops skills in auditory discrimination.)

Learning the Alphabet and Recognizing Letter Names Educators disagree about whether it is necessary for children to name letters and know them in alphabetical order prior to beginning reading. If letter names will be used during beginning reading instruction, they should be learned first. Below are suggestions for those teachers who wish to include this skill in their readiness program:

1. Either capital or lower case letters may be first. Some teachers teach both forms of each letter together. Durrell (1956) suggests an order for learning capitals from easiest to hardest:

   O, X, A, B, T, C, L, R, I, S, P, N, F,
   E, H, D, M, K, Z, J, Y, W, G, Q, U, V.

   For lower case letters the order is:

   o, x, s, c, i, p, t, m, k, z, e, w, r,
   j, y, f, n, a, h, v, u, b, d, l, g, q.

2. Point to a letter and say, "This is *b (B).*" Then associate the *b* with a key word. (It is a good idea to have classroom alphabet cards with a picture for every letter; the word is used for that picture, such as *b* as in *boy.*) Teach the letter with its sound, explaining that the letter *b* is the first sound in *boy.*
3. Use ABC picture books and picture dictionaries to reinforce letter names and sounds.
4. Use worksheets in which children must match capital and lower case letters or trace over one letter and color a picture whose first sound is the sound of the letter.
5. Play letter recognition games.

Developing Left-to-Right Orientation Children must acquire the habit of looking from left to right along a line of print and proceeding from the top of the page to the bottom. Marchbanks and Levin (1965) and Timko (1972) found that the first letter was the most important clue in recognizing words for first-grade children. Kindergarten children in Marchbank's study also used the first letter in recognizing words. However, kindergarten boys used the last letter almost as much as the first letter. Without proper training they could develop the habit of looking at words from right to left *(ball)*. Habits of left-to-right and top-to-bottom orientation can be taught at various opportune times during the school day. Most children will gradually establish this orientation. Special practice can also be given to a few children who experience unusual difficulty with it. The teacher can:

1. Teach children the terms *left* and *right* not only in reference to their hands, but also in reference to the chalkboard, bulletin board, and pages in a story book. Singing games such as "Looby-Lou" and direction games like "Simon Says" will be more useful than formalized drills.
2. Constantly repeat the idea of left to right by moving the finger or a pointer along chalkboard messages, experience chart stories, and so on when reading the words.
3. Use readiness workbooks and other picture books for practice in working from left to right. Each child has his own copy and follows along with the teacher. Careful teacher monitoring is needed in this exercise.
4. Cut apart a series of pictures and paste them on heavy cardboard. The pictures are mixed up and a child is asked to put them in the correct order from left to right.
5. Make or buy special practice worksheets in which the child must draw various straight or curvy lines from left to right. Example:

Developing Motor Skills The value of motor skill training in readiness programs is controversial. Although motor development has little relationship to success in reading, exercise in body coordination may prove helpful to normal but grossly uncoordinated children and to children with cerebral palsy or brain damage (Spache and Spache, 1973). To ensure developing pre-reading abilities, this author suggests connecting motor skill training as closely as possible to other pre-reading activities. The following suggested exercises are taken from a program developed by Peake (1972). They show how reading readiness can be fostered in other lessons besides reading.

1. Draw a square grid on a gym mat 4' 3" by 8' 7" and print a different letter of the alphabet in each square. Ask a child to jump to certain letters.
2. Write the following words on cards: *leap, backwards, forwards, slide, turn, skip, gallop, jump, stretch, shrink, run, walk, hop, crawl, kick,*

throw, catch, stop, and *go.* Ask the children to react according to the action of the word shown. At first, show each word and read it aloud. Later the children can read it themselves.

3. To a drum beat children do any one of the following actions or a combination of several to form a sequence: sit and clap, stamp feet, clap and stamp feet (standing), step in time, jump in time, run in time, run (quick soft beat) followed by a step (loud drum beat), twirl around, crawl, skip.

4. After reading aloud a short story with no more than five actions involved, ask the child to interpret it through body movement.

5. Make cue cards with a picture of an animal and its first letter below. Hang the cue cards on the wall. Put the corresponding letter cards in a hat box. Each child, in turn, draws a card from the box and matches it with the cue card letter hanging on the wall. The children then act out that animal for several minutes until it is the next child's turn to select a card.

Fine eye-hand coordination can be taught through coloring, cutting, pasting, tracing, and copying activities. The teacher might provide some special training in how to hold scissors for cutting and a crayon or pencil for drawing and printing. However, these fine muscle activities can usually be taught together with another skill. For instance, the child can be given a worksheet in which he must visually match identical letters by drawing a circle around them. Encircling the letters gives practice in hand-eye coordination.

Using Experience Charts

Developing experience charts is one of the more widely used techniques for helping children make a smooth transition from pre-reading to reading. The charts are compositions based on meaningful shared experiences and produced cooperatively by children and their teacher. Class discussions about what to include in the charts can extend children's experiences and oral language. The children are not necessarily required to read the charts. The teacher points to what he is reading so the children can follow along. At the same time, he develops (1) directional orientation—left-to-right and top-to-bottom; (2) more refined visual discrimination skills; (3) concepts of words and sentences (he may say, for example, "What should we say in our next sentence?" or "Who wants to read the sentence I've just pointed to?"), and (4) the idea that reading is meaningful and is talk written down. The charts can also provide the teacher with excellent opportunities to informally diagnose how the above readiness skills are progressing.

Using Commercial Programs

There is a vast array of commercially published materials that the teacher may use to supplement her readiness program. Below are listed three different types with examples of each type.

1. Colorful games, audio-visual aids, records, charts, and worksheets designed to provide practice in strengthening various readiness skills add variety to any readiness program. The following are representative examples:

   Picture Readiness Game. Champaign, Illinois: Garrard Press. This is a lotto game consisting of six cards with pictures on them. Children are supposed to develop attention and perceptual skills by matching a picture to its duplicate on the card.

   Continental Press Reading Readiness Program. Elizabethtown, Pennsylvania: Continental Press Incorporated. A series of twelve sets of worksheets that are sold in liquid duplicator form to be reproduced for classroom use. Rhyming, beginning sounds, visual motor skills, visual discrimination, thinking, and independent activities are stressed. Various levels of difficulty are provided for each skill.

2. Commercial programs have been developed to teach one particular skill. For example:

   The First Talking Alphabet. Chicago: Scott, Foresman and Company, 1967. This program was developed to teach the phoneme-grapheme (sound-letter) relationship. The program includes records, worksheets, individual picture and letter cards for each child, and a teacher's manual. The children listen to the recorded instruction and follow along on their card by pointing to pictures and repeating and tracing the letters.

3. Some commercial programs provide training in a variety of skills. Most of the companies which publish basal reading series also have readiness programs to be used specifically with that series. However, these programs can often be adapted for use with other types of first grade instruction. An example of a readiness program used in connection with a basal series is:

   Getting a Head Start and *Getting Ready to Read.* Boston: Houghton Mifflin Company, 1971. The first level of the pre-reading series *Getting a Head Start* claims to develop language facility, broaden conceptual backgrounds and readiness for a decoding strategy. The second level *Getting Ready to Read* introduces word attack skills—distinguishing letter forms, using spoken context, listening for initial sounds in words, making letter-sound associations, using spoken context and first letter of a printed word, and matching end sounds and letter forms. The series is accompanied by teacher's guides, "Big Books" for large-group instruction, pupil workbooks, letter cards, letter form board, Letto cards and Word cover (bingo-like games), plastic objects and set of twenty-two boxes to practice discrimination between sounds and letters, picture and key cards, letter-picture solitaire, word cards (the pre-reading series presents fifteen words), and a pocket chart.

Commercial Programs—A Mixed Blessing Reading educators often consider commercial readiness materials and programs a mixed blessing. Many have observed with dismay the abuses involving these programs in classrooms across the country. Commercial programs lend themselves neatly to an oversimplified approach to preparing children for reading. It is easy for teachers to say, "I teach reading readiness. Look, every morning between nine and ten o'clock I have my children take out their *ABC Easy Reading Readiness Workbooks* and we do three pages." Commercial materials should never be considered the entire readiness program. Neither should they dictate what skills are to be taught or the pace at which they should be learned.

Another oversimplified practice which is often linked with commercial programs is having all the children in the class go through all the steps of the program whether they need them or not. The teacher treats all pupils as though they were alike, insisting that even the one or two children who are reading books complete all the readiness activities. At the other extreme, there are children who are not ready to learn the readiness activities in the commercial program, but these too are forced to join in, although they cannot possibly benefit and may be harmed by being pressured through the program. Even though there may be only five children in the room who really need to use a particular activity, everyone is forced to waste time on it. Requiring a whole class or each group to go through the *entire* commercial program regardless of individual differences in skill needs, learning rates, and level of achievement is a waste of valuable learning time.

Frequently commercial materials are misused by being made into "busywork." This is especially true of the many master duplicator materials which are run off in tall stacks for classroom use. In some classrooms preparation for reading consists of a steady diet of these every day. Although some of these worksheets may provide good skill building activities, they must be used in moderation. They may be good activities to keep children busy and quiet, but every teacher should keep asking herself, "Is the child learning something from this, or is it just busywork?" Learning time is too precious to be wasted on the latter.

Although commercial programs claim to teach a number of skills—visual perception, auditory discrimination, sound-letter relationship, and so on—several studies, such as Ollila (1970) and Jacobs (1968), have found that a child is not necessarily better prepared in those skills because he used *one* particular program. In Ollila's study of three commercial readiness programs, no one training program was more effective in teaching the skills of visual perception and auditory discrimination than the other two. This result is of special interest considering that one program was designed specifically to develop visual perception and did not attempt to develop any auditory discrimination skills. Findings such as these should make the teacher look carefully at his commercial readiness program. Is it really doing the job it should be doing? Is it really helping to make each child more ready for reading?

Commercial materials must be chosen with an eye on the beginning reading program. Does the beginning program place a premium on any skill? If so, the teacher should choose readiness materials that provide lessons and practice in that skill. For instance, a beginning reading program with heavy doses of phonics can be supported by readiness materials emphasizing sound-letter relationships. It does not make much sense to use commercial materials to teach the traditional alphabet in kindergarten and then teach beginning reading with the initial teaching alphabet (i.t.a.) in first grade. Kindergarten and first-grade teachers should discuss their readiness and reading programs and coordinate their materials.

If commercial materials are used well, they can add valuable interest and variety to a readiness program. Readiness workbooks and books provide experiences in handling and caring for books and help in developing left-to-right orientation to reading. For the few children who may need a long extended period of readiness, these books and workbooks provide certain psychological advantages. As these children see their peers beginning to read books, they will want books, too, so they will feel that they are making progress. Readiness books and workbooks can provide some tangible evidence of their progress (McKim and Caskey, 1963).

Commercial readiness materials can also be sources of sequenced lessons and extra practice materials. Some teachers, especially beginning teachers, may not have the time, background, or experience to develop a large variety of sequential skill building lessons. While one child may learn a skill in one lesson, another child may need thirty practice sessions. Commercial materials can provide those thirty practice lessons, saving the teacher hours of preparation time. Even if a teacher chooses not to use commercial materials in her readiness program, she may want to develop a collection of them and occasionally scan them for ideas. They frequently provide reference lists of other materials and books as well.

If the teacher decides to use commercial programs, and according to most surveys the chances are good that he will, the materials should be adapted to fit the class. Remember, there is no rule that says the teacher must use the entire program as is. The more closely the materials are fitted to individuals in the class, the better the program will be.

Pre-school and Kindergarten Training Programs

Reading readiness instruction is an integral part of the average North American first-grade classroom. Many kindergarten teachers are also involved in teaching reading readiness skills. Ching (1970), in a survey of California kindergarten teachers, reported that 80 percent said they provided a "planned sequential reading readiness program" in their classrooms. Reaching down the ladder to three- and four-year-olds, readiness programs are now being experimented with in an increasing number of pre-schools. The following section explains how children are currently being prepared in nursery schools, kindergartens, and pre-schools for the culturally disadvantaged.

Reading in the Nursery School

As reading-related experiences in the nursery school are a new development, programs and instructional strategies for promoting reading for three- to five-year-old children are varied and experimental. Research to support the value of such early training has become available only in recent years. Obviously nursery school teachers (those qualified with a background of reading courses) can help prepare children for reading in many of the ways used in the kindergarten. For instance, discussions between children and between teacher and child can help develop oral language abilities which are important to reading. Developing a rich background of experience, promoting healthy emotional and social growth, and encouraging children to think and to be curious about their environment will indirectly prepare children for reading. Nursery schools can have library corners available for those children who want to use them. Teachers can share story books with children who are interested.

Other reading educators have suggested more direct instruction for children who are *interested.* Durkin (1973) recommends that "children's interests and reactions dictate materials and methods" (p. 6) used to help those children who *wish* to learn to read. She suggests experience charts and other homemade material, individual attention and small group work, and a combination of planned and on-the-spot teaching.

In contrast to the above proposals, several experimental, highly structured formal group approaches to teaching readiness and reading skills have been developed and shown to be of some benefit (Di Lorenzo and Salter, 1968). Characteristics of these programs include short blocks of time set aside daily for direct group teaching of skills like oral language and visual and auditory discrimination. The teacher presents the skills to the children and then directs their activity.

Reading in the Kindergarten

Readiness and formal reading are presented in kindergarten classrooms in a striking variety of ways. Organization, content, method, and materials differ widely from one class to another. This can be easily illustrated by the variety of answers given by kindergarten teachers when asked in recent surveys such as Ching (1970) and LaConte (1970) about the reading readiness programs in their classes. Some teachers said that all their children were included in readiness programs; others said that none were. A majority felt that most kindergartners would profit from training. Teachers disagreed on which readiness skills were most valuable for kindergarten and most deserving of instructional time. When asked about the type of program they thought was most effective, most teachers agreed that a combination of planned materials and workbooks plus informal activities and direct experiences was best; however, some teachers used one approach exclusively. Ching found that 25 percent of the teachers who taught readiness also taught reading to their kindergartners. Other surveys, such as LaConte (1970), have found even fewer kindergartens involved in direct reading instruction. Here again ways of teaching reading to kindergartners were as varied as any found in first-grade classrooms.

Kindergarten teachers today are seeing a widening gap in the knowledge of kindergarten beginners. With increased opportunities via television, records, and books to become acquainted with letters and words, a growing number of children already can, for instance, recognize certain alphabet letters and letter sounds on entering kindergarten. On the other hand, there are children at the other end of the spectrum who are obviously unprepared for reading. The kindergarten teacher must work toward individualizing instruction to help meet the needs of all the children in the class.

To what degree can the kindergarten teacher practically and effectively organize readiness and reading instruction that will meet the needs of each child? Downing (1971), who reports successful experiments with early readers in Great Britain, maintains that "the younger the pupils, the greater the need of an individual approach." In most current kindergartens, however, with their high pupil-teacher ratio, wide range of differences in readiness and experience, and limited class time, it is difficult to organize readiness programs that not only fit the situation but also fit the needs of the child. A common procedure in kindergartens is the mass instruction approach, in which all the kindergartners in the class are taught together in the same readiness or reading program. But it is highly unlikely that all children in any one kindergarten class will profit from the same early reading instruction given at the same pace. Many critics are skeptical of the way the concept of early reading has been translated into classroom practices. Hymes (1970) and Sheldon (1964) express deep concern over the serious, no-nonsense atmosphere, the silent, passive learning, the pencil-pushing activities, and the irrelevant materials which all too frequently creep into these programs. Critics also argue that some current kindergarten readiness and reading programs are actually poorly diluted copies of first-grade reading programs without adequate adjustments for kindergarten differences.

Probably the most realistic key to individualizing the kindergarten teacher's program is flexible grouping. In smaller group settings it is easier for the teacher to differentiate readiness and reading instruction. Paraprofessionals, when available, can be most helpful in supervising some of the class at another activity while the teacher works intensely with one particular group. Some school systems, as mentioned earlier, are exploring different classroom organizations to prepare children for reading. One example of this is the Transition Room. Suppose a child has completed kindergarten but is still judged quite unready for first grade. He is not a slow learner. His intelligence is probably average or above. Yet he will probably have trouble learning to read in an average first-grade classroom. So he is put into a Transition Room—a step up from kindergarten, but not as advanced as first grade. Classes are small—many number around fifteen. Children get more individualized instruction. Towards the end of the year, many Transition Room children begin formal reading and have a better chance for success in beginning grade one.

Using Parents in Pre-schools and Kindergarten

One of the most promising trends in pre-reading education is for the schools to reach out and involve the parents and community in their children's education. The relationship between the parent and the child's reading and the reason why parents should be involved in reading activities is summed up in a position paper on the Right to Read (1972):

> Realistic programs to stimulate reading must have parental and community support. Most agree that the child's intellectual and cognitive capacity is largely established by age three, before most enter a classroom. Even then only 10.6 percent of a child's time is devoted to formal

schooling. Parents, like it or not, have a role as educators; the only question is how well they educate. The home environment may stimulate the child's sense of self, his interest, his perception, his desire to experiment—or it may suppress these qualities. Parents may encourage the skills associated with reading and cognitive activity—or they may provide no inspiration, or even stifle incentive. . . . While influence of parents on learning may be compared to that of teachers, most parents are completely untrained in supporting school learnings, and have no way to get training and understanding for their role if they want to (p. 9).

What can the school do to help parents prepare their children for reading? With the help of federal and local funds a number of programs have been planned and developed to involve parents in the education of their child. Special programs have been designed to teach parents how they may foster in their children the social, emotional, and intellectual growth necessary for learning to read. Many of these are directed at the culturally different or disadvantaged, though there are some pre-school programs for other children. These programs are extremely diverse—both in the type of parental activity and in the degree of parent involvement. This is partly because each school needs to develop a program for its particular parents and community setting and partly because any new program requires constant experimentation. In many schools the parents are involved only in the school. In others, teachers and paraprofessionals are sent into the parents' homes. Some pre-schools rely on interested parents coming and enrolling their children. Other pre-schools actively conduct door-to-door campaigns, listening for children's voices, and ferreting out prospective parents with pre-schoolers. These pre-schools reason that frequently those parents and children least likely to come will benefit most from the program.

Parent involvement, as interpreted by various schools, includes a variety of educational, observation, and participation programs.

Educational Programs Parental involvement usually takes two forms: (1) educating parents in ways and means of preparing children for reading; and (2) providing clear explanations of the school's pre-reading program. Many kindergarten programs provide booklets and other handouts on reading readiness for parents. Typical of these suggestions are the following: provide proper rest and diet for the children, have many books and magazines in the home, read frequently to the child, set an example by reading yourself, show interest in school, take the child on trips, give him many and varied experiences, play records of stories, poems, and songs, praise and encourage, give the child responsibilities. While reading educators agree with these commendable suggestions, they also see some flaws in this approach. Handouts are frequently left unread or just glanced at.

Ideas in them are vague. Consider the suggestion, "Take many trips." Why is this important to reading? Often no explanation is included for the parents. For the culturally disadvantaged some of the activities suggested are impractical.

Many educators are exploring other methods of parent education. Some are beginning to move away from a complete reliance on handouts and formal teacher-talking-down-to-parents programs to a more informal and frequent exchange of ideas between parents and teachers. Typically, these involve demonstrations and discussions of desirable ways to prepare children for reading and ways to avoid undesirable behavior, such as babytalk. These meetings may take place on a regular or infrequent basis in the school or parents' home. They may involve the teacher with one parent, or a small or large group. In several pre-school programs for the culturally disadvantaged, teachers and paraprofessionals visit each house on a regular basis (Palmer, 1972). Sometimes these visits are mainly for discussion; other times special educational toys and games are lent to families after the teacher demonstrates their use.

Although studies (Swift, 1970) have shown that these parent education programs are effective, they must be undertaken cautiously. Some parents get highly anxious and involved trying to teach their child to "do it right." Teachers should warn parents that this may happen and suggest that when they feel these anxieties and emotions rising they discontinue the lesson.

Besides teaching parents specific ways in which the home and the school can cooperate, schools must also interpret the existing school program to parents. Parents value frequent communication on the child's progress in the reading program.

Observation and Participation Schools encourage different degrees of parental involvement. Some schools specify a few days on which parents may come and observe. Other schools follow an open door policy. Some schools permit observation only, while others offer superficial participation—mothers may pour juice or put on coats and hats. In some schools parents participate by occasionally reading a story, leading the children in some game, or writing captions on children's pictures. In a few pre-schools parents are invited to relate as they wish with the children.

In a growing number of pre-schools, the parents help plan and develop the school's educational program. For instance, parents in some programs help in choosing educational experiences—suggesting field trips, class visitors (doctor, dentist, fireman), activities for various lessons—and help to set up and participate in volunteer aide programs.

Parents are also frequently involved in ordering, making, and selecting toys, games, books, and consumable materials (paint, paper, etc.)

for the classroom. Sometimes parents are in charge of book and toy lending libraries connected with the school.

Many educators foresee good results from the trend toward more direct involvement for parents in school programs. Involved parents better understand how to help their children develop skills basic to reading. They tend to be more interested and sympathetic to the schools, and they can play an important role as part of the child's instructional team.

Using Paraprofessionals in the Pre-school Program

Another trend in pre-reading programs, as well as other educational programs, is to provide teachers with classroom assistants. These extra helpers are called by a variety of names—"paraprofessionals," "teacher aides," or "auxiliary personnel." Some help only one teacher, others work for several. Some get paid, while others are volunteers. Some help for one hour or so, others the full day's program.

Qualifications of the paraprofessionals vary too. Many are women, but there are also a number of men assistants, especially in programs for disadvantaged. Educational background varies, ranging from elementary school dropouts to high school and college students to college graduates. Parent helpers are frequently used, many in programs for the disadvantaged. Some programs have made considerable use of the talents of senior citizens also.

The type of person employed and the kind of work he does in the classroom frequently depends on the kind of pre-reading program and the needs of the community where it is located. For instance, a number of school dropouts from disadvantaged neighborhoods have been found to be effective teacher's aides. One such helper (*N.E.A. Journal*, 1967) explained why children saw her as similar to the adults at home and tended to take their problems to her. For the same reason, she had an advantage in explaining the school's program to adults.

The type of help paraprofessionals give to the teacher varies. Most teachers rely on them to do many of the non-instructional jobs in the classroom. Work like arranging bulletin board displays, taking attendance, supervising children on the playground, helping with the light cleaning chores, and getting materials ready for projects is often assigned to helpers. The teacher, not having to devote valuable class time to such tasks, is freed to concentrate on teaching. Some paraprofessionals help the teacher with selected instructional activities. For instance, the teacher may point out a specific problem to the paraprofessional, such as a child's inability to visually distinguish *d* from *b*. With the teacher providing background suggestions, the paraprofessional helps the child to overcome this problem.

In another case, the paraprofessional may supervise some type of free play or independent work activity already introduced by the teacher, while the teacher helps individuals or groups with reading instruction. In some pre-school programs paraprofessionals visit homes, demonstrating and explaining ways of improving reading skills.

Important to any effective paraprofessional is a thorough orientation and training program. Much of the training is done "on the job," but many schools also give in-service workshops or training sessions. Teachers and aides must have a good working relationship. Aides, to be effectively used, must understand what is expected of them. This helps avoid misunderstandings, as with the aide who resentfully washes paint brushes, complaining, "I came here to help children, not to do things *you* don't like to do" (*N.E.A. Journal*, 1967, p. 19).

Most teachers who have had the help of a paraprofessional in their classroom have positive comments about it. However, paraprofessional involvement is still a controversial topic. What should be the role of paraprofessionals in the classroom? Should they be kept to strictly non-instructional, clerical jobs? Or should they be given some instructional responsibility also? Some teachers feel threatened by paraprofessionals, others do not. Ransom (Chapter Five) provides further information about the use of paraprofessionals.

Pre-reading Programs for the Culturally Disadvantaged

One of the principal efforts in pre-school education has been the development of programs for the culturally disadvantaged. Many of these programs are still in the process of evolving. The characteristics of programs mentioned are largely those of Project Head Start and Project Follow Through, programs that actively stress the teaching of pre-reading skills. The more comprehensive of these is Head Start, which, since its beginning in 1964, has provided pre-school programs to over one-half million disadvantaged children (Evans, 1971). Project Follow Through was formulated in 1967 to serve the many Head Start graduates. Its purpose is to maintain and extend earlier gains.

It should be noted, however, that other programs, while not stressing reading readiness as such, do indirectly prepare the culturally disadvantaged child for reading. Some programs are primarily social. They attempt to help the child adjust to the classroom, teach him how to react with the teacher and other authority figures, and help him achieve a sense of personal worth and self-control. Other programs emphasizing general "learning how to learn" skills (how to use school materials, how to solve problems, and so on) will also provide good preparation for reading.

Content of the Programs The content of many pre-school pre-reading programs for the culturally disadvantaged is based on (1) the pre-reading skills and abilities that are lacking in culturally disadvantaged children as reported in the research, and/or (2) the skills that any child needs in order to experience success in an average school. Many programs stress all of the following: concept and vocabulary expansion, oral language skills, desire to read, motivation, and perceptual-motor skills. A few add visual and auditory discrimination skills, and sound-symbol correspondence.

The Teacher's Role Basic to the learning of pre-reading concepts in most programs is a warm, understanding relationship between the teacher (or other adult authority figure in the classroom) and the disadvantaged child. First and foremost, the teacher has to genuinely enjoy working with these children. "Teachers who feel that disadvantaged children are stupid, or who cannot like them because they are shabby, dirty or smelly, or use shocking language should not be working with them" (*High Points*, 1966). Edwards (1965) outlines the job of the teacher of the culturally disadvantaged: "Mere exposure [to the new learning] is not enough, particularly for the culturally disadvantaged student who has had severely limited experience in learning independently . . . [the teacher must] direct the attention, the perception, and the interpretation of the student in the learning situation. In addition, the mediator [teacher] provides encouragement in attacking a learning task, correction and encouragement when incorrect responses are made and confirmation and praise when correct responses are made" (p. 510). The teacher also acts as a model for the child. Mills (1966), in describing the children's first days in the Illinois Nursery School Project, highlights this:

> One of our most startling discoveries was the way these children used equipment. They threw everything they could pick up! A hole is to dig; a stick is to throw. A book isn't much different from a stick if you have never seen a book and don't know what it is for or how to use it. Slowly, step by step, we had to model how these concrete objects could be used (p. 348).

Modeling is particularly important in developing oral language skills. The child will probably emulate the teacher's speech; it should be worthy of emulation.

Importance of Parental Involvement Many pre-school programs emphasize that parents of culturally disadvantaged children need to get involved in the education of their children. Several researchers (McCarthy, 1969; Willmon, 1969) have reported much greater success in helping when programs make efforts to educate and involve the parents.

Methods and Materials for Teaching Pre-reading Skills Most of the materials and methods used in teaching the culturally disadvantaged are also used in pre-school programs for other children. However, there are a few differences—mostly in emphasis.

A number of programs, noting that disadvantaged children often take a physical approach to learning, capitalize on this by teaching skills through games, educational toys, models, miniatures and various combinations of games, spontaneous play, and tutorial and direct instruction. One very highly structured, fast-paced approach is the Direct Instructional Systems for Teaching Arithmetic and Reading, or *Distar* (Bereiter and Engelmann, 1969). The teacher is given a manual of specific structured tasks. Included in the manual are directions which the teacher is to follow precisely, questions the teacher is to ask, and answers considered acceptable.

In teaching oral language skills, many of the programs start out by encouraging the child to talk freely in his own dialect. If the teacher attempts to change speech patterns right from the start, spontaneous expression may be lost. Later, when the child feels at ease, he will gradually develop his language skills by imitating the teacher, by memorizing various poems and songs, and by listening to stories. Most programs stress a high level of verbal interaction between child and teacher. Teachers help disadvantaged children develop better communication skills as the children play with toys, puppets, flannel board characters, and so on. The teacher does not have to draw attention to the child's dialect. Frequently, he can merely listen to what the child has to say and then paraphrase it back to him in more standard English.

In developing concepts and expanding vocabularies, these programs emphasize that the teacher must help disadvantaged children understand what they have seen and heard. The teacher does not just say, "This is a dog, and this is a horse." She must explain similarities and differences. Careful consideration must be given to choosing basic learnings from which the culturally disadvantaged child can advance. Often backgrounds of experience are quite limited. Topics such as food, clothing, and shelter are good for teaching the various pre-reading skills. These are meaningful to the child.

What Does Research Say about
Programs for the Disadvantaged?

Researchers have not come to a general agreement on the effectiveness of programs for the disadvantaged. Evans (1971), summarizing current research on Head Start, concludes: "On the basis of research findings to date general programs within Head Start have been apparently ineffective or only moderately beneficial in facilitating cognitive and affective changes of the magnitude necessary to ensure academic success" (p. 95). Most researchers, however, feel that programs which last a full year or longer are far more beneficial than short-term summer programs. These studies have also shown the need for meaningful parental involvement in such programs.

Some pre-reading programs for the disadvantaged have been shown to be more effective than others (Stanchfield, 1972; Evans, 1971). Part of the reason seems to be that they clearly define the skills to be taught and then begin systematic procedures to teach them. A well thought out and developed program, a competent teacher, and good home-school relations are basic elements for success in pre-school programs for the disadvantaged, as they are for any other pre-school program. In the end, there is no such thing as *the* program for the disadvantaged. Each program must be designed for a particular circumstance. There are great differences among the various kinds of children termed "disadvantaged." One must teach individuals.

The Author's Viewpoint

There is no one best method or program for preparing all children for formal reading instruction. Some children will learn better with one program than with another; some teachers can teach one program quite well but have trouble obtaining the same success with another. Although there is no one best readiness program for all situations, there are certain features common to all good programs. Such programs start with a competent teacher who is thoroughly acquainted with both the school's reading program and the child's instructional level. From this base the teacher develops and organizes a readiness program geared to fit the needs of the children, keeping in mind general long range and specific daily objectives. In some readiness programs the children are exposed to skills that they already know, or skills that have no value as prerequisites to the skills needed in the initial reading task. It is important for teachers to assess what they are doing constantly, asking themselves, "Is this activity really helping this child become more ready for reading?"

A good readiness program gives children many opportunities to become acquainted with the act of reading and helps children to feel that reading is personally important to them. But the most crucial part of the program is the teacher, who, by giving the child praise, encouragement, and success, nurtures a positive attitude toward learning to read.

References

Anderson, I. H.; Hughes, B. O.; and Dixon, W. R. "The Rate of Reading Development and Its Relation to Age of Learning to Read, Sex, and Intelligence." *Journal of Educational Research* 50 (1957): 481–494.

Armstrong, R. D. "Language: The Essence of Readiness." In *Education 6.* Toronto: W. J. Gage, 1964–1967, pp. 57–61.

Bereiter, C., and Engelmann, S. *Distar.* Chicago: Science Research Associates, 1969.

Blakeley, W. P., and Shadle, E. M. "A Study of Two Readiness-for-Reading Programs in Kindergarten." *Elementary English* 38 (1961): 502–505.

Bond, G. L., and Dykstra, R. *Final Report of the Coordinating Center for First-grade Instruction* (USOE Project X-001). Minneapolis: University of Minnesota, 1967.

Browne, P. M. *An Exploratory Study of Teacher-Pupil Verbal Interaction in Primary Reading Groups.* Unpublished doctoral dissertation, University of Alberta, 1972.

Ching, D. *The Teaching of Reading in Kindergarten.* Paper presented at the International Reading Association Convention, Anaheim, California, 1970.

Davidson, H. P. "An Experimental Study of Bright, Average and Dull Children at the Four Year Mental Level." *Genetic Psychology Monograph* 9 (1931): 119–289.

Deutsch, M. "Minority Group and Class Status as Related to Social and Personality Factors in Scholastic Achievement." *Monographs of the Society for Applied Anthropology,* 1960, No. 2.

Di Lorenzo, L. J., and Salter, R. "An Evaluative Study of Prekindergarten Programs for Educationally Disadvantaged Children: Follow Up and Replication." *Exceptional Children* 35 (1968): 111–119.

Downing, J., and Thackray, D. V. *Reading Readiness.* London: University of London Press, 1971.

Durkin, D. "Children Who Learned to Read Before Grade 1: A Second Study." *Elementary School Journal,* 64 (1963): 143–148.

Durkin, D. *Teaching Young Children to Read.* Boston: Allyn and Bacon, 1972.

Durkin, D. *Teaching Them to Read.* Boston: Allyn and Bacon, 1974.

Durkin, D.; Butler, A.; Cole, E.; Nurss, J.; Smethurst, W.; and Sparrow, S. "Day Care and Reading." *The Reading Teacher* 26 (1973): 2–8.

Durrell, D. *Improving Reading Instruction.* New York: Harcourt, Brace and World, 1956.

Eames, T. H. "Physical Factors in Reading." *Reading Teacher* 15 (1962): 427–432.

Edwards, T. J. "Learning Problems in Cultural Deprivation." *Reading and Inquiry*, 10. Newark, Del.: International Reading Association Press, 1965, 256–261.

Evans, E. D. *Contemporary Influences in Early Childhood Education*. New York: Holt, Rinehart and Winston, 1971.

Frymier, J. R. "The Effect of Class Size Upon Reading Achievement in First Grade." *Reading Teacher* 18 (1964): 90–93.

Gates, A. I. "The Necessary Mental Age for Beginning Reading." *Elementary School Journal* 37 (1937): 497–508.

Getman, G. N. *How to Develop Your Child's Intelligence*. Luverne, Minnesota: Announcer Press, 1962, pp. 18–19.

Harris, A. J. *How to Increase Reading Ability*. 4th ed. New York: David McKay Company, 1961.

High Points. "Reading Help for the Disadvantaged." 48 (March 1966): 51–54.

Hymes, J. L. *Teaching Reading to the Under-Six Age: A Child Development Point of View*. Paper presented at the Claremont Reading Conference, Claremont, California, 1970, p. 76.

Jacobs, J. N.; Wirthlin, L.; and Miller, C. "A Follow-up Evaluation of the Frostig Visual Perceptual Training Program." *Educational Leadership Research Supplement* 26 (1968): 169–175.

LaConte, C. "Reading in the Kindergarten: Fact or Fantasy?" *Elementary English* 47 (1970): 382–387.

McCarthy, J. "Changing Parent Attitudes and Improving Language and Intellectual Abilities of Culturally Disadvantaged Four-Year-Old Children Through Parent Involvement." *Contemporary Education* 40 (1969): 166–168.

McKim, M. G., and Caskey, H. *Guiding Growth in Reading in the Modern Elementary School*. 2nd ed. New York: Macmillan, 1963.

Marchbanks, G., and Levin, H. "Cues by Which Children Recognize Words." *Journal of Educational Psychology* 56 (1965): 57–61.

Mickelson, N. I., and Galloway, C. G. "Verbal Concepts of Indian and Non-Indian School Beginners." *Journal of Educational Research* 67 (1973): 55–56.

Mills, Queenie B. "The Preschool-Disadvantaged Child." *Vistas in Reading*, Part 1, 1966 Convention Proceedings, pp. 345–349.

Morphett, M. V., and Washburne, C. "When Should Children Begin to Read?" *Elementary School Journal* 31 (1931): 496–503.

N.E.A. Journal. "How Teacher Aides Feel about Their Jobs." 56 (1967): 17–19.

N.E.A. Journal. "How the Profession Feels about Teacher Aides." 56 (1967): 16–17.

Ollila, L. *The Effects of Three Contrasting Readiness Programs on the*

Readiness Skill of Kindergarten Boys and Girls. Ph.D. Thesis, University of Minnesota, 1970.

Palmer, F. H. "Minimal Intervention at Age Two and Three and Subsequent Intellectual Changes." In *The Preschool in Action,* edited by R. K. Parker. Boston: Allyn and Bacon, 1972, pp. 437–465.

Paradis, E. E. "The Appropriateness of Visual Discrimination Exercises in Reading Readiness Materials." *Journal of Educational Research* 67 (1974): 276–278.

Peake, L. "Skills and Practices for the Primary Years." Handbook, University of Victoria, 1972.

Peters, H. B. "Screening with a Snellen Chart." *American Journal of Optometry and Archives of American Academy of Optometry* 38 (1961): 487–505.

Reid, J. F. "A Study of Thirteen Beginners in Reading." *Acta Psychologica* 14 (1958): 295–313.

Right to Read, Report of Forum 7. *The Reading Teacher* 25 (1972): 9.

Robinson, H. M. "Perceptual Training—Does It Result in Reading Improvement?" In *Some Persistent Questions on Beginning Reading,* edited by R. C. Aukerman. Newark, Del.: International Reading Association, 1972, p. 145.

Sheldon, W. D. "A Modern Reading Program for Young Children." In *Teaching Young Children to Read,* edited by W. G. Cutts. Washington: United States Department of Health, Education and Welfare, Office of Education Bulletin No. 19, 1964, pp. 31–37.

Spache, G. D.; Andres, M. C.; Curtis, H. A. et al. *A Longitudinal First Grade Reading Readiness Program.* Cooperative Research Project No. 2742, Florida State Department of Education, 1965.

Spache, G. D., and Spache, E. B. *Reading in the Elementary School.* 2nd ed. Boston: Allyn and Bacon, 1973.

Stanchfield, J. M. "Development of Prereading Skills in an Experimental Kindergarten Program." In *Some Persistent Questions on Beginning Reading,* edited by R. C. Aukerman. Newark, Del.: International Reading Association Press, 1972, pp. 20–32.

Swift, M. S. "Training Poverty Mothers in Communication Skills." *Reading Teacher* 23 (1970): 360–367.

Timko, H. G. "Letter Position in Trigram Discrimination by Beginning Readers." *Perceptual and Motor Skills* 35 (1972): 153–154.

Vernon, M. D. "Specific Dyslexia." *British Journal of Educational Psychology* 32 (1962): 143–150.

Weber, E. *Early Childhood Education Perspective on Change.* Worthington, Ohio: Charles A. Jones Publishing Company, 1970.

Willmon, B. "Parent Participation as a Factor in the Effectiveness of Head Start Programs." *Journal of Educational Research* 62 (1969): 406–410.

Chapter
Ten

Preview

Discussions of "coding" emphases versus "meaning" emphases in reading programs eventually converge upon a point of fundamental agreement: one must know what the marks on a page signify before one can respond to them. Word analysis skills, therefore, are important in any reading program. The authors of this chapter provide the teacher with a thorough background of research evidence on this topic, and offer a variety of teaching suggestions as well. They cover the development of meaning vocabulary, sight vocabulary, and word recognition skills, and discuss the necessity for a balance among these three areas. Some aspects of this subject are controversial. Arnold and Miller explain the differing points of view, at the same time making their own position clear.

Both authors have worked with pupils who became successful readers and with those who did not. Their experience gives them a firm foundation for the view they express here—that learning to read requires the mastery of a set of complex and interrelated skills. Helping pupils acquire these skills and become more sophisticated in their application is among a teacher's most important tasks.

Reading:
Word Recognition Skills

Richard Arnold, Purdue University
John Miller, Wichita State University

Objectives

After you have read this chapter, you should be able to:

1. Recognize the interrelationships among meaning vocabulary, sight vocabulary, and the various word recognition skills.
2. Outline a scope and sequence of word recognition skills such as the one listed in this chapter.
3. Define these word recognition skills: meaning clues, visual analysis, structural analysis, phonics, and dictionary skills.
4. Differentiate among these meaning clues: expectancy, picture, and context.
5. Differentiate among the structural analysis skills: derivatives, variants, and compounds.
6. Differentiate among phonics, phonetics, and phonemics.
7. Differentiate between synthetic and analytic phonics.
8. Recognize the importance of developing a balance among the word recognition skills.
9. Understand the importance of developing a flexible hypothesis testing approach to decoding.

On the first day of school, when a teacher arrives in a new classroom, he will be confronted with many faces with which he cannot associate names. Some children's names he will learn in the first few hours of school, because of a child's striking physical features, or because of the unusual way a child reacts. Other names he will learn because he makes a concerted effort to do so. Unfortunately, there will always be those names and faces that are not readily associated. Jimmy's and Jeff's names, which the teacher confused on the first day, may continue to be confused some time into the school year. Eventually, however, all the names and faces are readily associated. In effect the name has become the face—recognition and association are instantaneous.

The child's task in recognizing words is somewhat analogous to the task described above. He must develop strategies for associating printed representations of words with pronunciations and meanings that he has stored. Initially the child may remember a word by some distinctive physical feature, such as the tail on *monkey*. He may form some associations because of the environment in which he encounters the words. He may recognize *stop,* for example, as the word on those red, eight-sided street signs near which mom and dad always stop the car. As reading instruction proceeds he will use word analysis skills to recognize words. As the child continues to meet these words in a variety of settings, the analysis and memory devices fall by the side as association and recognition become automatic. The visual representation of the word automatically cues the language referent and meaning. The word becomes a part of the child's sight vocabulary. As with the teacher's confusion of Jimmy and Jeff, there will be "problem" words which the child will have difficulty in raising to the automatic sight recognition level. Efficient reading depends on having a vast store of words that are recognized at sight.

The ultimate goal of reading instruction is to develop efficient, mature readers, but beginning readers must learn how to study words. Four major long-term goals of word study are: (1) building a meaning vocabulary; (2) building a sight vocabulary; (3) developing a set of word recognition skills; and (4) establishing for each child a balance among these: meaning vocabulary, sight vocabulary, and word recognition skills.

Building a Meaning Vocabulary

Research indicates that many children enter school with extensive listening vocabularies (Shibles, 1959) and language structures (McCarthy, 1954; Templin, 1957). These abilities should enable children to understand, at the oral language level, the words and sentences contained in printed matter for young children. However, this does not assure the teacher that all children will know all the meanings for all the words to be taught in a lesson. So the development of word meanings becomes a vital segment of the reading lesson. It does little good for a child to know how to decode a word if, after the word is decoded, he is unable to verify its existence in his meaning vocabulary.

As a child matures he begins to use reading as a way to add to his meaning vocabulary. But the shift from learning to read to reading to learn does not usually occur until he has learned word recognition skills quite well, typically in third or fourth grade. Even then, teaching word meanings is important. The development of special and unique meanings for words goes on throughout the school day in all content areas.

Techniques of teaching word meanings, which are described in more detail elsewhere, should be considered highly relevant to the overall scheme of developing proficiency in word recognition.

Building a Sight Vocabulary

To be an efficient reader one must learn to perceive many words and phrases quickly and effortlessly. A skilled reader decodes automatically (Samuels and Dahl, 1973) and pays little attention to visual stimuli—letters, words, and phrases. He has committed thousands of words to his sight vocabulary and can recognize them instantly and with minimal visual cues.

Building a sight vocabulary is a major goal of reading instruction, and the teacher should actively pursue it early in the reading program. Every new word (or common word part) to which a child is introduced should be considered a candidate for his sight vocabulary. Each time a child sees a word he should become more familiar with it, so that ultimately he will recognize it instantly. Many children commit words to their sight vocabulary very quickly with a minimum of effort. Others need more practice. The number of new words a child is asked to learn in a given period of time can be critical. Teaching too few words may slow children's learning, but teaching too many new words too fast can also create problems. A child who is not learning new words to the point of instant recognition is likely to develop into a disabled reader. If he has learned to analyze words but has little or no sight vocabulary he is probably an over-analytical reader (Bond and Tinker, 1973). An over-analytical reader reads slowly and laboriously, "sounding out" nearly every word. Remedial teachers see many children who need a sight vocabulary component built into a corrective program.

Teaching Sight Vocabulary

The process of word recognition has three phases. At first, the child does not know a word when he first encounters it in graphic form. Later he recognizes it partially but must analyze the word to discriminate those graphic components which can cue a meaningful response. Finally he reaches the point of immediate recognition, and the word becomes part of his sight vocabulary.

Repetition is a key concept in building sight vocabulary. The word recognition skills to be discussed later provide a good opportunity for this, under structured conditions. But probably the most natural and effective way to expose children to words repeatedly is through recreational reading. After children study a word in a reading skills lesson, meeting it in the reader and in other books provides the repetition they need.

Continued exposure also helps children to distinguish each word's unique visual characteristics. Some words, such as *house* and *baby,* are relatively easy to discriminate. Others, such as *house* and *horse,* will take more practice. It is especially difficult to discriminate between words like *house* and *home,* which have similar visual characteristics and similar meanings.

The teacher can use many kinds of activities to develop sight words. Children can make or use picture dictionaries, illustrate word cards, trace and copy new words, and match or compare word cards. Two excellent sources for activities to develop sight vocabulary and other word recognition skills are *Spice* by Platts (1960), and *Reading Activities for Child Involvement* by Evelyn Spache (1972). Lists of common sight words readily available are the Dolch (1953) list of 220 words, the longer Stone (1956) list of 679 words, and the list of high frequency words (Moe, 1972a, 1972b) based on a computer analysis of words in children's literature.

Developing Word Recognition Skills

The following is a list of word recognition skills which children should learn early in their reading careers. The skills are grouped into five major categories:

1. Meaning Clues
   a. expectancy clues
   b. picture clues
   c. context clues
2. Visual Analysis
   a. configuration
   b. striking characteristics
3. Structural Analysis
   a. variants
   b. compounds
   c. derivatives
4. Phonics
   a. initial single consonants
   b. short vowels
   c. final consonants

    d. long vowels and vowel combinations
    e. consonant combinations—two- and three-letter blends and digraphs
    f. *r*-controlled vowels
    g. syllabication
    h. auditory blending
5. Dictionary Skills
    a. location skills
    b. pronunciation skills

Authorities in the field of reading tend to agree that the above skills are important and should be taught. However, considerable difference of opinion exists about the labels applied to the skill categories and about the importance of each category. It is our opinion that all five categories listed are important, that none should be excluded from the word recognition skills program, and that the categories are quite clear, though some may wish to use other labels.

We have ordered the skills according to their usefulness. We believe that meaning clues and visual characteristics are used through the years by the mature reader as major techniques for word recognition—more so than structural analysis, for example, because the reader can probably use meaning-related skills most quickly and efficiently for minor corrections in analyzing unknown or misread words in context. Similarly, the mature reader will probably resort to structural analysis more frequently than phonics in his efforts to analyze an obscure or misperceived word. Phonics is probably a "last resort" for an able reader, though it is an important skill to have and use when needed. Using the dictionary is a special skill which usually involves learning the meaning of a new word; it is not considered exclusively a word recognition skill.

Sequencing Word Recognition Skills

The order in which word analysis skills should be taught has not been empirically established. Reading experts do not agree on this issue, but they do tend to sequence word analysis skills according to frequency of encounter and ease of learning. Reliance upon these two major ideas has produced many similar sequences. While a few special programs start with the teaching of vowels (usually short first, then long), the majority of reading programs begin by teaching initial consonants.

It is important to recognize that most eclectic programs include the teaching of several skills at the same time. Often beginning consonants, limited spelling patterns, variant endings, picture clues, and the like are introduced simultaneously, so the child, even early in the first grade, is developing a variety of word analysis skills to help him.

Also important to remember is that word analysis skills—especially phonics skills—taught early in the reading program are often those that have the least value in terms of the mature, efficient reader. While no one can deny the importance of sound-symbol correspondence in initial decoding instruction, for a mature reader it is probably the most time-consuming method of approaching an unknown word.

Table 12 is a compendium of word analysis skills by grade level. Deviations will occur from one reading program to another but usually the general sequence is quite similar. *It is important for the reading teacher to know the content of the reading skills program.* Not only should he be aware of the scope and sequence of the skills at the grade level he is teaching, but he should also have a general knowledge of the skills that precede and follow the level he teaches. The publishers of reading programs often include scope and sequence charts; the teacher should study these carefully to gain a broader perspective of the reading goals for the materials used in his school.

Table 12 Word Recognition Skills—Scope and Sequence Chart

Readiness
 1. Learning letter names.
 2. Developing awareness of sound-symbol relationships.
 3. Hearing similarities and differences in initial phonemes.
 4. Hearing rhyming sounds.
 5. Developing left-to-right orientation.
 6. Tracing, matching, and copying letters and words.
 7. Developing sentence sense.
 8. Developing listening comprehension.

First Grade (Pre-primer and Primer)
 1. Grapheme-phoneme correspondence (consonant).
 2. Begin consonant digraphs.
 3. Begin consonant blends.
 4. Begin short vowels.
 5. Begin spelling patterns.
 6. Begin using initial consonants with context.
 7. Begin final consonants.
 8. Begin initial and final consonant substitution.
 9. Begin inflectional endings.
10. Picture dictionary.

First Grade (First Readers)
 1. Continue grapheme-phoneme correspondence.
 2. Continue consonant digraphs.
 3. Continue consonant blends.

4. Continue short vowels.
5. Begin long vowels.
6. Continue spelling patterns.
7. Continue final consonants.
8. Initial and final consonants with context.
9. Initial and final consonant substitution.
10. Inflectional endings.
11. Begin suffixes.
12. Begin compound words.

Second Grade
1. Review and continue grapheme-phoneme correspondence.
2. Unusual consonants (*c* and *g*, silent *t*) and consonant digraphs.
3. Continue consonant blends, initial and final positions.
4. Unusual vowels *(y)*.
5. Vowel digraphs and diphthongs.
6. Schwa.
7. *r*-controlled vowels.
8. Syllabication (correspondence between # of vowel sounds and # of syllables).
9. Compound words.
10. Suffixes.
11. Prefixes.
12. Spelling changes involved in suffixes and inflected endings.
13. Using phonic elements with context.

Third Grade
1. Review grapheme-phoneme correspondence.
2. Difficult consonant blends, including triple clusters.
3. Unusual and difficult vowels and vowel combinations.
4. Structural analysis, including roots and affixes, compounds, and larger word elements.
5. More complex spelling patterns.
6. Syllabication—two- and three-syllable words.
7. Learning important phonics rules and their application.
8. Verification of phonics through use of context.
9. Simple dictionary skills; begin diacritical markings and pronunciation spellings.

This scope and sequence chart does not contain a list of word recognition skills taught beyond third grade because few, if any, new decoding skills are introduced in the intermediate grades. When such skills are taught, it is usually as review and for reinforcement purposes. It is extremely important that teachers of older children recognize the need for skill review.

In a typical fourth-grade classroom, for instance, the majority of the students will progress nicely with a review of the skills provided. Some children, however, will be ready only for third-grade word recognition skills, and it is quite likely that two or three children will be working below third-grade level. These children need instruction in materials at their respective levels—they need corrective or remedial reading. This area is too complex to discuss here; the interested reader is referred to Karlsen, Chapter Five, and to the many texts (Harris, 1975, Bond and Tinker, 1973) and university course offerings for further study.

Meaning Clues

The use of meaning clues is very important in word recognition. Such clues help the reader to anticipate words that he will encounter in the reading selection. The efficient reader uses these clues regularly, in conjunction with the other word recognition skills. An insufficient use of meaning clues often results in a slow, careful analysis of many words that should have been read with a minimum of inspection.

Three major types of meaning clues have been identified: expectancy, picture, and context. Expectancy clues are related to a given topic. When a person thinks about a general topic or concept he develops a "psychological set" for that topic. Certain ideas, and especially words, rise to the threshold of his consciousness ready to be used. This process is called *expectancy*. When a child discovers, for example, that he is going to read a story entitled "David's Airplane Ride," the title in itself should cause him to "expect" to run across such words as *airport, pilot, sky, clouds, takeoff, fly,* and so on. Words associated with airplane rides can be anticipated in this story more than in a story entitled "David's Trip to the Farm."

Picture clues may be considered a special class of expectancy clues (Artley, 1943; McCullough, 1943). The words and concepts included in the verbal discussion of the story, both before and during the reading lesson, can often be enhanced and augmented by pictures. A picture can clarify concepts and present information to children. Pictures may draw children's attention to objects and to the tone of the story, and they can make a simple story more interesting and vivid. For example, in the story "David's Airplane Ride," a picture could show whether David is riding on a commercial airliner or in a small aircraft at the county fair. Pictures should not be used to carry the story line, however, even in the pre-primer stages of reading.

A few authors of children's readers (Bloomfield and Barnhart, 1961) believe that children should not be allowed to use picture clues. They believe that pictures detract from the task of decoding. The authors of this chapter believe a child should not be denied any reasonable method for analyzing unknown words, including picture clues, although excessive use of pictures—especially those which carry the story—can be detrimental to learning word analysis skills (Samuels, 1967).

Another important purpose that pictures serve in reading materials is to help build concepts. It is much more efficient to show a picture of an aardvark than to describe one, particularly in print.

A context clue is much more specific to the material being read than an expectancy or a picture clue. A context clue is the arrangement of words in a sentence (or paragraph) in such a manner that only one word is likely to fit into a particular slot in that sentence. Essentially it is a method of limiting alternatives. In a complete sentence, if a word is missing (or unknown) the choice of the missing word is limited by the words surrounding it. We encounter this phenomenon frequently in reading a section in the newspaper where the paper has been creased or torn and we supply the missing word. We guess at the word and then confirm its "fit" by re-reading the sentence (or paragraph) to see if it makes sense.

This process is similar to the skill children need when they run into an unknown word. Consider, for example, this sentence:

David wants to _____ in an airplane.

If a child knows all the words in the sentence except the one represented by the blank, he should be able to infer that the new word is probably *fly* or *ride*. The inference can be confirmed easily and quickly if the initial consonant *r* is used as an additional cue:

David wants to r_____ in an airplane.

Teaching Meaning Clues

Expectancy The skillful teacher develops expectancy as a new story is introduced. Having in mind the new words to be learned by the pupils, the teacher introduces the topic and carefully elicits those words from the students. As the children relate their personal stories, the teacher writes the relevant words on the chalkboard, preferably underlined in phrases or sentences. To continue with the example of "David's Airplane Ride," the teacher might start the lesson as follows: "Boys and girls, I wonder what it is like to ride on an airplane?" Usually such a question is sufficient to begin a lively discussion. Through guided questioning, the teacher can lead the discussion through nearly all the content needed to introduce the new words. An additional bonus for the pupils is that many more words contained in the story are likely to be discussed, some of which the children may not know. Such a discussion prior to reading the story or section can be properly labelled reading readiness in the broader sense, because it is preparing the child to meet concepts covered in the reading selection.

A child will probably have trouble with expectancy clues if he is unable to anticipate what words might appear in a certain type of story. If, for example, the teacher asks Mark what words he thinks might be in a story about a lost letter and he cannot think of words such as *post office, mailbox,* and *stamp,* he probably is not going to be using expectancy clues too well and will need careful, direct instruction.

Many kinds of exercises can be designed to build expectancy clues through knowledge of a topic:

1. Circle the words below that are things you can expect to find in a kitchen:

pan	dress	stove
bed	dish	meat
tree	sink	pond

2. Put an x by the words you might expect to find in a newspaper story about a violent earthquake:

    ____ Geiger counter ____ typhoid fever
    ____ Richter scale ____ death and destruction
    ____ gas lines ____ troops on the border

Picture Clues Most children need very little teaching to begin to use picture clues. Even before formal reading instruction, most of them have discovered the relationship between the words on the page and the characters in the illustrations. Television often introduces the concept of the interrelationship between auditory stimulus and visual stimulus. The child easily realizes that neither the words without the picture nor the picture without the words is a *complete* television program. Movies, magazines, and other mass communication media imprint the fact that pictures can enhance stories.

Informal observations will help the teacher identify those children who are over-reliant on picture clues. A child's head may bob back and forth from the printed page to the accompanying page of illustrations. Some children will invariably look at pictures before words as they turn pages. The child who "reads" the pictures first may be attempting to maintain a story line without using word analysis skills. Thus, the task of the teacher is to help the child develop a balance between using picture clues to anticipate new words and overusing picture clues to gain meaning without reading the selection.

Context The use of context clues—that is, the use of surrounding words to determine an unknown word's pronunciation and meaning—is a most effective strategy. Context limits possible alternative word selections. Students should know that they can decode an unknown word more easily if they use context clues to limit the number of words that might fit into a specific language structure. Children should be taught to verify a freshly decoded word by insisting that the word "makes good sense" in the sentence. This training begins with the development of sentence sense at the oral language level in many readiness programs.

Taylor (1953) presented a technique known as the *cloze* procedure. Cloze involves filling in blanks that have been created by the deletion of words from a prose passage on some regular basis. The creative teacher can devise many logical methods to utilize the cloze technique as an aid to decoding through context. In fact, modified cloze procedures have been historically synonymous with exercises to teach the use of context clues.

In some instances the teacher will wish to center the student's attention on a specific language clue. Here a modification of the cloze technique may be used effectively.

1. Using context to verify a word ending, constrained by a word in a previous position in the sentence:

> Yesterday, the man walk___ ___ home.
> The man is run___ ___ ___ ___ home.
> I saw two little dog___.

2. Verbs constrained by subjects and prepositions:

> The dog ___ ___ ___ ___ ___ ___ over the fence.
> The bird ___ ___ ___ ___ over the fence.
> The snake ___ ___ ___ ___ ___ ___ ___ ___ under the fence.

3. Initial consonant plus context:

> Jim hit the b___ ___ ___ over the fence.
> The old m___ ___ became very tired.
> When the b___ ___ ___ rings it is time for lunch.

4. Triple consonant cluster plus context:

> Thr___ ___ strikes and you are out!
> We str___ ___ ___ ___ ___ the coiled spring.
> We stretched the coiled spr___ ___ ___.

The examples are only a small sample of many possible exercises. The teacher must be aware that he is teaching context clues informally when he draws upon the child's previous experiences with language. He is not teaching grammar.

Emans and Fisher (1967) listed the different kinds of deleted-word exercises in order of difficulty (from most to least difficult):

1. No clue given other than context.
2. Beginning letter given.
3. Length of word given.
4. Beginning and ending letter given.
5. Four word choice given.
6. Consonants given.

In addition to varying the specific skill to be focused on, the teacher may wish to vary the degree of complexity of the task through the amount of information supplied. Three of the many possible formats are:

1. Multiple choice: This requires the child to read and mark.

> Circle the correct word:
>
> In the _____ the streets are icy.
>
> A. summer   B. running   C. winter

2. Context only: This requires the child to write the word. Beginners will probably find this task more difficult because they have yet to develop proficiency in writing and spelling.

> Fill in the blank:
>
> In the _____ the streets are icy.

3. Initial consonant supplied: This exercise asks the child to verify initial consonant with context. Exercises of this type teach the child to use more than one skill to analyze unknown words.

> Fill in the blank:
>
> In the w_____ the streets are icy.

Teachers of young children should be careful to avoid selecting exercises which require an undue amount of writing. By varying both specific skills and the complexity of the task, the teacher can develop a store of exercises that can be beneficial, on an individual basis, to all the children in the classroom (McKee, 1966). Published materials such as Continental Press *Reading-Thinking Skills* (Maney, 1963) and Barnell-Loft's *Specific Skills Series* (Boning, 1962) also provide a good source of cloze worksheets.

In addition to using cloze exercises the teacher should seek every opportunity to discuss the relationship between various language units with the students. Students need to be made aware that the strings of words (usually sentences) they decode while reading must make sense. One simple method of demonstrating that words have relationships with other words in a sentence is to isolate a certain verb and subject in the child's reading material. For example, consider this sentence:

The boy *prayed* for help.

The verb pray requires a certain type of subject. The subject must be an animate being, and furthermore it must be human. The teacher may ask the students to make a list of things that pray (boy, girl, mother, and so on). During the course of the discussion certain things that do not pray may be mentioned. These items should be fitted into the sample sentence framework.

The _____ prayed for help.

dog   car   mother

The teacher must acknowledge that there are exceptions to many of our language rules. It is quite possible that a bright child will point out to the class that a mantis prays but is not human. In this manner children can begin to formulate hypotheses about the relationships and constraints that exist among words, and they may begin to use these language clues to help them decode unknown words.

Visual Analysis

The importance of vision to reading is obvious, but the need for a child to learn systematic visual analysis of new words is sometimes underestimated or overlooked. Visual study of words does not always need to be used in conjunction with other word analysis skills. This is particularly true for the more skilled reader. For example, if a child encounters a word that he has not completely mastered, all he may need to do is inspect the word carefully without resorting to other more time-consuming processes of word analysis.

The major task is to visually identify word units in the unknown word which will help the reader crack the code. The units identified are often word parts—discussed later in the sections on structural analysis and phonics. Obviously, then, skill in identifying visual cues often operates in conjunction with other word analysis skills. Often the exercises that teach phonics and other skills fail to communicate to the child that words must be visually segmented into smaller units before they can be properly identified and analyzed. The teacher must help children develop the habit of careful, flexible visual inspection of the problem words, always seeking possible cues for identification.

Children need to look especially carefully at words when they are taught by spelling patterns (Bloomfield and Barnhart, 1961; Fries, 1963) or word families. Consider what might happen if careful visual study of the following patterns is not encouraged.

cap   gap   nap   rap   tap

sit   set   sat   sad   sod

Exercises that are first begun in reading readiness programs—often labelled visual discrimination exercises—form the beginnings of careful visual inspection of words. Teachers need to continue with this type of exercise that encourages careful visual examination of words.

Two of the most common visual analysis skills taught are general configuration (shape) and specific striking characteristics of words. Able readers read many words by their general shape, particularly if they know the word well. Also some words do not lend themselves well to the usual analytical techniques, and they must be learned from their general shape or specific characteristics. Children study these as sight words and learn them from repeated exposure to their graphic form. Common examples are *the, together,* and *who.* They are learned as single visual units and may need to be seen thirty to fifty times before they are learned, depending on the individual child (Huey, 1908).

Teaching Visual Analysis Skills

The purpose of studying words visually is to develop two primary abilities: visual memory and discrimination. Memory requires the child to recall what particular words or word parts look like. Discrimination involves differentiating between units: letters, groups of letters, and words. Many reading experts feel that visual analysis skills are very important. The exercises advocated for teaching visual analysis, however, have yet to be shown truly effective in the development of word analysis skills. Consider exercises such as the following:

Draw a circle around the little words in these bigger words:

electricity   uncanny   sifter

Finding little words in big words may sometimes be helpful. But it may also be confusing, particularly in isolated words—for example, *father, earth,* and *pigeon.*

We know that people read from visual cues derived from the upper portion of words much more so than the lower portions (Huey, 1908),

Father is a big man

Sister is a little lady.

and that visual cues are much easier to deduce when lower case letters are used rather than upper case (Patterson and Tinker, 1946).

SEE HOW THEY RUN

See how they run

Yet the teaching of word shape or word configuration seems to have limited direct value in making children aware of the differences between words. For example:

Draw a box around these words:

season   happy   baby

Such an exercise draws a child's attention to the box (or configuration) rather than to the letters of the words themselves. Since there are nearly as many shapes of boxes as there are words, it is probably more profitable to learn the words.

A better technique to get children to attend to visual differences may be for the teacher to talk about how the new words look different. "Boys and girls, our words today are *bird* and *some*. Notice how flat the word *some* looks" (teacher draws a line above and below the letters of *some*), "and the word *bird* has two tall letters—*b* and *d*" (teacher draws a line over *b, i, r,* and *d* to emphasize the difference in the way the two words look). This focuses attention on the difference in the visual characteristics of the words rather than the shapes of boxes.

Words that are "look-alikes" require special study. "We have a couple of tough ones today, kids. You know why?" (Teacher writes *when* and *then, quite* and *quiet*.) "Yes! Because they look so much alike. We need to be very careful when we read these words because they are easy to get mixed up." (Continue class discussion, pointing out the parts that look alike and the parts that are different.) Considerable practice with look-alikes will probably be needed before some students can recognize the differences with a minimum of effort.

Learning words on the basis of striking characteristics is also of questionable value. The child may learn that *monkey* has a tail on the end; but so do *money* and *donkey*. The fact that the word *Ohio* is round on both ends and *hi* in the middle is of limited usefulness.

Perhaps the greatest strength of this teaching procedure is that it helps children be aware that almost every word in our written language has its individual, idiosyncratic graphic representation. And perhaps the greatest problem in learning words from this technique is that what is learned about a particular word is not conducive to generalization to other unknown words. With other word analysis skills, the child finds certain characteristics in words that he may apply usefully to decoding other new words. In learning words on the basis of striking characteristics, the opposite is probably true.

Locational Errors

Some children develop faulty habits in their visual study of words. Certain error patterns become apparent. These error patterns are often called locational errors. That is, a child will make frequent errors in the initial, medial, or final positions of words. The teacher then must choose or design special exercises which require the child to focus on the part of the word where he is consistently making errors.

When a child is observed erring in word beginnings, the teacher should prescribe exercises that draw attention to the initial elements of words. For example:

> Circle the correct word:
> We hear the little pig _____.
> heal   meal   squeal

> Draw a line around the words that begin like *break*:
> bring   train   bread   bash

Exercises in alphabetizing and simple dictionary work also help students focus on word beginnings. Many workbooks from basal reading series (Fay et al., 1972; Evertts et al., 1973) contain exercises of this type.

Other children may be having difficulty with the middles of words. Often these children observe the initial and final word sections but tend to hurry over the midsection—especially with longer words. Exercises should be designed to focus on the medial position of words. For example:

> He's the new sixth grade _____.
> teamster   teacher   temper

Sometimes children regularly make errors in the medial position of words because they are having trouble differentiating vowels. Exercises should focus attention on vowels in the middle of words. For example:

> Here is Mom's shopping _____.
> list   last   lost

Children sometimes have trouble with word endings. Qualitatively speaking, ending errors are not usually as serious as initial or medial word errors. Good readers tend to make more errors in the final position than in the initial or medial positions. Nevertheless, when needed, exercises requiring the child to attend to word endings are recommended. For example:

> Draw a circle around the words that end with *elt*:
> melt   sail   felt   tame   . belt

The teacher should be cautious in the use of exercises emphasizing word endings; they may confuse some children's left-to-right orientation.

Structural Analysis

Breaking a large word into smaller units is often a useful way to analyze it. There are two major categories of skills that deal with analysis of smaller word units: structural analysis and phonics. Structural analysis deals with those word parts that carry some element of meaning. The smallest meaning units in English are morphemes. For example, the word *walked* is made up of two morphemes. One meaning unit refers to the act of locomotion, the other to the fact that walking took place in the past. Similarly, *ran* is also made up of two morphemes, although the *ed* is not present in the irregular form. Morphemes may be combined into new, larger meaning units frequently referred to as derivatives, variants, and compounds.

Derivatives

In analyzing a derivative the student looks for a meaning-bearing unit affixed to the beginning or end of a root that also has meaning. The emphasis on meaning is essential when considering such examples as:

uneven   under   uncover

Which word or words have a prefix? The student must examine the root for meaning to determine that *under* is one morpheme, or meaning unit, while *un* + *even* and *un* + *cover* are derivatives containing two morphemes. *Un* can either be a morpheme or a phonogram (as in *under* or *run*), a unit which is discussed in the section on phonics. For decoding purposes, it makes little difference whether the unit is properly labelled a morpheme or a phonogram. What is important is that the *un* unit is familiar and therefore more easily decodable. In the study of word meanings, however, it is very important that the child recognize that the morpheme *un* has a meaning roughly equivalent to *not*.

Variants

Variants are words which contain a root and a variant or inflectional ending. The terms *variant* and *inflectional* are interchangeable, and for the purpose of early instruction in word recognition skills will be defined as words ending in *s, es, ed, ing, er,* and *est.* Variant endings perform a largely grammatical function. They change the root to allow it to conform to its grammatical environment. The following are examples:

Verb—time agreement

| talk | talks, talked, talking |
| cry | cries, cried, crying |

Nouns—number agreement

| book | books |
| glass | glasses |

Adverbs—degree

| slow | slower, slowest |
| high | higher, highest |

Adjectives—comparison

| funny | funnier, funniest |
| small | smaller, smallest |

In actual reading, knowledge of roots and variants will help children analyze words. Visual study is important here, to identify the root and variant. This takes place prior to the actual analysis of the word structure, although frequently these processes are so rapid that their sequence is not evident.

Compounds

Compound words require perhaps the closest combination of visual and structural analysis skills. A compound word is one in which two mor-phemes, both of which could stand as root words, are combined to form one new word. The new word may be very similar in meaning to the sum of its two roots, as in *police* + *man* = *policeman,* or the relationship may be obscure to the child, as in *turn* + *pike* = *turnpike,* or perhaps not evident at all, as in *dog,* + *wood* = *dogwood.* In what appears to be the vast majority of compound words the meaning is similar to the sum of the roots; so in the majority of encounters with compounds, structural analysis for meaning will make the reader more efficient. The initial visual clues, however, cannot be overlooked. The child must find just the right place to segment *dogwood.* Otherwise he may never get to the two roots. If he attempts to segment the word *backstop* into *backs* + *top* he may become confused.

Teaching Structural Analysis Skills

Derivatives Mere listings of common suffixes and prefixes to be memorized will not improve students' structural analysis skills in dealing with derivative words. The child must be interested—he must encounter these words in the spirit of a "word detective." Then he can figure out meanings through structural analysis, as well as build new words by adding affixes to roots.

The teacher may be wise to begin his introduction of affixes with suffixes rather than prefixes. In normal left-to-right progression the child will encounter the root word before a suffix (*care + less*). Initially, seeing the familiar root before the affix may facilitate meaningful structural analysis.

Three suffixes that are generally consistent in meaning are *less, ful,* and *ness.* These suffixes afford the teacher an adequate starting point. The teacher may seize the opportunity to discuss the fact that Phil was *shoeless* on the playground, or that Adrienne had been *careful* with the paints in art class. Examples such as "Mark's new dog has brought his family great *happiness*" should be avoided initially because of the spelling change from *y* to *i* in *happiness.* The discussion should proceed on the basis of meaning, looking at the differences the suffixes have caused in the total meaning of the derivative word.

shoe	care
shoeless	careful

It is not necessary, of course, that all suffixes be mastered before any prefixes are introduced. The prefixes *un, dis,* and *re* will provide adequate regularity for initial introduction to prefixes. This introduction can proceed in much the same manner as the introduction of suffixes. The teacher should choose concrete examples of the derivative words to be discussed, then point up the meaning changes while simultaneously displaying the graphic difference between the root alone and the root with prefix.

Goodman (1965) explained that children increase their ability to use context clues as they progress through the primary grades. Ramanaskas (1972) has demonstrated that these context clues operate between sentences as well as within them. Providing children with meaningful context is an immeasurable aid in helping them use acquired structural analysis skills.

Tom struck out three times in the baseball game.
This made him *unhappy.*

As the student becomes more proficient in analyzing roots with one affix, the more complex task of analyzing roots with multiple affixes may be attempted. These derivatives may take the form of a root with one prefix and one suffix.

happy

un + *happy*

un + *happ(i)* + *ness*

The derivative with multiple affixes may also be a root and two suffixes.

care

care + *less*

care + *less* + *ly*

The major difficulty with this type of structural analysis resides in the multiple meaning changes the root may undergo. The following is a four-step checklist which may help the student in his structural analysis of derivative words:

1. Find the meaning of the root word.
2. Find the prefix and the resultant meaning change.
3. Find any and all suffixes and consider their meaning changes.
4. Test the derivative word in context.

The ways of constructing structural analysis activities are numerous.

Make a word that means the opposite of its root by adding a prefix:

un   _____comfort

ir   _____happy

dis   _____regular

Make a word that means the same as the word the root is paired with by adding a prefix:

sad   = _____happy

bumpy = _____even

raw   = _____cooked

The teacher can construct word wheels or word strips with common roots and affixes. In addition to these lists there are many published games, activities, and workbook pages to reinforce the teacher's explanation of derivative words. The study of structural analysis is an excellent example of how language study can be successfully combined with the development of word recognition skills. It further reinforces the intimate relationship of language arts and reading.

Variants Variant forms of common roots are in the speaking vocabularies of the great majority of beginning readers. The child is familiar, for example, with the oral-aural representations of plurals. The instruction he needs is in recognizing the graphic form of the word and connecting it with the already familiar pronunciation and meaning. Hanson (1966) found variant endings (*s, ing, ed, er*) successfully taught in pre-primers, primers, and first readers.

The variant endings *s* and *es* are used to change root words in two ways: (1) the conversion of a singular noun to its plural form (*dog* to *dogs* or *dish* to *dishes*), and (2) the conversion of a verb to third person singular (I walk, you walk, he walk*s*, or I fly, you fly, he fli*es*). There are certain phonetic principles concerning the pronunciations of *s* as [s], [z], or [əz]; since the vast majority of children have incorporated these "rules" into their speech patterns long before entering school, that need not be of concern here. It is important, however, to make the child aware of the parallel uses of *s* and *es*.

The teaching of variant endings need not be difficult. The teacher should be certain to select roots the students can already read and then explain what adding the plural or third person does. This can be clearly exemplified by requiring the student to make comparisons with his oral language. Initially, the teacher may employ cloze exercises at the oral level.

"I have one dog, but Mary has two _____."

After the student has had a brief encounter with the oral representations of these, he should progress to the important graphic recognition level. For example:

Fill in the missing endings:

He like___ the ten little pup___.

The teacher should begin with nouns that are clearly defined by context as being plural, as in the above sample.

The past tense of regular verbs is formed by adding *ed*. As with *s*, there is a variation in pronunciation with *ed*—[t] as in *asked,* [d] as in *pulled*, and [əd] as in *dusted*. If the teacher concentrates his instruction on recognizing the visual form, the child's incorporated language rules should give him the pronunciation.

The student also needs to be introduced to *ing*. This variant, when added to a verb root, forms a word that can either be used in the noun or verb position in a sentence. It may be wise to use it in the verb position in contrast to the *ed* past tense form. Exercises designed in this manner exemplify the uses of the two forms.

Lincoln began to walk.

He walk*ed* all day.

He was walk*ing* to his new home.

The teaching of the variant endings *ing* and *ed* is much the same as with *s* and *es*. The teacher should be sure that the root word is in the reading vocabulary of the student. The meaning of the variant ending should be discussed, and the instructional time should be balanced between recognizing visual forms and oral discussion.

The *er* ending is added to modifying words (adjectives or adverbs) and to nouns. In either case the student must once again be careful to analyze the root for meaning. In the following example *moth* is not a root.

faster   mother   hunter

A purely visual analysis of each of the above words would yield these patterns: *cvcc* + *er* (consonant, vowel, consonant, consonant + *er*). In fact when the *er* is removed all three words do contain a meaningful root—*fast*, *moth*, and *hunt*; however, a final check in meaningful context reveals that *mother* is, indeed, a single morpheme. Such an example, a sight word ending in *er* when the *er* is not used as a variant ending, may help the child recognize the necessity for using meaningful units in structural analysis. It is also an excellent example of an exception to a rule.

The variant ending *est* may be added to adjectives such as *tall*. This *est* form may well be introduced in conjunction with *er*. Numerous games can be constructed with a deck of adjective roots and a deck of *er* and *est* endings. If a root card can be paired (and named) with an *er* and *est* ending then the "book" may be played. The games may follow the rules of the card games "Rummy" and "Go Fish."

Variants may be introduced and taught in much the same manner as derivatives with a root and suffix. The fact that variants usually clue only the grammatical function of the root makes them easily discernible to the child if he is reminded to test their use in context *via* his speaking vocabulary.

Compounds Recognizing compound words can be relatively easy for the student if the teacher begins instruction with two simple sight words that may be combined to form a compound. Initially this may be easiest with monosyllabic words.

into   sunset   gunman   outside

This skill should not be associated with the practice of looking for small words in larger ones. The concern must be with finding two meaningful units that combine to form a new unit with a similar meaning. If this is not stressed, the child may begin to view some words inappropriately—*together* as *to* + *get* + *her*, for example.

After some of the simpler compounds have been introduced the sequence may progress to those compounds in which either or both of the roots have more complex spelling patterns.

stagecoach   windshield   corkscrew

Finally, the more difficult compounds, those in which the combined meaning of the two roots is obscured or totally different from the compound word, may be introduced.

broadcast   tadpole   wholesale

These words depend more on visual analysis than any other category of words discussed in structural analysis skills, because meaning units may not be evident. When a child encounters an unknown compound he will not know it is a compound until, through visual inspection, he discovers one or both of the smaller roots.

Numerous card and board games can be constructed for teaching compounds, variants, and derivatives. Published materials and workbook exercises are also plentiful and enumerated in such sources as Schubert and Torgerson (1968).

Structural analysis is among the most important word analysis skills. An efficient reader must learn to use this set of skills in combination with other word analysis skills, especially context, in decoding unknown words.

Phonics

Phonics instruction can be defined as a system in which the student learns the relationships between graphic symbols (letters and letter combinations) and the speech sounds they represent. Many teachers of reading confuse or misuse the terms *phonics*, *phonetics*, and *phonemics*. Smith (1971) draws the following distinctions:

> Phonics is not phonetics, which is the scientific study of the sounds of a language, and which has nothing at all to do with writing. . . . phonetics is to phonics what brain surgery is to cutting-and-pasting.

> Phonics is not phonemics, which is the study of the classes of sounds that do constitute significant differences in a language. In English there are about 46 phonemes (pp. 159–160).

The discussion here will pertain only to phonics—that is, symbol-sound correspondences, particularly as they relate to the process of learning to read.

In addition to confusion over the terminology of phonics, there are numerous misconceptions about what phonics can or cannot do, what

should or should not be taught in phonics instruction, and so on. Wardhaugh (1969b) attempts to dispel some of the misconceptions:

1. Letters do not have sounds. . . . Letters are letters, and sounds are
   sounds; they must not be confused with each other.
2. Statements are often made about syllabication which only hold true for
   word-breaking in writing, but not for pronunciation.
3. Statements are often incorrectly made about children mispronouncing
   words, when in reality the pronunciations are acceptable as a part of
   their dialect.
4. Long and short vowel sounds have nothing to do with the duration of
   pronunciation.
5. Lessons in articulation are not a part of phonics instruction. Phonics is
   not a matter of teaching children the sounds of their language (p. 82).

In order to achieve efficiency in reading, the student needs to establish
independence in word recognition skills. Phonics, or more appropriately
phonics in conjunction with other word recognition skills, is an invaluable
tool in achieving a degree of independence. Phonics is by no means a
cure-all; nevertheless, it has an extremely important function in decoding
words.

Unfortunately, authors disagree as to how phonics should be taught.
Presently there are at least two quite different approaches to phonics
instruction. Frequently they are characterized as synthetic and analytic
phonics.

Synthetic phonics is concerned with the teaching of isolated symbol-
sound correspondences. First the student learns the name of each letter,
then the sound each letter represents. Once these two skills are mastered
the student is expected to be able to sound out and blend an unknown
word. Three variations of synthetic phonics are:

1. Sounding and blending of each letter (Brunner, 1968):

c-a-t

kuh-a-tuh

2. Sounding the initial consonant and vowel together, then blending the
   final consonant sound (Cordts, 1953; Gillingham and Stillman, 1956):

ca-t

ka-tuh

3. Sounding the initial consonant, then sounding the vowel and final
   consonants together (Wylie and Durrell, 1970):

c-at

kuh-at

One of the most common problems associated with synthetic phonics is that the child often produces extraneous sounds which tend to distort the pronunciation of the word. This problem is most apparent in words containing unvoiced consonants:

p-u -m-p

puh-uh-m-puh

Synthetic phonics involves the synthesis of small units, letters, into larger units, words. Analytic phonics, on the other hand, starts with words and proceeds to smaller units, letters.

Gates (1947) was one of the early proponents of analytic phonics. This is the position that is most often represented in present basal reading programs. It also is the approach taken most frequently in schools today. Although analytic phonics has many ramifications, it can be explained broadly as making use of the sounds of known units or words to unlock the pronunciation of an unknown unit or word. For example, if the new word is *cat*, the child may recognize that the word begins with the same letter, and possibly the same sound, as another word he knows—*can*. Furthermore, he may recognize that the ending is the same as the ending of *bat*. So he may analyze cat as:

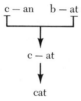

To analyze words in this manner, the student must have some sight vocabulary to serve as referents.

In this chapter we will discuss primarily the analytic approach to phonics instruction, since this is the direction of current trends.

Various generalizations about the sound-symbol correspondences have been formulated over the years. The work of such authors as Emans (1967), Clymer (1963), Bailey (1967), and Burmeister (1968a, 1968b) have revealed that a few of these generalizations have a great deal of utility while others have very little. The teacher must be careful to select examples which conform to the more useful generalizations.

Generally, basal reading programs and phonics workbook materials strive for vocabulary control by means of phonic regularity. Essentially this means that as a phonic generalization is introduced, the reading assignments will emphasize words which conform to the generalization. For example, the student may be introduced to the "silent *e* generalization." Essentially this rule refers to instances in one-syllable words where two vowels are separated by a consonant. The second vowel is an *e* which is not sounded and the first vowel is given the long sound.[1] At this point the reading material will emphasize new words such as *late* rather than *love*, which is obviously an exception to the rule. The teacher must also maintain this kind of control in phonics exercises.

After the child has learned to identify the letters of the alphabet rapidly, phonics instruction generally begins. Learning the sounds represented by initial consonants in readiness activities is usually the beginning of the program, and it extends through advanced concepts such as *r*-controlled vowels and triple consonant clusters. In between, final consonants, short and long vowels, consonant blends and digraphs, diphthongs, and vowel combinations are learned. Essentially, the child is instructed in a method of analyzing word elements for sound, blending these sounds together, and reaching an approximate pronunciation of the unknown word which should in turn cue a meaning association. Extensive practice is necessary for learning each phonic element to a level of instant recognition.

Teaching Phonics Skills

Beginning Single Consonants Many basal readers and initial reading programs contain activities that present several pictures of objects, the names of which all begin with the same consonant. It is suggested that the program begin with the consonants *b*, *d*, *h*, *j*, *m*, *n*, *p*, *t*. For various reasons that will be presently discussed, these consonant sounds produce less confusion than the others. Pairing the beginning consonant with pictures is wise because it avoids the confusion in blending that may arise from learning letter sounds in isolation. The concept that *b* is the letter that represents the beginning sound in *baby*, *book*, *ball*, and *bell* may cause less difficulty later than learning that *b* represents the sound *buh*.

After the letters and sounds have been discussed, the teacher should progress to pairing the initial sound to a printed word which begins with the consonant in question, in this case *b*. The words used to illustrate may well be children's names in the class—Bill, Bernie, or Beth. The word might also be one of the initial sight words that the children have already learned as a whole word by configuration or picture association. In either case the teacher should list these words that begin with *b* on the chalkboard. The child's attention should be focused first on the visual similarity of the words—they all begin with the same letter. Then the teacher should focus on the auditory similarity—they all begin with the same sound.

The consonants *c* and *g* were not included in the beginner list because they vary in pronunciation according to the environment they are in: [c]-*cat*

---

[1] Some linguists prefer to use the terms *glided* and *unglided* instead of *long* and *short*.

or [c]-*city* and [g]-*gum* or [g]-*gem*. The consonants *f, l, r,* and *s* were not among those first introduced because they are often more difficult for children to pronounce correctly. *K* and *q* were omitted from the initial list because in many environments they have quite similar pronunciations, as in *queen* and *keen*. This problem is just the opposite of *c* and *g*, where there is one symbol with two pronunciations. *W* and *y*, because they may be sounded as semi-vowels as well as consonants, are also confusing. Finally, *v, x, y,* and *z* can be very confusing; their pronunciation varies greatly with the environment. The letter *x*, for example, represents many pronunciations ([xylophone], [exam], [box]).

Short Vowels In this section, the terms *short* and *long* will be used because the reader is probably most familiar with these terms. The authors are aware, however, that some linguists (Wardhaugh, 1969a) think these terms are unscientific and confusing.

When the students have grasped the concept of symbol-sound relationships with some of the initial consonants, they may be introduced to short vowels, which are more consistent in their pronunciation than long vowel sounds. The short sound of *a* is commonly introduced first.

Once again the words selected to illustrate short *a* should be listed on the chalkboard, the visual similarities noted, and the sound similarities noted. The list might include:

cap   lap   bat   am   Sam   Pat   tan

Picture associations may often be useful. The pictorial form, the graphic form, and the auditory form of the word may all be displayed at the same time.

Final Consonants After students have attained some degree of mastery over initial consonants and short vowels, they may be introduced to consonants in the final position, which will enable them to use phonic attack to decode monosyllabic, closed syllable (cvc) words. Although many children may generalize the sounds of consonants from the initial to the final position, consonants in this position can cause difficulty for poor readers (Harris, 1975).

At first it may be prudent to select words in which the initial consonant is repeated in the final position:

dad   tot   nan   bib

As soon as these words have been illustrated, the introduction may proceed to those closed syllable words that are formed from initial consonants, short vowels, and familiar ending consonants which are different from the initial consonant:

Dan   top   nap   bit

Once the child has learned these sound-symbol correspondences, numerous methods of instruction in phonic attack can be employed. The child has attained enough phonic decoding skill to begin to isolate elementary generalizations. These may well take the form of looking at words in terms of families (also called phonograms or spelling patterns).

_at_	_ap_	_it_	_ot_	_am_
cat	lap	pit	lot	ham
fat	cap	sit	cot	jam
sat	sap	hit	got	dam
hat	tap	lit	not	Pam
rat	rap	fit	tot	ram
bat	map	bit	dot	Sam

This gives the child practice with a consistent ending phonogram and also with the initial consonants that have been substituted in the pattern. Word wheels prove very useful in reinforcing this decoding skill. The outer portion of the wheel contains various consonants, while the inner wheel contains phonograms. The child may choose one initial consonant and rotate the phonograms to form different words. Various other strips or wheels may be constructed in which the medial vowel or the ending consonant changes. Although at this point the closed syllable, cvc spelling pattern is the only one directly and completely decodable by phonic attack alone, students will be able to build from this unit when they have learned other sound-symbol correspondences and syllabication. By the time children have reached this level of knowledge in phonics, they will probably have attained some proficiency in using context for word analysis. Conjointly, context and phonics skills are powerful decoding tools.

Long Vowels and Vowel Combinations Long vowels vary far more than short vowels in pronunciation. Emans (1967) found that a vowel in the initial or medial position of a closed monosyllabic word represented the short sound 80 percent of the time. The exceptions occurred largely in words containing _i_ or _o_ followed by double consonants (for example, _right, thigh, blind, cold, toll, hold_). Because long vowels and vowel combinations are much less regular, the child must learn to try various sounds to see if they complete a word that he has stored in his meaning vocabulary. For example, _ea_ has the sound of [e]-_beak_ approximately one-third of the time, but it is also pronounced as [a]-_great_, [e]-_dead_, and in other ways (_wear, earn, hear_).

The vowels which do not represent a sound but rather change the sound of another vowel in the word (silent vowels) serve to further confuse the issue. Although the silent *e* in monosyllabic, cvc spelling pattern words is highly consistent (*hope, like, cake,* etc.), combinations with silent vowels such as *ea* are sometimes long *e*, silent *a* (*neat*); they are also often short *e*, silent *a* (*bread*).[2]

The difference between single-letter long vowel sounds and vowel combinations is apparent visually, but diphthongs need to be distinguished from other vowel combinations. A diphthong is a combination of sounds that is perceived as very nearly one sound. This sound is graphically represented by two letters. The most regular are: *au* (*caught*), *aw* (*law*), *oi* (*boil*), and *oy* (*toy*). The numerous other vowel combinations are less regular than the highly consistent diphthongs.

The teaching of long vowels and vowel combinations must account for irregularity of pronunciation. "Rules" may often be of little value when their validity is constantly challenged. If "rules" are encompassing enough to be useful they are in many cases too complex to be learned and applied. It is better for the child to be willing to forward reasonable guesses, using all available language clues.

Burmeister (1968b) points out that phonemes for vowel pairs tend to fall into these categories:

1. The first vowel may do the talking as in *ai, ay, ea, ee, oa,* or *ow* and say its name. *Ea* may be long *e* or short *e; ow* may be long *o* or *ow.*
2. The two vowels may blend as in *au, aw, oi, oy, oo; oo* may sound as in *lagoon* or *wood.*
3. The two vowels may represent a new sound; *ei, ow, ey, ew.*
4. Vowel pairs may separate (p. 449).

As the student meets new words in which the similarity or difference in the pronunciation of a given spelling pattern is exemplified, and as he learns some guidelines (such as those cited by Burmeister), he will begin to internalize some pronunciation generalizations of his own. If this internalization and experimentation with sound-symbol relationships is encouraged by the teacher, the child's proficiency with long vowels and vowel combinations will doubtlessly increase.

Consonant Combinations Consonants are combined in words in four main ways: (1) two-consonant blends, (2) two-consonant digraphs, (3) three-consonant blends, (4) three-consonant trigraphs. A consonant blend is

---

[2] Terms such as *often, highly regular, irregular,* and so on are used in conjunction with phonic generalizations because various studies have reported somewhat different percentages of utility. Long *a* and long *i* are sometimes considered diphthongs by linguists. The reason will be evident if you say these in a prolonged fashion.

formed by two or three letters that are combined together but maintain the distinction of their individual sounds in the blend (for example, [bl]-*blend*, or [str]-*strong*). Digraphs, on the other hand, are formed when two or more letters are combined to represent a single phoneme or speech sound that is different from the sound either letter typically represents (for example, [wh]-*when*, or [ght]-*bought*). Some consonant letter combinations are highly regular, such as *ng*. It is pronounced as in *ring* and occurs only in the ending position of a syllable or word. *Ch* is far more irregular. It stands for four different sounds [ch, j, sh, k] and occurs in the beginning of words or syllables as well as the middle and ending positions.

Two-letter consonant blends should be introduced in the initial position. Essentially they have the same characteristics as the beginning single consonant in monosyllabic words. The teacher may use pairs of cvc or ccvc words to demonstrate the use of blends.

> fat–flat   pan–plan   lot–blot

As with initial consonants the visual as well as auditory differences should be pointed out. The entire presentation can be very similar to that of initial consonants. Many of the same teaching materials are also applicable. The outside wheel of the word wheel containing single consonants may now be replaced with one containing blends.

The consonant blends occurring in the final positions should also be introduced in monosyllabic words. The techniques are the same as for beginning blends.

Children will learn the consonant blends *sch, scr, shr, spl, spr, str,* and *thr* more easily if they are familiar with the concept of two-consonant blends. Then they can proceed to the concept of blending three sounds and learning the sounds' corresponding visual representation.

Learning digraphs requires quite a different concept. The child must recognize that two or more consonants may combine to form one speech sound. The problem is complicated by the fact that certain digraphs have different sounds depending on their environment. *Gh* may be pronounced as in [ghost] in the initial position, or as in [enough] in the final position, or it may be silent as in [bough].

Teachers should present only words which conform to one pronunciation of the digraph at a time. Then the child may learn the environments in which second and third pronunciations occur. The teacher will be wise to check reading materials being used to determine which pronunciation is most common and teach that generalization first.

Triple-consonant combinations, or trigraphs, are rare; *ght* is the most common. It may be learned as pronounced in [right] or [bought].

R-Controlled Vowels Vowels that are followed by the letter *r* often are represented by a sound that is different from the sound the same vowel would make in a different environment. Two generalizations concerning the principle of r controls are regular enough to be useful to the child:

1. a followed by an r and the final e represents the sound heard in *dare*. Some words conforming to this generalization are *care, hare, mare*, and so on. A word such as *are* is an exception. Bailey, Clymer, and Emans all found the utility of this generalization to be 90 percent or greater.

2. r gives the preceding vowel a sound that is not the normal short or long sound. Some words representing this generalization are *born, worn, darn, bar*, and so on. A word such as *tire* is an exception. Bailey, Clymer, and Emans found this generalization to have a utility ranging from 78 to 96 percent.

Children need not be concerned with committing these generalizations to memory; but they should know that when they encounter a vowel followed by an r, the vowel may have a sound different from that which might normally be expected. Children should be encouraged to adopt a flexible attitude toward decoding. As they must be encouraged to make hypotheses regarding words in order to use context clues, they must also be encouraged to formulate hypotheses about the sounds that certain graphic symbols represent. Once they begin to develop a willingness to take a chance on various symbol-sound correspondences, they need to be reminded to search for sound combinations that form words they have in their listening vocabulary.

Syllabication

A syllable is a group of sounds pronounced as a single unit. It always contains a minimum of one vowel and can contain a combination of vowels and consonants, but syllables must be pronounced in a single "chest pulse." In written form a syllable can be a single letter (*I, a*) or a combination of consonants and vowels (*aye, me, bout*). It is important for teachers to differentiate between spoken syllables and written syllables, as they do between letters and the sounds they represent.

Knowledge of syllables is probably most important in two non-reading areas of the language arts—spelling and writing. Many spelling programs stress syllabication practice to help children break down long words into more manageable units. In spelling, the word is known, in terms of reading it, and it is pronounced quietly by the child to aid him in sequencing and writing the letters in known syllabic utterances. In writing, syllabication helps a child tell how to divide a word correctly at the end of a line. In writing, the word is already known in the child's listening, speaking, and reading vocabularies, but the restrictive conventions of the written language, the end of line dividing point, is unknown.

When decoding new words in reading, the child may use syllabication to break down longer words into smaller, more manageable (pronounceable) units, then decode the smaller units (syllables) and blend them together to approximate the pronunciation of the word.

The value of syllabication for decoding has been questioned (Glass, 1965), however, because it seems that students use the sounds represented in the words to determine the number of syllables, rather than vice versa. If this is the case, syllabication used as a word analysis tool is of little value. Another criticism of syllabication as used in word recognition (Wardhaugh, 1966) is that there is very little value in syllabicating words because the dividing point between syllables often is not at all clear. For example, the word *rabbit* appears in many dictionaries with the syllables divided between the *bb,* when in fact the word is probably spoken as [rabb/it] (or do you say [ra/bbit]?).

Nevertheless, there seems to be some pragmatic value in teaching syllabication as a word recognition tool, though probably the point of the instruction should be to help students approximate reasonable breaking points in polysyllabic words. Segmenting unknown words as described above may be argued to be part of visual analysis, since the student breaks words apart on the basis of visual inspection, looking for clues such as double consonants.

In recent years considerable effort has been made to reduce the number of syllabication rules from many and questionable to a few that are widely generalizable.

George and Evelyn Spache (1973), for example, suggest children should be taught seven concepts relevant to syllabication, but the concepts are far from the traditional rules suggested by many experts in the past. In fact only one concept could be considered a rule of syllabication.

Four syllabication generalizations seem dependable enough to be considered for direct teaching purposes:

1. Compounds usually are divided between the two smaller words.
2. Affixes usually form a syllable.
3. Double consonants usually mark the division point between syllables . . .
4. Except for certain clusters such as *sh, ch, th, ph,* and *ck.*

It is important to stress flexibility in teaching syllabication. The pupil must be encouraged to try different ways of breaking a word apart. With the word *rabbit,* for example, it matters little whether the word is divided between the *ab, bb,* or the *bi.* If the child divides it so as to come up with *rabbit,* he has used syllabication effectively.

Auditory Blending

When a pupil is asked to analyze a long, polysyllabic word he does not know, he must first separate the word into smaller units, such as syllables, affixes, and roots; he must then attempt to pronounce these units; and finally he must blend these units together to orally reconstruct the word which triggers a meaningful response. This blending of word parts is a necessary skill for successful decoding. Without the ability to blend sounds together, phonics skills in general are of little value because isolated word parts are meaningless unless they can be synthesized. Blending is even more critical in synthetic phonics.

Many children have no trouble blending sounds. However, the child who seems to be learning his sound-symbol correspondences and still has trouble with phonics in general may well be experiencing auditory blending difficulties. He can say the word parts but cannot put them together.

The teacher can identify this problem by asking the child to pronounce isolated parts of words. When it is clear that the child knows the individual parts, the teacher asks him to blend these parts together to make a word.

Initially, this can be done by presenting a written word, broken into parts, to be pronounced.

oc   to   pus

au   to   mo   bile

After the child has pronounced the individual parts correctly he is shown the word without separation and is asked to say the whole word.

octopus

automobile

If he fails on this task the teacher should proceed to the oral language level, pronouncing the word slowly, part by part, and asking the child to say what the whole word is.

Teacher: ad   van   tage

Child: advantage

If the child cannot do this, it is fairly clear that he has auditory blending problems and will experience difficulty with what is typically assumed to be part of phonics instruction. Some children with this problem will benefit from training in blending. Others may have difficulties so severe that phonics instruction may be far less profitable than instruction in other word analysis skills, such as context and visual analysis.

Exercises for beginners should expose children to word parts they already know and that form a familiar word.

in to   into
a   way   away

Working with known words and word parts will help the child understand the usefulness of blending. After this has been understood, the child may begin to work with blending word parts into unfamiliar words.

se cret   secret
le ver age   leverage

The most difficult form of auditory blending is with nonsense or unknown words. But this is the "acid test" of auditory blending and phonics in general. If a child is able to break a large "word" he does not know into small parts, pronounce those parts, and then blend them together to arrive at an acceptable pronunciation—even with a nonsense word—it can be assumed this child has command of blending skills.

The teacher can make the real value of auditory blending clear to children by using words that are in the child's oral vocabulary but not yet in his written vocabulary. Arranging the unknown word in context (usually a sentence), so that all words but the target word are known, also helps the child recognize the importance of blending.

Dictionary Skills

The more children read, the more unfamiliar, undecodable words they will encounter. These words may be irregular and therefore difficult to deduce. Other words may be decodable for sound but not in the child's meaning vocabulary. When the child has exhausted his decoding skills on all the available clues to pronunciation and meaning, he needs an outside reference. Since the goal in word recognition is developing efficient, mature, independent readers, this source must be one which the child uses on his own.

The dictionary meets these requirements. However, dictionary usage slows the reading process significantly and must be viewed as a final alternative in decoding unknown words.

Teaching Dictionary Skills

Spache and Spache (1973) suggest that training in dictionary use may begin as early as third grade, but selected experiences with the dictionary may begin earlier. Many basal readers provide a glossary of "new" words that may also prove to be a beneficial tool prior to the third-grade level. Numerous publishers produce picture dictionaries that provide initial dictionary experiences.

In order to use the dictionary as a word recognition tool the student must become familiar with two skill areas, *location skills* and *pronunciation skills.* The child must be able to find the word he cannot decode, and he must be able to pronounce the word to determine if he has already learned its meaning.

When the child uses the dictionary as a word recognition tool, he has encountered the unknown word in its written form. Therefore, there is no question as to how the word is spelled. The child must know the alphabetical organization of the dictionary and how to use this organization to find the word. Then he is ready to use pronunciation skills.

The child may have difficulty using diacritical marks to determine the pronunciation of a word for two reasons. First, different dictionaries and glossaries use different diacritical markings. The teacher must teach those markings used in the instructional materials he is working with. Second, knowledge of diacritical marks alone will not ensure that the child can read the word. He still has to use regular phonics on those units not diacritically marked. The child must learn that the unknown word, as written in traditional orthography, is one representation of a given sound, and the phonetic spelling in the dictionary is merely another way of writing the same word. The phonetic spelling may also be a useful method of writing the word, because it may lead the child to the correct pronunciation when the traditional orthography may not. In this case the phonetic spelling cues the meaning response. If it does not, the problem is one of word meaning as well as word recognition.

Establishing Balances in Word Recognition Skills

We have discussed various strategies for decoding unknown words. While all of these strategies are important for efficient, mature, independent reading, they can and must not develop in isolation. Consideration must be given to relationships that exist between the various skills. Bond and Tinker (1973) state five important balances in word recognition:

1. *Balance between the establishment of word recognition techniques and the development of meaning vocabulary.* In order to decode a word for sound, the child need not know its meaning. However, because the sound

alone is without meaning, the child who does not know a word's meaning may not realize he has arrived at a correct pronunciation. Teaching solely analytical techniques with no development of meaning vocabulary may well reach a point of diminishing returns. The result may be what is termed a "word caller." Similarly, if meaning is emphasized and word analysis skills are neglected (Schell, 1967), children may not be able to decode words.

2. *Balance between sight vocabulary and word recognition skills.* Although it is extremely important to be able to analyze words, continued practice with these words is necessary to elevate them to the sight recognition level. The child who has adequate analysis skills but a limited sight vocabulary is often a slow, laborious reader. He lacks the ability to read fluently and concentrate on gaining meaning, because he must continuously devote attention to word analysis. Some children, on the other hand, commit all words to their sight vocabulary and fail to develop skills in context, visual, structural, and phonic analysis. This may result from the old "look-and-say" teaching method. The more words the child commits to his sight vocabulary, the fewer he needs to analyze.

3. *Balance between meaning clues and analytical aids.* Proper decoding requires the use of clues within words as well as clues between words. The child who is over-reliant on context may deviate from the printed text, and, as the deviations mount up, stray from the meaning intended by the author. The child who depends too greatly on analytical aids and fails to use context as a check for meaning, however, may have poor comprehension of what he has read. He becomes so involved with decoding that he loses sight of meaning.

4. *Balance among the analytical techniques.* Some words are more readily decoded by one technique of word analysis than another. The student needs to have mastered several techniques in order to be most efficient. Sometimes context clues provide enough information to determine the pronunciation and meaning of an unknown word; however, a phonic clue in addition to context will often be far more useful. Children need to develop all the decoding skills and use them in combination, not independently of each other.

5. *Balance between emphasis placed on knowledge of word parts and the orderly inspection of words along the line of print from left to right and from the beginning of the word to the end.* Prolonged, concentrated effort on isolated word parts may cause the child to look for familiar parts rather than inspect the word in an organized sequence from left to right. For example, if continued stress has been placed on word endings, the child may begin to analyze words from their ends, rather than their beginnings. Such an emphasis could cause serious reversal errors or other unfortunate habits.

The resourceful football coach knows that his most valuable players are those who have mastered running, passing, and kicking. Those with only one or two of these skills may or may not be successful players, and those who have not mastered any of them will probably sit on the bench. The same is true of word analysis skills. The efficient reader uses all of them together.

The Authors' Viewpoint

Word recognition skills should always be taught along with meaning and sight vocabularies. If children are to learn new words in the reading lessons they must know those words at the oral language level. Otherwise they have no practical method of checking the decoded word in context to verify its accuracy. We also believe that many children have reading problems because they learn how to decode words and word parts, but they do not learn the words they decode to the level of instant recognition. These students spend a great deal of time and effort continually decoding instead of reading to gain information. Overemphasis of word analysis skills in the reading program can produce this result.

Students will decode most effectively if they develop a large set of word analysis skills. No one skill should be taught to the exclusion of others; they are all important and should be developed more or less simultaneously so the child has a combination of techniques to attack unknown words. The skills should be balanced, and the child should use them flexibly, viewing the task of word analysis as a form of hypothesis testing. If a word as he decodes it does not make sense in context, he should accept that effort as a possible error and try a different analytical approach.

A skill program to develop word recognition techniques is a critical part of every reading program. These skills are not an end in themselves. But they are a means to very important goals—reading for information and enjoyment.

References

Ames, W. S. "The Development of a Classification Scheme for Contextual Aids." *Reading Research Quarterly* 2 (1966): 57–82.

Artley, A. S. "Teaching Word Meanings through Context." *Elementary English Review* 20 (1943): 68–74.

Bailey, M. H. "The Utility of Phonic Generalizations in Grades One through Six." *The Reading Teacher* (Feb. 1967): 413–418.

Bloomfield, L., and Barnhart, C. L. *Let's Read: A Linguistic Approach.* Detroit: Wayne State University Press, 1961.

Bond, G. L., and Tinker, M. A. *Reading Difficulties: Their Diagnosis and Correction.* New York: Appleton-Century-Crofts, 1973.

Boning, R. *Specific Skills Series.* New York: Barnell-Loft, 1962.

Brunner, E. C. "The DISTAR Reading Program." *Proceedings*, College Reading Association, Fall 1968, p. 9.

Burmeister, L. E. "Usefulness of Phonic Generalizations." *The Reading Teacher* (Jan. 1968a): 21.

Burmeister, L. E. "Vowel Pairs." *The Reading Teacher* (Feb. 1968b): 5.

Clymer, T. "The Utility of Phonic Generalizations in the Primary Grades." *The Reading Teacher* (Jan. 1963): 252–258.

Cordts, A. D. *Readiness for Power in Reading.* Chicago: Berkeley-Cardy, 1953.

Dolch, E. *Dolch Basic Sight Vocabulary.* Champaign, Ill.: Garrard Publishing Company, 1953.

Emans, R. "The Usefulness of Phonic Generalizations above the Primary Grades." *The Reading Teacher* (Feb. 1967): 419–425.

Emans, R., and Fisher, G. M. "Teaching the Use of Context Clues." *Elementary English* 44 (1967): 243–246.

Evertts, E.; Hunt, L.; Weiss, B.; and Cruikshank, S., eds. *The Holt Basic Reading System.* New York: Holt, Rinehart, and Winston, 1973.

Fay, L.; Ross, R.; and LaPray, M. *The Young American Basic Reading Program.* Chicago: Lyons and Carnahan, 1972.

Fries, C. C. *Linguistics and Reading.* New York: Holt, Rinehart and Winston, 1963.

Gates, A. I. *The Improvement of Reading.* New York: Macmillan, 1947.

Gillingham, A., and Stillman, B. *Remedial Training for Children with Specific Disability in Reading, Spelling and Penmanship.* New York: Author, 1956.

Glass, G. G. "The Teaching of Word Analysis through Perceptual Conditioning." *Reading and Inquiry*, IRA Proceedings, 1965, p. 10.

Goodman, K. S. "A Linguistic Study of Cues and Miscues in Reading." *Elementary English* (1965): 42.

Gray, W. S. *On Their Own in Reading.* Glenview, Ill.: Scott, Foresman, 1960.

Hanson, I. W. "First Grade Children Work with Variant Endings." *The Reading Teacher* 19 (April 1966): 505–507.

Harris, A., and Sipay, E. R. *How to Increase Reading Ability.* New York: David McKay, 1975.

Hester, K. B. *Teaching Every Child to Read.* New York: Harper and Row, 1964.

Huey, E. B. *The Psychology and Pedagogy of Reading.* Boston: Massachusetts Institute of Technology Press, 1908 and 1969.

McCarthy, D. "Language Development in Children." *Manual of Child Psychology.* New York: John Wiley, 1954.

McCullough, C. M. "Learning to Use Context Clues." *Elementary English Review* 20 (1943): 140–143.

McFeely, D. C. "Syllabication Usefulness in a Basal and Social Studies Vocabulary." *The Reading Teacher* 27 (1974): 809–814.

McKee, P. *Reading: A Program of Instruction for the Elementary School.* Boston: Houghton Mifflin, 1966.

Maney, E. *Reading-Thinking Skills.* Elizabethtown, Pa.: The Continental Press, 1963.

Moe, A. J. *High-Frequency Words.* St. Paul, Minn.: Ambassador Publishing Co., 1972 (a).

Moe, A. J. *High-Frequency Nouns.* St. Paul, Minn.: Ambassador Publishing Co., 1972 (b).

Patterson, D. G., and Tinker, M. A. "Readability of Newspaper Headlines Printed in Capitals and in Lower Case." *Journal of Applied Psychology* 30 (1946): 161–168.

Platts, M. E. *Spice.* Stevensville, Mich.: Educational Services, Inc., 1960.

Ramanaskas, S. "The Responsiveness of Cloze Readability Measures to Linguistic Variables Operating over Segments of Text Longer than a Sentence." *Reading Research Quarterly* (Fall 1972): 7.

Samuels, S. J. "Attentional Processes in Reading: The Effect of Pictures in the Acquisition of Reading Responses." *Journal of Educational Psychology* 58 (1967): 337–342.

Samuels, S. J., and Dahl, P. "Automaticity, Reading and Mental Retardation." U.S. Office of Education, Bureau of Education for the Handicapped, Occasional Paper No. 17, Project No. 332189, 1973.

Schell, L. M. "Teaching Structural Analysis." *The Reading Teacher* 21 (Nov. 1967): 133–137.

Schubert, D. G., and Torgerson, T. L. *Improving the Reading Program.* Dubuque, Iowa: William C. Brown, 1968.

Shibles, B. H. "How Many Words Does a First Grade Child Know?" *Elementary English* 41 (1959): 42–47.

Smith, F. *Understanding Reading.* New York: Holt, Rinehart and Winston, 1971.

Spache, E. B. *Reading Activities for Child Involvement.* Boston: Allyn and Bacon, 1972.

Spache, G., and Spache, E. *Reading in the Elementary School.* Boston: Allyn and Bacon, 1973.

Stone, C. R. "Measuring Difficulty of Primary Reading Material: A Constructive Criticism of Spache's Measure." *Elementary School Journal* 51 (1956): 36–41.

Taylor, W. L. "Cloze Procedures: A New Tool for Measuring Readability." *Journalism Quarterly* 30 (Fall 1953): 360–368.

Templin, M. "Certain Language Skills in Children, Their Development and Relationship." University of Minnesota, Institute of Child Welfare, Monograph Series No. 26, 1957.

Wardhaugh, R. "Syl-lab-i-ca-tion." *Elementary English* 63 (Nov. 1966): 785–788.

Wardhaugh, R. *Reading: A Linguistic Perspective.* New York: Harcourt, Brace and World, 1969 (a).

Wardhaugh, R. "The Teaching of Phonics and Comprehension: A Linguistic Evaluation." In *Psycholinguistics and the Teaching of Reading,* edited by K. S. Goodman and J. T. Fleming. Newark, Del.: International Reading Association, 1969 (b), pp. 79–90.

Wylie, R. E., and Durrell, D. D. "Teaching Vowels through Phonograms." *Elementary English* 47 (1970): 787–791.

Chapter
Eleven

Preview

Few deny the importance of comprehension in reading. Without it, reading has no value. However, considerable controversy exists concerning what comprehension is, and how it should be taught. Guszak defines comprehension and considers theoretical models and taxonomies.

He describes comprehension problems in detail, and discusses the reasons for these problems. And he emphasizes the importance of teachers' questions, defining the teacher's role in setting purposes, stimulating various levels of comprehension, and controlling pupil responses.

Ways of planning the comprehension program and strategies for teaching comprehension skills are discussed thoroughly, and in a way which is directly applicable in the classroom. Guszak shows how varied reading-thinking skills, cloze technique, and critical reading skills may be developed.

This chapter represents a synthesis of new ideas about comprehension. The author presents these in a contemporary, creative, and practical manner.

Reading:
Comprehension Skills

Frank J. Guszak, University of Texas

Objectives

After you have read this chapter, you should be able to:

1. List and discuss the outcomes described in Barrett's Taxonomy of Cognitive and Affective Outcomes.
2. List and discuss linguistic backgrounds, reading materials, instructional methodology, and primary learning disabilities.
3. Specify steps in the planning of a reading comprehension program, including the following: establishing realistic goals, building a tracking system for following pupil skills growth, acquiring needed subsystems, and scheduling direct teaching and pupil-managed learning components.
4. Describe effective means for establishing purposes or sets for reading, questioning, using cloze techniques, and stimulating critical reading.

Thorndike (1917) put reading comprehension in proper perspective with the simple statement, "Reading is thinking." A discussion of reading comprehension, therefore, must examine first the nature of thinking and second the application of thinking to the reading act. Basic definitions of *thinking, reading, comprehension,* and interrelated terms provide the background for this chapter. With basic definitions established, models of reading comprehension or "reading-thinking" are discussed and synthesized and some of the more common reasons for reading comprehension failure are explained. The last step is the pragmatics—how to plan reading comprehension programs and strategies for developing specific comprehension skills.

Definitions of Terms

Thinking is the inferred mental activity that takes place when a person senses and makes discriminations among people, objects, places, and ideas in his environment. Thinking can progress through varying levels of difficulty, such as cognition, memory, divergent thinking, convergent thinking, and evaluation.

Reading is thinking in response to selective graphic cues. As Goodman (in Harris and Smith, 1972) states, it involves the partial use of available minimal language cues selected from perceptual input on the basis of reader expectation.

Cognition means the discovery or rediscovery of something.

Memory is the retention for some period (long or short term memory) of that which is cognized (discovered or rediscovered).

Intelligence is often defined as a person's innate capacity for generating thought.

Comprehension refers to the process of generating thought. As pointed out in the definition of reading, that process is stimulated in reading by the response to selective graphic cues.

Models of Reading Comprehension

Some of the models which follow will illustrate some of the *processes* involved in comprehension, while others will detail some of the main *products.* Because of the immense complexity of the processing act, which is essentially unknown and only inferred, the reader may wish to give primary attention to the products, which are evident and describable.

Guilford—Structure of the Intellect

Guilford's model (1959) has become a classic for educational psychologists, curriculum makers, and others interested in thinking because it provides a three-dimensional model of the *operations* of thinking, the *contents* of thinking, and the *products* of thinking. It is difficult to talk about the processes of thinking without telling whether those processes are operating on symbolic, figural, semantic, or behavioral contents.

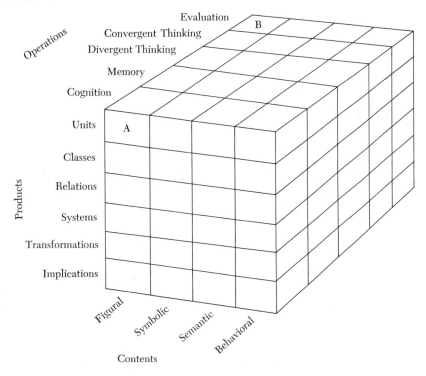

Figure 11.1   Guilford's Model.

Source: J. Guilford, "The Three Faces of Intellect" from *The American Psychologist* 14 (1959). Copyright 1959 by the American Psychological Association. Reprinted by permission.

In reading a story, we are carrying out the various *operations* listed in Guilford's model—most frequently, cognition, memory, and convergent thinking, that is, the process of reasoning or reaching likely explanations. Certain passages, however, remind us of related things, so that we see other possibilities (divergent thinking). All of these mental operations are taking place as we view some type of reading *material*, which may contain figural elements as well as symbolic (letters) and semantic (meaning association) elements. Reading material is not simply a set of meaningless letters (with sound counterparts) but rather a set of elements that triggers expectations and familiar meanings.

The result of the interaction of *thinking operations* upon *contents* (materials) produces thought products. Guilford describes these products in terms of units, classes, relations, systems, transformations, and implications. As we shall see in the following discussion of these theories, thought products are also described in other terms.

Bloom—Taxonomy of Educational Objectives: Cognitive Domain

The *Taxonomy of Educational Objectives: Cognitive Domain* (Bloom, 1956) grew from the efforts of examiners to standardize the various types of examinations that were being written to evaluate pupil understandings. In order to deal with the widely different types of thinking necessary to perform certain tasks, the group worked out a model of a taxonomy of thinking behaviors that could be built upon indefinitely.

Now an educational landmark, the Bloom Taxonomy serves as a guide to thousands of educators. They describe their educational goals in terms of the following progression of thinking skills:

1. *Knowledge*: The knowledge category is broken down in terms of increasingly difficult types of knowledge—for example, knowledge of specifics and knowledge of ways and means of dealing with specifics.
2. *Comprehension*: Comprehension is the ability to understand or generate logical thoughts about one's knowledge. The taxonomy differentiates between increasingly difficult comprehension tasks: translation, interpolation, and extrapolation.
3. *Application*: Application suggests that the individual can actually apply the knowledge and understandings to a simulated or real situation—for example, rebuilding a car engine or writing a short story.
4. *Analysis*: Analysis is the ability to analyze elements, relationships, and organizational principles.
5. *Synthesis*: Synthesis is the ability to take the elements of analysis and synthesize them into a unique communication (for example, a critique of a play), a plan, or a set of abstract relations (a novel mathematical formula, a working design of an invention).
6. *Evaluation*: Evaluation is the ability to place value on some thing or idea by judging it according to internal logic (logic within it) or by comparing it with other elements of the same type (external evaluation).

Sanders—Taxonomy of Questions

In a book called *Classroom Questions: What Kinds?* Sanders (1966) has developed a most valuable group of suggestions on questioning pupils for the various levels of thinking. For the teacher seeking further detail, such a reference is quite valuable.

While Bloom and his associates focused upon a classification of objectives, Sanders looked more closely at teachers' questions. The results of Sanders's view are seen in the following revised categories of the original Bloom taxonomy.

1. *Memory*: Memory is the process called for by teacher questions that require the recognition or recall of information—for example, "In what year did the American Revolution begin?"
2. *Translation*: Translation is the ability to change information into different symbolic form or language, called for in a question such as, "Would you summarize the events that led up to the American Revolution?"
3. *Application*: This is the ability to solve a "lifelike problem that requires the identification of the issue and the selection and use of appropriate generalizations and skills." A student might apply the lessons learned in a study of revolutionary history to potential causes of current revolutions in the world.
4. *Analysis*: Analysis is the ability to solve problems by examining the elements of the problem and using logical forms of thinking—for example, "Can you analyze the specific causes that are creating tension in the Middle East? Can you detail the historical tensions between Arabs and Jews?"
5. *Synthesis*: Synthesis is the ability to solve a problem that requires "original, creative thinking"—for example, "What kind of peace agreement might be negotiated in the Middle East which would satisfy the major combatants?"
6. *Evaluation*: The student evaluates something as good or bad, right or wrong, in accordance with some standards that he has developed—for example, he makes a judgment about the relative merits of the political party platforms in the election.

Barrett—Taxonomy of Cognitive and Affective Dimensions of Reading Comprehension

After analyzing and synthesizing the ideas of Bloom, Sanders, and others, Barrett (in Clymer's chapter, *1968 National Society for the Study of Education Yearbook, Part II*) developed a taxonomic structure that would describe the specific outcomes of reading. His taxonomy also attempted to describe the affective dimensions of reading. Consequently, the structure might permit the measurement of both understandings and feelings about various types of reading.

Essentially, Barrett's Taxonomy ordered reading outcomes as follows:

1. *Literal Comprehension*: Literal comprehension focuses upon those elements explicitly stated in the selection. It involves, for example, recognizing a piece of information or remembering a story character's name. The category is broken down into two major sub-elements—recognition and recall. Elements of recognition include recognition of

details, recognition of main ideas, recognition of a sequence, recognition of a comparison, recognition of cause and effect relationships, and recognition of character traits. Recall is the reproduction from memory of ideas that were explicitly stated in the selection read. Recall tasks, in increasing difficulty, include: recall of details, recall of main ideas, recall of a sequence, recall of a comparison, recall of cause and effect relationships, recall of character traits.

2. *Reorganization*: Reorganization is the analysis, synthesis, and/or organization of ideas or information explicitly stated in the selection. Reorganization tasks, graduated in difficulty, are as follows: classifying, outlining, summarizing, synthesizing.

3. *Inferential Comprehension*: Inferential comprehension involves the inferences that students make after reading explicitly stated materials. Such inferences might be either *convergent* or *divergent* thoughts that go beyond the statements on the pages. The hierarchy of inferential comprehension skills is: inferring supporting details, inferring main ideas, inferring sequence, inferring comparisons, inferring cause and effect relationships, inferring character traits, predicting outcomes, and interpreting figurative language.

4. *Evaluation*: Barrett's evaluation category is substantially the same as Sanders's. The reader must make evaluative judgments on the basis of either external criteria (comparisons with other sources) or internal criteria (comparisons within, such as internal logic or consistency). Evaluative thinking includes the following: judgments of reality or fantasy, judgments of fact or opinion, judgments of adequacy and validity, judgments of appropriateness, judgments of worth, desirability, and acceptability.

5. *Appreciation*: Appreciation, according to Barrett, involves all the previously described cognitive dimensions because it deals with the aesthetic impact of certain things on the reader. One reader may be deeply touched by a beautiful description at one moment, angered by a slanted argument at another moment, and delighted by a whimsical bit in the next paragraph. Many emotions cross the reader's mind as he reads for different purposes—including emotional response to the content, identification with characters or incidents, and reactions to authors' use of language and imagery.

Obviously, it is not necessary to hold every dimension of Barrett's Taxonomy in mind in order to develop written and oral comprehension tasks for children. Rather, the teacher needs to be aware of the various major groupings and seek to provide reading-thinking situations in each one.

A popular misconception is that "literal comprehension" questions are unimportant. This is nonsense, because literal comprehension forms the basis for higher level comprehension skills. The Bloom, Sanders, and Barrett taxonomies are not for the purpose of eliminating literal comprehension but rather emphasizing a need for the recognition and development of varied types of thinking.

Synthesis of the Reading Comprehension Models

Each of the previously discussed models provides a useful means for describing the products of reading comprehension. Perhaps some are more useful than others because of their explicit application to the outcomes of the task we call *reading*. The products, units, and classes of the Guilford model leave many of us thinking, "What's that again?" The Bloom and Sanders descriptions, though clearer, fall somewhat short of describing the kinds of observable behaviors that we might want to measure after our pupils read something. Probably the Barrett classifications give us the clearest set of descriptors of this group.

Common Explanations of Comprehension Failure

Why do some children have trouble with reading? Some of the most common answers blame linguistic backgrounds, conceptual backgrounds, inadequacy of reading materials (because of implied or demonstrated cultural bias), poor instructional methodology, confused goals, and limited instructional means.

While reading failures are probably the product of a number of factors, we have singled out the following major factors for brief discussion.

Linguistic Backgrounds

We no longer need sociologists to tell us that our Puerto Rican population is concentrated in certain areas of the country, that the black population is concentrated in large metropolitan areas, that migrant families are resettling in certain areas, and that white, middle-class families are moving to the suburbs. America is not the melting pot that it has been called. Instead, many groups are maintaining identification with their own and are turning inward more and more. Our concern here is not whether this trend is desirable or not but rather the implications of such a trend upon reading comprehension.

The melting pot concept is based on the assumption that the intermixing of various cultural groups produces a language common to all the groups and therefore fosters communication. In reality, however, communication problems abound. As far as schools are concerned, it has been charged that: (1) teachers cannot understand or readily communicate with their linguistically different pupils (Horn, 1970); (2) pupils cannot understand or relate to certain concepts in textual materials; (3) pupils cannot understand or relate with teachers who are linguistically different from them.

As a result of these charges, attention has been focused upon teacher preparation (Horn, 1970), the development of reading materials addressed to the needs of linguistically different groups (Robinett, 1965; Horn, 1970), and the development of a wide array of language development projects. Some of these have been notably successful (Bond and Dykstra, 1967; Cohen, 1970; Coleman, 1966).

Because reading comprehension is premised upon the pupil's conceptual backgrounds, some type of assessment of these backgrounds must be made before pupils begin reading the available materials. However, because of the difficulty of designing a speedy and effective measurement device, teachers are without means for making such assessments.

Specific measures of concept attainment do exist. One, the *Common Concepts Test* (Banathy et al., 1962) provides some assessments of specific concepts in parallel English and Spanish forms. Essentially, the tests are listening tests; the children are instructed orally to follow the direction of the examiner and perform some marking task. They are told, for example, "Mark the big ball."

Because tests such as the *Common Concepts Test*, as well as any number of listening subtests (as in some of the more popular reading readiness batteries and the *Durrell-Sullivan Reading Capacity Test*, 1970) require the specific language referents of certain concepts, it is possible that they measure some important elements in the child's acquisition of and progress toward linguistic maturity. Of course, it is possible that he might have the concept but not the language referent (for example, "far away"). However, if the child is to successfully read certain materials, he must have the language referents.

The most practical way to assess a pupil's ability to understand the materials he will be required to read is simply to read sections of such material and question the child about them. If he can retell the main portion of what he has heard or answer a majority of the questions (providing they are reasonable), the teacher has ample evidence of his ability to understand the material. This procedure will not indicate whether he has the necessary word recognition skills, but will end any speculation about the presence of understanding skills and receptive language skills.

It is important for teachers to realize that the language and cultural background of "linguistically different children" is not always responsible for their reading failures. Time after time, this author has seen these pupils reach frustration levels in reading but subsequently understand a majority of the material when it is read to them. Their reading problems are obviously not accounted for by linguistic differences or intelligence factors but rather by difficulties in managing the basic word recognition tasks.

Reading Materials

Pupils identify most readily with reading that stimulates their curiosity. The publishers of the major basal series have tried to make their books sure-fire interest generators, but they have not yet succeeded. When the adequacy of a given book or set of books is under question, the teacher should ask:

1. Can various cultural groups identify with this written material?
2. To what extent does the material have holding power for various children (cultural groups)?
3. To what extent do the linguistic structures of the material parallel the pupils' oral language structures (Strickland, 1962; Ruddell, 1965)?
4. To what extent can interest be generated while vocabulary and syntax are controlled for mastery in beginning reading instruction?

Added to these are concerns relative to the sex roles of boys and girls in stories, the roles of various cultural groups, the presence or absence of moral rules, and so on. Consequently, those who prepare materials must be cognizant of such things as the following:

1. Do the texts portray women in ways which stereotype them as mothers, maids, and playmates of men?
2. Do the texts illustrate women in such important roles as doctors, lawyers, and engineers?
3. Do the texts portray men in differing roles (male nurse, beautician)?
4. Do the texts portray minority group individuals in stereotyped roles (for example, blacks as custodians and bellhops)?
5. To what extent do the children see real life situations depicted in their readers (as opposed to idealized stereotypes)?

Instructional Methodology

Instructional methodology is shaped by the teacher's perception or definition of reading. A teacher who has a narrow definition of reading (one
which limits it to the sound-symbol decoding aspects) will teach children
primarily to relate sounds to symbols. Conversely, a teacher who considers
meaning most important will be mainly concerned with directing pupils to
realize that their oral statements can be reproduced in writing (Stauffer, in
Kerfoot, 1965). This is the language-experience approach, described in
greater detail in Chapter Seven. Here we will describe instructional
methodology designed to increase reading comprehension skill in terms of
two other approaches: the guided reading approach, and the workbook
approach.

Guided Reading Approach Authors of basal readers usually insert guiding
questions in the teacher's manuals. These questions are designed so that
the teacher can help the child understand the selection through the use of
(1) questions asked before the child reads a selection (or portion of a
selection), and (2) questions asked at the end of a selection (paragraph,
page, story, etc.).

The guided reading strategy grew from the work of Thorndike (1917),
and Judd and Buswell (1922), and others who found that pupils and
teachers alike were fixed on calling the words as opposed to determining
their meanings. In guided reading, the emphasis is on silent reading for
specific facts and ideas.

While the guided reading technique has been a highly accepted
methodology, it is not without its critics (Chall, 1967; Frase, 1967; Goudey,
1969; Guszak, 1971). They charge that in this method *teachers* tend to do all
the talking, few children actually respond to the guided questions, and the
thinking sets stimulated by the guided questions are too limited. These
failings and their avoidance will be discussed in a later section.

Workbook Approach Just as the guided reading portion of a basal program
has been a long-standing format, the accompanying workbook has been
considered a "must." Pupils reading from a certain basal often use a
supposedly parallel workbook that is intended to develop the various types
of reading skills. Comprehension skills in these workbooks frequently
include short stories utilizing the vocabulary and syntax patterns taught in
the reader, followed by a few questions (with multiple choice, open blank,
and true-false formats). There may also be questions in various forms
relating back to a story in the reader.

Some workbook pages provide excellent tasks for measuring and
stimulating various levels of comprehension. Other pages seem exceedingly

questionable. Perhaps one of the greatest problems is that the same tasks are administered to pupils with dissimilar needs. Few workbooks provide for individual differences.

Confused Goals

Definitions of reading and their implications for teaching continue to influence reading instruction. While most teachers agree that their primary reading objectives concern reading comprehension, the practice of measuring reading skill through the use of the "barber shop" style of round-robin oral reading continues to exist (Austin and Morrison, 1963; Barton and Wilder, 1964; Farr et al., 1969; Spache and Spache, 1969).

Perhaps most teachers are clear on the goal—efficient silent reading—and it is only the means which get confused. Nevertheless, the practice of emphasizing oral reading has to be at the expense of silent reading, if such oral reading forces the child to concentrate on pronunciation and expression.

Oral reading sessions involve numerous questionable practices that seem capable of short-circuiting reading comprehension. These include:

1. Excessive teacher interruption of the reading-thinking act.
2. Cueing on factors that do not require teacher prompts.
3. Excessive attention on the part of the child to precise pronunciation as opposed to precise understanding.
4. Damage to interest in reading which may result from tediously long sessions where good readers have to listen to poor readers.
5. Restricting the eye to travel only as fast as the voice (eye-voice span notion).

Watching teachers, parents, and other instructors of reading directing oral reading sessions, the author has observed (1) direct correction whenever the pupil deviates from the precise wording of the page, (2) the request or demand to sound out most unknown words, and (3) frequent impromptu sessions within the reading session to show the pupil how to attack the word (while the story is left hanging). Not only do these actions impede comprehension, they communicate to the pupil that the primary purpose of reading is accurate pronunciation. If comprehension is the foremost goal, teachers should seek to limit what they say while the pupil is reading. The purposes of their suggestions should be to get a pupil to reread something that does not make sense, read ahead to pick up additional cues, and so on.

Limited Instructional Means

Typically, the primary influences on comprehension development have been the teacher and the basal reader comprehension program (as detailed in the teacher's manual and pupil workbook). To a lesser extent, specialized comprehension materials such as the S.R.A. Reading Laboratories (Parker, 1961) have been a part of the set.

If programs are going to be tailored to individual pupil needs, direct teacher actions and pupil-managed comprehension tasks are going to have to be greatly expanded.

Direct Teacher Actions Direct teacher actions are those tasks that teachers employ in instruction. Because a very wide range of comprehension levels may be present in a single classroom, the teacher, for maximum effectiveness, must interact with more than one, two, or even three reading groups. He must instead learn means of working with a large number of groups and individuals, delegating questioning responsibilities, delegating checking responsibilities, assigning individualized, self-paced tasks, as well as sharpening specific techniques of stimulating reading-thinking skills.

All of us have seen dynamic teachers who can pose sharp questions, stimulate reflective responses, and create exciting learning experiences. Despite their dynamic qualities, we have seen their efforts go for naught when applied to inappropriate groups. The key to success, then, is the appropriate use of direct teacher actions.

Pupil-Managed Comprehension Tasks Direct teacher instruction alone cannot deal with the varying comprehension needs of children in a classroom. Increasing attention must be given to procuring and constructing "pupil-managed comprehension sets" such as the following:

1. Short story material with accompanying questions (available commercially in various formats).
2. Specific comprehension skill tasks, such as locating, remembering, following directions, and getting the main idea (available in separate skill materials formats).

If a wide array of such materials is available, pupils can be guided toward the appropriate skills materials, taught to use them, and ultimately taught to check and record the scores in a central folder. As a result of delegating these responsibilities, teachers can spend more time on direct teaching tasks, support tasks for learning problems, and specific skills.

Planning a Reading Comprehension Program

Like so many things, good reading comprehension programs seldom "just happen." They are the result of careful planning and execution. Because program execution is dependent upon sound planning, this portion of the chapter examines some crucial planning decisions. These decisions concern:

1. Establishing realistic goals.
2. Building a tracking system.
3. Acquiring needed subsystems.
4. Scheduling direct teacher- and pupil-managed components.

Establishing Realistic Goals

Comprehension goals are sometimes difficult to decide on. Different authors use different labels and list varying numbers of skills. The ultimate recipient of the confusing goals is the teacher who sees the following:

Basal Program's Goals

Identifying meaning of:
    word
    phrase
    sentence
Identifying story problem
Making and checking inferences
Grasping implied meanings
Anticipating actions
Perceiving relationships
    analogous
    cause-effect
    general-specific
    sequence
Forming sensory images
Sensing emotional reactions
Evaluating actions
Following plot
Comparing and contrasting

Teacher Goals

Literal
Inferential

Some teachers prefer to rely on intuition rather than on a list of specific goals. Inadvertently, they often neglect to develop many basic comprehension skills—locating information in reference texts, for example. Others may fail to develop some skills for the opposite reason—they are fearful of departing from the basal manual and rely too little on their own judgment. Obviously, neither extreme is satisfactory for the teacher who wants to develop the full range of comprehension skills.

Realistic comprehension goals must be those which the teacher internalizes and understands. The teacher should ask:

1. Can the behaviors be described easily (so they can be recognized)?
2. Can the behaviors be measured with relative ease?
3. Are such behaviors developed in the available reading materials?

The Barrett Taxonomy provides the most usable set of reading behaviors in terms of outcomes that can be described and measured. A teacher can work first from the major skills: literal comprehension, reorganization, inference, evaluation, and appreciation. Then he can determine how the parts of his reading program might contribute to the development of each skill. A first grade teacher might choose to focus upon a few basic skills of inference and literal comprehension. A fifth or sixth grade teacher might look into the various categories for more sophisticated skills—inferring main ideas, appreciating certain types of rhyme, and so on.

Since the behaviors are described rather precisely in the Barrett Taxonomy, they can easily be measured. The teacher must decide how the measurement should be done. He might use the following methods, for example:

1. Literal comprehension: Ask pupils to mark a specific sentence, tell what happened, or put cut-out sentences in order (as determined by story read previously).
2. Reorganization: Ask pupils to summarize orally or in writing, sequence cut-out pictures and sentences (representing outline of story), put items under organizers.
3. Inference: Ask students to predict from pictures or sentences, fill in details in outline story, or create visual representations of next event (after hearing preceding events).
4. Evaluation: Ask students to draw lines between inconsistencies in story, detect fallacious reasoning, mark unsupported claims.
5. Appreciation: Ask students to describe feelings for character, action, plot, description, and so on.

Often there are teacher questions listed in the basal manual, specific workbook pages, and other supplemental comprehension skills materials that can be used to test and develop the desired skills.

Building a Tracking System

Once a teacher establishes a set of realistic goals and writes them down, then what? The next step is to make a plan for tracking the various pupil needs and developments of the various skills. With so many children, skills, and materials, it seems improbable that any teacher can keep an accurate *mental* account of each child's needs and developments. Tracking systems such as the *Reading Skills Checklist* provide the teacher with means for noting increasingly complex skills.

Listed on the fourth level of the *Reading Checklist* are five major comprehension skills: predicting/extending, locating information, remembering, organizing, and evaluating critically. Each of these large skill areas is broken down into sub-skills.

By testing pupils for the specific skills on the checklist, the teacher can make appropriate entries on an individual pupil's *Comprehension Checksheet*. Figure 11.3 indicates that John needs to work on locating stories in the table of contents and remembering the sequence of the story.

As John masters the various comprehension skills, the teacher will put a plus (+) sign by each one. More skilled readers can note their own progress and needs on the checksheet.

Figure 11.4 reveals a more sophisticated set of comprehension skills.

The teacher has noted that Mary has specific needs in four of the five comprehension areas. First of all, she needs to sharpen her closure skills. Consequently, cloze tasks employing an every-fifth-word cloze pattern are prescribed. Presumably, such tasks might be needed because Mary is not inferring well enough to read efficiently.

Mary apparently needs work in locating words in the dictionary that involve going to the third letter for identification, work in rapid location in a phone directory, as well as location work using the legends of a topographic map.

The notation "Loft D" under *Remembering* suggests that Mary might profit by doing remembering tasks in a commercial specific skills series. Mary will read a brief selection and then answer questions about it.

Organizing needs indicated for Mary on the checksheet include the outlining of a story in sentences. She might outline a chapter in her geography book. Frequently, outlining will be preceded by comprehension tasks that involve the selection of the main events, ideas, or components.

Such tracking systems as the *Reading Checklist* and *Checksheet* cannot ensure that pupils will receive proper instruction. They can,

Predicting/Extending	Locating Information	Remembering	Organizing	Evaluating Critically

Predicts convergent outcomes from:
  pictures
  picture and title
  title
  oral description
  story situations
 	
Predicts divergent outcomes
 	
Explain story character actions
Explain gadget operations
Generalizes from sets of information in story(ies) (Include task of identifying an unstated **main idea**).
 	
Restores omitted words in context
 	
Labels feelings of characters, i.e. sad—glad
 	
Explains why story characters hold certain viewpoints
	Locates specifics within written materials
	  phrase(s)
	  sentence(s)
	  paragraph(s)
	  page numbers
	  parts of a story (beginning, middle, end, etc.)
	
	Locating information with book parts
	  titles
	  stories
	  table of contents
	
	Locating information with reference aids
	  picture dictionaries
	  maps (political)
	  dictionaries
	  encyclopedias
	  atlases
	  globes
	  telephone books
	  newspapers
		Remembering simple sentence content
		
		Remembering the content of two or more simple sentences in sequence
		
		Remembering the factual content of complete and complex sentences and sentence sets
		
		Remembering paragraph content
		
		Remembering story content
			Retells:
			  sentence
			  sentence set
			  paragraph
			  story
			
			Outlines orally the sequence of the story
			
			Reorganizes a communication into a:
			  cartoon
			  picture
			  picture sequence
				Makes judgments about the desirability of a:
				  character
				  situation
				
				Makes judgments about the validity of a:
				  story
				  description
				  argument, etc.
				by making both **external** and **internal** comparison
				
				Making judgments about whether stories are fictional or non-fictional by noting:
				  reality
				  fantasy
				  exaggeration
				
				Making judgments about whether the author is trying to amuse, bias, etc. the reader.
				
				Detects in reading materials the following propaganda techniques:
				  —bad names, **e.g.** wallflower
				  —glad names, **e.g.** superstar

4 COMPREHENSION

Figure 11.2   Reading Skills Checklist: Comprehension.

Source: *Reading Skills Checklist*, Services in Education, 300 E. Huntland Dr., Austin, Texas 78752. Copyright © 1972.

Predicting/Extending	Locating Information	Remembering	Organizing	Evaluating Critically
	Loc. stories in contents	Remember sequence of story events.		

COMPREHENSION CHECKSHEET

John

Figure 11.3   Comprehension Checksheet: John.

Predicting/Extending	Locating Information	Remembering	Organizing	Evaluating Critically
Restore every omitted word in _Zany Times_ (5ᵗʰ word closure)	Locate: - words in dict. (through 3rd letter) - phone nos. in phone dir. - topographic info. on map	Details in _Loft D_	Outline story in sentence outline Outline events in chapter	

Mary

COMPREHENSION CHECKSHEET

Figure 11.4   Comprehension Checksheet: Mary.

however, assist the teacher in making a systematic needs assessment. Identifying these needs can help the teacher determine the skills materials which must be purchased, borrowed, or constructed.

Once the materials are acquired they need to be made operable. When many different children are working in a variety of materials (as they should), the teacher does not have time to personally select the needed materials for each pupil on a daily basis. Rather, the effective teacher must: (1) organize the materials into a system whereby each pupil can readily find what he has to do, and (2) establish checking systems that permit pupils to get immediate feedback as to their success or failure.

Usually the range of skills within a given classroom will be so great that the teacher will need to set up a wide range of materials (from readiness tasks to involved evaluations). This requires that space be made available and organizer boxes arranged, and that the system be readily accessible to all the pupils. Consequently, the teacher may wish to build a series of boxes to house graded levels of difficulty, as shown below.

Through the use of individual contracts such as the following, the teacher might easily send pupils to the various boxes to do tasks unique to their needs.

Monday
P-6
R-5

This would mean that the student would be expected to go to the *Predicting* box, pull out P–6, perform the skill task, look up the answer(s) on the self-checking answer key, and then write down some description of his task accuracy in a manner similar to that suggested in the diagram below.

Monday	
P-6	$\frac{6}{8}$
R-5	$\frac{4}{4}$

The notations 6/8 and 4/4 would indicate that the pupil got 6 of 8 items correct on P–6 and 4 of 4 correct on R–5.

Acquiring Needed Subsystems

Tracking systems can have little value if the pupils do not have access to suitable tasks for developing the various types of comprehension skills they need. Many teachers lack the necessary materials; others may have such materials but lack the organization necessary to make them usable.

Some teachers are eager to make their own comprehension materials. While the attitude is admirable, the logistics frequently make such a task very difficult. Consequently, the emphasis here is upon the acquisition of commercially prepared materials which may prove less costly in the long run.

Major Skill Area	Specific Materials	Publishers
Predicting	Specific Skills Series (Using the Context, Drawing Conclusions)	Barnell-Loft, Ltd.
	Kaleidoscope Readers	Field Educational Publications
	Reading-Thinking Skills	The Continental Press
Locating	Specific Skills Series (Locating Information)	Barnell-Loft, Ltd.
	Study Skills Labs (Reference FFF)	Educational Development Laboratory
Remembering	Specific Skills Series (Getting the Facts)	Barnell-Loft, Ltd.
	New Reading Skilltexts	Merrill
	Reading for Meaning	J. B. Lippincott
	Reading Laboratories	SRA
Organizing	Reading Skills Laboratory	Houghton Mifflin
	Reading-Thinking Skills	Continental Press
	Reading for Meaning	J. B. Lippincott
Evaluating	Reading-Thinking Skills	The Continental Press

While such materials can be helpful, they can also accumulate on shelves if not organized into a working system. Such systems are not built over a weekend but require careful, deliberate planning. It is well to plan to work on one element at a time.

Scheduling Direct Teacher- and Pupil-Managed Components

Teachers often put too much time into comprehension tasks that have a low yield—certain guided reading tasks, for example. Since teachers have limited amounts of time, they need to use that time wisely.

One efficient method of organization is to program all children onto completely individualized contracts (which include comprehension tasks). This means that each child has a written contract or guide that he can readily understand. The contract directs him toward certain types of tasks to perform during the reading period (or larger contract period). It is his responsibility to perform the tasks called for on the contract, to check the correct answers from an answer key, and to record his score on the contract.

If the teacher has arranged the room with subsystems and all pupils are taking care of their own needs, then the teacher can plan the *direct teaching role* in terms of the following:

1. Direct teaching of small groups with common skills needs (or individuals with a particular need).
2. Determining the appropriateness of contract tasks.

Few teachers will be able to program their time so well that no direct teaching of small groups is necessary. Rather, the teacher's concern is to pull small groups together on the basis of need, quickly teach the needed skill element, and immediately send the group back to its individual contracts. Thus, small group meetings with the teacher might last five, ten, or fifteen minutes, seldom longer.

Daily planning by the teacher is crucial if he is to meet a wide array of needs. The following schedule shows what a single day's schedule might entail:

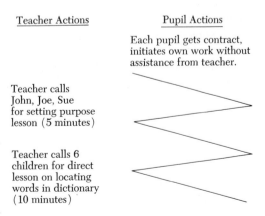

Teacher Actions	Pupil Actions
	Each pupil gets contract, initiates own work without assistance from teacher.
Teacher calls John, Joe, Sue for setting purpose lesson (5 minutes)	
Teacher calls 6 children for direct lesson on locating words in dictionary (10 minutes)	

The teacher might pull six or seven such groups during this day's reading period. The following day, he might pull some of the same groups as well as other groups. Some groups might meet as few as one or two times a week with the teacher for direct teaching instruction. These latter pupils can learn as easily or more easily without direct teacher intervention, so they are contracted to do so.

The teacher must also plan the time to *determine the appropriateness of each pupil's contract* and his work on it. Essentially, this means that the teacher must build some so-called "float time" into his schedule—time during which he is freed from direct teaching to move among the pupils as they perform their contract tasks. The following outline schedule shows both *direct teaching* and *determining* functions.

	Teacher Actions	Pupil Actions
8:30		Each pupil gets contract, initiates own work without assistance from teacher.
8:40	Teacher works with John, Joe, Sue on setting purposes.	
8:45	Teacher works with 6 students on dictionary.	
8:55	Teacher works with 5 students on main idea.	
9:05	Teacher floats.	
9:10	Teacher works with Tom & Henry on task.	

Using this schedule, the teacher can pull small groups daily, bi-weekly, or weekly for direct teaching of skills that are not as easily taught through pupil-managed tasks.

In the final analysis, the success of a comprehension program depends on the quality of the teacher's decisions about individual needs, provisions for meeting those needs (including materials and decisions about direct teaching tasks), and provisions for feedback to children about their accuracy and progress.

Strategies for Developing Comprehension Skills

While there must be a myriad of strategies for developing reading comprehension skills, the following were chosen because they are adaptable to most instructional settings:

1. Establishing purpose or set
2. Teacher questioning techniques
3. Cloze techniques
4. Critical thinking

Establishing Purpose or Set

Although it has often been said that "you can't judge a book by its cover," many people do make such judgments. They purchase a book on the basis of the pictures, the title, the author, the publisher, or various other bits of information. With experience, we can often weave several such pieces of data into rather good hunches about the contents of the book. Then we read the book to check our hunches.

Often, poor readers come to a book with no hunches, interests, or other motivation to find out what it is all about. After reading a paragraph, page, or chapter, these readers are uncertain of what they have read and where their reading is going. If, in beginning reading instruction, unusual emphasis is placed upon the correct pronunciation of the words, pupils frequently have little or no notion about the substance of the story.

There is little need to go through much of a ritual for setting purposes for interested pupils; the desire to find out is ample motivation. For students without such interest, however, a careful structuring of what to look for is useful.

Recognizing the importance of teaching children to anticipate and to use available data, Stauffer (1969) described the D-R-T-A (Directed-Reading-Thinking-Activity) Process. He suggested that a reading group should be composed of pupils reading at about the same level of competency in the same material. In Stauffer's words:

> The teacher sets the climate for a D-R-T-A and directs the process. This she does by the frequent use of three questions: "What do you think?" "Why do you think so?" and "Can you prove it?" While the children are reading, she remains available constantly to provide help as needed in word recognition or comprehension.

Group sizes considered most acceptable for good teaching range from eight to twelve members. Groups of this size permit pupils to compare and contrast their thinking with that of others in the dynamics of interacting minds. Each can observe how others use evidence, make assumptions or educated guesses, adapt rate, provide proof, and perform creatively.

The D-R-T-A process is usually initiated by the teacher, who gives the children a title, partial picture, or some other stimulus and asks them to speculate as to what they think it is, what it means, what will happen. Speculations are fielded from a number (or possibly all) the children in the group. Then the teacher asks them to look at more information and check their initial speculations for accuracy. The process is repeated, so that pupils learn to anticipate what might be happening on the basis of the given information.

Teacher Questioning Techniques

Teacher questioning usually involves the literal, interpretative, and evaluative dimensions. In the section which follows, we discuss each of these dimensions, asking, "How *do* we measure it?" and "How *should* we measure it?"

How Do We Measure Literal Comprehension? Literal comprehension is measured through the student's ability to recognize or recall some literal element of his reading.

Typically, basal reader programs include recognition questions designed to guide the pupil's understanding of the stories. Frequently referred to as the "guided reading strategy," this technique places the teacher in the role of a guide, asking leading questions in advance of a page or story. As the students respond to the task by searching out the element, the teacher can observe those who are succeeding as well as those who are not. The teacher asks questions to check out her observations. The whole task goes something like this:

Teacher: Find the name of the story.
  Child: "The Trip."
Teacher: Right! Now read the first page and find out when the Parks were taking a trip and where they were going. (Silence as pupils read.)
  Child: On June first.
Teacher: Good, and where were they going?
  Child: To the mountains.

Such questions guide pupils to the primary elements of the story and help them learn how to identify these elements themselves in a variety of reading materials and tasks.

This approach will be most valuable if:

1. The questions direct the pupils to the most important elements.
2. The directing questions are appropriate because they direct only when necessary.
3. A majority of the pupils provide their share of the answers.

Guidelines for recall-type questions are similar to those listed above. Teachers should be careful not to program children to look for insignificant information or to remember insignificant facts to the neglect of basic considerations.

How Should We Measure Literal Comprehension? Before questioning pupils, teachers should assess the reading content as to its most basic concepts and its sequence of events (and their relative importance). Such an assessment can indicate how many questions should be asked, and which are the most pertinent questions. Nothing is more defeating than to squeeze a multitude of questions out of something that has relatively little significance or meaning to the readers or, conversely, to miss many basic points in something of particular interest or importance. The first step to better assessment is to know the content, the backgrounds of the students, and the interrelationships of the two.

In oral questioning of the recognition type it is a good idea to *spot different tasks* by saying:

John, please find out why they were taking this trip.

Mary, find out where they were going and how long they were going to stay.

Sue, see if you can find things that tell how each of them feels about the trip.

Bob, I'm hoping that you can find out . . . .

Because students may complete these assignments very quickly, it is useful to *set purposes in advance* by writing them on the chalkboard and ask the students to *use a marker technique* (such as a paper clip) to mark the specific elements as they find them in their reading. This way the rapid readers can complete the assignment and go on to something else while the slowest readers have time to finish. A variation of this has the children jot down the page, paragraph, and sentence number of certain elements.

For purposes of measuring recall, group response instruments such as a color wheel can permit the teacher to find out precisely which students know the answers to specific fact questions. Each child holds a color wheel, and the teacher asks a question which may be answered by one of three colors.

Teacher: The real winner of the game was Tom, Bill, or Joe. Show blue for Tom, red for Bill, and white for Joe.
Pupils: (The pupils flash the color on signal to the teacher, who notes the responses.)

How Do We Measure Reorganization? Research and observation by the author suggest that we do not measure reorganization skill often enough. A study of the questions asked by certain second, fourth, and sixth grade teachers (Guszak, 1967) showed that less than one percent of the questions were of the reorganization type.

In all fairness to the teachers, we must acknowledge that it is difficult to measure reorganization skills by means of the oral techniques that characterize reading group discussions. Such tasks take time; when a single student is asked to summarize a story, for example, there is little left for the other group members to do but to make some additions or corrections.

How Should We Measure Reorganization? Silent strategies such as the following are good ways to measure reorganization:

1. *Sequence tasks*: Students are given pictures, sentences, or paragraphs and are asked to order them by their occurrence in the story. Teachers can construct the sequence sets themselves or use the ones that appear in basal workbooks.
2. *Synopsis, summary tasks*: When writing skills are fairly well developed, the pupils can go beyond the ordering of pictures and sentences and do their own summaries.

Reorganization is an important skill. It develops the student's ability to produce precise (short and accurate) reorganizations essential to effective communication.

How Do We Measure Inferential Comprehension? Before allowing the children to turn to the next page, the teacher asks, "Well, what do you think Jack's going to do?" Instantly the children respond: "He's going to swing from the rope." Inferential training is certainly useful; we can think and read more ably when we can accurately anticipate what is coming. By constantly anticipating and seeking verifications of our anticipations we can increase both the speed and accuracy of our reading.

Unfortunately, though, most teacher-pupil exchanges of the sort described above do not test inference but rather whether or not the students have (1) listened to another reading group encountering the same bit, (2) flipped ahead to see the picture, (3) read the next page. Consequently, much of the value of the exercise is lost. This will happen unless we rigidly hold every child to the same reading selection and page-turning pace.

How Should We Measure Inferential Comprehension? Through the use of D-R-T-A, teachers can guide pupils to make inferences on the basis of the smallest of clues, beginning with the title of a story, or a picture. After pupils make their inferences, they test them by reading. Upon verification, they make further predictions and set about further verification.

The following conditions are essential to carrying out D-R-T-A strategy:

1. The availability of multiple sets of readers, so that the fastest readers will not always preview the stories for the slower readers (multiple adoptions will allow for this).
2. The choice by the teacher or group leader of a significant organizer for inference—for example, a suggestive title or clue.
3. The sampling of a wide variety of conjectures so as to increase children's interest and sense of participation.
4. The accurate verification of the most precise conjecture.

Pupils will learn to sense when to apply convergent conjectures or divergent conjectures. At times, they will realize that they totally missed the significant cues that might guide their anticipations. Still, the exercise will refine the processes of anticipation that are capable of making us either strong or weak readers.

How Do We Measure Evaluation? Have you ever heard or used any of these questions?

Well, how did you like that story (ending, character, etc.)?
Would you like to be in a situation like that?
What kind of boy do you think Bill was?
Which story did you like best in this unit?

If you have, then you have surely heard the droning "yes" and "no" answers, as well as the "goods," "bads," and other judgment terms.

How Should We Measure Evaluation? There's nothing wrong in asking for evaluations if we ask for support for the evaluative statements. All too often, according to the author's research and that of others, we fail to plug in the "why" follow-up questions, such as:

Why did (or did not) you like the story?

Why would (or would not) you like to be in a situation like that?

Why do you think Bill was that kind of boy (whatever kind was indicated)?

Why did you like that story best?

Cloze Techniques

The cloze technique as discussed earlier not only provides the teacher with a valuable means of assessment, it provides him with a useful teaching tool.

When a pupil is tested with the cloze technique, his task is to effect closure in a selection such as the following:

It was the last _____ game of the year. _____ boys wanted to make _____ good showing before the _____ town crowd. Everybody would be in _____ stadium at the eight _____ kickoff time.

Tom laced up his _____ while Bill adjusted his _____ pads so they wouldn't _____ blisters. Most of the team _____ already dressed and were _____ up and down so _____ wouldn't feel so tense. A few boys were _____ the ball back and _____ across the dressing room.

The following are the steps involved in the preparation, administration, scoring, and judging of a cloze test.

Preparation

Step 1. Select a relatively free-standing selection of at least 275 words (55 cloze blanks) from the portion of the book you plan to use for instruction. (Free-standing means the beginning of a section, chapter—material that does not depend too much on previous information).

Step 2. Delete every fifth word.

Step 3. Type up the cloze test, being sure to allow the same number of spaces for every deleted word. The spaces should be large enough for the students to write in the longest words.

Administering, Scoring, and Judging

Step 1. Hand a test to each individual and ask him to write in the blank spaces the words he thinks should be there. Indicate that you realize the task is difficult and that it will probably be necessary for him to erase and change words as he works on the problem. Encourage the students to complete every blank. *Do not provide a time limit, as this is a power test.*

Step 2. When the tests are completed, mark every word that is not exactly the same as the deleted word from the story. Total up the number of correct responses (unmarked) and place that score at the bottom of the paper.

Step 3. Determine the difficulty level of each pupil's effort on the following scale (established by Rankin and Culhane, 1969):

Independent level—the student correctly replaces 61 percent or more of the deleted words. (Thirty-three words or more correct.)

Instructional level—the student correctly replaces 41 percent or more of the deleted words. (Twenty-two words or more correct.)

Frustrational level—the student correctly replaces 40 percent or less of the deleted words. (Less than twenty-two words correct.) *Note:* Bormuth (1967) recommends other percentage criteria for making such determinations.

Although the preceding testing may seem complex, it is actually rather easy from the standpoint of the examiner, as he has only to make a deleted word selection, administer it, and then compute the scores. The technique seems most appropriate for upper-grade teachers in assessing the readability of a multitude of instructional materials such as *My Weekly Reader* and content area texts (geography, science, English), as well as the assigned reading materials. In addition to the advantages of wide content sampling, cloze testing is rather simple in terms of administration and scoring. Among the disadvantages are the frustrating nature of the task (especially to children below fourth-grade level) and test score variation that appears more akin to topic content than vocabulary and sentence difficulty.

Teaching tasks which have been found to be successful are the following:

1. Pre-reading pupils can be taught to listen and insert the next word. For example:

   Familiar rhyme: Jack be nimble, Jack be _____.
         Sequence: One, two, _____, here we go.
         Expected: It became dark and the wind began to blow very _____.

2. *Cloze words* are those words that are covered on the pocket chart as the teacher seeks to get good "guesses" from pupils as to the missing words. For example:

Tom can _____ ball.

Mary _____ Tom can run.

3. *Cloze readers* are any pupil readers where flip tabs are placed over strategic words. The pupils are asked to read the readers and guess the covered words. Then they are to look and verify their guesses (presuming that they know the covered words).

4. *Cloze transparencies* can be made, in which every fifth word or so is omitted and a square of the word left in its place. The teacher can have children read aloud together or independently to provide closure words. Someone (probably the teacher) can write in the words suggested and change the words as pupils see a better word subsequently.

Critical Reading

If there is one thing all experts would agree upon, it is that we should teach our children to read critically. However, if we were to ask what "reading critically" means we might hear several different explanations, such as: (1) detecting propaganda devices in printed material, (2) differentiating fact from fiction, (3) measuring the validity of statements, or (4) evaluating what is read.

Wolfe, King, and Ellinger (1967) define critical reading as an analytical and evaluative process which requires the reader to make rational judgments about both the content and style of writing based upon valid criteria. Readers vary the criteria in accordance with the type of material and their purpose for reading it. For instance, if you were to read a sworn statement against you by another party, you would sift each statement carefully against the evidence that you had first hand. Thus, you would apply tests (criteria) of the accuracy of the statements. This definition of critical reading comes under "evaluative reading" in the Barrett Taxonomy. We could represent it in a formula as follows:

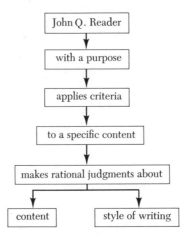

Suppose that John Q. Reader has received an advertising offer to buy a waterfront lot at the bargain price of $600. Because he would like to own such a lot, John reads carefully in order to determine whether the offer is legitimate or not. His purpose is to find out the following things:

Is a specific lot offered?
Are there hidden costs that are not represented in the brochure?
Is a valid title of ownership provided?
Is the lot actually above water, usable, etc.?
Is this strictly a come-on to get a prospective purchaser?

He will apply many criteria. He will, for instance, check the validity of the offering firm through the Better Business Bureau. He will check the wording of the brochure to determine what is specifically offered. He may check the offer out with his attorney to determine its legal basis. All these things will help him determine the *internal* as well as *external* validity of the offer.

On the basis of his findings, John will make a rational judgment as to whether the offer is good or bad. In this instance his judgment will primarily concern the content of the brochure, although the style of writing may influence him as well.

Two of the most important teaching applications of critical thinking or critical reading are set forth in the studies of Taba (1965) and Wolfe et al. (1967). We will discuss each briefly.

Taba Taba sought to design teaching strategies that would affect cognitive development. Two groups of teaching functions were identified: (1) teacher questions or statements which are managerial, and (2) teacher questions or statements which give direction to discussions and are related to the logic of the content and of the cognitive operations sought. This latter group included focusing questions, extending thought on the same level, lifting the level of thought, and controlling thought. Taba gives examples of teachers managing the thinking levels in various kinds of discussions. In order to be effective, the teaching strategy had to be carefully managed so as to allow for variation in the pacing of each step, determining how long to continue on the plateau of each step, and deciding when to make a transition to the next one. Because all of this was done in class discussions, it is difficult to see how Taba assessed the impact of the program on the individuals in the class.

Wolfe et al. Wolfe and her associates did the most extensive study of critical reading undertaken to date. Their research involved the teaching of critical reading strategies to children in the first six grades.

Initially, the researchers determined that the primary forms of content were (1) informational and persuasive materials and (2) literary materials. Obviously, different criteria had to be applied to the different types of material, so the authors determined the following criteria:

I. Informational and Persuasive Material
   A. Semantics in Writing
      1. Distinguishing between vague and precise words.
      2. Recognizing the difference between connotative and denotative meanings of words.
      3. Recognizing the persuasive use of words through such devices as name calling, glittering generalities, and plain folks. (Note: These are the commonly mentioned propaganda techniques used to brand rival politicians, show why one soap is the best, etc.)
      4. Evaluating the effectiveness of the use of words according to the author's purpose.
   B. Logic in Writing
      1. Recognizing and evaluating the validity of writing (examining validity of an argument, classifying into groups and sub-groups, determining appropriate use of all, some, and none statements, discovering unstated premise and conclusions).
      2. Recognizing and evaluating the reliability of printed materials (testing the reliability of information, determining soundness of premises and conclusions, detecting material fallacies such as hasty generalizations and false analogies, recognizing illogical reasoning in persuasive writing such as testimonial, band wagon, and card stacking, distinguishing between objective and subjective evidence, judging the reliability of information).
   C. Authenticity in Writing
      1. Recognizing adequacy of information or the necessity of suspending judgment.
      2. Comparing relevant information from multiple sources to recognize agreement or contradiction.
      3. Recognizing authoritative sources and evaluating them according to established criteria.
      4. Evaluating the qualifications of an author.
      5. Recognizing the publisher and sponsor's commitments.

II. Literary Materials
   A. Literary Forms
      1. Recognizing characteristics of various genres of fiction, such as: fantasy, realistic fiction, historical fiction, and biography.
      2. Distinguishing among variants of a particular form of fiction, e.g. fantasy, forms of make believe, fairy tales, etc.
      3. Developing criteria for evaluating each type of fiction.

   4. Recognizing the characteristic forms of poetry, e.g. narrative, lyric, haiku.
   5. Developing criteria for evaluating poetry.
B. Components of Literature
   1. Identifying and evaluating characterization.
   2. Identifying and evaluating plot structure.
   3. Identifying and evaluating setting.
   4. Identifying and evaluating theme.
C. Literary Devices
   1. Identifying and evaluating author's use of language.
   2. Identifying and evaluating mood of writing.
   3. Identifying and evaluating point of view.

Wolfe and her associates applied the preceding elements in a program and found that elementary school children (grades one through six) could be taught to read critically through the application of logical reasoning skills. While grade level did have a bearing upon the development of different types of skills, it was apparent that even the youngest children were capable of certain critical skills. Furthermore, the researchers concluded that instruction in critical reading had no apparent ill effect upon the children's growth in other reading skills.

Summary

Our definition of reading comprehension has a major influence on our classroom reading comprehension program. We have defined comprehension as a process of generating thought from selective graphic stimuli. The next step is to see what types of thought are involved in this process.

The Barrett Taxonomy of Reading Outcomes organizes comprehension skills into categories: literal comprehension, reorganization comprehension, inferential comprehension, evaluative comprehension, and appreciation. It is possible to break down these areas of thinking into the sub-skills of reading comprehension.

Reading comprehension development has been hindered by many factors. Most frequently, students' failures have been attributed to linguistic differences, poor matches between instructional materials and pupil backgrounds, erroneous instructional methodology, confused curricular goals that put emphasis in the wrong place (on oral reading, for example, or accuracy in pronunciation), unrealistic achievement expectations (expecting all pupils to achieve at the same rate in the same material), and limited instructional means (direct instructional skills, independent pupil comprehension materials).

To plan an effective comprehension program, teachers must establish realistic goals, build tracking systems whereby they and the students can gauge student progress through a program of increasingly difficult skills, acquire the necessary types of reading comprehension skills materials, and finally develop a plan that will make the best use of the teacher's direct teaching actions and the pupil's independent efforts.

Teachers may use many strategies for developing the desired skills, such as establishing differing sets for reading, using questioning strategies for developing varied reading-thinking skills, using cloze teaching techniques, and finding means for stimulating critical reading skills.

References

Allen, R., and Allen C. *Language Experiences in Reading: Teacher's Resource Book.* Levels 1 through 6. Chicago: Encyclopaedia Britannica Press, 1965–1967.

Aschner, M. J. et al. *A System for Classifying Thought Processes in the Context of Classroom Verbal Interaction.* Champaign: Institute of Research on Exceptional Children, 1965.

Austin, M., and Morrison, C. *The First R; the Harvard Report on Reading in the Elementary School.* New York: Macmillan, 1963.

Banathy, B. et al. *Common Concepts Foreign Language Test.* California Test Bureau, 1962.

Barrett, T. *Innovation and Change in Reading Instruction,* edited by H. Robinson. National Society for the Study of Education Yearbook, Part II. Chicago: University of Chicago Press, 1968, pp. 19–23.

Barton, A., and Wilder, D. "Research and Practice in the Teaching of Reading: A Progress Report." In *Innovations in Education,* edited by M. Miles. New York: Teachers College, Columbia University, 1964, pp. 361–398.

Bellack, A. et al. *The Language of the Classroom.* New York: Institute of Psychological Research, Teachers College, Columbia University, 1963 (mimeographed).

Bloom, B. S. *Taxonomy of Educational Objectives: Handbook 1, Cognitive Domain.* New York: David McKay, 1956.

Bloomfield, L. "Linguistics and Reading." *Elementary English Review* 19 (1941): 125–130.

Bond, G., and Dykstra, G. *Final Report: Coordinating Center for First Grade*

Reading Instruction Programs. Cooperative Research Project X-001. Minneapolis: University of Minnesota, 1967.

Bormuth, J. "Comparable Cloze and Multiple Choice Comprehension Test Scores." *Journal of Reading* 10 (1967): 291–299.

Botel, M., and Granousky, A. "A Formula for Measuring Linguistic Complexity: A Directional Effort." *Elementary English* 49 (1972): 513–516.

Cohen, S. In *Reading for the Disadvantaged: Problems of Linguistically Different Learners,* edited by T. Horn. New York: Harcourt, Brace and World, 1970, p. 212.

Coleman, J. *Equality of Educational Opportunity.* Washington, D.C.: U.S. Department of Health, Education, and Welfare, 1966.

Chall, J. *Learning to Read: The Great Debate.* New York: McGraw-Hill, 1967.

Chomsky, C. "Reading, Writing, and Phonology." *Harvard Educational Review* 40 (1970): 287–309.

Chomsky, N., and Halle, M. *The Sound Pattern of English.* New York: Harper and Row, 1968.

Durrell, D., and Sullivan, H. *The Durrell-Sullivan Reading Capacity and Achievement Tests, Primary Form A.* New York: Harcourt Brace Jovanovich, 1970.

Farr, R. et al. "The Problem with Reading: An Examination of Reading Programs in Indiana Schools." *Bulletin of the School of Education,* Indiana University, 1969.

Frase, L. "Learning from Prose Material: Length of Passage, Knowledge of Results, and Position of Questions." *Journal of Educational Psychology* 59 (1967): 266–272.

Fries, C. et al. *Merrill Linguistic Readers.* Columbus: Charles E. Merrill, 1966.

Frost, J., and Rowland, T. *Curricula for the Seventies.* Boston: Houghton Mifflin, 1969.

Gibson, E. "The Ontogeny of Reading." *American Psychologist* 25 (1970): 136–143.

Goldberg, L., and Rasmussen, D. *Science Research Associates Basic Reading Series.* Chicago: Science Research Associates, 1965.

Goodlad, J. "The Schools Versus Education." *The Saturday Review,* April 19, 1969, p. 59.

Goodlad, J., and Anderson, R. *The Nongraded Elementary School.* Revised ed. New York: Harcourt, Brace and World, 1963.

Goudey, C. "A Comparison of Children's Reading Performance under Directed and Nondirected Conditions." Unpublished Ph.D. dissertation, University of Minnesota, 1969.

Guilford, J. "Three Faces of Intellect." *American Psychologist* 14 (1959): 469–479.

Guszak, F. *Diagnostic Reading Instruction in the Elementary School.* New York: Harper and Row, 1972.

Guszak, F. *Reading Skills Checklist.* Austin, Texas: Educational Program Development, 1971 (a).

Guszak, F. "Strategies for Measuring Students' Understanding of Written Materials." In *Diagnostic Viewpoints in Reading,* edited by R. Liebert. Newark, Del.: International Reading Association, 1971 (b), pp. 41–47.

Guszak, F. "Teachers' Questions and Levels of Reading Comprehension." In *The Evaluation of Children's Reading Achievement, Perspectives in Reading No. 8,* edited by T. Barrett. Newark, Del.: International Reading Association, 1967, pp. 97–110.

Guszak, F. *Reading and Realism,* edited by T. Figurel. Newark, Del.: International Reading Association, 1969, pp. 110–116.

Harris, L., and Smith, C. *Reading Instruction through Diagnostic Teaching.* New York: Holt, Rinehart, and Winston, 1972.

Horn, T., ed. *Reading for the Disadvantaged: Problems of Linguistically Different Learners.* New York: Harcourt, Brace, and World, 1970.

Judd, C., and Buswell, G. *Silent Reading: A Study of the Various Types.* Supplementary Education Monographs, No. 23. Chicago: University of Chicago Press, 1922.

Kerfoot, J., ed. "First Grade Reading Programs." *Perspectives in Reading Number 5.* Newark, Del.: International Reading Association, 1965.

Lee, D., and Allen, R. *Learning to Read through Experience.* New York: Appleton-Century-Crofts, 1963.

Lundsteen, S. "Teaching Abilities in Critical Listening in the Fifth and Sixth Grades." Unpublished Ph.D. dissertation, University of California (Berkeley), 1963.

Manuel, H. *Pruebas de lecturas.* Austin, Texas: Inter-American Test Series, 1962.

Money, J. *The Disabled Reader: Education of the Dyslexic Child.* Baltimore: Johns Hopkins Press, 1966.

Parker, D. *Science Research Associates Reading Laboratory 1.* Chicago: Science Research Associates, 1961.

Rankin, E., and Culhane, J. "Comparable Cloze and Multiple Choice Comprehension Test Scores. "*Journal of Reading* 13 (1969): 193–198.

Robinett, R. "First Grade Reading Programs." In *Perspectives in Reading Number 5,* edited by J. Kerfoot. Newark, Del.: International Reading Association, 1965, pp. 132–149.

Ruddell, R. "The Effect of Oral and Written Patterns of Language Structure on Reading Comprehension." *The Reading Teacher* 18 (1965): 270–275.

Russell, D. *Children Learn to Read.* Boston: Ginn and Company, 1961.

Sanders, N. *Classroom Questions: What Kinds?* New York: Harper and Row, 1966.

Smith, F. "Phonology and Orthography: Reading and Writing." *Elementary English* 49 (1972): 1075–1088.

Smith, F. *Psycholinguistics and Reading.* New York: Holt, Rinehart, and Winston, 1973.

Spache, G. *Reading in the Elementary School.* Boston: Allyn and Bacon, 1964.

Spache, G., and Spache, E. *Reading in the Elementary School.* 2nd ed. Boston: Allyn and Bacon, 1969.

Stauffer, R. *Directing Reading Maturity as a Cognitive Process.* New York: Harper and Row, 1969.

Stauffer, R. *Teaching Reading as a Thinking Process.* New York: Harper and Row, 1969.

Stauffer, R. *The Language Experience Approach to the Teaching of Reading.* New York: Harper and Row, 1970.

Strickland, R. "The Language of Elementary School Children: Its Relationship to the Language of Reading Textbooks and the Quality of Reading of Selected Children." *Bulletin of the School of Education, Indiana University,* 1962.

Taba, H. "The Teaching of Thinking." *Elementary English* 42 (1965): 534–542.

Thorndike, E. "Reading as Reasoning: A Study of Mistakes in Paragraph Reading." *Journal of Educational Research* (1917): 323–332.

United States Office of Education. Seminars on Reading in the 70s. Washington, D.C.: System Development Corporation, Room 3318, 2500 Colorado Avenue, Santa Monica, California, 1970.

Wolfe, W. et al. *Critical Reading Ability of Elementary School Children.* Project No. 5-1040, U.S. Office of Education, 1967.

Chapter
Twelve

Preview

In this chapter, Roselmina Indrisano discusses three important aspects of the reading program: oral reading, reading in the content areas, and study skills.

She places oral reading in perspective, listing the major values of this important facet of the reading program. She also provides a great deal of information on the use of oral reading as a diagnostic tool and suggests teaching strategies for an effective oral reading program.

The remainder of the chapter focuses on reading in the content areas and study skills. The author believes these to be essential tools for independent learning. She offers practical suggestions for teaching strategies and appropriate materials.

This chapter will be of special value and of particular interest to those teaching or preparing to teach in middle schools or departmentalized elementary schools where expeetations of independent learning are high.

Reading:
Specialized Skills

Roselmina Indrisano, Boston University

Objectives

After you have read this chapter, you should be able to:

1. Describe the place of each of the specialized skills within the total reading curriculum.
2. Analyze the components of each specialized skill and the interrelationships among them.
3. Prepare diagnostic strategies to assess individual strengths and weaknesses in each area.
4. Utilize diagnostic findings to design instructional strategies aimed at enhancing strengths and overcoming weaknesses.

Historians tell us that the number of discoveries made between the birth of Christ and 1750 has been approximately equalled in each decade of the latter half of the twentieth century. Many of these discoveries have yielded knowledge new to human endeavor. Others require a re-evaluation of that which is known, a redefinition of truths held constant for centuries. This rapid growing and changing of human knowledge requires the contemporary citizen of the world to learn, unlearn, and relearn at a pace never before demanded. At such a time, the old dictum of "reading to learn" becomes as new as tomorrow.

Jenning's classic, *This Is Reading* (1965) provides a poetic guide:

Our theme must be repeated here: the value of a book in the changing world is in its ability to hold things still long enough for them to be understood, until fear and confusion can be replaced by something less paralyzing. The book can make yesterday's seven thousand years a golden tapestry for the hero's hall. With it we can measure today's dilemma against yesterday's defeats. It may not diminish the press of our anguish, nor tarnish the glow of our achievements but it can show us connections. It can give us perspectives (p. 75).

This chapter is concerned with the specialized skills required to gain those perspectives: oral reading, study abilities, and the processes required for effective reading in the academic disciplines.

Oral Reading

The Place of Oral Reading in the Curriculum

The classroom teacher introduces oral reading into the curriculum for several purposes. The oral reading program allows the *teacher* to:

1. Observe oral reading behavior as evidence of students' strengths and weaknesses and as clues to causes of reading disability.
2. Provide a model for effective oral reading, particularly the aesthetic aspects of voice, enunciation, and expression.
3. Share literary and informative materials with children for the purpose of motivating them to read independently.
4. Broaden children's knowledge in a given area or awaken interest in a new area.
5. Introduce disabled readers to literature and information at their listening level, though their reading level does not permit them to decode the symbols that contain the message.
6. Provide mutual opportunities for teacher and children to enjoy reading.
7. Introduce new readers to the process.

Oral reading helps the *learner* to:

1. Understand more fully the message conveyed by the poet or dramatist who writes for the voice rather than the eye.
2. Share an aesthetic experience with others through interpreting a piece of literature.
3. Exchange information or present a different point of view.
4. Motivate others to enjoy the printed word.
5. Serve as a model for younger children or less able readers.
6. Analyze personal reading behavior as a means of self-improvement.

Values and Limitations of Oral Reading

In any discussion of values and limitations, it is well to remember that both beneficial and detrimental effects are often a product of the teacher's efforts rather than the process itself. It is the teacher's sensitivity to the nature of the processes of reading and learning that makes it possible for the values to be realized and the limitations overcome.

Shortly after the death of Adlai Stevenson, Norman Cousins (1965, p. 12) wrote an editorial about the scholarship of the late statesman. Cousins wrote, "A book to him was not just a reading experience, but was an opportunity for dialogue." This phrase, "opportunity for dialogue," describes the essence of the potential values of oral reading. The benefits for both teacher and learner may be analyzed as: (1) diagnostic, (2) instructional, (3) motivational, (4) cognitive, and (5) aesthetic. We will discuss each of these values below.

Diagnostic Values The oral reading process is an effective diagnostic tool. It provides a fine opportunity for assessment by the teacher and for self-analysis by the learner. Because silent reading *is* silent, that process lends itself only to analysis of level, rate, mechanics, and comprehension and recall. Furthermore, the greater part of the analysis can be done only after the student has finished reading, although the skillful diagnostician becomes an astute observer of signals students emit while they read. By contrast, in the oral reading process, every word is vocalized; word identification and the communication aspects such as phrasing, voice, enunciation, and expression are immediately audible to the diagnostician and can provide clues to comprehension difficulties. The teacher may also test comprehension directly, by questioning students after they read or at any point during the reading. Detailed procedures for developing, administering, scoring, and analyzing oral reading through a teacher-devised informal test are included in the next section of this chapter.

For the *learner*, self-analysis has been found to improve both motivation and performance (ASCD, 1962):

> Perhaps some blocks to learning could be prevented by early confrontation and assessment and by positive approaches to improvement in self and content learnings. In any event, more positive views of self are possible when one is able to feel and know his needs and values more precisely. He can then begin to take charge of experiences for changing them. Thus the individual can begin to move away from an inadequate concept of self toward a sense of can-ness (p. 112).

Oral reading can help students toward this goal. By listening to taped samples of their reading, children can analyze their strengths and weaknesses as a means of improving their reading. To facilitate this process, suggestions are provided in the section on teaching strategies.

If oral reading is to be an effective diagnostic tool, it must be an ongoing part of the reading program, and teachers should base their instruction on the findings. Teachers may plan for periodic oral reading inventories, perhaps taped so students may play back previous samples for the purpose of noting improvement and redefining goals. The use of the tape technique facilitates a cooperative relationship between teacher and learner. This sharing can be extended to the instructional setting if the teacher will take the time to explain the relationship between the teaching materials or strategies to be used and the diagnosis mutually discovered.

Instructional Values If teaching materials or strategies are ineffective, the value of oral reading can be limited. In selecting materials, teachers should consider the ability and experiential background of the child. Material should be appropriate to the instructional level and to the learner's language and concept development. Building a meaningful background by providing children with real and vicarious experiences before they read makes oral reading more valuable.

Evidence and experience have shown that some teaching strategies are effective, and others should be avoided. An effective strategy is to have the student prepare his presentation through purposeful silent reading, even if that purpose is simply to rehearse his performance. Related to this performance is a strategy to be avoided. If every child in the group has his own copy of the material, why should one member read orally? Unless the material is to be read by several readers, as in a play, or is beyond the reading level of the other members, the content could be more efficiently read silently by the group than by an oral reader.

Oral reading is most valuable, then, when there is meaningful preparation by the reader and meaningful response by the audience. Under these conditions, oral reading provides the teacher with a promising instructional tool, particularly when used with beginning and disabled readers. The openness of the process permits the teacher to share much of the experience with the child.

Effective oral reading instruction focuses not only on the mechanics of the process, but more importantly on the content of the material. An oral reading lesson is the natural setting for assisting children to build concepts and associate them with the labels which are words. Oral reading is a language process, and therefore a thinking process with great potential for learning.

For a learner, particularly one who is just beginning to read or one who has difficulty in mastering the process, oral reading brings the security of immediate assistance. Silent reading can be a lonely puzzle unless one is willing to ask for help, but oral reading is a shared experience, affording mutual learning for the teacher and the child.

Additionally, oral reading provides for the development of language and speech skills and is often a youngster's first opportunity to gain insight into the interrelationships among the language arts. He listens while others read and uses his own speaking powers to read what another has written. Thus he may begin to understand that reading is that magic process which allows him to communicate across time and space, with a man who lived long ago and with a child who is seated next to him.

Motivational Values For the teacher, the value of motivating children to be open to learning cannot be underestimated. Krathwohl (1964, p. 57) has stated, "One of the main kinds of affective-domain objectives which are sought as means to cognitive ends is the development of interest as motivation."

To introduce youngsters to Mr. and Mrs. Mallard or to Charlotte and Wilbur is to initiate a friendship with Robert McCloskey (1941) and E. B. White (1952) as well. Such company can make children want to read well in order to widen their circle of acquaintances in the world of books. To introduce children to oceanography and outer space is to show them that the world in which they live can be extended, through books, below its surface and beyond its horizons. Daily oral reading by a teacher who enjoys the experience is one promising means to the cognitive end of effective reading.

Recent interest in the learner as teacher suggests the motivational value of youngsters' reading to others, perhaps cooperatively in teams or in small groups, or to an audience of younger or less able readers. The content may be selected from library shelves, from the youngster's own creative writing, or from pupil specialty reports completed as a result of research and inquiry.

Cognitive Values In his classic, *How to Read a Book*, Adler (1972) has written:

> The art of reading, in short, includes all the same skills that are involved in the art of discovery: Keenness of observation, readily available memory, range of imagination, and, of course, a reason trained in analysis and reflection. . . . To whatever extent it is true that reading is learning, it is also true that reading is thinking (p. 43).

This relationship between reading and thinking has been well established. In reading orally to children, teachers can stimulate concept development for all youngsters and especially for those whose listening ability is better developed than their reading ability. They can also provide the opportunity for children to experience vicariously places they have not visited, events they have not witnessed, and people they have not met.

Thoughtful questions about content can stimulate the development of thinking at all levels, from memory to evaluation. Sanders (1966) has provided insight into the effect of teachers' questions on the cognitive development of children. Chapter Eleven deals with this issue in detail.

For a learner, giving voice to the printed word in oral reading can clarify concepts which were ambiguous before or relationships among concepts already familiar.

A research project or a collection will gain added value if a youngster is allowed to share his knowledge with others. The oral reading of such reports affords opportunities for youngsters to gain new insights into the concepts they prepare to explain to others. Piaget (1964, p. 18) has written, "Learning is possible only when there is active assimilation."

Aesthetic Values It is important for the teacher to keep in mind the interrelationships among the language arts in relation to oral reading. These interrelationships are perhaps nowhere more apparent than in material written for speaking and listening—poetry, drama, and some aspects of humor.

These art forms are created for the human voice and can only be fully appreciated when expressed orally. To present "Jonathan Bing" to a child for silent reading is like presenting a Neil Simon comedy in paperback to an adult. Each must have the benefit of the nuances of speech to be fully enjoyed.

Participation in choral reading of poetry and cooperative reading of plays stimulates an aesthetic reaction while enhancing the meaning of the content.

Applying oral reading activities to other creative arts is a logical extension of the process. A child who creates illustrations or puppets to accompany his presentation, or who selects background music for his performance, is discovering the relationships between art, music, and reading.

Perhaps one value of oral reading that encompasses all others is sharing humor. Of the art of teaching, Highet (1950) says:

> When a class and its teacher all laugh together, they cease for a time to be separated by individuality, authority, and age. They become a unit, feeling pleasure and enjoying the shared experience. If that community can be prolonged, or reestablished, and applied to the job of thinking, the teacher will have succeeded (pp. 56–57).

Comparison of Oral to Silent Reading

In comparing oral to silent reading, Russell (1961) states,

> Oral reading, like silent reading, involves comprehension, vocabulary, speed, and accuracy. In it knowledge of vocabulary and accuracy are

almost synonyms. Comprehension and speed, however, operate differently in oral reading and silent reading . . . (p. 122).

Comprehension Language and thinking are the essential components of reading—both oral and silent. The reader must decode the language symbols and respond cognitively in order to recreate the author's meaning. In oral reading, however, the purpose is to share that meaning with others, and the reader must not only comprehend the message, he must convey it effectively. The added dimensions of phrasing, voice, expression, and enunciation make oral reading the more complex process. An analysis of the relationship of each of these factors to comprehension is essential for the teacher of oral reading.

Phrasing is the product of comprehension, since phrases are units of thought. Proper phrasing is the result of understanding the author's message and perceiving the relationship of the parts (or phrases) to the whole (sentences, paragraphs).

Proper expression is the product of comprehension and interpretation, since expression is an indication of the reader's insight into the deeper meaning of the message. The voice is the instrument for expressing that insight. Enunciation and pitch are also related. Enunciation is the speech skill which results in clear and accurate diction, while pitch implies meaning through the rise and fall of the voice. It may be said that enunciation and pitch are tools of the voice; the voice is the tool of expression and phrasing; and expression and phrasing are tools of communication.

It must be added here, however, that the oral reading process is dependent upon physical and affective factors as well as cognitive factors. Symptoms such as a high-pitched voice may not necessarily indicate faulty comprehension, but rather, tension. Similarly, problems in enunciation may be the result of a speech problem which is physiological or psychological in origin. In observing oral reading behavior, the teacher will need to be aware of the possible relationship of the communication abilities to factors other than comprehension.

Rate The essential differences in rate of oral and silent reading were discovered early in the history of reading research. The earliest standardized tests, published in 1915, included measures of speed of reading (Smith, 1965, p. 161). Recently, our technological society has become increasingly interested in rate of reading, but the emphasis has shifted. Today's teachers of reading encourage youngsters to be flexible in both rate and style of reading, and to use different rates and styles for different purposes.

McDonald (1963) explains the relationship between rate and flexibility as follows:

The flexible reader, as the result of his attention to purpose, difficulty of material, complexity of theme, and background knowledge, makes many adjustments of reading approaches and specific techniques. These adjustments may be made within a single section or even a single paragraph of an article. . . . Variability in rate, however, is *not* the *cause* of flexible reading. Rather, rate variability is the result of flexible reading approaches (p. 83).

Two processes are especially important in a discussion of rate of oral reading: listening and speaking. While the average speaker can comfortably utter 250 words per minute, the average listener can, depending upon concept load, comfortably receive an average of 150 words per minute (Taylor, 1964). The effective oral reader presents the material at a rate appropriate for his audience.

Though the rate of the average speaker exceeds the rate of the average listener, the mature oral reader can never approximate the potential speed of the mature silent reader. Oral reading, dependent upon the voice, must be slower than silent reading, which is dependent upon the eye.

Durrell (1956, p. 174) compares the rate of oral and silent reading of elementary children:

Grade	1	2	3	4	5	6
Oral Reading	45	80	110	135	150	170
Silent Reading	45	78	125	156	180	210

For beginning readers, there is little or no difference between the rates of silent and oral reading. As children develop maturity in reading, the difference increases as a result of increased proficiency in the decoding process.

Reading researchers are agreed on the following guidelines with regard to rate of reading:

1. Flexibility is a major goal.
2. Silent reading lends itself to the development of more rapid rates than oral reading.
3. Rate of reading is not emphasized at the primary level.
4. No attempt should be made to increase rate until basic skills and abilities have been mastered.
5. The reader's purpose should be the basis for decisions regarding rate and style of reading.

Stauffer (1969, pp. 41–42) has designed a process to enhance reading and cognitive abilities and to teach youngsters to adjust rate to purpose and to use oral and silent reading as group and individual needs indicate. The process follows these steps:

1. Identifying purposes of reading.
2. Learning to adjust rate of reading to the purposes declared and to the nature and difficulty of the material.
3. Observing the reading.
4. Developing comprehension.
5. Fundamental skill training activities: discussion, further reading, additional study, writing.

Since the effectiveness of any teaching strategy depends upon the teacher's ability to adjust the approach to the individual needs of the learners, the next section will deal with procedures for diagnosis.

Procedures for Diagnosing Oral Reading

Two types of diagnostic tools are available—formal published tests and informal, teacher-created tests. The former are generally administered by a trained reading specialist, but it is well for the classroom teacher to be aware of their availability and their functions. Of very real benefit to the classroom teacher are the informal, teacher-constructed tests created from classroom materials and designed to meet the individual needs of the children for whom they are planned.

Published Tests The tests listed below include (1) measures of oral reading and (2) diagnostic tests which include subtests of oral reading.

Tests of Oral Reading

Gilmore Oral Reading Test:

Author	John V. Gilmore
Publisher	Harcourt Brace Jovanovich, Inc.
Date	1951–1968
Range	Grades 1–8
Scores	accuracy, comprehension, rate
Time	15–20 minutes
Forms	C, D

Gray Oral Reading Tests:

Author	William S. Gray
Publisher	The Bobbs-Merrill Co., Inc.
Date	1963–1967
Range	Grades 1–16 and adults
Scores	accuracy, rate, comprehension
Time	(untimed)
Forms	A, B, C, D

Tests Including an Oral Reading Subtest

Diagnostic Reading Scales:

Author	George D. Spache
Publisher	California Test Bureau/McGraw-Hill Book Co.
Date	1963–1972
Range	Grades 1–6 and retarded readers in grades 7–12
Scores	(oral reading)
Forms	(one)

Durrell Analysis of Reading Difficulty:

Author	Donald D. Durrell
Publisher	Harcourt Brace Jovanovich, Inc.
Date	1933–1955
Range	Grades 1–6
Scores	(oral reading)
Forms	(one)

Gates-McKillop Reading Diagnostic Tests:

Author	Arthur I. Gates and Anne S. McKillop
Publisher	Teachers College Press, Columbia University
Date	1926–1962
Range	Grades 2–6
Scores	(oral reading)
Forms	I, II

Informal Tests One of the most useful techniques for diagnosis is the informal oral reading inventory. It is constructed by the teacher from instructional materials and administered in the classroom setting. The following are suggested guidelines for the preparation, administration, scoring, and analysis of a teacher-made oral reading test.

1. *Preparation*
   a. Select a series of three graded passages, one at the level of the grade placement, one at the level above, and one at the level below. These three passages will meet the needs of the majority of children, but for significantly advanced or disabled pupils, additional paragraphs will be necessary.

      The content should be appropriate for the experiential background of the children to be tested; for example, children who live in urban environments might be provided with material which describes an urban setting. Whatever the content, each passage should present a meaningful whole. The number of words should be increased at successive levels.

Primer–Level 1	50– 75 words
Levels 2–3	75–100 words
Levels 4–6	125–150 words

b. Prepare a series of questions for each passage. The types of questions should be appropriate for the content and provide the teacher with opportunities to evaluate several levels of comprehension (Barrett, 1968, pp. 19–23).

To assist the teacher in preparing an informal oral reading test, a sample is included here. The material is taken from a literature series at the fourth level; it is non-fiction, selected for its universal appeal to youngsters in urban, suburban, and rural settings.

History of the Ice Cream Cone

Until the turn of this century, ice cream sold by street vendors was served in glass dishes, which required a great deal of washing and care. And customers were always breaking the glasses or walking away with them.

This unsatisfactory and expensive means of serving ice cream was changed in 1896 when the first ice cream cone was invented. The inventor was an Italian immigrant, named Italo Marchiony, who sold ice cream from a pushcart in the streets of New York City. Mr. Marchiony got tired of washing his serving dishes and buying new ones to replace those that had been broken, so he decided to make a new kind of container for ice cream. He baked a thin cookie and rolled it up into the shape of a cone. Then he scooped ice cream into the cone (Martin and Brogan, 1972, pp. 200–201).

Questions:

Contextual

1. What is a *vendor*?

Literal comprehension

2. What did the vendors use to bring the ice cream to the streets where it was sold?
3. How was the ice cream served before the cone was invented?

Reorganizational

4. Pretend you are writing a news story of the invention of the ice cream cone. Tell who—what—when—where.
5. Describe the steps in making the first ice cream cone.

Critical

6. Why was the ice cream cone invented?
7. Why did the inventor decide upon a cone shape?

Evaluative

8. How does this information compare to what you know about ice cream cones?

Table 13   Oral Reading Test Questions

Fiction	Primer–Level 1	Levels 2–3	Levels 4–6
Contextual	1	1	1
Literal	1	2	2
Inferential	1	1	2
Creative	1	1	2
Appreciative	1	1	1
Total	5	6	8

Non-fiction	Primer–Level 1	Levels 2–3	Levels 4–6
Contextual	1	1	1
Literal	1	2	2
Reorganizational	1	1	2
Critical	1	1	2
Evaluative	1	1	1
Total	5	6	8

2. *Administration*
   a. The oral reading test must be administered individually. The teacher must therefore plan for the other children to be meaningfully occupied during the testing. It is recommended that the purposes and procedures of the testing situation be explained to all the children in order to create an optimal testing situation—a feeling of ease on the part of the child being tested and a spirit of cooperation among the children who have had their turn or who are waiting for it.
   b. It may be helpful to tape-record the child's reading for more careful analysis at a later time. Such a tape may also be shared with the child as a vehicle for self-analysis.
   c. When beginning the test, select a passage at the level of probable success and ask the child to read the material without prior silent reading. If the passage appears too difficult, the teacher explains that she will select a more suitable paragraph and provides the child with

a passage at a lower level. The reverse procedure may be adapted if the material appears too easy for a given child.

d. Establish the instructional level at the point where the child makes no more than one error in twenty running words with good comprehension.

e. At the instructional level, the teacher asks the comprehension questions and notes the child's reading and comprehension abilities on the checklist provided in the next section.

f. For children who are experiencing real difficulty, it is helpful to analyze errors more closely. The following marking system will assist teachers in this process. It is recommended that a record blank be prepared by typing a copy of the material the child will read, leaving triple spaces for marking.

Marking System for Errors

substitutions—~~in~~ (cross out word or phrase; write child's pronunciation) [it]

words added—in the house (∧ plus added word) [little]

words omitted—~~in the house~~ (– – – through the word or phrase omitted)

words unknown—house (write *P* above the word pronounced for the child) [P]

Marking System for Habits

phrasing—in/the/house/ (vertical line indicates phrasing)

hesitation—in the house (*H* to show a pause of two seconds or more) [H]

repetition—in the house (*R* above word or phrase repeated) [R]

punctuation ignored—X (*X* through the mark ignored)

3. *Analysis*
   a. While the determination of the instructional level is the major purpose of the informal oral reading inventory, there is much to be gained through a careful analysis of the child's reading behavior. Such an analysis can provide a blueprint to guide the teacher in individualizing instruction. Using the checklist below, the careful diagnostician may observe these factors:

Word Identification
   1. phonic, structural patterns in errors
   2. phonic, structural patterns in unknown words

3. visual patterns in unknown sight vocabulary
4. effect of words omitted and/or added on meaning
5. effect of substitutions on meaning

Communication
1. effect of word identification on phrasing, voice, and enunciation
2. effect of comprehension on phrasing and expression
3. effect of repetition, enunciation, and phrasing on comprehension
4. effect of experiential deficiencies on comprehension
5. tension—cause or effect?

Oral Reading Checklist

Word Identification

_____ words omitted
_____ words added
_____ substitutions
_____ sight vocabulary inadequate
_____ word analysis inadequate
_____ no attempt at analysis

Communication
_____ phrasing inappropriate
_____ phrasing inadequate (word by word)
_____ repetition of words or phrases
_____ punctuation ignored
_____ voice high pitched
_____ voice too soft
_____ enunciation difficulties
_____ inadequate expression
_____ language background inadequate
_____ tension

Comprehension

(Fiction)
_____ contextual
_____ literal
_____ inferential
_____ creative
_____ appreciative
(Non-fiction)
_____ contextual
_____ literal
_____ reorganizational
_____ critical
_____ evaluative

In selecting teaching strategies and materials, teachers should be guided by the needs revealed in the diagnosis. Specific needs may be translated into instructional goals. The succeeding sections of this chapter will offer instructional strategies.

Teaching Strategies

As defined here, reading is a language process, a cognitive process which enables a reader to communicate with a writer through the medium of symbols, or words. In the domains of learning, reading is both cognitive and affective, demanding the active involvement of the thoughts and feelings of the reader. Guidelines are suggested and strategies planned with a view to the needs of the child as well as the requirements of the process. Reading is an interaction between reader and writer. Learning to read is an interaction between child and process.

General Guidelines for Teaching Oral Reading

1. The *climate* is open, the potential for the active involvement and success of each learner is inherent in the plan.
2. The *goals* are real and realistic for teacher and learners, with purposes clearly defined and attainable, though not necessarily identical for each child.
3. The *material* is suitable for the children, the content is inherently interesting, and the level is appropriate for instruction.
4. *Experiential background* is provided through real or vicarious experience.
5. *Decoding* is facilitated through adequate preparation, assisting youngsters to utilize phonic patterns, structural elements, and/or context as aids to word recognition.
6. Meaningful *silent reading* precedes the oral presentation.
7. *Presentation* requires effective oral reading by providing an audience for the reader.
8. *Questions* for discussion are prepared to facilitate the development of thinking abilities and to increase and evaluate comprehension.
9. *Evaluation* is positive, designed for the purpose of learning about learning, and shared by teacher and learner.
10. *Follow-up* activities are based on the evaluation, planned to meet individual purposes and needs.

Strategies for Effective Oral Reading

1. *Class News Report:* A daily or weekly newscast is prepared by a group of editors and read to the class by a group of reporters. Categories are selected on the basis of the maturity and abilities of the children. Some possibilities are:

   international, national, local, school, and class news
   editorials and rebuttals
   weather analyses and forecasts
   human interest stories
   announcements of community, school, and class events
   sports news and commentaries
   fashion reports
   reviews of movies, books, and television programs
   advertisements

2. *Variations on a Theme:* The group selects a topic and each member shares something which contributes to their knowledge of the topic. As

the ideas are discussed, conflicting viewpoints are analyzed. Follow-up activities could include films, filmstrips, and television documentaries on the topic.

3. *Getting to Know Authors:* The group selects an author and reads his books with emphasis on discovering the author through his words. Each child reads from the book the sections he has found particularly insightful. The group discusses the material read orally. On another occasion, each child could become "expert" on one author and share his insights by reading to the group.

4. *Children as Authors:* Children contribute their creative efforts to the library collection. Readers may choose from among all the authors whose works are on the shelves, including classmates. The reader may interpret the story by reading it to a selected group; the writer may then read the story and the group may discuss the differences in the two interpretations.

5. *Creative Arts:* Children select favorite stories to present to the group, and the group decides how to interpret the material through the creative arts—for example, through illustrations, murals, cartoons, dioramas, filmstrips, photographs; costume design; selection of background music.

6. *Choral Reading:* Choral reading is especially valuable for developing an appreciation of poetry, since preparation includes pre-reading to determine appropriate patterns, voice, pitch, expression, and interpretation. The following poems are good for different kinds of choral reading:

Unison:	"Jabberwocky" by Lewis Carroll
Refrain:	"The Mysterious Cat" by Vachel Lindsay
Choir:	"I Met a Man That Was Coming Back" by John Ciardi
Sequence:	"The King's Breakfast" by Lewis Carroll
Line-a-child:	"Bunches of Grapes" by Walter de la Mare
Part-speaking:	"If I Were a . . ." by Karla Kuskin

Strategies for Improving Specific Components of Oral Reading These strategies will focus on the aspects of oral reading which are unique to that process—phrasing, expression, voice, and enunciation.

In order to improve these aspects, the teacher must recognize the student's deficiency and understand its relationship to the total reading process.

One model for self-analysis is a diagnostic checklist, adapted from the teacher's version, designed to assist the child to recognize his strengths and weaknesses in oral reading.

Pupil Checklist

Check your good points. Circle your goals for improvement.

Reading the Words
_____ words to know by sight   (this)
_____ words to study   (hippopotamus)
Sharing with Others
_____ phrasing   (to the circus)
_____ punctuation   (. ? ,)
_____ voice   (high/low)
_____ pronunciation   (going to . . . gonna)
_____ expression   (Where *are* you going?)
Understanding
_____ stories   *(The Five Chinese Brothers)*
_____ information   *(All About Dinosaurs)*

In developing a checklist for children, the teacher must take the reading and maturational levels of these "diagnosticians" into account. Adaptations might take the form of a simplified version, a rebus for younger children, or a more detailed inventory for older children.

A second major consideration in the use of self-analysis techniques is the affective domain. The teacher must make sure that the youngsters maintain a positive self-concept even when they identify their weaknesses. Strengths as well as weaknesses should be emphasized, with weaknesses converted directly into goals for improvement. Since the self-concept is defined as a "mirror image" (Combs, 1962), the attitude of the teacher is significant. A teacher who shares the youngster's goals for improvement, and communicates confidence in the child's potential for realizing his goals, creates a welcome view in the child's mirror.

An ideal instrument for self-analysis is the tape recorder. It allows the child to listen to his reading and to review his progress at regular intervals. The use of ear phones allows total privacy for youngsters who prefer not to share this experience with others. The child should be free to decide when, where, and with whom he will share the analysis process.

In introducing this technique, the teacher will need to be certain the children understand the aspects of oral reading. Role playing can be helpful here. Children may read, on purpose, with a voice which is too high or too low, pronunciation which is faulty, or expression in need of improvement. They may practice listening to tapes made by other, anonymous children and analyze the reading. Finally, they may practice analyzing their own tapes.

In introducing the checklist, have children focus on only one aspect of the checklist at a time, lest they become discouraged at the prospect of too few "good points" and too many "goals for improvement." This way each item of the checklist becomes a short range goal leading to the larger goals.

It has been suggested that children tape samples of their oral reading at regular intervals. The youngster may begin his recording by giving the date of the taping. Checklists may also be dated and placed in a folder. The dated tapes and checklists then become a permanent record of the youngster's progress toward his goal of improved oral reading.

As a general rule, materials used for this purpose should be one level below the instructional level to avoid unnecessary distraction caused by decoding difficulties. The material should also be interesting to the child, conveying a message he deems worthwhile. An excellent guide to children's reading interests at various stages of development has been provided by Huck and Kuhn (1968, pp. 30–36).

1. *Phrasing*
   a. *Can You Do This?* The child reads silently a set of directions, marking the phrasing, with particular attention to reading the procedures step by step. Then he reads the directions orally to a group of children. The listeners follow the directions in reality or imaginatively and identify the procedure (for example, tying a shoe, putting on a coat).
   b. *Minute Mysteries:* The reader is given a riddle or mystery, cut in phrases. He reads the phrases to his listeners, who must solve the riddle or mystery in one minute. (A kitchen timer is an added incentive.)
   c. *Have You Heard?* The child prepares a news report and reads it to the class, modeling his performance on those of the television news-casters he has heard. In preparation for this activity, the children may wish to listen to commentators and tape the reporting to study the phrasing and expression.
2. *Expression*
   a. *Story Tellers I Have Heard:* The child listens to the records of the talented readers who have prepared records for children. Then he tapes his reading of the same story in an attempt to provide for others the pleasure he experienced in listening to the story.
   b. *How Are You Today?* The reader prepares a short paragraph, introducing himself or another child. His reading of the paragraph expresses a mood—happy, sad, excited. The listeners must tell how the person introduced feels today.
   c. *Play-Say-Become:* Plays, choral reading, and role playing are all tried and true vehicles for improving expression.
3. *Voice*
   a. *Auditions:* The children prepare a selection for choral reading by experimenting with voice pitch. Individual children then audition for the parts by demonstrating their ability to pitch voices to the desired level.
   b. *Who Said That?* A group of children decides what kind of voice the

characters in a story (Stuart Little, Ping, Christopher and Pooh) might have. Each child then selects a character and reads the appropriate dialogue using the character's voice.

c. *Filmstrip Producers:* Children may add their own captions to filmstrips, tape record the captions, and share the filmstrip and tape with the class. Variations include using slides or photographs as the visual medium.

4. *Enunciation*

a. *Puppet Theatre:* Tension is diminished through the magic of a puppet. Each child makes a puppet of a well-known story character and selects some dialogue for oral reading. The reader first presents the dialogue without showing the puppet. Then the listeners must guess who is speaking. When the secret is discovered, the reader shares another bit of dialogue, this time holding the puppet. The characters may be from different stories or the same one.

b. *Echo—echo:* A teacher, a teacher aide, or an older child tapes a series of simple tongue twisters. The child reads each tongue twister, modeling his enunciation on that of the taped voice.

c. *Read Me a Story:* The child selects a simple story and tapes it for younger children for the purpose of helping them to read the book. Careful enunciation becomes a vital matter when the reader is helping first graders to learn.

Applied Skills

The Place of the Applied Skills in the Curriculum

The new education must teach the individual how to classify and reclassify information, how to evaluate its veracity, how to change categories when necessary, how to move from the concrete to the abstract and back, how to look at problems from a new direction—how to teach himself. Tomorrow's illiterate will not be the man who can't read: he will be the man who has not learned how to learn (Toffler, 1970, p. 414).

Alvin Toffler, writing in *Future Shock*, describes a basic goal of contemporary education. It is applied reading skills which permit the individual to "classify," "reclassify," "evaluate," and "move from the concrete to the abstract."

The Network of Applied Abilities

The study skills have been variously described and classified in the literature. Although the many schemata differ in content, they have one characteristic in common. Each depicts the applied abilities as a network of sub-skills, interrelated and interdependent. As a basis for our discussion of diagnostic and teaching strategies for this phase of reading, we present this author's interpretation of the network of applied reading abilities.

The four major abilities are (1) setting the purpose, (2) collecting and evaluating information, (3) classifying and ordering information, and (4) application.

Setting the Purpose The initial task of the investigator, whether he is a first grader searching through a picture book or a sixth grader using the *Readers' Guide*, is to define his purpose. This ability usually involves one of the following processes:

Identifying a problem to be solved.

Determining an objective to be realized.

Stating a question or a series of questions to be answered.

Setting purposes is not restricted to the reading program but requires the development of skills and attitudes common to all aspects of learning. It involves both cognitive and affective domains and requires basic problem solving skills—skills the child will need in all aspects of life. Sears (1966) writes:

A child must learn to recognize when a new situation is a problem situation; that is, he must first of all understand that problems exist and that they can be solved. He must learn how to perceive a problem and categorize it as such. A corollary of this perception is that he must have search techniques which he can call upon in seeking a solution (p. 4).

Collecting and Evaluating Information Having identified the problem and set his purpose, the reader now engages in a search for sources of information which are particularly suited to his needs. Since the world abounds with sources of information, the evaluation of the ideas discovered is as significant as the discovery itself.

This complex phase of the network of applied skills may be divided into four major skill categories and a myriad of sub-skills. Because it is vital for the teacher to be aware of the sources of information and the problems of selection, the sub-skills will be listed in detail.

1. Knowing the availability of a variety of sources of information, including print and media, and human and environmental resources.

   a. *printed materials:*

     (1) reference works: books, dictionaries, thesaurus, encyclopedias, almanacs, atlases, anthologies, periodicals, letters, diaries.

     (2) reference sources: card catalogues, reference systems (Dewey Decimal or Library of Congress), *Readers' Guides,* bibliographies, indexes.

     (3) current sources: newspapers, magazines, pamphlets, bulletins.

     (4) graphic aids: maps, charts, tables, graphs, figures, diagrams, time lines, pictures, cartoons. (For a more detailed discussion, see *Reading Social Studies,* p. 76.)

   b. *media:* photographs, slides, films, filmstrips, records, tapes, radio, and television.

   c. *human resources:* specialists, collectors, artists, craftsmen, travelers, exchange students, teachers, parents, government officials, community service workers, professionals, business, and industry.

   d. *environmental resources:* museums, historical sites, points of local interest, and conservation areas.

2. Locating appropriate information through the use of the sources and resources indicated.

   a. understanding the *function* and *format* of each type of printed material.

   b. using *reference sources,* such as the card catalogue.

   c. knowing the variety of topics under which the desired information may be located.

   d. determining the value of each source and resource in contributing particular types of information.

3. Mastering the various techniques of collecting information.

   a. selecting the appropriate *style* and *rate* of reading for the task:

     (1) scanning or skimming at a high rate to locate.

     (2) literal reading at above average rate to comprehend.

     (3) critical reading at a normal rate to interpret, evaluate, and elaborate.

   b. *following directions:* attention to key vocabulary, main ideas, sequence, relating parts to whole and whole to parts, retention of significant ideas.

   c. *using a book:* careful analysis of each part of the book in relation to its known function—for example, title page (including author's name and credentials, publisher); publication date (noting effect of date on content); preface; table of contents; lists of tables, charts, and illustrations; major and minor chapter headings and other typographical features; footnotes; tabular and graphic materials; summaries; bibliography; glossary; appendix and index.

   d. *using a dictionary:* ability to determine "approximate" spelling; knowledge of alphabetical order, guide words, diacritical markings, pronunciation key; selection of appropriate meaning and/or origin of word; use of special sections.

   e. *using reference materials:* understanding the format of multi-volume resource, location of material within volume, reference to related topics.

   f. *interviewing:* ability to arrange meeting, plan questions, establish rapport, note responses, all with attention to courtesy and concern for the person being interviewed.

4. Determining the relevance, significance, and adequacy of the information.

   a. *logical thinking* to determine cause and effect relationships and relate the parts to the whole.

   b. *critical thinking* to evaluate the accuracy of the information by comparing the content to other sources and to experiences, real and vicarious; noting the author's point of view, or biases; and distinguishing fact from opinion.

   c. *elaborative thinking* to determine the contributions of the ideas to the stated purposes and to know when the purposes have been accomplished.

Classifying and Ordering Information The applied study procedures included in this phase of the network of skills are notetaking, outlining, and summarizing. These procedures are, in essence, variations of the same process; the product is the major difference. The reading-thinking skills required for effective notetaking are identical to those required for outlining; the only additional requirement is the formal outline structure. The third variation, the summary, is, in essence, an extension of the outline; it uses the same organized content as the basis for an expository piece.

The reading-thinking skills common to the classifying and ordering phase are:

1. Awareness of sentence and paragraph structure and the structure of the whole selection.
2. Discerning relevant and irrelevant ideas.
3. Determining the main ideas, minor ideas, and details and perceiving the interrelationships among these components.
4. Generalizing, noting the relationship of the parts to the whole and the whole to the parts.
5. Perceiving sequence and chronology.

Application The final phase, application, is closely allied to the first phase, goal setting, since the application represents the successful conclusion of the "search." The process is completed when the student presents the solution to the problem, the product of the stated objectives, or the answers to the questions posed.

If the application is to be shared, the teacher will help the student decide on the content to be presented, the audience to be addressed, and the mode of presentation. On the basis of these considerations, the student may choose the oral or written form of sharing.

Diagnostic Teaching Strategies

Perhaps in no area of reading is Strang's (1969) term "diagnostic teaching" as appropriate as in the applied or study skills. Diagnosis and teaching are best perceived as points along a circular continuum. Diagnosis is an integral part of the instructional process and teaching a vital component of the diagnostic process. The teacher evaluates as he teaches, instructs as he tests.

In this section, the procedures for diagnosis will not be described apart from ideas for teaching. Rather, the strategies will be suggested in relation to the goal to be achieved and the child to be served.

General Guidelines for Diagnostic Teaching Earlier in this chapter, several guidelines for teaching oral reading were suggested. Most are generalizable to all aspects of the instructional program and those of particular relevance to the applied skills will be briefly reviewed here. They are:

1. An *open climate,* affording maximum potential for involvement and success.
2. Setting *goals,* clearly defined and attainable.
3. Suitable *material,* appropriate in content and level.
4. *Experiential background,* real or vicarious.
5. Adequate decoding and comprehension *skills.*
6. Positive *evaluation,* a basis for growth.
7. Meaningful *follow-up.*

The nature of the applied skills requires a few additions:

8. An awareness of the *total network of the applied reading skills* as a basis for determining those appropriate to the developmental level of the children.
9. Determination of each child's *readiness* to apply the basic decoding, comprehension, and thinking skills to the reading-study tasks.
10. Familiarity with the appropriate *sources and resources* required for teaching the study abilities, including those outside the classroom, such as the school library or instructional materials center; the town or city hall; the parents who have hobbies or special collections.
11. A master *plan* for the diagnostic teaching of the selected skills.

These special requirements are particularly suitable for cooperative effort on the part of two teachers of the same grade level—or all the teachers in an entire school. The greater the number of persons involved, the less expenditure of time is required on the part of each individual.

One possible plan is suggested here:

1. Using the network of applied skills provided on pp. 420–423, prepare a master checklist of these skills. Under *Level,* indicate the approximate developmental point at which the skill will be included in the instructional program. These columns function in two ways: (1) as an indication of sequence, and (2) as a checklist on which to record progress. A sample follows:

Checklist of Applied Reading Skills

Child's Name _____   Grade or Level _____

Skill	*Level**		
	I	II	III
I. Setting the purpose			
A. Identifying problem	____	____	____
B. Determining objectives	____	____	____
C. Stating questions	____	____	____
II. Collecting and evaluating information			
A. Knowing availability of sources	____	____	____
1. Printed materials	____	____	____
a. Reference works	____	____	____
books	____	____	____
dictionaries	____	____	____
thesaurus	____	____	____
encyclopedias	____	____	____
almanacs	____	____	____
atlases	____	____	____
anthologies	____	____	____
periodicals	____	____	____
letters	____	____	____
diaries	____	____	____
b. Reference sources			

*I. Readiness (pre-reading and beginning reading)

 II. Introductory level (primary unit)

III. Refinement (intermediate or middle unit)

2. Reproduce sufficient copies to provide one for each child. It is advisable to use sturdy material, since the checklist will be used as a permanent

record during the elementary years, showing a youngster's proficiency at each level.

3. On the individual checklist, correlate the information available from other sources, such as standardized tests, informal inventories, and criterion-referenced tests, to determine the child's readiness in the areas of decoding, comprehension, and thinking. This information should guide the selection of the material to be used in an instructional program in the applied reading skills.

4. Prepare a master list of classroom, school, and community resources (see the network of applied skills, *Collecting and Evaluating Information*, pp. 420–422). A simple questionnaire sent to parents will yield information regarding the interests, hobbies, and talents they would be willing to share. In many schools this type of parental involvement has enriched the lives of all who participate in the program.

5. From all of the information, the checklists, and the master list of resources, prepare a plan for an instructional program in the applied skills. Plans may be made for a month, a half-year, or a full year, but it is important that each unit be planned to achieve short range goals leading to the fulfillment of the stated goals for that level.

Strategies for Diagnostic Teaching of the Applied Skills To assist the teacher in realizing the values of a diagnostic-teaching program, the specific strategies will be classified according to the network of applied skills. The ideas are offered according to three developmental levels: (1) readiness (pre-reading and beginning reading), (2) introduction (levels 2 and 3), and (3) refinement (levels 4 through 6). These refer to the developmental level of the child, rather than the grade placement, although the two may be identical for the average child.

1. *Setting the purpose*

   Summary of sub-skills:

   Identifying the problem(s)

   Determining the objective(s)

   Stating the question(s)

In the discussion which follows, the teacher helps the children understand how purposes for learning are set.

Level 1

Learning to Learn: The teacher arranges a series of picture books about a given topic, and asks the children what they might learn from the books. The teacher writes down the responses as with an experience chart, in three columns:

To find out (problems)   To do (objectives)   To answer (questions)

Why We Came Today: At the beginning of the school day or session, the teacher assists the children to set their purposes for the day. Again the ideas may be grouped so that the children understand the possibilities for goal setting. This process, begun as a class activity, may become a small group, then a team, and finally an individual activity as the children grow in proficiency.

Curiosity Box: A box is placed in the classroom into which a child may place a picture of something which arouses his curiosity. As a small group activity, the box is opened and the children help the curious child refine his curiosity into objectives—things to find out, activities to do, questions to answer.

Level 2

One or Many? The children write problems or questions on individual cards or slips of paper. In a discussion group (and later in teams) the cards are read and sorted into two categories: those which will have many right solutions or answers, and those which will have only one. For example, "How many children have a birthday in March?" will have one answer. "What is the best birthday present you can give to a friend?" will have many.

That's a Good Question: The teacher notes the ideas the children question. On separate cards, several possible patterns of questions are listed. The children discuss the questions and choose the one which will be most effective in guiding a search for answers. Questions about rain, for example, might include, "What about rain?" and "Why does it rain?"

Level 3

Read and Discover: A unit in a content area book is selected. The children skim the material and set their purposes for reading the content. The aim is to state *specifically* problems, purposes, questions. A list is made and checked off as the purposes are realized.

A Plan for Tomorrows: Each youngster makes a personal list of problems, objectives, and/or questions related to an area of interest. The list is used to guide personal reading, project planning, and independent research activities.

2. *Collecting and evaluating information*

Summary of sub-skills:
    Familiarity with sources and resources.
    Using sources and resources to locate appropriate information.
    Mastering techniques for collecting information.
    Evaluating information for relevance, significance, and adequacy.

A. *Collecting*

Level 1

Ways to Know: With the help of the teacher, the children prepare a class chart of all the sources and resources which provide information at their level. The chart is an ongoing activity; new entries are made as children discover new ways to know. A rebus may be used to assist children who are not yet able to read.

A Class Picture Dictionary: Using chart paper or a large scrapbook, the teacher labels each page with a capital and corresponding lower case letter. As children discover new words beginning with each letter, pictures of the objects are drawn or pasted on the appropriate pages. Until the children learn to write, the teacher labels the object, but the children provide the artistic work from the beginning of the effort.

People and Places: In preparation for a class visitor or field trip, the children review simple interview techniques and decide what questions to ask. Each child is assigned one question. Later, with the aid of the teacher, the children record their findings and write a thank-you note to the visitor or host.

Level 2

Word Collections: In a notebook or scrapbook, each child writes his own dictionary and thesaurus. This is an ongoing process, which grows as the child's abilities in reading and writing develop. The pages are labelled, pictures are drawn or pasted on appropriate pages, words are entered under the pictures, sentences are added each time a new meaning for the word is discovered, and word classifications are identified *(People, Words to describe feelings, Words to give* pretty *a rest).*

Experts: Each child selects a topic of special interest and becomes an expert on the sources of information about that subject. Through a class scrapbook, each child shares his expertise with others who are interested in the topic. To assist the process, the children may first discuss the available sources and resources. (The outline on page 421 may be used to guide the discussion.)

Level 3

Librarians: The children enter the classroom at the beginning of the year to find the books arranged on tables. Together they discuss procedures for creating a library from the stacks of books. They plan the work and assign tasks, such as classifying, arranging within categories according to author, numbering, creating a card catalogue, and devising a lending system. The result is a classroom library.

Authors and Editors: During the academic year, each child creates or edits one or more books, including in each as many features of a book as his ability permits. Children may write and illustrate a fiction or non-fiction work, or they may serve as editors of anthologies, gathering material from discarded readers, literature series, children's magazines, or newspapers. Possible topics for anthologies include: Animal Tales, Adventures in Space, The Boston Bruins. Each completed work is classified, catalogued, and added to the library.

B. *Evaluating*

Level 1

Logical thinking: Riddles, puzzles, simple science experiments.

Critical thinking: Distinguishing real from make believe; for example, "The bears lived near Goldilocks" vs. "The bears lived in a zoo."

Elaborative thinking: Selecting from a collection of pictures the ones which contribute to the topic under investigation.

Level 2

Logical thinking: Minute mysteries, brain teasers, math problems.

Critical thinking: Distinguishing fact from opinion in advertisements, newspaper features, parts of newspapers and magazines.

Elaborative thinking: Listing all the possible uses for which one source or resource might be used—*The Junior Book of Authors*, for example.

Level 3

Logical thinking: Acrostics, crossword puzzles, analogies.

Critical thinking: Detecting the author's bias, noting the effect of emotionally laden words, comparing sources, such as a news article and an editorial about the same topic. Writing an article to advance a point of view.

Elaborative thinking: Creating a bibliography of sources and resources for a given topic, including all possible types. Later the sources may be rank ordered according to their potential value for the specific purpose.

3. *Classifying and ordering information*

Summary of sub-skills

Notetaking

Outlining

Summarizing

Level 1

Notetaking: From a series of objects, the children select the one which tells about the story the teacher read.

Outlining: The class makes a mural to depict a favorite story. Class discussions precede the activity as children decide the most important scenes and later what will be included in each scene. A popular variation is the dramatization of a story using the same procedure.

Summarizing: The class plans an experience story to tell about an experience, an activity, or a field trip.

Level 2

Notetaking: From a simple, non-fiction account, such as an article in a children's newspaper, the children write three important ideas to remember.

Outlining: After discussing the form of an outline, the children arrange a cut-up outline, comparing their version to the original. The outlines used for this practice should be very simple, including only a limited number of items in each category.

Summarizing: After reading a favorite book, the child prepares a book jacket, including the information for the front flap, a summary of the story or content, and the information for the back flap—a brief account of the author's life.

Level 3

Notetaking: The children preview a taped selection of an expository piece and decide the important ideas and details. The tape is played again and the children take notes. Later they compare their notes to a written version of the material. As proficiency grows, the preview may be unnecessary.

Outlining: Crossley[1] has suggested a highly effective procedure:

1. Present a skeletal outline, including the main topics. The child reads to fill in the minor ideas.

    Music in Colonial Days
    I. Jamestown Colony and Virginia
        A. . . . .
        B. . . . .
        C. . . . .
    II. New England
        A. . . . .
        B. . . . .
        C. . . . .

2. Provide the minor ideas. The child reads to fill in the major ideas.

[1] Crossley, B. A. "Can We Help Children Write?" *Journal of Education,* 139, 3 (1957), pp. 10–11. Copyright by the Trustees of Boston University.

Music in Colonial Days

   I. . . . .
     A. Ballads
     B. Chants
     C. Rounds
  II. . . . .
     A. Psalmody
     B. Folk songs
     C. Ballads

3. Present the structural organization. The child reads to fill in the parts of the outline.

   I. . . . .
     A. . . . . : . .
     B. . . . .
     C. . . . .

4. Finally the child writes an original outline.

Each step represents the culmination of several practice sessions, using increasingly detailed material. The final step may not come until after several months of concentrated discussion and practice.

Summarizing: Each student selects a topic of particular interest—a scientific phenomenon, the life of a famous person, a current event—and researches the subject. He outlines his findings and prepares a written account which might be published in a class newspaper or an oral account to share with selected classmates.

4. *Application:* The application of the study abilities is best accomplished in relation to the stated goals, the content of the material and the preferences of the investigator. It may be that the student has accomplished his purpose simply by solving the stated problem or answering the questions posed. These outcomes alone may justify the search. In other instances, however, the researcher may wish to share his findings. The teacher will then guide the selection of the optimal mode of presentation, oral or written, for one or many, formally or informally. The Pupil Specialty, introduced by Durrell and Savignano (1956), presents a promising plan for such sharing. Procedures and suggestions for the development of the pupil specialty will be presented in the final section of this chapter.

Reading in the Content Areas

The Place of Reading in the Content Areas

Forecasters of the educational climate have been predicting recently that one day books will be replaced by something more efficient. Perhaps the day will come when reading books will no longer be necessary for learning. Until that day, however, reading remains vital to learning and living.

For centuries, man's knowledge has been preserved through the medium of written language. The history of the traditional academic disciplines—literature, mathematics, science, and social science—is the history of civilization. As knowledge has advanced, and ideas have changed as a result of new discoveries, the content of the disciplines has reflected the changes. Each of the content areas represents a history of the thought within the discipline, a compilation of current thinking and inferences for the future, inviting the person who is able to read effectively in the academic disciplines to recreate the past, participate in the present, and gain insight into the future.

An analysis of the sources of learning in each of the disciplines reveals similarities and differences in two major aspects: concept-bearing vocabulary and structure. In every type of writing, the reader is confronted with units of meaning, words, and with the structure selected by the author as a means of organizing the units. In every type of reading, the basic process is the same: the reader decodes the units, comprehends the meaning intended by the author, and responds cognitively and/or affectively to the message.

The differences in the content are the result of the unique words and structures required to convey various kinds of meanings. These differences require adaptations in the basic reading process. The reader must understand the concept represented by the unit or word, make use of the higher thinking skills to comprehend the structure, and apply the study skills required for cognitive and/or affective response or application.

As a basic for a discussion of diagnostic and teaching strategies, we will again rely on an analysis of the process of reading in the content areas. Bruner's insights regarding "general policies" for education in our day provide a framework for that discussion. The first two conclusions are particularly applicable:

1. "Principal emphasis in education should be placed upon skills—skills in handling, in seeing and imagining, and in symbolic operations. . . ."
2. "A curriculum should involve the mastery of skills that in turn lead to the mastery of still more powerful ones, the establishment of self-reward sequences" (1966, pp. 34–35).

Units and Structures Effective reading in the content areas demands a set of abilities common to all disciplines and additional sets of abilities unique to each discipline. The abilities are determined on the basis of the content to be read.

To interact with the author, the reader must first be able to read and understand the basic unit of meaning, the word. This task may be more difficult than it seems, given the variety of possible meanings represented by a single word. One of the most common words in the language, a simple three-grapheme unit, *run,* has more than fifty meanings. The degree to which the reader will be confused or intrigued by the possibilities is determined, to a large extent, by the real and vicarious experiences he brings to the content, regardless of the nature of the discipline. Through skillful use of that experiential background, the reader is able to comprehend a *run* on an athletic field in one context and the *run* of a play on Broadway in yet another context.

In approaching the content areas, the youngsters will be confronted with a variety of challenges to vocabulary development: (1) words in general usage which are in the listening-speaking vocabularies but not in the reading-writing vocabularies, (2) words in general usage which are in all four vocabularies, (3) specialized words which are in the listening-speaking vocabularies but not in the reading-writing vocabularies, (4) specialized words which are in all four vocabularies, (5) specialized words in the various vocabularies which are known in another context and therefore may cause confusion. For example, the word *culture* may be known in social studies but not in science, and *civil* may be known in literature but not in social studies.

The responsibility of the teacher, then, is to be certain that the child has the experiential background to understand the general and the specialized words in the particular context to be read and understood. In the academic disciplines, the specialized vocabulary is particularly important since one word may represent a key concept upon which the total paragraph, chapter, or unit depends—*satire* in literature, for example, *integer* in mathematics, *solid* in science, *democracy* in social studies.

Glaser (1968) has stated the goal clearly:

> One of the functions of education and of school learning is to transmit relatively definite meanings of certain concepts, and at the same time transmit the ability to amend and revise concepts, as well as the ability to recognize instances of experience into newly discovered or personally held concepts (p. 3).

Just as the word may be described as a basic unit of meaning, so the sentence may be perceived as the basic unit of the structure of language. The basic sentence patterns and the variations and expansions are used by all writers, but the structure of each discipline demands a different style of writing. The storyteller's style is fluid; the mathematician's is terse and precise. The task of the writer is to choose the style most appropriate to his content; the task of the reader is to discover the structure, the better to comprehend the content.

Strang (1967, pp. 314–315) enumerates the sentence types used by authors of content area materials: (1) generalization, (2) summary, (3) percept, (4) law or principle, (5) comparison, (6) contrast, (7) analogy, (8) simile, (9) metaphor, (10) cause, (11) effect, (12) judgment, (13) enumeration, (14) whole–part, (15) definition, (16) coordination–subordination, (17) procedure, (18) conjecture and prediction, (19) problem-solving, and (20) transition.

These sentence types demand literal comprehension of the material as the beginning, not the end, of comprehension. Basic understanding merely provides the framework for the higher level thought processes—critical thinking (comparison); creative thinking (analogy); and elaborative thinking (conjecture and prediction). The applied reading abilities are also required: evaluating, classifying, ordering, and application.

In summary, the major considerations for the teacher of reading in the content areas are the units of meaning, particularly the specialized vocabulary, and the structure of the content, particularly as it relates to the higher thought processes and the applied reading abilities.

Since all effective teaching begins with knowledge of the learner, the next section will provide procedures for determining a youngster's ability to deal with the units and structures of any given content material.

Diagnostic Strategies

Although there is a growing trend toward using multiple resources for learning in the content areas, most teachers presently use a basic text with other resources as supplementary material. Therefore it is wise to assess each youngster's ability to read the basic text effectively. Informal vocabulary and silent reading tests (the latter a variation of the oral reading test described on pages 410–414) have proven useful to many teachers.

Vocabulary Test Select a random sample of twenty words from the glossary or word list in the text. Type the list, double spaced, in a column on a card or sheet of paper to be placed in a tachistoscope (teacher-made or on individual index cards). Prepare a record blank for the teacher's use according to the format in the sample on page 435.

To administer the test, the teacher uses the tachistoscope or card to expose the first word briefly. If the child reads the word accurately, the teacher records a plus (+) in the *Recognition* column and asks the child to define the word or use it in a sentence. Again, an accurate response is recorded as a plus, this time in the *Meaning* column. If the child fails to provide an accurate meaning for the word, a minus (−) is recorded. When the child is unable to recognize a word at sight, the word is revealed again for analysis. A correct identification on this trial is recorded as a plus in the *Analysis* column; an incorrect identification or no response is noted as a minus. (Here as in other tests, it is well to record the incorrect response wherever possible, since an analysis of errors often yields significant information.) If the child analyzes the word correctly, the meaning is asked and the response recorded. An incorrect analysis or no response requires the teacher to identify the word for the child in order to test his knowledge of the meaning of the word. Again the outcome is recorded in the *Meaning* column. The procedure outlined above is continued for the entire list of words.

The teacher will gain insight into individual differences and needs through analysis of strengths, weaknesses, and patterns of errors. For example, a student may show evidence of skill in word meaning and deficiencies in analyzing words, thus revealing strength in the listening vocabulary and weakness in the reading vocabulary.

A sample of the teacher's record blank of a vocabulary test devised from a fifth-grade social studies text is given in Table 14.

Silent Reading Test Select material from the text to be used and prepare the test and questions according to the guidelines provided for the grade level and content type, non-fiction, in the directions for preparing the oral reading test found on pages 410–412. Reproduce enough copies of the selection and questions for each child.

To administer the test, distribute individual copies of the material and instruct the children to read silently and answer the questions on the sheet. Ask the youngsters to underline words they cannot read, indicating that anyone who must underline ten words in the first two sentences should ask for the teacher's help. As the test is being administered the teacher moves about the room, noting individual difficulties. Requests for help or observations of need should be the basis for selecting children who will listen to a taped version of the material and answer the questions orally. This will yield information about the child's listening ability in contrast to his reading ability.

Analysis Viewed together, the performances on the vocabulary and silent reading tests will suggest general guidelines for teaching. Viewed separately, the findings will help the teacher select specific strategies to enhance the strengths and overcome the weaknesses of individual children.

Teaching Strategies

Each aspect of the reading program makes use of general guidelines to produce optimal conditions for learning and more specific strategies for realizing the particular goals of a learning experience.

Some general guidelines for teaching reading in the content areas of mathematics, science, and social studies follow. (Literature is also consid-

Table 14   Word Abilities Inventory

Name _____   Level _____

Date _____   Scores:
                                                    Word Identification _____
                                                    Word Meaning _____

Word	*Recognition*	*Analysis*	*Meaning*
adapt	_____	_____	_____
analysis	_____	_____	_____
census	_____	_____	_____
conditioning	_____	_____	_____
custom	_____	_____	_____
democracy	_____	_____	_____
environment	_____	_____	_____
goal	_____	_____	_____
habit	_____	_____	_____
influence	_____	_____	_____
irrigate	_____	_____	_____
manufacturing	_____	_____	_____
population	_____	_____	_____
psychologist	_____	_____	_____
republic	_____	_____	_____
role	_____	_____	_____
society	_____	_____	_____
supply	_____	_____	_____
treaty	_____	_____	_____
value	_____	_____	_____

Vocabulary sample from: *The Social Sciences: Concepts and Values.* New York: Harcourt Brace Jovanovich, 1970.

ered a content area, but since the next chapter focuses specifically on that topic, it will be omitted from this discussion.)

General Guidelines for Teaching Reading in the Content Areas Each teaching-learning activity begins with *goal setting.* (Strategies for helping children set goals are described on pages 425–426.)

1. The *material* is selected on the basis of the readiness of the learner, the goals to be accomplished, and the content to be investigated.
2. The learners have acquired the real and/or vicarious *experience* necessary for comprehending the general and specialized *vocabulary.*
3. The teacher has made provision for the meaningful reinforcement and application of the *study skills* appropriate to the goals and the content.
4. The children are guided in selecting the *rate and style* of reading appropriate to their goals and the content of the material.
5. The activities focus on the application of critical, creative, and elaborative *thinking,* rather than the exclusive use of literal comprehension and recall.
6. *Evaluation* includes the *application* procedures of reporting, debating, discussion, summarizing, and testing.

Strategies for Developing Specialized Vocabulary

This technical language of a subject generally causes communication problems for students. The language is new to them and the words have special meanings, and sometimes even different meanings within the same subject depending on concepts being studied. Then, to compound the problem, students find, as they progress through the grades within a given subject, that new meanings are applied to old and familiar words. Moreover they are confronted daily with words they have never considered before, appearing in material they are required to read. Since they do not know the meanings of these words, they derive little benefit from their reading. Their teachers assume these students have reading problems when, in fact, they are having language problems; that is, they do not know the language of the subject and therefore cannot participate in the communication of its concepts (Herber, 1970, p. 151).

In analyzing the technical vocabulary, Herber has not only identified the potential problem, but has provided a clue to its prevention. Since the specialized vocabulary is potentially a language barrier, the students must be actively interested in discovering meanings of the words they encounter. To awaken this interest, the teacher may introduce students to semantics (Why do we call this a chair? What would happen if everyone in the room decided to change the word *chair* to *op?* What would you do if I asked you to count the *ops* in the room?), to the history of the language (Where did we get the words *kindergarten, cookie, ballerina?* and *Coke* and *Kleenex?* and *sinister* and *martial?*), and to social history (Why do we still need the word *horse* when we have *airplane?* Why did we replace the word *icebox* with the word *refrigerator?*). The search begins and a budding linguist may be the result.

Books are potentially powerful motivational devices. Consider the variety of dictionaries, glossaries, thesauruses, indexes, and books of quotations. Publishers now provide a plethora of such materials at a variety of levels, so that every child can locate resources appropriate to his needs. Opportunities for language learning are infinite when a child makes effective use of the basic materials and the special sections to become acquainted with multiple meanings, word derivations, synonyms, antonyms, prefixes, suffixes, root words, parts of speech, figurative language, and idioms.

The use of these and all other printed resources in the content areas depends upon the application of the basic word skills: phonic analysis to decode the phoneme-grapheme relationships; structural analysis of prefixes, suffixes, and root words to provide clues to meaning; and contextual analysis to indicate the precise meaning intended by the author.

Finally, if language is to be an active process, the student must communicate not through the silent processes of reading and writing alone, but also through the vocal processes of listening and speaking. Some specific suggestions follow:

1. *A personal dictionary/thesaurus:* Each child compiles his own dictionary/thesaurus of specialized vocabulary for each content area, including a cross reference for each word that appears in more than one collection.

   How much *change* will John get from his dollar?

   What causes the weather to *change*?

   Why was there a *change* in the attitude of the citizens?

2. *Word elements:* The class develops lists of prefixes, suffixes, and root words, antonyms and synonyms related to topics being investigated. Specialized meanings are discussed.

Common prefixes:	*anti*	*de*	*dis*	*in*	*mis*	*pre*	*pro*	*re*	*sub*	*un*
Common suffixes:	*al*	*ate*	*ful*	*ish*	*ism*	*ous*	*tion*			

3. *Media makers:* The children create their own slides, films, tapes, photographs, or video to make abstract concepts more concrete—for example, attributes (mathematics), environment (science), behavior (social studies).

4. *Key concepts:* The class makes use of personal experience and identification to "live" the key concepts. They may develop, for example, a monetary system for the class store, a science laboratory, or a system of

government for class management. Each experience is described in a class newspaper or reported on a class TV or radio newscast requiring youngsters to use the language in reporting, editorializing, advertising, and so on.

5. *Word games:* The solution or creation of word games using specialized vocabulary—riddles, crossword puzzles, adaptions of *Scrabble* and *Spill and Spell*, and analogues such as:

> inch : foot : : ounce : pound
> apple : fruit : : carrot : vegetable
> president : democracy : : king : monarchy

Strategies for Developing Reading-thinking Abilities in Mathematics, Science, Social Studies The teacher who wants to teach youngsters to read effectively in the academic disciplines must be aware of the reading-thinking abilities required. There is a cluster of abilities unique to each discipline.

The reading-thinking abilities common to mathematics, science, and social studies are:

1. Understanding the specialized vocabulary.
2. Determining the rate and style of reading appropriate to the reader's purpose.
3. Following directions.
4. Perception of relationships among ideas:

cause and effect	classification
comparison and contrast	sequence
relevant vs. irrelevant	chronology
fact from opinion	main idea and details
whole to parts	parts to whole

5. Critical and creative thinking:
   synthesize
   generalize
   analyze
   infer
   conclude
6. Interpretation of appropriate graphic material.
7. Application of the study skills.

Mathematics requires, in addition:

1. Understanding symbols and formulas.
2. Awareness of key words which give clues to processes.
3. Determination of the relationship between the words and mathematical symbols.
4. Substitution of symbols for words.
5. Ability to infer the range of an accurate response.
6. Appreciation of the human and aesthetic dimensions of mathematics.

Science demands:

1. A scientific attitude of suspended judgment.
2. Understanding the scientific method.
3. Elaboration upon the findings to a practical application.
4. Awareness of the implications of a given discovery.
5. Sensitivity to the humanism of science, the aesthetics of science.

Social studies requires of its readers:

1. Understanding concepts of time and space.
2. Relating the new to the familiar, the past to the present.
3. Comparison of sources: coordinating information.
4. Distinguishing fact from opinion, validity of sources.
5. Awareness of recurring themes or trends.
6. Perceiving the interrelatedness of the social sciences, such as economics and geography.
7. Effective interpretation of graphic materials.

A comprehensive analysis of social studies skills, classified according to grade level, has been prepared by Johns and Fraser (1963, pp. 310–327).

The ideas that follow are intended as examples of the types of strategies appropriate for each discipline. In designing specific activities, the teacher must be cognizant of the level of the individual needs of the learners, selecting materials at the appropriate reading level and activities at a suitable developmental level.

1. Mathematics

   Translate: A sheet of paper is divided into three columns. The problem is written, in phrases, in the first column. In the second column, the numbers facts are listed; in the third column the facts are translated into operations.

   Communicate: Write a problem for a friend to solve. Help him by underlining key phrases which will provide clues to the operations needed for a solution.

   Eliminate: Read a problem and eliminate by crossing out all the irrelevant information. Rewrite the problem including only the essential facts.

2. Science

   Investigate: Using an appropriate form of the scientific method, cite a problem and proceed through the steps to a solution. The problems may be selected from a text or from queries raised by the class.

   Experiment: Describe an experiment (orally or in writing) for a friend to conduct. Keep a record of the process and of the findings. Provide a second set of directions for another classmate. After they have conducted the experiment, compare the findings of the two scientists. In the event of discrepancy, check writer and readers on main ideas, details, sequence, and accuracy in following directions.

Elaborate: Select a given scientific fact or discovery. Elaborate on the implications of these findings for people and the way they live. Raise additional questions for future investigation.

3. Social Studies

Compare: Select a single historical event. Compare the information provided through a variety of sources—a biography, an autobiography, a letter, a novel, a newspaper (editorial and news story), a history text.

Validate: Note two opposing points of view. Investigate the background, academic qualifications, and experience of each of the authors. Form a judgment. Consult additional sources to verify the decision.

Interrelate: Make use of the various graphic aids to interrelate information on a variety of topics: make a map of the classroom and later include it in a map of the school; make a time line of one day's activities, leading to a time line of a week's activities; keep a graph of the weather for each month, leading to a graphic analysis of the seasonal temperature for a year.

Each of these activities provides practice in applying the appropriate reading-thinking skills to a given academic discipline. The ultimate achievement is the ability to interact with any writer one chooses, understanding the vocabulary and analyzing the structure in a near automatic response to the content.

The Pupil Specialty A recent educational idea affords youngsters the opportunity to develop expertise in one aspect of a content area and in so doing become more skillful readers. This is the pupil specialty, initially introduced by Durrell and Savignano as "a desirable way to give the child experience in directing his own learning" (1956, p. 2). The pupil specialty has evolved, over the intervening years, into a viable means of applying the reading-study abilities to the content areas of the curriculum as individual learning needs indicate.

Specialties enable the pupil to make his own correctives in the educational offering. If he considers the school content too vague and distant, his own specialty may be intensely practical. If there is too much talking and too little doing, his specialty may emphasize constructive activities. If vocational improvement is desired, his specialty can be vocational. If his interest is caught by any phase of the curriculum, he may pursue that subject more deeply (1956, p. 6).

The pupil specialty, then, is a vehicle for learning and for learning to learn. It provides an opportunity for one child, a team, or a small group of children to become expert in one area of knowledge and to share their discoveries with others. In so doing, each learner is engaged in the meaningful use of the network of applied skills, in the exploration of content area materials, and in the preparation of an oral and visual presentation. The main purpose of using curriculum-related pupil specialties is to *provide for individual differences.* While more and more teachers are using a multi-text, multi-resource approach to the content areas, many teachers have only one set of texts in each of these areas. While individualized reading is used in more and more classrooms, many youngsters have only one source through which to learn mathematics, science, or social studies. Teachers who are sensitive to individual differences adapt and augment "the series" as knowledge, resources, and time permit, but the task is substantial.

Since the pupil specialty encourages students to pursue their own interests in their own ways, children are free to select from available resources as individual needs and talents indicate. Visual learners can use media and graphic materials, while auditory learners conduct interviews and listen to tapes and records. The teacher becomes a guide to these resources, providing direction, making suggestions, and assisting youngsters in their search. The learners share in the responsibility for extending the curriculum beyond the textbook to people and places, print and media.

Multiple resources also serve individual learning levels. Youngsters of below average ability are free to make use of high-interest, low-vocabulary books, picture collections, and site visits, while those of superior ability add depth and dimension to the basic knowledge provided by the text through exploration of original data, interviews with experts, and comparison of multiple sources. Team and small group situations provide for learners of varying abilities to work together, each contributing in his own capacity by assuming tasks appropriate to his style and level of learning. For example, a youngster of superior ability might provide a critical comparison of information provided by a biography, an editorial, a news article, and a text on the subject of Lincoln's assassination, while a youngster of low ability might assist in making a chart to depict the findings.

Rates of learning are taken into account, since the duration of the investigation and the subsequent report is determined on the basis of the child's cognitive ability to investigate and synthesize and his affective ability to pursue the task and sustain motivation. A useful guide is to provide five minutes' reporting time for every week of investigation—ten minutes following two weeks of investigation, twenty minutes following one month.

A second value of the pupil specialty is that the student uses the network of applied skills in meaningful learning situations. In order to develop the specialty, the pupil must set his purposes, determining the directions and nature of his efforts. Having set his purpose, the specialist collects and evaluates information from a variety of sources. Next, he classifies and orders his findings in preparation for the final step, the application, a report to be shared with his classmates. Required for the presentation is a summary on which to base decisions regarding the report, an outline for the oral presentation, media to enhance the presentation, and a visual display to add clarity and interest.

In the process of utilizing the full network of applied skills, the specialist is also engaged in *a total language experience*. He reads and listens in order to discover, speaks and writes in order to share; the audience reads and listens in order to share, speaks and writes in order to discover. Each is active in the process of learning and of learning to learn.

The following section provides a detailed guide for the accomplishment of the pupil specialty.

Preparation: The teacher and children together determine the curriculum content from which the specialties will evolve. The topics may relate generally to the subject matter or more specifically to a given unit of study. Examples of topics generally related to mathematics are: famous mathematicians, architecture and mathematics, problem-solving. Topics related to a specific unit in social studies, such as Africa, might include: famous people or present day citizens; the educational, monetary, or governmental systems; the art, music, or literature of a given country.

Such topics might be listed to generate ideas for self-starters or to offer choices to those who need more direction. Pupils are given time to declare their choice of topic and working relationships—that is, whether they would like to work with one child, a team, or a small group.

Setting the purpose: After this first planning phase, the teacher meets with each working individual or group to assist in refining the topic and setting specific purposes in the form of sub-topics to be investigated or questions to be answered. On the basis of the cognitive and affective abilities represented by the group, a time period and reporting date are determined.

Collecting and evaluating information: The pupils set about the task of discovery, first determining all the resources and sources appropriate to the task. The teacher may wish to reproduce the resource list on page 421 to be used by the specialist, first to indicate the sources to be investigated, and later as a checklist of accomplishments. The checklist might also serve as a guide for the teacher when he meets periodically with the children to check progress and assist in this phase of the program. During the first specialty experience, such meetings may be scheduled frequently; as youngsters grow in proficiency, fewer conferences will be required.

Pupils gather information both in and out of school. As they make discoveries, they take notes on cards, including simple bibliographic data on the source of the information. Later, the cards are color-coded with marking pens to indicate the sub-topic or question to which the information relates.

Midway to the reporting day, the specialists evaluate the material to determine how effectively they have accomplished the goals. They seek additional data if necessary and hold a final conference with the teacher to evaluate this phase of the program.

Classifying and organizing information: The information is sorted into sub-topics or questions, according to the color code previously determined. A sequence is then established by ordering the categories and the material within each category. The total body of information is then reviewed to determine which portions will best be presented (1) in the oral report, (2) through media, and (3) within the display. The oral report is outlined, the media planned and prepared, and the display gathered and designed.

Application: The color-coded cards function as the basic information for the outline and supporting media and display. Students determine responsibility for each role: the oral reporter, the media technician, the guide for the display, the respondee for the question period. If the specialty has been prepared by one child, he will choose assistants to help with the media and display. Taped interviews, overhead transparencies, and pictures shown on the opaque projector are promising media to enhance a specialty report. Since the display is to be viewed at leisure by the audience, it may include books, magazines, maps, dioramas, works of art, craft projects, and collections.

All specialists should be afforded the privilege of choosing the audience to whom they will present their reports. Some may wish to speak to the entire class; those who are more reticent may choose to present to a small group of friends. Another alternative for the latter group is a taped presentation, prepared in advance at a listening station or at home. Since one aim of the specialty report is to provide a feeling of accomplishment, it is best to provide the child with optimal conditions for success.

The audience, as well as the specialist, should be prepared for the brief question period which follows the presentation. The audience is responsible for asking relevant questions; the specialist is responsible for investigating questions to which he does not have a ready response. The question-answer period encourages active listening on the part of the audience and mutual participation in the concluding phase of the report.

Evaluation: A checklist for evaluating the specialty may be prepared by the class, by individuals, or by small groups. The checklist may be used by the child for self-evaluation, by the teacher, and/or by students selected by the specialist. One basic guideline is recommended: a negative comment must be accompanied by a suggestion for improvement. Possible areas for evaluation include: the content of the report, the media, the display; the quality of the oral presentation; the effectiveness of the media; the interest created by the display; the participator in the question-answer period.

Each specialist retains his evaluations and suggestions to use when he prepares for the next specialty. Areas to be improved are included as goals to be accomplished.

Adaptations: Although the pupil specialty is usually included in the curriculum of the intermediate grades, primary level teachers may adapt the procedures to the level of development of younger specialists. Even a beginning reader can locate picture books, view filmstrips, and talk to collectors. A special interest such as sea shells may be investigated, a simple display added, and a report taped or presented personally for others to enjoy. The rebus technique can be used to provide a simple evaluation guide.

In describing aspects of Piaget's theory which have implications for teacher education, Celia Stendler Lavatelli (1970) reminds teachers:

> As Piaget puts it, knowledge is not a copy of reality; to know something is to modify external reality. Knowledge always involves a mental operation which permits one to transform what one sees in the light of what one already knows (p. 38).

The pupil specialty is a promising approach to "seeing" and to "knowing."

Summary

This chapter focused upon the specialized skills (1) oral reading, (2) the applied or study skills, and (3) reading in the content areas.

Some topics are common to each area: a process analysis to establish relationships among components of the curriculum and an inventory of sub-skills to facilitate the planning of diagnostic and teaching strategies.

Other issues relate more particularly to one area and were discussed within the appropriate section: (1) a comparison of oral and silent reading, and the values and limitations of oral reading, (2) the network of applied skills, and (3) the pupil specialty.

The real value of this chapter must be determined by its effect not only on the teacher, but more significantly, on the learner, for the specialized abilities described here are the tools of independent learning. These skills must be so expertly taught in the elementary school that the learner will develop the cognitive abilities and affective attitudes to make learning a lifelong experience.

In describing a philosophy of education as self-renewal, Gardner (1964, pp. 21–22) provides an insightful view of the role of the teacher:

> We are beginning to understand how to educate for renewal but we must deepen that understanding. If we indoctrinate the young person in an elaborate set of fixed beliefs, we are ensuring his early obsolescence. The alternative is to develop skills, attitudes, habits of mind and the kinds of knowledge and understanding that will be the instruments of continuous change and growth on the part of the young person. . . . The ultimate goal of the educational system is to shift to the individual the burden of pursuing his own education.

References

Adler, M. J. *How to Read a Book*. New York: Simon and Schuster, 1972.

ASCD Yearbook Committee. *Perceiving, Behaving, Becoming*. Washington, D.C.: Association for Supervision and Curriculum Development, 1962.

Barrett, T. C. "Taxonomy of Cognitive and Affective Dimensions of Reading Comprehension." In *Innovation and Change in Reading Instruction*, edited by T. Clymer. National Society for the Study of Education, 1968 (Part II).

Bruner, J. *The Process of Education*. New York: Random House, 1960.

Bruner, J. *Toward a Theory of Instruction*. Cambridge: Belknap, 1966.

Combs, A. W. "A Perceptual View of the Adequate Personality." In *Perceiving, Behaving, Becoming*. Washington, D.C.: Association for Supervision and Curriculum Development, 1962.

Cousins, N. "Memories of A.E.S." *Saturday Review*, July 31, 1965, p. 12.

Crossley, B. A. "Can We Help Children to Write?" *Journal of Education*, Whole No. 3 (1957): 139.

Durrell, D. D. *Improving Reading Instruction*. New York: Harcourt, Brace and World, 1956.

Durrell, D. D., and Savignano, L. J. "Classroom Enrichment through Pupil Specialties." *Journal of Education*, Whole No. 3 (1956): 138.

Gardner, J. W. *Self-renewal*. New York: Harper and Row, 1964.

Glaser, R. "Concept Learning and Concept Teaching." In *Learning Research and School Subjects*, edited by R. M. Gagne and W. J. Gephart. Itasca, Ill.: Peacock, 1968.

Herber, H. L. *Teaching Reading in the Content Areas*. Englewood Cliffs, N.J.: Prentice-Hall, 1970.

Highet, G. *The Art of Teaching*. New York: Random House, 1950.

Huck, C. S., and Kuhn, D. Y. *Children's Literature in the Elementary School*. New York: Holt, Rinehart and Winston, 1968.

Jennings, F. G. *This Is Reading.* New York: Teachers College, 1965.

Johns, E., and Fraser, D. M. "Social Studies Skills: A Guide to Analysis and Grade Placement." In *Skill Development in Social Studies*, edited by H. Carpenter. Washington, D.C.: N.E.A., 1963.

Krathwohl, D. R. *Taxonomy of Educational Objectives, the Classification of Educational Goals, Handbook II: The Affective Domain.* New York: David McKay, 1964.

Lavatelli, C. B. Stendler. "Aspects of Piaget's Theory That Have Implications for Teacher Education." In *Educational Implications of Piaget's Theory*, edited by I. Athey and D. Rubadeau. Waltham, Mass.: Ginn-Blaisdell, 1970.

McCloskey, R. *Make Way for Ducklings.* New York: Viking Press, 1941.

McDonald, A. S. "Flexibility in Reading." In *Reading as an Intellectual Activity*, edited by J. A. Figurel. Proceedings of the International Reading Association Conference, 1963, pp. 8, 81–84.

Martin, B., Jr., and Brogan, P. "History of the Ice Cream Cone." In *Sounds of Language.* New York: Holt, Rinehart and Winston, 1972.

Piaget, J. "Development and Learning." In *Piaget Rediscovered*, edited by R. E. Ripple and V. N. Rockcastle. Ithaca, N.Y.: Cornell University, 1964.

Russell, D. H. *Children Learn to Read.* Boston: Ginn, 1961.

Sanders, N. M. *Classroom Questions.* New York: Harper and Row, 1966.

Sears, S. "Introduction." In *Learning about Learning*, edited by J. Bruner. Washington, D.C.: U.S. Department of Health, Education and Welfare, 1966, pp. 3–8.

Smith, N. B. *American Reading Instruction.* Newark, Del.: International Reading Association, 1965.

Stauffer, R. G. *Directing Reading Maturity as a Cognitive Process.* New York: Harper and Row, 1969.

Strang, R. *Diagnostic Teaching of Reading.* 2nd ed. New York: McGraw-Hill, 1969.

Strang, R.; McCullough, C.; and Traxler, A. *The Improvement of Reading.* 4th ed. New York: McGraw-Hill, 1967.

Taylor, S. E. *Listening.* Washington, D.C.: American Education Research Association, 1964.

Toffler, A. *Future Shock.* New York: Random House, 1970.

White, E. B. *Charlotte's Web.* New York: Harper and Row, 1952.

Chapter
Thirteen

Preview

This chapter will inspire as well as inform its readers. Strickler and Eller focus on a fundamental point: children should learn that reading is a joyful process, and learning to read should be fun. Concerned teachers often lose sight of this in their eagerness to instruct. They forget that reading skills are not ends in themselves.

The authors begin by describing the reading habits of adults, adolescents, and children. They discuss reading interests and what determines them, and they explain how teachers may develop positive attitudes toward reading in their students.

In the next section of the chapter the authors deal with interest inventories and other ways of assessing attitudes and interests. They show how teachers may use literature as a vehicle for stimulating and maintaining pupils' interest in reading.

Finally, Strickler and Eller suggest ways to create a classroom climate conducive to developing and sustaining lifelong interest in reading. This is the basic goal of the contributors to this text, and should be the goal of those who read it.

Reading:
Attitudes and Interests

Darryl Strickler, Indiana University
William Eller, State University of New York at Buffalo

Objectives

After you have read this chapter, you should be able to:

1. Explain the rationale for placing a major emphasis within the elementary school reading program upon children's affective development in relation to reading.
2. Describe the interrelatedness of reading interests, attitudes toward reading, reading habits, and interest in reading.
3. List the major research findings on children's reading interests and preferences.
4. Identify and describe those factors within the home and school environment that have the greatest influence on the development of reading attitudes and interest in reading.
5. Describe numerous strategies that can be used within the elementary school setting to increase children's interest in reading.
6. Construct and administer an interest inventory appropriate for a specific individual or group of elementary school children.
7. Establish a classroom library containing a wide range of reading material appropriate for a given elementary school grade.
8. For a given elementary school grade, design and implement a component of a language arts program that deals with the development of reading interests and positive attitudes toward reading.

What have they gained if children leave school knowing how to read, but don't know why to read, what to read, when to read—or worse—don't care to read at all?

The above question is intended to serve as the main focus of this chapter. Most of the preceding chapters have quite appropriately been devoted to instructional strategies for developing and refining children's ability to read. But while the development of children's reading skill is unquestionably one of the teacher's major responsibilities, an equally important responsibility is the development of positive attitudes toward reading and a lifelong interest in reading. If children are to develop attitudes toward reading that result in an interest in reading and in personally constructive reading habits, they need other reading-related experiences in addition to direct instruction in reading skill. They must experience the excitement and personal fulfillment, as well as the practical value, of learning through reading.

The major emphasis of this chapter is upon the affective dimension of reading. The first part of the chapter provides the teacher with pertinent research information on reading habits, interests, and attitudes. By analyzing such information we can gain insights into the ways in which reading interests and attitudes influence interest in reading and reading habits. Building upon this information base, the second part of the chapter presents specific programs and strategies for developing children's reading attitudes and interests.

Reading Habits

American schools have frequently been accused of producing generations of people who can read, but do not. Huck (1971, p. 37) used the term *illiterate literates* to describe such people—they are able to read but lack the interest and desire to do so. It is clear that if the teaching of reading continues to be directed solely to the development of reading skills, and no attempt is made to influence children's reading attitudes and interests, our efforts may well result in still another generation of illiterate literates.

Reading Habits of Adults

Although we can take little comfort from the fact, some evidence suggests that the reading habits of Americans do not differ greatly from the reading habits of citizens of several Western European nations of similar cultural and technological advancement. Data presented by van der Brink (1968) indicate that, on the average, literate Americans read about three more books per year than their Western European counterparts. However, research into the reading habits of Americans conducted by the University of Michigan's National Opinion Research Center over the past decade indicates that less than half (49%) of all literate adults in the United States actually choose to read books (Ennis, 1965). In another comprehensive survey of the reading habits of persons over sixteen years of age, which was undertaken by the Educational Testing Service in 1971, it was found that the most frequently reported reading activity was reading newspapers. The next most frequently reported reading activity was reading mail, followed by reading magazines. Only one-third of the more than 5000 individuals interviewed had read a book on the day prior to the interview (Trisman, 1972). And, while 54 percent of the respondents indicated that they had read for "recreational purposes" during the previous day, Trisman noted that "by far the most frequently mentioned recreational, or free-time, reading activity was the reading of words and sentences on the TV screen . . ." (Trisman, 1972, p. 10).

By combining the results of large-scale surveys (van der Brink, 1968; Ennis, 1965, 1966; Trisman, 1972; and Sharon, 1972) of the reading habits of American adults, it is possible to construct a composite profile. Most of the reading done by the "typical American adult" is confined to the newspaper, on which he spends approximately one-half hour per day. He is likely to spend a small amount of time reading bills, statements, advertisements, and—to a lesser degree—personal letters that he receives by mail. If he reads a magazine, it is likely to be one of general interest, or one that contains news and editorials. He has only about a 50 percent likelihood of choosing to read for recreation or to occupy his free time. He reads very few, if any, books, although he tends to read more books than does his counterpart in Western Europe. If he does read a book, it is most frequently fiction, either classic or current, or it is related to a sport or hobby, or to history. It is not too likely that he will read a book pertaining to science, a book of plays or poetry, or a book related to the social sciences.

Of course, not every American fits this pattern. Certainly we have all known—or perhaps are ourselves—the type of person who reads widely on a variety of topics, from a variety of sources, and for many reasons. Unfortunately, the surveys of adult readership in the United States tend to indicate that such persons are few.

Reading Habits of Adolescents

We might expect that teenagers' reading habits would be different from adults'. However, the findings of several surveys have indicated that this is not the case (Campbell, 1969; Trisman, 1972). The data from these surveys suggest that the reading habits of adolescents and adults are not significantly different. The majority of both groups tend to read newspapers and magazines, but very few books. And just as adults frequently use reading skills in a functional way—while traveling or commuting, or while shopping—teenagers in school frequently read notices, bulletin boards, and announcements. It appears that, as a group, both adolescents and adults seldom choose to read as a recreational activity.

Reading Habits of Children

It is more difficult to generalize about children's reading habits because of the lack of large-scale representative surveys such as those of adolescent and adult reading habits. However, from the available studies of children's media habits and their use of leisure time (Feeley, 1973; Jung, 1967; Long and Henderson, 1970; and Witty, 1965, 1966), and from general observation, we can readily conclude that children spend far more time watching television than they do reading. And, while it is quite possible that watching television can, potentially, broaden children's interests and experiences and lead to increased reading, it is more likely that television is a self-perpetuating medium. In other words, the viewing of television leads to more viewing rather than more reading—particularly if no attempt is made to capitalize upon interests developed through television viewing.

King (1972) reviewed and summarized various studies pertaining to children's reading habits. She noted that girls tend to read more than boys, and that the amount of reading done by both boys and girls increases with each succeeding year in elementary school. On the basis of the studies she reviewed, King stressed that the home environment and the availability of books are important influences upon children's reading habits.

Attitudes toward Reading

The present body of knowledge pertaining to attitude formation is rather limited. Nevertheless, we can identify several factors that appear to influence significantly the development of children's attitudes toward reading. It is particularly important that the teacher be aware of these factors because of their relationship to the formation of reading habits.

Influences within the Home

Among the influences on a child's attitude toward reading, research has indicated that an early exposure to books and reading within the child's home is particularly important. If someone has read to the child frequently during his pre-school years, and if he has seen his parents, siblings, or other persons significant to him engaged in reading-related activities, he is likely to have developed at least the readiness for a positive attitude toward reading.

Several research studies have indicated that the amount of time a child is read to during his pre-school years is proportionally related to later measurements of his IQ and school achievement (Bloom, 1964; Sutton, 1964). Studies of children who learned to read before entering school have also demonstrated the importance of early experiences with books and reading (Durkin, 1962; Plessas and Oakes, 1964). And, while these studies dealt with the influence of early experiences upon school achievement and the attainment of reading skill, the relationship of early experiences within the home to later attitudes toward reading has also been investigated. Hansen (1969, 1973) conducted a study of the "early home literary environment" of fourth-grade students in an effort to determine what specific factors influenced their attitudes toward reading. He found that such factors included parental help and encouragement; their assistance in selecting books; their discussion of books; and the regularity with which they read to their child. All of these influenced positively the child's later attitude toward reading, as evidenced by the number of books the child read independently.

Television viewing also appears to have considerable potential influence upon reading attitudes. And, although it is not possible to speak definitively about specific relationships between television viewing and attitudes toward reading, it is probable that television's influence is both positive and negative, and that the degree and direction of influence varies considerably from child to child.

Little doubt exists that the reading attitudes of some young viewers have been positively influenced by such programs as "Sesame Street" and "Electric Company," both of which include reading-related sequences in their programming. Through such programs many young viewers have been introduced to numbers, letters, and words in a visually exciting and rapidly-paced format. They have also listened with rapt attention while such "stars" as Bob, Easy Reader, or Mister Rogers have modeled reading habits for them.

While television may enrich the pre-school experiences of many children, it is doubtful that it can fully compensate for what is otherwise lacking in a child's home environment. Present research findings related to "Sesame Street," for example, have led to some speculation that it has actually widened the gap between more advantaged children and children from less advantaged home environments.

Television as a medium also has considerable potential impact on young viewers in relation to reading attitudes. Since television is often the first form of mass media with which children come into sustained contact, it is probable that they tend to judge other media—including printed media—in relation to television (Feeley, 1973). For sheer visual stimulation, the act of reading is hardly a match for a show such as "Electric Company," which is easily one of the most sophisticated shows on television in terms of the special electronic effects used in its production. Similarly, there is quite a contrast between the way in which reading-related activities are presented in some children's television shows and the way in which such activities are presented in schools.

Although many adults would certainly consider the rewards of reading much more significant than the short-term entertainment provided by television, the amount of time that the average child spends watching television would indicate that not all children agree. Children who have spent a great deal of time watching television during their pre-school years—to the exclusion of reading-related activities—may come to school with less well-developed attitudes toward reading. Such children need additional exposure to books and reading in order to orient themselves to printed media and to discover the personal benefits that reading can provide.

Influence of the School

It is frequently assumed that a child's attitude toward reading and, in turn, his interest in reading, is irreversibly determined by his home environment. But reading attitudes and, indeed, most attitudes are dynamic; they can change over a period of time in relation to new experiences. Within the school setting, teachers can plan and conduct numerous activities for children that will contribute to the formation of positive attitudes toward reading. In order to do this the teacher must be aware of the more subtle, and often unplanned, occurrences within the classroom that can negatively influence children's attitudes toward reading.

In their desire to develop children's reading skill, well-intentioned teachers have sometimes overlooked the necessity for developing reading attitudes. In classrooms where there is an overemphasis on skill development and little attention to attitudes, children often feel that it is the acquisition of reading skill per se that is valued and not the application of the skill for deriving information or enjoyment through print. A child might easily intuit such a message in a classroom where he spends many hours per week engaged in activities designed to develop and refine his skill in reading, but is provided little time within the school day to use his reading skill to pursue his own interests and purposes. It is well to remember that what is "caught" is often as important, and in some cases more important, than what is taught.

Children's exposure to "formal reading instruction," which typically occurs at the end of kindergarten or the beginning of first grade, often alters their attitudes toward reading. If one were to ask a group of kindergarten children near the beginning of the school year how many of them would like to learn to read, the chances are good that a large percentage would enthusiastically respond in the affirmative. After children have been introduced to reading instruction in the first grade their response to such a question may be quite different. Fewer are likely to respond as enthusiastically.

Both the amount of difference and the specific factors that account for the difference between the attitudes of kindergarten and first-grade children toward reading vary greatly from one school situation to another. It is probable, however, that kindergarten children perceive the question of learning to read in relation to their previous experiences with reading and books. Most kindergarten children want to learn to create for themselves the kind of positive experiences they have gained from being read to by parents and teachers. The first-grade children, on the other hand, having been exposed to reading instruction, would more likely respond to the question on the basis of how they perceived that instruction. The fact that children's attitude toward reading often appears to change after they are introduced to "formal reading instruction" points to the necessity of developing reading attitudes concurrently with reading skill.

The reading instructional program, or system, used can also influence children's reading attitudes. More important than the program itself, however, is the way in which the teacher uses the program and materials. With few exceptions, authors and publishers of basal reading instructional systems recommend that teachers judiciously select and adapt appropriate activities from the variety of teaching suggestions provided in teacher's manuals. Yet, in practice, some teachers apparently feel compelled to use many of the suggestions provided without adapting them to the specific children with whom they are working. Perhaps this is due to a lack of self-confidence, or an inability or unwillingness to make necessary adjustments. Whatever the reason, slavish adherence to teacher's manuals often results in instruction that is inappropriate for a specific group of children.

One outstanding example of inappropriate reading instruction is instruction on skills that children have previously mastered. When this occurs too frequently, children are likely to lose interest. The danger here is not only that they may become bored with reading instructional activities, but that they may generalize their dislike for reading instruction and develop negative attitudes toward reading as a process of gaining information and enjoyment. Anyone who has heard the statement made by a child that he "hates reading" cannot help wondering whether the child is referring to the instruction he receives in school, or to the process of learning, discovering, and experiencing through the medium of print. In most cases he is probably referring to the former and has, unfortunately, been provided with very little assistance in truly discovering the latter.

Another significant influence on reading attitudes is the readability, or reading difficulty, of instructional materials provided for children. If children are to learn to enjoy reading—or the process of gaining new insights and experiences through reading—the readability of textbooks and other printed materials they are expected to use must be appropriate for them. Few people enjoy activities that are too difficult; yet too often children are expected to use instructional materials that require reading skill beyond their present competence. When a child experiences continual difficulty due to material containing vocabulary and concepts far beyond his level of understanding, obviously he is not likely to develop a positive attitude toward reading.

The use children are permitted to make of classroom and school libraries and the amount of time they are permitted to read self-selected books can also influence their reading attitudes. If, for example, a teacher regularly schedules his class to use the school library for selecting books for voluntary reading, he should also use some of the valuable time within the school day to allow children to read and discuss the books they have selected. Despite the pressure many teachers feel to "cover" the essential elements of the curriculum, time used by children for reading and discussing self-selected books is time well spent. Children derive clues to what is valued within the school setting by the amount of time and attention devoted to a given activity or area of instruction. If books are merely made available, and no specific time is allotted for reading and sharing them, children are not as likely to view books and reading as being worthy of their attention.

Depending upon the degree to which the child responds to or is affected by peer pressure, his reading attitudes may be altered by a peer reference group. Since the elementary school is one of the primary settings for peer interaction, the teacher must be particularly aware of the ways in which children influence each other's perceptions and attitudes toward reading. Such an awareness can be gained through attitude questionnaires and informal observation techniques (which are discussed later in this chapter), and through sociograms, which indicate the peer interaction and friendship patterns of children in the classroom. After such data are gathered the teacher can regroup children within the classroom for reading-related activities that involve interaction among children with varying attitudes toward reading. If, for example, a teacher finds that several children appear to view reading, or reading instruction, rather negatively, he should make a concerted effort to structure situations that will allow these children to interact with other children in the class who have developed more positive attitudes. In this way, the teacher can affect reading attitudes through peer influence, which, for some children, is a stronger influence than the teacher's.

Teachers often provide subtle clues to their own attitude toward reading, which over a period of time can greatly influence their students' views of reading. For example, a teacher might tell his pupils that after they finish their "work" they may read whatever they wish. Here children may get the message that the work is important and the reading is merely something to do to occupy time. Furthermore, it is usually the more able pupils who finish their work first and have more time for reading.

Finally, and perhaps most important, is the matter of children's interest in the specific content of what is to be read. If children are to discover the value of reading, both as an information-gathering process and as a process of self-fulfillment, they must be provided with reading materials and reading-related activities in which they are interested. Of equal importance is the teacher's ability to stimulate children's interest in specific topics or reading materials through readiness and motivation-building activities. It may not always be possible to provide for every child's interests in every classroom activity. Nor is it always possible to develop the interest where it is lacking. However, a teacher can, through his knowledge of the interests of each child, structure follow-up and enrichment activities geared to individual interests. The degree to which this is done will have considerable influence on children's attitude toward reading.

Children's Reading Interests

Because of the significant relationship between children's interests and their attitudes toward reading, literally hundreds of research studies have been undertaken during the past fifty years in an effort to determine the nature of children's interests, and specifically their reading interests. While the research methodology employed has varied widely, such studies have typically used library circulation records, questionnaires, interviews, and teacher and pupil records of books read to study the reading interests and preferences of large groups of children of various ages. A child may prefer to read one kind of material over another, but have no interest in reading anything. The criterion is action, that is, what is actually read. Because of the method of data collection used in many of the studies that purport to investigate "reading interests," they could more appropriately be considered studies of reading preferences (Weintraub, 1969).

The findings of research studies have been useful in establishing general guidelines, which teachers, librarians, authors, and publishers can use for selecting reading material—particularly when the specific children who will use such materials are not known beforehand. It should be recognized, however, that generalized findings from studies of large groups of children are of limited usefulness when applied to an individual child. For example, the fact that many fifth-grade girls report that they are interested in "horse stories" is obviously no guarantee that a specific girl in fifth grade will be.

On the basis of the various reviews of research on children's reading interests and preferences (Beta Upsilon Chapter of Pi Lambda Theta, 1974; Getzels, 1966; Huus, 1964; King, 1972; Purves and Beach, 1972; Weintraub, 1969; and Zimet, 1966) we can make the following generalizations: Primary grade children appear to prefer stories of humor and fantasy, animal stories, stories related to nature and living things, and realistic stories based upon everyday experiences involving children. It has been well established that reading interests change as children mature. Studies have shown that intermediate grade children are generally interested in mystery and adventure, biographies, animal stories, stories of family life, sports, and stories that would come under the general topics of science and social studies.

Until approximately third grade there appear to be few differences between the reading interests of boys and girls. However, clearly defined differences appear at about the age of nine. Girls show an increasing interest in fiction of a romantic nature and stories related to home and school, while boys rank action, adventure, biographies of sports figures, and stories of science and invention as major interests. In general, boys express a wider range of interests than do girls. This is not to say that boys are necessarily interested in more topics, but that within any given group of boys there is likely to be less agreement as to what is "interesting" to them.

While girls may be likely to read what would generally be considered "boys' books," the opposite is seldom the case. This undoubtedly arises from socially patterned behavior, since there appears to be a taboo in our society that in effect prohibits boys from reading "girls' books." Indeed, there is considerable evidence that the reading preferences expressed by children are heavily influenced by sex stereotyping.

In addition to the generalizations regarding topical preferences and reading interests of children by chronological age and sex, various research studies have yielded information about children's preferences for specific literary forms. This research has indicated that elementary school children generally prefer fiction to non-fiction, although the demand for realistic treatments of objects, people, and situations increases through the elementary grades (Peltola, 1965). Also, children appear to prefer narrative materials having a suspenseful plot, and those containing a generous amount of action, nonsense, and humor.

Elementary school children generally demonstrate less interest in poetry than in other narrative forms, although girls show a greater interest in poetry than do boys. Nelson's (1966) analysis of favorite poems of primary-grade children indicated that such poems contained a minimum of description while maintaining a clearly defined story line. They also contained much action and humor and dealt with experiences of children.

Children's interest in poetry tends to decline as they proceed through the elementary grades. And, while the reasons for this decline of interest are unclear, research has indicated that intermediate grade children dislike poetry that includes overly complex sentence structure and abstract, figurative language.

There has also been much research on children's preferences for and interests in specific types of illustrations. Generally, most primary grade children prefer realistic illustrations that they can readily interpret. Line drawings may be as effective, or perhaps more effective, than photographs since photographs are likely to include some extraneous details. The extent to which each illustration depicts action or some element of the story line also appears to be important. For kindergarten children especially, illustrations are at least as important a factor as the book's content in arousing children's interest. Older children appear to be less influenced by the amount and type of illustration. However, some older children may avoid a book with numerous illustrations—even when the content interests them—possibly because they feel that the book was written for younger children.

Teachers should remember, however, that these are all generalizations. A story or poem having all the elements of content, form, and illustration that children generally prefer may be poorly received by a given individual or group. At the same time, a teacher may select materials to be read to, or by, children that contain none of these preferred elements, and still be able to stimulate children's interest. The teacher's own enthusiasm for the particular material, and his manner of dealing with it, can do a great deal to generate interest.

Creative teachers are frequently able to "sell" a book to children as a result of their own enthusiasm for it. But, while this is certainly helpful in stimulating children's interest in reading, the most desirable and productive means of creating long-lasting interest in books and reading is by introducing children to books that have particular relevance to them—books that speak to them on a highly personal level.

Developing Reading Attitudes and Interests

The first part of this chapter presented background information on reading habits, attitudes, and interests. These topics were dealt with separately to facilitate analysis and discussion of each, but in reality they are highly interrelated. It is of limited value, for example, to consider reading attitudes and interests independently of reading habits, since a major purpose of reading instruction and other reading-related activities in the elementary school should be to help children develop reading habits that are both purposeful and personally constructive. Reading habits should serve some function—whether utilitarian or recreational—and aid personal growth.

The attitudes and interests an individual develops in relation to reading exert a significant influence upon his reading habits. Further, there is considerable evidence that the reading habits an individual develops while he is in elementary school will set the pattern for his reading habits in adulthood. For this reason, developing children's attitudes and interests within the elementary school is a primary means of affecting their reading habits. In the second part of this chapter specific programs and strategies are described that can be used to develop children's reading attitudes and interests and in turn their reading habits.

Before considering these strategies, however, it is necessary to examine some of the assumptions upon which they are based. The efficacy of the strategies described will depend on the acceptance—at least in principle—of the following assumptions:

1. One of the primary goals of a reading program is to help the individual child to develop purposeful and personally constructive reading habits.
2. An individual's reading habits can be influenced by providing him with appropriate activities and experiences within the school setting.
3. A primary means of effecting interest in reading—and, consequently, reading habits—is by determining an individual's interests so that reading materials and/or reading experiences can be provided that are aligned to those interests.
4. An individual's attitude toward reading contributes directly to the formation of purposeful and personally constructive reading habits.
5. The degree to which an individual discovers personal relevance and value in what he reads will, to a large extent, influence his attitude toward reading and, in turn, his reading habits.

Although not all of the above assumptions can be tested directly through experience or research, the literature on reading habits, interests, and attitudes that was reviewed in the preceding part of this chapter adequately justifies their acceptance.

Keeping in mind the long-range goal of developing purposeful and personally constructive reading habits, the basic question the teacher faces is "how to turn kids on to reading." Just as there is no single approach to teaching children *how* to read that has been found to be consistently more effective than another approach, there is also no single most effective approach to developing children's attitudes and interests. For this reason, many approaches and strategies are detailed in the following sections.

The following general guidelines are suggested for the teacher who wishes to build his students' interest in reading. Some of the guidelines refer to aspects of the reading/language arts program, some refer to the classroom climate for reading, and others imply teacher behaviors that encourage children to read independently.

1. Get to know each of your students well. Determine what interests each one and provide materials and activities that are aligned to those interests.
2. Provide for early and continued success in mastery of reading skills. Develop needed skills sequentially, teaching only those skills that have not been previously mastered. Make learning to read enjoyable. Integrate instruction in all areas of language: reading, writing, speaking, and listening.
3. Read to children often, not only when you have time. *Make* the time. Expose children to creative and colorful use of language in poetry and narrative. Introduce them to the sounds and rhythms of language. Select what you will read with the same care you use in selecting your own reading material.
4. Become familiar with the best in children's literature. Use your knowledge of children's books to select books for your classroom and to recommend books to your students. Use children's literature to supplement learning of, and interest in, content areas of the curriculum, such as social studies and science.
5. Be a reader yourself, not only of children's books, but of materials that have personal relevance to you. Share your enthusiasm for reading with children. Be caught "red-handed" in the act of reading for pleasure.
6. Provide a great quantity, and quality, of books and other reading material within your classroom—especially paperback books. Beg, buy, borrow, or make books, but by all means make them available to children.
7. Provide time for sustained silent reading and for discussions among children of the books they have read. Structure "sharing" and "celebrating" activities through which children can stimulate the interest of their classmates.
8. Help children discover that reading is not a "subject they had in school," but a valuable tool for expanding and clarifying their own experiences. Help them learn *why* to read as well as how to read—that is, help them to uncover their own purposes for reading.

Within the guidelines listed above are many specific strategies that can be effectively applied in an elementary school reading/language arts program. In the following sections of this chapter these guidelines are expanded to include suggested activities and strategies.

Determining Children's Reading Interests and Attitudes

A major means of building the kind of interest in reading that helps form constructive reading habits is to provide children with reading materials and reading-related activities that interest them. The degree to which this can be done successfully depends, of course, upon the teacher's knowledge of each child's interests. Unquestionably, the best way of determining what interests a child is by getting to know him well. Although this may seem like an over-simplification, the importance of knowing each child personally cannot be emphasized too strongly.

The most useful information about interests and attitudes is that which is gathered by the teacher daily. Within every school day there are countless opportunities for determining children's interests and attitudes, and the teacher who employs diagnostic teaching techniques can capitalize upon them. Conversations between children, products of their creative activities, class projects, trips to the library, group sharing activities, and a variety of other situations in which children are involved in self-initiated activities provide rich sources of information about their interests and attitudes toward reading. The teacher who is aware of the opportunities that all of these situations provide will not only make a concerted effort to observe and interact with children in a variety of learning situations, but will also spend as much time as possible talking informally with individual children. Time spent with one child looking through and discussing various books in the school or classroom library can not only provide the teacher with greater insight into the child's interests and attitude toward reading, but can also communicate to the child the teacher's genuine concern and interest in him as a person.

Determining Reading Interests and Preferences While there is no real substitute for first-hand knowledge about the child that is gathered through informal observation and interaction, there are various techniques and instruments the teacher can use to discover children's interests. Interest inventories, questionnaires, structured and informal interviews, auto-biographies, circulation records from school or classroom libraries, and records of books the child has read provide valuable clues to reading interests and preferences.

Included under the general category of interest inventories are a wide variety of specific instruments. Basically, interest inventories consist of a series of questions or incomplete sentences, which are designed to elicit responses from the child about his experiences, his likes and dislikes, his hobbies, and his use of free time. Most interest inventories are not copyrighted. Sample copies of such inventories can usually be obtained from school district language arts coordinators, from reading clinic personnel, or from college and university teacher education program faculty.

An interest inventory may be administered orally or used as an outline for an interview conducted by the teacher, or it can be duplicated so that children may read it by themselves and record their own responses. Whichever method of administration is used, it is usually desirable to have the child respond as spontaneously as possible so that he does not spend undue time and energy speculating on what response the teacher would *like* him to give. If the child is asked to respond rapidly, this so-called "halo effect" will, hopefully, be reduced. Since the usefulness of the child's responses will be determined by his candidness in answering the questions, it is also important the inventory be administered in such a way that the child feels free to respond frankly.

In addition to the *Interest Inventory* (*Table 15,* p. 464), an incomplete sentence, or open-ended, inventory may prove to be very useful to the teacher. Following are several examples of items which might be included in an incomplete sentence interest inventory:

I like.......................
It's fun to ....
After school.................
Reading.....................
TV.........................
I think that school ....
I would read more often if .....

Again, this type of inventory may be administered orally, or read and completed by the child. As with the question-type inventory, it is important to have the child respond as spontaneously as possible.

Whatever the format or method of administration, the most valuable interest inventory is the one the teacher himself constructs to use with a particular individual or group. Such an inventory can be related to a specific purpose the teacher has, and the vocabulary used in the items can be adjusted for the particular children who will use the inventory. Items to be included in a teacher-made inventory should be selected carefully to avoid embarrassing particular individuals.

To make the best use of an interest inventory, the teacher should review and summarize the child's responses, listing several topics or even specific reading materials or books in which the child may be interested.

Table 15   Interest Inventory

Name: _____ Age: _____ Date: _____

Grade: _____ Teacher: _____ School: _____

(Check One):   Read to child: _____   Read by child: _____

General Interests

1. What do you like to do in your free time?
2. What do you usually do after school?
3. What are your favorite TV shows?
4. Do you have any hobbies?
5. Do you collect anything? What?
6. What things do you like to make?
7. Do you belong to any clubs or scout groups?
8. What games or sports do you like best?
9. What kind of places do you like to visit?
10. Have you taken any trips with your family? Where?
11. Do you have any pets at home? What kind?
12. What kind of work do you want to do after you finish school?

Reading Habits and Interests

13. Do you go to the public library (or bookmobile)? How often?
14. Do you have any books of your own? About how many?
15. Does someone read to you (or with you) at home? Who?
16. What things do you like to read about?
17. What is the title of the best book you ever read?
18. Do you read comic books? Which ones?
19. Do you read magazines? Which ones?
20. If you were to write your own book what might it be about?

This summary can then be recorded on a file card so that it can be readily referred to for planning instructional strategies, or for helping the child select reading materials.

The teacher can also find valuable clues to children's interests in library circulation records and records of books the children have read—kept either by the teacher or the children themselves.

Discussions with parents about the interests of their child are another important source of information. Informal contacts with parents as well as questionnaires and parent-teacher conferences provide opportunities for the teacher to learn a great deal about the child that could not be learned in the school setting.

The above strategies for determining individual children's interests will provide useful information in most cases. However, within any given classroom there are likely to be some children who appear to have no well-defined interests that can be capitalized upon for building interest in reading. While it is certainly true that some children lack the desire to read—or at least are not interested in those things that teachers think they should be—it is equally apparent that every child is interested in something. No matter how difficult it may be for the teacher to determine what that something is, the effort is well worth expending since it is often the case that those children who appear to lack well-defined interests also require the most assistance in discovering the personal value of reading.

Interests, like attitudes, are constantly subject to change as a result of new experiences. The teacher must not just survey children's interests at the beginning of the year, and then assign, or ascribe, areas of interest to a given child. Certainly a major aspect of the teacher's role includes helping children to expand their present areas of interest and providing experiences that help them to develop new interests.

Assessing Attitude toward Reading The extent to which a child discovers the personal benefits of reading will affect, and be affected by, his attitude toward reading. That is, a child who has developed a negative attitude toward reading and/or reading instruction may also develop an "avoidance reaction" that could preclude his development of constructive reading habits.

The first step in positively influencing a child's attitude toward reading is the collection of relevant data. The primary means of gathering data about a child's reading attitude is by observing his responses to reading in a variety of instructional and non-instructional situations. Rowell (1972) developed an observation instrument that can serve as an aid to the teacher in gathering attitudinal data related to reading.

Other means of assessing reading attitudes are also available. Numerous questionnaires have been developed that are intended to "measure" children's attitudes toward reading. Although the results of some of these questionnaires are generally no more valid than data derived from continued observations by an experienced teacher, questionnaires can provide potentially useful information about children's attitudes toward reading.

An example of an attitude questionnaire that has been widely used is the *San Diego County Inventory of Reading Attitude* (San Diego County Department of Education, 1961). It consists of twenty-five "Do you like to . . . ?" items in a written format. The child's *yes* or *no* responses to the items yield a stanine score that is supposedly indicative of his attitude toward reading. Another attitude questionnaire—one which the teacher of older children may find useful—was developed by Estes (1971, 1972). It contains twenty statements related to reading; the child indicates his agreement or disagreement with each item on a five-point scale.

Fiddler (1973) constructed and standardized an instrument for assessing attitude toward reading, which differs markedly from other attitude questionnaires because of the rigorous validation procedures used in its construction and because of the way in which it is administered. Of the 100 items in the questionnaire, only twenty are directly related to reading attitude. These twenty items are based upon Fiddler's adaption of Krathwohl's (1964) taxonomy of the affective domain. Because the purpose of the Fiddler questionnaire is disguised by the eighty "distracting" items, the probability of a "halo effect" is greatly reduced. Therefore this questionnaire is likely to yield a more accurate indication of a child's attitude toward reading.

The data gathered through informal observation or attitude questionnaires must be used to plan reading-related activities if it is to affect children's reading habits. If, for example, you have some children in your class who appear to view reading quite positively, but who lack the basic reading skills, it will be necessary to spend additional time diagnosing and correcting their specific reading deficiencies so that their positive attitudes can be maintained. If, on the other hand, you find that several children in your class appear to view reading and/or reading instruction rather negatively, it will probably be more beneficial for these children if you place greater emphasis on developing their attitudes toward reading. This can be done through informal counseling or group therapy where reading attitudes and habits are the focus of the discussion, and through the use of the various strategies in this chapter that are designed to develop children's interest in reading.

Providing Early and Continued Success in Reading

Many children enter school eager to learn to read. In fact, for some children, starting school and learning to read appear to be synonymous. At the same time, it is often difficult for children to understand that the ability to read cannot be mastered instantly. The fact that children want to be able to read on the first or second day of school presents the kindergarten or first-grade teacher with the difficulty of maintaining children's enthusiasm for learning to read while developing initial reading skills. The way a teacher deals with this dilemma will have considerable potential impact on pupils' attitude toward reading.

Children need to experience some degree of success with reading even before they are able to employ decoding strategies independently. No matter what approach or specific instructional materials are to be used for initial reading instruction, early success with reading can be provided by developing "experience charts" that contain stories or experiences that are dictated by the children and recorded by the teacher on the chalkboard or chart paper. Similarly, children can dictate captions or brief stories related to their creative artwork. The experience charts or captions are then "read" either by individuals, or chorally by the group. Through such activities children can develop a number of important concepts and pre-reading skills while experiencing the visual and mental processing skills involved in reading. As children recall the words they have dictated, they begin to understand that their speech can be represented by printed symbols that are graphically produced and visually processed in a left-to-right sequence. In addition to exposing children to such conventions of English orthography as capitalization and punctuation, experience charts also help children make associations between printed symbols and the concepts and objects those symbols represent.

The labelling of items in the classroom such as chairs, tables, and windows can also help children associate words with concrete objects. Such labels also help children establish sound-symbol correspondences and sight recognition of the visual form of words.

While the above strategies are often associated with what is known as the "whole-word" or "sight-word" approach to beginning reading, we do not suggest that such an approach be used exclusively. The above "language-experience" strategies can be used in conjunction with virtually any method or approach to beginning reading instruction. By using experience charts, writing captions to pictures, and labelling classroom objects, children can experience some degree of early success with reading even before they can actually employ a decoding strategy. Perhaps too often teachers have dutifully begun teaching decoding skills and have apparently overlooked the importance of providing experiences and activities for children that sustain their interest in learning to read.

Maintaining children's interest in learning to read and in improving their skill in reading is, of course, not only important during the initial stages of reading skill acquisition, but throughout all grade levels. As has been noted previously, the way children are taught how to read—that is, the way reading instruction is managed in the classroom—can have a major effect upon their attitudes toward reading.

Obviously, it is important that children experience success and enjoyment in learning to read. They must experience the same degree of success that all of us need to continue in demanding tasks. Children cannot reasonably be expected to develop positive attitudes and interest in reading if they continually experience difficulty with the basic word recognition and comprehension processes.

To help ensure that each child will develop the skill he needs to read efficiently, a "management system" can be employed in the reading instructional program. Such a system might be based upon the "skills strand" of a basal reading series, or on one of the various "systems approaches" to teaching reading; but, hopefully, it would be based on the teacher's own understanding of the developmental aspects of learning to read. Whatever form it takes, the use of a management system implies that reading instruction is based upon the diagnosed needs of individuals. It further implies that reading instruction is both differentiated and personalized, although it does not necessarily mean that each child is actually taught individually.

The terms *management system* and *systems approach* may seem to have Orwellian connotations; actually, however, they describe highly humanistic methods. What is more humanistic than helping children learn what *they* need or want to learn? And what is more demoralizing than failing to help them develop skill in the uniquely human ability to read?

The use of a reading instructional management system does not prescribe or proscribe any single method or approach to teaching reading. Nor does it require that reading skills be developed through "dreary, demeaning, dreadfully dull, dry drill." It merely implies that the teacher knows the developmental level of each child, and that provisions are made for the child's continued growth and success.

The teacher should be aware not only of the reading skill needs of each child in the class but also of the need for developing the reading attitudes and interests that contribute to constructive reading habits. Some teachers seem to feel that reading skills should be developed first and that interest in reading will follow naturally. As well as being unrealistic from a child's point of view, such a perception is both limiting and short-sighted. Reading programs based on this position—whether by design or by practice—fail to capitalize on the motivation generated when the child is helped to uncover the many and varied uses he can make of his reading skill. When he is engaged in reading that is aligned to an existing interest, or generates a new interest, the child is far more likely to see the usefulness of reading.

Reading to Children

Perhaps the best way of inspiring a young child with a desire of learning to read is, to read to him, with proper intervals, some interesting story, perfectly intelligible, yet as full of suggestion as communication; for the pleasure of discovering is always greater than that of perceiving.

(Horace Mann, 1838)

Horace Mann's advice is as cogent and timely for children of the electronic age as it was for the children of Massachusetts in 1838. Although he referred to building children's desire to learn to read, his advice is equally applicable to sustaining and building interest in reading.

Most teachers and parents would agree that reading to primary grade children can provide them with many benefits that they cannot derive for themselves because of their lack of reading skill. Yet for many reasons—not the least of which is lack of time—the practice of reading to children seems to decline rapidly when children reach the upper primary and intermediate grades. Children of all grade levels can profit from and enjoy being read to.

Reading to children serves many purposes. In addition to the more obvious purposes of modeling good oral reading habits and building children's listening skills, reading to children allows them to experience literature which they might not be able to read or be inclined to read for themselves. Oral reading to children can also whet their appetite to read more on their own. For example, an exciting chapter of a book that is read aloud can often stimulate children to read the entire book themselves. In addition to providing exposure to specific books, reading to children can also introduce them to creative and colorful use of language in prose and poetry, introduce new vocabulary and concepts, and acquaint children with the variety of language patterns found in written and oral communication.

For the individual child, being read to and reading to himself are very different. Because he is freed from the visual processing aspects of reading, and because he can think much faster than the reader can read orally, the child can devote greater attention to the images evoked by the story or poem being read to him. He can, for example, imagine that he is living the part of one of the characters in the selection; or he can see, smell, hear, taste, or feel what the author describes.

Much of the message of reading orally to children is communicated by the medium itself. For this reason, how a selection is read is often as important as what is read. When you read to children, let your own enthusiasm for the material show. Your voice inflection, intonation, and facial expressions will not only add interest and meaning to the selection, but will also convey your own attitudes toward reading and books.

Certainly you can do a great deal to add interest to a story that is to be read to children by pre-reading it several times to practice the mechanics of reading it orally. It is doubtful, however, that mechanical perfection alone will achieve the purpose for which such reading is intended. If you yourself do not have a genuine interest in the selection you read to children you are less likely to secure their interest. For this reason it is obviously very important to select books to read aloud that you find especially appealing. With the variety and quality of children's books available this should not be difficult.

Before you begin reading to children, it is helpful to spend a few minutes building their readiness for the selection. This might be done by leading children into a discussion of prior experiences pertinent to the selection, or by giving them some basic information such as the title and asking them to speculate upon what the story might be about. Interesting biographical information about the author might also be used. In other cases the use of "realia" (tangible objects) or pictures and illustrations might be helpful. Readiness activities should be brief and should build interest while introducing or reviewing concepts contained in the selection to be read.

If the main objective of reading to children is to build their interest in reading, any discussion of the selection that follows the reading should reflect this purpose. Few adults would enjoy being closely questioned about what they have read, yet some teachers have an inclination to interrogate children after reading a story to them. And, while the use of effective questioning strategies can do a great deal to build comprehension skills, it is possible to "beat a story to death" by asking too many of the wrong types of questions. It is better to ask a few well-selected questions that serve as a stimulus for discussion of the major concepts developed or implied in the selection. In addition to reviewing some of the major aspects of the selection, such questions should also focus upon the feelings and emotions the selection evoked, as well as some of the elements of form or theme that make the story or poem especially appealing. A discussion of E. B. White's *Charlotte's Web* could, for example, focus primarily upon the concepts of "true friendship" and "the cycle of life." And, while it is true that the events in the story are essential for the development of these concepts, the children's feelings about the events are of greater importance.

Exposing children to literature through reading aloud need not be limited to the situation where the teacher or librarian reads to the entire class. Many excellent cassette tapes, phonograph records, films, and correlated filmstrip and tape recordings of children's books are commercially available and can be used independently by children. For example, a cassette recording of Sendak's *Where the Wild Things Are* (Weston Woods)—as well as other recordings—could be placed in the classroom reading corner or language arts center along with several copies of the book and a tape recorder. An individual child or a small group of children using a listening station with jacks for multiple head sets, could then listen to the recording while reading along in the books. This type of activity can generate a great deal of interest in a variety of selections while providing another medium through which children can experience literature.

The current state of school finance should not keep the resourceful teacher from providing activities of this type for children. It is not necessary to achieve the studio quality of commercially prepared tapes. Teachers can make homemade tapes, either of an entire selection or just enough to stimulate children to finish reading it on their own. A recording made by a child who is reasonably fluent in oral reading can also be used to stimulate other children's interest in a book.

Having children read to other children in a "live" situation can also build interest in reading. While this can be done within the classroom among classmates, it is often mutually beneficial to have older children read to younger children. This not only provides the older children with an eager audience for whom to refine and use their skill in oral reading, but it also widens the younger children's experience with literature and allows them to see older children modeling reading behaviors they can emulate.

Whether or not you can recall the specific *content* of stories or poems which were read to you in the elementary grades by a parent, teacher, or librarian, you can no doubt remember such experiences. For the most part, the recollections of these experiences evoke positive feelings. Perhaps this is because people who frequently read to children seem to do so because they are convinced that children can benefit by experiencing literature in this manner. The positive feelings you remember are also likely to be partly the result of the skill and enthusiasm with which the selection was read, and partly the result of the person having carefully selected what was read to you.

Becoming Familiar with Children's Books

Literally thousands of children's books are published each year. Current estimates of the number published annually place the figure at more than 3000. While this figure may be somewhat misleading since some of these are reprints of books published in previous years, the responsibility of teachers to familiarize themselves with children's books is no less formidable an undertaking.

Keeping Informed about Books The sheer number of children's books on the market might be somewhat intimidating, since a teacher cannot reasonably hope to read all of them. Because the time required to read children's books and the availability of the books are important constraints that teachers face in familiarizing themselves with children's literature, the numerous sources of book reviews and other compilations of children's books are very helpful. Most periodicals pertaining to elementary education include reviews of children's books. Reviews can be found, for example, in *Language Arts, The Reading Teacher, Childhood Education, The Instructor, Grade Teacher, Early Years,* and *Learning.* In addition there are several periodicals devoted almost exclusively to children's literature. The *Horn Book Magazine, Bookbird, Bulletin of the Center for Children's Books, Booklist,* and the *School Library Journal* include current reviews as well as recommended, and in some cases non-recommended, titles. Reviews of children's books can also be found in the *New York Times,* the *Chicago Tribune,* and in *Saturday Review.* The *New York Times* also publishes an annual supplement devoted to children's literature.

In addition to these book review sources, numerous reference publications contain annotated lists of recommended children's books. Some of these publications that the teacher will want to consult are listed at the end of the chapter. (See "Aids for Selecting Children's Books.")

Another useful source in selecting children's books is a listing of Newbery and Caldecott award winners. The John Newbery Award is presented annually to the author whose book is most highly evaluated on the basis of literary merit, while excellence in illustration is the criterion used in awarding the annual Randolph Caldecott Medal. Generally speaking, many of the Newbery Award books are most appropriate for independent reading by children in the intermediate grades, but could be read to younger children. Many Caldecott Medal books, on the other hand, are geared to the interests and preferences of pre-school and primary grade children, since they contain numerous illustrations of a very high quality.

In addition to the Newbery and Caldecott awards, several other awards for outstanding children's books are presented on a regular basis. Information about these awards is contained in the Children's Book Council publication entitled *Children's Books: Awards and Prizes.* While most of these awards are determined by committees of adults, the Young Reader's Choice Award, which is presented annually by the Pacific Northwest Library Association, is based upon the preferences of children in the northwestern United States and British Columbia.

Finally, teachers who are skeptical of book reviewers and children's book award committees, and who subscribe to the "best seller" method of determining which children's books are read most frequently, will want to consult Kujoth's *Best-Selling Children's Books* (1973). Although this publication is very useful, it should be kept in mind that most children's books are probably purchased by adults.

Reading book reviews and reference lists will unquestionably conserve a great deal of time and energy which might otherwise be spent searching through the stacks of a library. Consulting a school librarian or the children's librarian of a university or public library will also be quite helpful. However, these references and resource persons are only a starting point. If you want to become truly familiar with children's literature, you will have to read it.

Reading Children's Books Before you embark on a continuing regimen of reading children's literature, stop for a moment to consider why you need to be familiar with books for children. How, for example, can you hope to interest children in books which you have not read yourself? How can you select the "right" books to read to your students if you are not aware of the many exciting possibilities? How can you refer an individual child to a specific book that could help him gain insight into a particular problem he has if you are not aware of the bibliotherapeutic qualities inherent in many children's books? Finally, how can you decide which books contain the "stuff of which childhood is made" if you have not sampled many of these books yourself?

Once you have convinced yourself of the importance of being familiar with children's literature and have developed a basic reading list, the next step is, of course, to begin reading. Read as many books as you have the time and interest to read. Visit an elementary school library and the children's book room of a university or public library. Check out books, and read them. Start your own file on children's books by selecting those books that you feel are the best. Briefly summarize the plot of the book on an index card; list some of the major concepts the book develops; and, where appropriate, list any bibliotherapeutic value you think the book might have for specific children. Make your book notes as detailed or as brief as you like so long as they help you to select books you want to read to children or help you recommend a specific book to a specific child.

In considering which are the best books to include in your classroom program, take into account the various aspects of literature normally used in literary analysis—style, theme, characterization, and plot. Most importantly, however, try to evaluate a book from a child's point of view. Ask yourself whether the book seems to be relevant to the lives of children in your classroom; whether it is likely to have some impact upon them; whether it meets some basic psychological need—including the need to laugh; and, equally important, whether it is simply fun to read.

Creating a Classroom Climate for Reading

The teacher's familiarity with children's literature is one of the basic ingredients of any program that succeeds in developing children's interest in reading. In addition, there are several other significant classroom influences upon children's reading attitudes and interests and, in turn, their reading habits. These include the attitude toward reading and books which the teacher demonstrates daily; the availability and accessibility of a wide variety of reading materials within the classroom; and multiple opportunities for children to read and share the pleasure they derive from books they read. The sum total of these factors is the primary indicator of what might be called the "classroom climate for reading." More broadly conceived, the climate for reading can extend far beyond the walls of the classroom.

Modeling Reading Habits As a teacher your own attitude toward reading will be one of the most significant factors in determining the classroom reading climate. And while you might be able to pretend to be interested in books and reading by affecting enthusiasm, you will probably not be able to fool many children for very long. Children are quick to detect insincerity, whatever form it takes. Regardless of what you say about reading in general or about specific books, your own personal behavior in relation to reading will speak loudest. So let your actions do the talking; let children see that reading is an important part of your personal life as well as a necessity in your profession. Bring your own reading to school to fill your spare moments—be they ever so few. Instead of going to the teachers' lounge during your free period, relax with a book in a comfortable chair in your own classroom reading corner. (And don't be afraid to be "caught" there when your class returns from their gym period.) Share your enthusiasm for reading with children. Catch up on some personal reading while children are reading; share what you have read with them. Let them know what reading has meant to you, how you feel about what you have read, and what difference it has made in your life. In short, be a model of the kind of reading habits children will want to emulate.

Making Books Available If children are expected to develop purposeful and personally constructive reading habits they must have a sufficient quantity and quality of books at their fingertips. Ideally, every elementary school classroom should contain its own collection of books suitable to the range of interests and preferences of each child in the class. A useful rule of thumb is to have at least fifteen books in the classroom collection for each member of the class. The fact that many elementary schools have adequate school library facilities and provisions for regularly scheduled visits by individual classes does not reduce the necessity for creating classroom libraries where books and other reading materials are invitingly displayed.

One way of starting a classroom library is to borrow a basic collection of books from the school library or the public library. Many public libraries have provisions for lending collections of children's books to schools. Such collections should be rotated frequently enough to provide a continually fresh supply throughout the year.

Paperback books are a particularly good source of supply for classroom libraries. The number of high quality, inexpensive paperbacks on today's market allows for the addition of many volumes to the classroom library with only a moderate investment. Many titles by such children's authors as E. B. White, Ezra Jack Keats, Laura Ingalls Wilder, and Maurice Sendak are currently available in paperback at prices well below the original hardcover editions. Many classroom teachers have discovered that paperback books appear to be less formidable to many children than hardbound books and therefore seem to have greater appeal. Whether this is because paperbacks seem more manageable or because hardbound books remind children of "school books," the special appeal of paperbacks should be capitalized upon to encourage independent reading. Fader and McNeil (1968) have described a successful reading program for reluctant readers built around the use of paperback books.

Children's book clubs that offer inexpensive paperback books provide another source of supply for classroom libraries. Many of these book clubs offer "dividend books" when a class orders a given number of books. These dividend books can be donated by the class to the permanent collection in the classroom. In addition, children are often willing to share their own books by donating or lending their personal copies of books to the classroom library so that other children can read them. Although it is probably wise to check with parents first, the practice of donating books can be encouraged by having children autograph the inside cover accordingly: "Donated by _____"; or, "On loan from the private library of _____."

In times of tight school budgets many teachers have purchased books for their classroom libraries at their own expense. In addition to being a good investment in "tools of the trade," such expenditures are usually tax deductible. The teacher who is fortunate enough to be given responsibility for allocating a portion of the school's materials budget to purchase items for his own classroom should seriously consider spending part of the allocation to augment the classroom library. Money that might be spent to purchase the latest "skills kit" or a new set of workbooks could be used to far greater advantage if it were allotted to the purchase of many inexpensive paperback books. Furthermore, such an investment will probably pay far greater dividends in the long run.

So far we have suggested that teachers beg, buy, or borrow books for the classroom collection. We have not recommended stealing books, but there is a fourth alternative—make them. Books written and illustrated by members of the class are often the hottest items on the shelves. Furthermore, there is usually no communication gap between the author and the reader of such books. It is fair to assume that children know what other children would like to read about, so there is no problem of a credibility gap either. If a child wants to know why a story written by one of his classmates turned out as it did, he can simply ask him.

Class bookmaking projects not only provide a creative outlet for budding authors, they also serve as a springboard for getting children into a whole range of related topics such as plot, theme, characterization, and illustration. The books produced in such projects can range from the first grader's collection of language-experience stories stapled between two sheets of construction paper to a fourth grader's elaborately bound "first edition," produced in the classroom from remnants of sewing fabric, cardboard, dry mount tissue and construction paper.

Allowing children to borrow books from the classroom library to take home is often a good idea, since this encourages more independent reading. A simple check-out system can be instituted by having the children sign their names on a file card or in a notebook kept in the classroom library. Some teachers have found that they can successfully use an "honor system" for lending books. Whatever system is used, it is a good idea to keep the loan policy flexible enough so that children will not be discouraged from borrowing books. You need not be too alarmed, for example, if the best books in your classroom library appear to be missing most of the time. In fact, if a book is not an expensive one and has been borrowed for an extended period of time by a child who was previously a reluctant reader, you might consider replacing the book with a new copy. While being too lenient may result in the loss of many of your books, it is equally probable that being too rigid may discourage independent reading. The question really becomes one of deciding where a given book might do the most good—in the hands of one child who does not have any books of his own, or in the classroom library.

Children need not start their own personal libraries at the expense of the classroom collection, however. Book ownership can be promoted through paperback book clubs, through school-wide "book fairs" where children can trade, buy, or sell used paperbacks, or through a program such as the Smithsonian Institution's Reading Is Fundamental Program which provides children with books either free of charge or at a substantially reduced cost. The experience of many teachers and the success of various Reading Is Fundamental projects throughout the country have adequately demonstrated that children's motivation to read can be substantially increased by emphasizing the pleasure of reading through personal owner-ship of books.

When stocking your classroom library do not overlook other sources of printed media such as pamphlets, magazines, and newspapers. Although comic books are still controversial, they can sometimes be used to attract the attention of reluctant readers. Paperback books containing cartoons, such as Schulz's "Peanuts" series, can often serve a similar purpose. Once children begin the habit of reading, they can be encouraged to undertake more substantive reading. The classroom library might also contain periodicals such as *Children's Digest, Highlights for Children, Jack and Jill, Cricket, Kids,* and *Child Life,* as well as copies of the daily newspaper.

It is also important to create an attractive physical environment in the classroom that encourages the development of reading habits. The classroom library collection should be housed in a prominent location in the "reading corner" or "language arts center." A carpet, some plants, a few lamps, and comfortable seating can make the classroom library more inviting to children. Furnishing the reading corner can be a real adventure. If no permanent shelving is available in the classroom, shelves can be made from bricks and boards, or from sturdy cardboard boxes covered with contact paper (such as liquor cartons). Revolving book racks of the type drugstores often use to display paperback books are particularly useful and can sometimes be obtained free of charge if you are willing to haul them away. Teachers who are particularly skillful at "scrounging" materials for their classrooms have found that an old bathtub filled with pillows, a refrigerator carton with one side cut out, or an industrial-type cardboard drum with a hole cut in its side will attract children to the reading corner. If extra tables and chairs are needed for the reading corner, they can be secured free of charge. Large telephone cable spools make particularly sturdy tables, while seating can be made from large potato chip cans padded on top and attractively painted. Also, do not overlook the local Salvation Army, Goodwill Industries, and used furniture stores as a source of low-cost furnishings.

Providing Time to Read and Share Books While the physical environment is important, even an attractively designed language arts center and a wide variety of reading material in the classroom will not accomplish the purpose of developing reading habits if there is no time for children to read and to share books with one another. Opportunities for sustained silent reading of self-selected materials must be built into the classroom schedule so that reading does not become merely something for children to do when they have finished their "work." At least as much time should be devoted to applying reading skills through independent reading as is devoted to the development of those skills through direct instruction. Regardless of what specific instructional program or approach is used to develop reading skills, independent reading within the classroom serves as a necessary and logical application of those skills.

Many of the features of the so-called "individualized approach" to reading instruction can be incorporated into any classroom reading program. In fact, many skillful teachers have successfully built their entire reading instructional program around self-selection of reading materials and sustained silent reading—both of which are associated with the individualized approach. This approach is based on the assumption that children's motivation to read, and their motivation to improve their skill in reading, can be increased if they select their own reading material.[1] In theory, the operation of an individualized reading program is rather straightforward, although in practice the successful operation of such a program requires considerable professional expertise as well as a working knowledge of the developmental aspects of the reading process.

As many variations of the individualized approach exist as there are teachers using it. Basically, however, many teachers who use this approach schedule most of the reading instructional period for children to read self-selected materials silently. If a child appears to need guidance or if he asks for specific suggestions of what to read, the teacher helps him select a book. While children are reading silently the teacher is free to hold individual conferences or conduct ad hoc skill development sessions with a small group of children as the need arises. Frequently in such programs children maintain their own "word banks," which contain new words they have selected from their reading. These individual word banks also serve as a basis for vocabulary development and word analysis exercises, which are conducted on an individual basis or with a small group.

Another significant feature of an individualized reading program— and one that should also be included in every elementary school reading program—is the "sharing" or "celebrating" which children engage in after they finish reading a book. Although such activities often carry the somewhat negative connotation of "book reports," there is no reason why the sharing of books should be limited to the standard oral or written reports. There are many creative ways in which children can share the books they have read. For example, they can make puppets; use flannel board figures to dramatize a story; create a colorful mural, collage, or mobile; make a poster or write a television commercial to advertise a book; produce a play based on the book; write book reviews for the school newspaper; or construct a diorama.

Other interesting means of sharing books include films, filmstrips, and videotapes. Scenes from a book, for example, can be dramatized or reconstructed using animation techniques, then recorded by children on "Super 8" film or videotape for later viewing. Filmstrips can be produced by drawing directly on exposed 35mm film with felt pens, or they can be produced photographically with a half-frame 35mm camera by shooting all frames horizontally and having the film developed as a continuous roll. "U-make-it" kits are also commercially available for producing filmstrips. Such multi-media methods of sharing are not always prohibitively expensive; it is surprising how inexpensively filmstrips, films, and videotapes can be produced and how much enthusiasm they generate among children.

In addition to the suggestions listed above, Jensen (1956) and Williams (1969) have listed many other creative means of sharing books.

[1] For a more detailed description of individualized reading programs see: Veatch, 1966; Duker, 1969; Hunt, 1967; and Aukerman, 1971.

To help children decide upon the best means to interest other children in the books they have read, the teacher may suggest several possible ways and discuss with them how and when each might be used. Several different means might be suggested during one period of time, and other means suggested later. As children gain experience with various methods, they can devise their own techniques to generate interest in the books they have read. They need only be reminded that their mission is to "sell" the book to their classmates.

Time must be scheduled not only for reading books, but for sharing books as well. Ideally, much of this sharing will be spontaneous and ongoing, although it is sometimes necessary to set aside specific time periods for sharing activities. The teacher who is able to make reading and sharing of books a naturally occurring part of classroom activities will find that time spent in this way pays off in the development of reading attitudes and interests.

Encouraging Children to Read The best advice for teachers who want to foster the development of children's reading habits is to direct their professional efforts toward *inspiring* rather than requiring. Although requiring students to read a given number of books may seem justifiable, there is considerable evidence that coercing children to "read for enjoyment" may actually be detrimental to their development of purposeful and personally constructive reading habits.

Certainly teachers can and should provide children with much external motivation to read by employing the strategies described in this chapter. Modeling good reading habits, exposing children to a variety of literature, making a wide range of reading matter available within the classroom, and providing time within the school day to read and share books are highly recommended practices. If creatively applied by the teacher, all of these strategies can be used successfully to encourage and inspire children to read independently. The use of competition among students to encourage independent reading is not, however, recommended.

Teachers have sometimes attempted to use competition among individuals as a form of external motivation. While competition may serve a useful function in some classroom activities, its use to encourage independent reading is of questionable long-range value. Because some children have been conditioned by prior experiences to compete fiercely with their peers, they may be inclined to try to read more books than other children in order to gain recognition. This is especially true if such competition continues to be encouraged by the teacher.

The teacher should discourage competition if he discovers that children are merely going through the motions of reading a large number of books for competition's sake alone. For example, rather than placing stars on a chart to indicate the number of books each child has read, it is preferable to focus upon the reading accomplishments of the entire class. This could be done by making a chart entitled "Books We Have Read," or by making the head of a "bookworm" which is placed on a colorful bulletin board under the caption "Help Me Grow by Reading." The children add body segments to the bookworm on which are printed the titles and authors of books they have read.

Care must be taken to see that independent reading and sharing activities within the classroom do not stress quantity over quality. Keep in mind that there is nothing sacred about a child completing a book he has begun to read. It is surprising how many adults are inclined to insist that children finish a book they have started, when they themselves have often begun reading a book, and, after reading a few chapters, have put it aside because it failed to hold their interest. Certainly children should be afforded this same privilege. They should also be allowed to re-read the same book several times if they wish, particularly if the book is one that might provide new insights with each subsequent reading.

Helping Children Learn Why to Read

Within the context of the elementary school, teachers can provide much external motivation to encourage children to read independently. However, only by replacing such external motivation with internal motivation—that is, by helping children learn why to read—can teachers develop purposeful and personally constructive reading habits in their students.

Learning why to read is primarily a matter of discovering for one's self the many purposes of reading in relation to one's own personal needs and value system. Helping children make this discovery is, of course, not something which can be accomplished in three easy steps; nor can it be accomplished by simply telling children why other people read. Each child must make this personal discovery for himself.

For a child, learning the varied purposes of reading begins early in life with the first exposure to the medium of print. Gradually, the pre-school child who is exposed to printed media by being read to, or through television programs such as "Sesame Street" and "Electric Company," realizes that books and other printed media contain meaning-bearing symbols that represent speech and that are arranged in an order that conveys information and/or enjoyment. In addition, most children see persons significant to them engaged in the act of reading. Whether that person is reading a newspaper, a magazine, a book, a recipe, or the *TV Guide*, through observation the child begins to form his own concepts of why people read. For this reason, it is extremely important for children to be exposed to adults and peers who read in a variety of situations.

Children who have not seen people read, or whom no one has read to, may be totally unaware of the many purposes and applications for reading. Opportunities should be provided throughout the elementary grades for them to develop their own purposes for reading. This can be done partially through discussions with individual children or small groups where the content of the discussion focuses directly on the various purposes for reading. Such discussions might center around the pleasurable aspects of reading as a potentially rewarding use of leisure time and the applications of reading for the acquisition of new knowledge and understanding.

In order for discussions of the purposes of reading to be most productive, they must be related to the circumstances of the children's lives. Teachers sometimes tend to refer rather abstractly to future applications of reading such as, "When you grow up you will need to read because . . . ." Although such references are undoubtedly made with good intentions, they are often difficult for young children to appreciate fully. Future oriented statements of this type also tend to convey the message that adulthood is the only time in one's life when reading is important. While education is viewed by some as "preparation for life," it must be remembered that children are living *now* and that they have a whole range of personal needs and interests to which reading can be related. Children who are fortunate enough to have teachers who help them discover the ways in which their reading skill can be applied to fulfill their current needs and interests are much more likely to learn why to read.

In addition to promoting discussions of the purposes of reading, the teacher must structure classroom activities in which children will turn naturally to reading as a source of information and enjoyment. The teacher's assumption of the role of a "stimulator for reading" and the accessibility of reading material within the classroom are particularly significant factors in building the kind of classroom climate in which children turn spontaneously to reading.

When the teacher assumes this role and when reading materials are readily available, many opportunities can be found within the school day to get children interested in reading and thereby help them discover for themselves why to read. Teachers who effectively stimulate children to read tend to make frequent and spontaneous references to reading such as the following: "Hey! Speaking of that, did you read that new book we just got in our classroom library?" or "Have you checked some of the reference books we have to find some information that would help you with your project?" or, "Here's a book you might be interested in reading. Why don't you take a look at it and see if you think it might be helpful."

When children continually meet the right book at the right time, they usually have no difficulty discovering the relevance of reading to their lives—that is, learning why to read. Helping to arrange such meetings through the creative application of the strategies suggested in this chapter is what the teacher's role as a stimulator of interest in reading is all about.

Summary

Children bring to school with them a wide variety of reading-related concepts, interests, and attitudes, which can be viewed as the "raw material" from which reading habits develop. And although teachers may have little control over the concepts, interests, and attitudes children bring to school, they can play a major role in influencing the reading habits children take with them when they leave school. Current evidence suggests that the reading habits an individual develops in elementary school set the pattern for his reading habits as an adult.

The most important long-range objective for reading instruction and reading-related activities that occur within the school setting should be to help children develop purposeful and personally constructive reading habits that will serve them throughout their lives. The fact that schools have in the past failed to fully attain this objective is evidenced by the large percentage of the adult population who are able to read, but who seldom read either for information or enjoyment. Perhaps this is because too many of these adults completed elementary school with the notion that reading was a "subject" they had studied for six or seven years and, as such, had little relevance to their lives. Or perhaps it is because they were "turned off" by too much reading instruction and not enough reading. Whatever the reason, children who leave school knowing how to read, but do not know why to read, what to read, and when to read, cannot make full use of their skill in reading.

The information and enjoyment derived from reading make an invaluable contribution to the continual process of learning and personal growth, which takes place throughout an individual's lifetime. Reading can help people learn more about themselves and their world, and can help them enlarge and clarify their own experiences. Whether people use the reading skill they have developed to the fullest extent in this learning and growth process will depend upon the degree to which they have discovered the value of reading. One of the primary responsibilities of a teacher is to help children make this discovery.

Suggested Activities

1. Design an interest inventory for a specific individual or group of elementary school children. Administer the inventory and summarize the results. Where possible, suggest specific selections to be read to the group and list specific books that you think may be interesting to specific individuals.

2. Design an attitudes survey that takes into account the child's experience with reading and books, factors within his home environment, and his television viewing habits.

3. Design a reading corner or language arts center for an elementary school classroom. List the title and author of books you would like to include in the classroom library; list other reading and writing materials; describe how you will organize your classroom schedule to encourage use of the center; and draw a sketch or floor plan that illustrates the physical arrangement of the center.

4. Outline a language-arts program component that is designed to develop reading attitudes, interests, and habits. Include descriptions of specific activities as well as statements pertaining to the structuring of the "classroom climate for reading."

5. Arrange to read a story or poem to a group of elementary school children. With the aid of the teacher, decide upon an appropriate selection and plan and conduct an introductory and follow-up discussion of the selection with the children.

6. Visit the children's room of the local public library. Examine circulation records or consult with the children's librarian to develop a list of the most frequently read titles.

7. Examine some of the sources listed under "Aids for Selecting Children's Books." Make a tentative list of books that you feel would be appropriate to be read to or by children at a given grade level.

8. Read a number of children's books with which you would like to become familiar. Write a brief summary of the books including title, author, illustrator, publisher, estimated reading level, plot summary, suggested uses for content area instruction, concepts developed, and a statement about possible bibliotherapeutic value of the book. Type the summaries (one-half page each) on duplicating masters so that multiple copies can be reproduced and shared with other class members.

9. Begin a file of poems for special occasions such as holidays, rainy days, the first snowfall, and seasons. A good sourcebook is *Poetry for Holidays*, edited by Nancy Larrick (Champaign, Ill.: Garrard Publishing Co., 1966).

10. Write to the Reading Is Fundamental Program (c/o Smithsonian Institution, Washington, D.C. 20560) to request program guides and book lists. Investigate the procedures for initiating a RIF project in your local area.

Aids for Selecting Children's Books

American Library Association. *Books for Children 1971–1972*. Chicago: The American Library Association, 1973. (Original edition 1960–1965; annual supplements published yearly.)

Arbuthnot, May Hill. *Children and Books*. 4th ed. Chicago: Scott Foresman, 1972.

Baker, Augusta. *The Black Experience in Children's Books*. New York: The New York Public Library, 1971.

Best Books for Children. New York: R. R. Bowker (annual publication).

Bowles, Catherine, ed. *Good and Inexpensive Books for Children*. Washington, D.C.: Association for Childhood Education International, 1972.

Catterson, Jane, ed. *Children and Literature*. Newark, Del.: International Reading Association, 1970.

Childhood Study Association of America. *Books of the Year for Children*. New York: Childhood Study Association of America (annual publication).

Children's Book Council, *Children's Books: Awards and Prizes*. New York: Children's Book Council, 1973.

Eastland, Patricia Ann. "Read-Aloud Stories in the Primary Literature Program." In *Individualizing Reading Instruction, A Reader*, edited by Larry Harris and Carl B. Smith. Chicago: Holt, Rinehart and Winston, 1972.

Gillespie, John T., and Lembo, Diana L. *Introducing Books: A Guide for the Middle Grades*. New York: R. R. Bowker Co., 1970.

Griffin, Louise. *Multi-Ethnic Books for Young Children*. Washington, D.C.: ERIC-NAEYC Publication in Early Childhood Education, National Association for the Education of Young Children, 1970.

Haviland, Virginia. *Children's Books*. Washington, D.C.: Library of Congress, 1973.

Hemsig, Esther D. *Good and Inexpensive Books for Children*. Washington, D.C.: Association for Childhood Education International, 1972.

Kujoth, Jean Spealman. *Best Selling Children's Books.* Metuchen, N.J.: The Scarecrow Press, 1973.

Ladley, Winifred C. *Sources of Good Books and Magazines for Children.* Newark, Del.: International Reading Association, 1970 (annotated bibliography).

Perkins, Flossie L. *Book and Non-Book Media: Annotated Guide to Selection Aids for Educational Materials.* Urbana, Ill.: National Council of Teachers of English, 1972.

Riggs, Corrine W., comp. *Bibliotherapy.* Newark, Del.: International Reading Association, 1971 (annotated bibliography).

Rollins, Charlemae, ed. *We Build Together: A Reader's Guide to Negro Life and Literature for Elementary and High School Use.* Champaign, Ill.: National Council of Teachers of English, 1967.

Root, Sheldon L., Jr., ed. *Adventuring with Books.* 2nd ed. New York: Scholastic Magazines, Citation Press, 1973.

Shor, Rachel, and Fidel, Estelle A., eds. *Children's Catalog.* 11th ed. New York: H. W. Wilson Co., 1966 (annual supplements, 1967–1974).

Smithsonian Institution. *Reading Is FUN-damental Booklist.* Washington, D.C.: Smithsonian Institution, 1973.

Smithsonian Institution. *RIF's Guide to Book Selection.* Washington, D.C.: Smithsonian Institution, 1971 (ERIC: ED 062095).

Smollar, Eleanor, ed. *Guide to Book Selection.* Washington, D.C.: Reading Is Fundamental Program, 1970.

Spache, George D., *Good Reading for Poor Readers.* Champaign, Ill.: Garrard Publishing Co., 1974.

Stensland, Anna Lee. *Literature by and about the American Indian—An Annotated Bibliography for Junior and Senior High School Students.* Urbana, Ill.: National Council of Teachers of English, 1973.

Sunderlin, Sylvia, ed. *Bibliography of Books for Children.* 1970 Edition. Washington, D.C.: Association for Childhood Education International, 1971.

Sutherland, Zena, ed. *The Best in Children's Books: The University of Chicago Guide to Children's Literature, 1966–1972.* Chicago: University of Chicago Press, 1973.

Tanyzer, Harold, and Karl, Jean. *Reading, Children's Books and Our Pluralistic Society.* Newark, Del.: International Reading Association, 1972.

Williams, Frank E. "Media Resource Book—A Total Creativity Program for Individualizing and Humanizing the Learning Process." Vol. 4, April 1973. (ERIC: ED 070 244).

Suggested Readings

Ashley, L. F. "Children's Interests and Individualized Reading." *Elementary English* 47 Dec. 1970): 1088–1096.

Athey, Irene. "Affective Factors in Reading." In *Theoretical Models and Processes of Reading*, edited by H. Singer and R. Ruddell. Newark, Del.: International Reading Association, 1970.

Beery, Althea, ed. *Elementary Reading Instruction: Selected Materials*, Second Edition. Boston: Allyn and Bacon, 1974.

Brown, Dale W. "A Selected Bibliography of Professional Materials Dealing with Children's Literature." *Elementary English* 46 (March 1969): 334–341.

Brown, Jennifer. "Reading Aloud." *Elementary English* 50 (April 1973): 635–636.

Busch, Fred. "Basals Are Not for Reading." *Teachers College Record* 72 (September 1970): 23–30. (Also in Sam L. Sebesta and Carl J. Wallen, *The First R: Readings on Teaching Reading*. Chicago: Science Research Associates, 1972, pp. 215–224).

Carlson, Ruth K. *Literature for Children: Enrichment Ideas*. Dubuque, Iowa: Wm. C. Brown Co., 1970.

Chomsky, Carol. "Stages of Language Development and Reading Exposure." *Harvard Educational Review* 42 (Feb. 1972): 1–33.

Dallman, Martha; Rouch, Roger L.; Lynette, Y.C.; and DeBower, John J. *The Teaching of Reading*. Chicago: Holt, Rinehart and Winston, 1974, ch. 11.

Darling, David W. "Evaluating the Affective Dimensions of Reading." In *The Evaluation of Children's Reading Achievement*, edited by Thomas C. Barrett. Newark, Del.: International Reading Association, 1967, pp. 127–141.

Dietrich, Dorothy M., and Mathews, Virginia H., eds. *Development of Lifetime Reading Habits*. Newark, Del.: International Reading Association, 1968.

Dillner, Martha H. "Affective Objectives in Reading." *Journal of Reading* 17 (May 1974): 626–631.

Donelson, Kenneth, ed. *Adolescent Literature, Adolescent Reading, and the English Class*. Urbana, Ill.: National Council of Teachers of English, 1972.

Elementary English 51 (Oct. 1974), entire issue.

Feeney, Georgiana. "The Ecology of the Bookworm." In *Claremont Reading Conference 34th Yearbook, 1970*, edited by Malcolm P. Douglass. Claremont, Cal.: The Claremont Reading Conference, 1970.

Gage, Thomas. "The Reader as Performer." Paper presented at the annual convention of the National Council of Teachers of English, November 1971 (ERIC: ED 073 414).

Geeslin, Dorine H., and Wilson, Richard C. "Effects of Reading Age on Reading Interests." *Elementary English* 49 (May 1972): 750–756.

Greer, Margaret. "Affective Growth Through Reading." *The Reading Teacher* 25 (Jan. 1972): 336–341.

Iverson, William J. "The Role of the Teacher in Developing Lifetime Readers." In Sam L. Sebesta and Carl J. Wallen, *The First R: Readings on Teaching Reading.* Chicago: Science Research Associates, 1972, pp. 342–351. (Also in *Development of Lifetime Reading Habits.* Newark, Del.: International Reading Association, 1968, pp. 5–13.)

Jackson, Philip W. "Reading and School Life." In *Claremont Reading Conference 34th Yearbook, 1970,* edited by Malcolm P. Douglass. Claremont, Cal.: The Claremont Reading Conference, 1970.

Lasser, Michael L. "Literature in the Elementary School: A View from Above." *Elementary English* 46 (May 1969): 639–644.

Markwell, Margaret. "Literature in the Elementary School—What For?" *Elementary English* 50 (May 1973): 739–744.

Martin, Sue Ann. "Techniques for the Creative Reading or Telling of Stories to Children." *Elementary English* 45 (May 1968): 611–618.

Monson, Dianne. "Humor in Children's Literature." In *Reading and Realism,* edited by J. Allen Figurel. Newark, Del.: International Reading Association, 1969, pp. 232–238.

Ohanian, Vera. "Cherished Books of Children: What Makes Them So?" *Elementary English* 47 (November 1970): 946–952.

Painter, Helen W., ed. *Poetry and Children.* Newark, Del.: International Reading Association, 1970.

Painter, Helen W., ed. *Reaching Children and Young People Through Literature.* Newark, Del.: International Reading Association, 1971.

Roeder, Harold H., and Lee, Nancy. "Twenty-five Teacher-Tested Ways to Encourage Voluntary Reading." *The Reading Teacher* 27 (October 1973): 48–50.

Spennato, Nicholas A. "Cause: Project Literary Fair/Effect: More Eager Readers." *Elementary English* 51 (Sept. 1974): 880–882.

References

Aukerman, Robert C. "The Individualized Reading Approach." In *Approaches to Beginning Reading.* New York: John Wiley and Sons, 1971, pp. 383–389.

Beta Upsilon Chapter of Pi Lambda Theta. "Children's Reading Interests Classified by Age Levels." *The Reading Teacher* 27 (April 1974): 694–700.

Bloom, Benjamin S. *Stability and Change in Human Characteristics.* New York: John Wiley and Sons, 1964.

Campbell, Laurence R. "Teenagers' Media Habits." ERIC: ED 033 955, September 1969.

Dejardins, Mary. "Reading and Viewing: A Survey." *School Libraries* 21 (Spring 1972): 26–30.

Duker, Sam, ed. *Individualized Reading: Readings.* Metuchen, N.J.: Scarecrow Press, 1969.

Dulin, Kenneth L., and Chester, Robert D. "A Validation Study of the Estes Attitude Scale." *Journal of Reading* 18 (Oct. 1974): 56–59.

Durkin, Dolores. "Children Who Read Before Grade 1: A Second Study." *The Elementary School Journal* 64 (Dec. 1962): 143–148.

Ennis, Philip A. "Adult Book Reading in the U.S." National Opinion Research Center, University of Chicago, 1965 (ERIC: ED 010 754).

Ennis, Philip A. "Book Reading Audiences and the Mass Society." Paper delivered to American Sociological Assoc., Miami, Florida, August 1966 (ERIC: ED 014 402).

Estes, Thomas H. "Assessing Attitudes Toward Reading." Paper presented at International Reading Association Convention, Detroit, May 1972 (ERIC: ED 063 007).

Estes, Thomas H. "A Scale to Measure Attitudes Toward Reading." *Journal of Reading* 15 (Nov. 1971): 135–138.

Fader, David N., and McNeil, Elton B. *Hooked on Books: Program and Proof.* New York: Berkeley Medallion Books, 1968.

Feeley, Joan T. *Interest Patterns and Media Preferences of Boys and Girls in Grades Four and Five.* Unpublished doctoral dissertation, New York University, 1972.

Feeley, Joan T. "Television and Children's Reading." *Elementary English* 50 (Jan. 1973): 141–148.

Fiddler, Jerry B. *The Standardization of a Questionnaire to Ascertain the Attitude Toward Reading of Sixth-Grade Pupils.* Unpublished doctoral dissertation, The State University of New York at Buffalo, 1973.

Hansen, Harlan S. "The Impact of the Home Literary Environment on Reading Attitudes." *Elementary English* 46 (Jan. 1969): 17–24.

Hansen, Harlan S. "The Home Literary Environment—A Follow-Up Report." *Elementary English* 50 (January 1973): 97–98, 122.

Huck, Charlotte S. "Strategies for Improving Interest and Appreciation in Literature." In *Reaching Children and Young People Through Literature*, edited by Helen W. Painter. Newark, Del.: International Reading Association, 1971, pp. 37–45.

Hunt, Lyman C., ed. *The Individualized Reading Program.* Proceedings of the 11th Annual Convention, vol. 2, pt. 3. Newark, Del.: International Reading Association, 1967.

Huss, Helen. "Interpreting Research in Children's Literature." In *Children, Books and Reading*, edited by Mildred Dawson. Perspectives in Reading No. 2. Newark, Del.: International Reading Association, 1964.

Jensen, Amy E. "Attracting Children to Books." *Elementary English* 33 (October 1956): 332–339.

Jung, Raymond. "Leisure in Three Cultures." *Elementary School Journal* 67 (March 1967): 285–295.

King, Ethel M. "Critical Appraisal of Research on Children's Reading Interests." In *Language Arts Concepts for Elementary School Teachers*, edited by Paul C. Burns et al. Itasca, Ill.: F. E. Peacock, 1972, pp. 258–271.

Krathwohl, David R. et al. *Taxonomy of Educational Objectives, Handbook II: The Affective Domain.* New York: David McKay Co., 1964.

Kujoth, Jean Spealman. *Best-Selling Children's Books.* Metuchen, N.J.: The Scarecrow Press, 1973.

Long, Barbara H., and Henderson, Edmund H. "Children's Use of Time: Some Personal and Social Correlations." 1970 (ERIC: ED 054 475).

Nelson, Richard C. "Children's Poetry Preferences." *Elementary English* 43 (March 1966): 247–251.

Peltola, Bette J. *A Study of the Indicated Literary Choices and Measured Literary Knowledge of Fourth and Sixth Grade Boys and Girls.* Unpublished doctoral dissertation, University of Minnesota, 1965.

Plessas, Gus, and Oakes, Clifton. "Pre-Reading Experiences of Selected Early Readers." *Reading Teacher* 17 (January 1964): 241–245.

Purves, Alan C., and Beach, Richard. *Literature and the Reader: Research in Response to Literature, Reading Interests, and the Teaching of Literature.* Urbana, Ill.: National Council of Teachers of English, 1972.

Rowell, C. G. "An Attitude Scale for Reading." *The Reading Teacher* 25 (February 1972): 442–447.

San Diego County Department of Education. "An Inventory of Reading Attitude." In *Improving Reading Instruction, Monograph 4.* San Diego, California: San Diego County Department of Education, November 1961 (ERIC: ED 028 893).

Sharon, Amiel T. "Reading Activities of American Adults." Paper presented at meeting of American Educational Research Association, Chicago, Illinois, April 1972 (ERIC: ED 061 013).

Smithsonian Institution. *RIF's Guide to Developing a Program.* Washington, D.C.: Smithsonian Institution, 1972 (ERIC: ED 062 094).

Sutton, M. "Readiness for Reading at Kindergarten." *Reading Teacher* 17 (January 1964): 234–240.

Trisman, Donald A. "Adult Readers: Activities and Goals." Paper presented at meeting of American Educational Research Association, Chicago, Illinois, April 1972 (ERIC: ED 061 024).

van der Brink, R. E. M. *Book Reading, Borrowing, and Buying Habits.* Eighteenth Congress, International Publishers Assoc., Amsterdam, The Netherlands, 1968 (ERIC: ED 059 736).

Veatch, Jeannette. *Reading in the Elementary School.* New York: The Ronald Press, 1966.

Weintraub, Samuel. "Children's Reading Interests." *Reading Teacher* 22 (April 1969): 655, 657, 659.

Williams, Lois E. *Independent Learning in the Elementary School Classroom.* Washington, D.C.: American Association of Elementary-Kindergarten-Nursery Educators, 1969.

Witty, Paul. "Studies of the Mass Media—1949–1965." *Science Education* 50 (1966): 119–126.

Witty, Paul, and Melis, Lloyd. "A 1964 Study of TV: Comparisons and Comments." *Elementary English* 42 (February 1965): 134–141.

Zimet, Sara F. "Children's Interest and Story Preferences: A Critical Review of the Literature." *Elementary School Journal* 67 (December 1966): 122–130.

Index